A Guide to Critical Reviews of United States Fiction, 1870-1910

Volume II

compiled by

CLAYTON L. EICHELBERGER

The Scarecrow Press, Inc.
Metuchen, N. J. 1974

Library of Congress Cataloging in Publication Data

Eichelberger, Clayton L. 1925-
A guide to critical reviews of United States fiction, 1870-1910.

1. American fiction--Book reviews--Bibliography.
2. Periodicals--Indexes. I. Title.
Z1225.E35 016.813'4'09 77-149998
ISBN 0-8108-0380-1 (Vol. I)
ISBN 0-8108-0701-7 (Vol. II)

CONTENTS

PREFACE

The rationale and method for this supplemental Volume II are consistent with those of A Guide to Critical Reviews of United States Fiction, 1870-1910 (Scarecrow Press, 1971). It lists in a simplified bibliographic form roughly nine thousand additional contemporary critical notices of fiction produced by United States writers and published during the 1870-1910 period, thus expanding the original listing to over twenty thousand items. The guide is still far from comprehensive, however, and should, accordingly, be regarded as preliminary and tentative.

To avoid the occasional flaws in identification incorporated in the first volume, I have in this case ignored the casual--and often misleading--clues to authorial nationality provided by the contemporary reviewers and literary columnists, and I have depended even more heavily than before for authentication of name, nationality, and title on three basic sources: Lyle H. Wright (American Fiction, 1851-1875 and American Fiction, 1876-1900), Oscar Fay Adams (A Dictionary of American Authors, 5th ed.), and W. Stewart Wallace (Dictionary of North American Authors Deceased Before 1950), in that order. When I found those sources lacking the information I sought, or in disagreement, I consulted the many standard dictionaries, encyclopedias, and biographical listings routinely available to the researcher. Generally I excluded authors I could not absolutely verify through the reference books available to me, but I treated minor title variations somewhat more tolerantly. Since this work is intended simply as a guide, and not a final statement, I felt justified in doing so.

The focus, which continues to be on adult fiction, again raised problems of definition previously discussed and not easily resolved. Especially troublesome is the fact that a vast portion of the fiction produced during the period was designed to appeal to both youthful and mature readers; therefore, one cannot justly assign all titles exclusively to one audience or the other. Writers such as Frances A. Humphrey, Lucy C. Lillie, Kirk Munroe, Mrs. Anna Raffensperger, James Otis--the complete list is extensive--wrote primarily for young people, and usually their books were reviewed as children's literature. But some contemporary reviewers seemed to conclude that their work was sufficiently mature in nature, or had enough appeal to an older audience, to justify being listed under fiction--without any juvenile qualifications attached. In an effort to be true to the period in this very complex situation, I followed the guidance of the reviewers and included "juvenile" titles when they were reviewed in adult fiction columns. I excluded reviews of books which the reviewers designated as exclusively for children.

Since _Harper's Magazine_ was supposedly covered by the first installment of this guide, explanation of the _Harper's_ items included here is in order. Between 1886 and 1900, first Laurence Hutton, and later John Kendrick Bangs, conducted a book review column called "Literary Notes" for the popular monthly magazine. It typically consisted of four double-column pages. Because it was separately paginated and bound between the main body of the magazine and the second installment of advertisements, binders, in gathering the issues into volumes, usually excised the "Literary Notes" along with the advertisements. Thus, most sets of _Harper's_ found on library shelves today include only occasional--one is tempted to say accidental--segments of this major review column. After an extensive search, I have assembled the complete sequence of "Literary Notes" and have included the reviews of United States fiction in this listing. Arrangements for facsimile reproduction of the generally inaccessible Hutton and Bangs reviews are being made.

MECHANICS OF COMPILATION

Arrangement of Entries. Titles are entered alphabetically under known authors' names or under identified pseudonyms or initials. Anonymous titles of established United States authorship are entered alphabetically with authors. Under individual book titles, reviews are arranged alphabetically by the title of the periodical in which the review appeared. When a periodical carried multiple reviews, the entries are chronological beneath the periodical title.

Bibliographic Form. The title of the work reviewed is followed by bibliographic detail in this sequence: the name of the periodical in which the review appeared, series designation if any, volume number in Arabic form, pagination (separated from volume number by a colon), and date of the periodical number in which the review appeared (month names have been uniformly shortened to the first three letters), thus:

Critic, NS 13:63, 8 Feb 1890

Square brackets around the name of an author indicate editorial identification of authorship for a work published anonymously or pseudonymously when a pattern of anonymous or pseudonymous publication is clearly established. Known pseudonyms are identified by the abbreviation "pseud." in brackets, and parentheses are used to identify the maiden name of married female authors.

Cross References. In cases of co-authorship, identified pseudonyms, and name changes resulting from marriage, cross references are included. Titles are listed under the author's actual name--Mark Twain appears under Clemens, Samuel Langhorne--or married name--Mary E. Wilkins is entered under Freeman, Mary E. (Wilkins).

Index of Titles. The titles in shortened form of all books reviewed and an indication of the page of the guide on which the review information appears are included in the Index.

15 August 1973 Clayton L. Eichelberger

Arlington, Texas

ACKNOWLEDGMENTS

Although fewer people were directly involved in the compilation of this volume than its predecessor, I am again indebted to many librarians and friends who assisted without knowing they were doing so.

I especially thank the people who staff the interlibrary loan departments of The University of Texas at Arlington, North Texas State University, Southern Methodist University, and Texas Christian University for arranging convenient access to necessary materials; Mrs. Leslie Branyon, who prepared a portion of the final typescript; and Randall Brunner, a patient and dedicated young man who assisted me in arranging and checking the complete list. I am grateful also to The University of Texas at Arlington for providing some financial assistance in the form of a Liberal Arts Organized Research grant, which greatly facilitated the project.

But most of all I thank four friendly comrades I know as Nancy, Julie, Joel, and Jon. It is they who merit a large portion of the credit for all I do.

C. L. E.

PERIODICALS COVERED

Catholic World, Jan 1870 through Dec 1910

Chautauquan, Oct 1880 through Dec 1910

Critic, 15 Jan 1881 through Sep 1906

Dial, May 1880 through Dec 1910

Galaxy, Jan 1870 through Jan 1878

Harper's "Literary Notes," Jan 1886 through Jan 1900

Independent, 2 Jan 1873 through 29 Dec 1910

Literary World, 1 Jan 1871 through Dec 1904

Literature, 23 Oct 1897 through 24 Nov 1899

Westminster Review, Jan 1870 through Dec 1910

GUIDE TO CRITICAL REVIEWS

Abbott, Charles Conrad
A Colonial Wooing
Chautauquan, 22:510, Jan 1896
Critic, NS 25:6, 4 Jan 1896
Independent, 47:1579, 21 Nov 1895
The Hermit of Nottingham
Literary World, 28:479, 25 Dec 1897
When the Century Was New
Critic, NS 27:421, 19 Jun 1897
Dial, 22:311-2, 16 May 1897
Literary World, 28:342-3, 2 Oct 1897

Abbott, Mary Perkins (Ives)
Alexia
Critic, NS 13:63, 8 Feb 1890
Dial, 10:216, Dec 1889
Literary World, 21:7, 4 Jan 1890
The Beverleys
Dial, 11:241, Dec 1890

Ackerman, A. W.
The Prince of Peace
Critic, NS 23:27, 12 Jan 1895

Acklan, William Hayes
Sterope
Independent, 44:1329, 22 Sep 1892

Adams, Andy
Cattle Brands
Critic, 48:571, Jun 1906
The Log of a Cowboy
Critic, 43:474, Nov 1903
Literary World, 34:209, Aug 1903
The Outlet
Independent, 58:1257, 1 Jun 1905
A Texas Matchmaker
Critic, 45:94, Jul 1904
Dial, 37:41, 16 Jul 1904
Literary World, 35:201, Jul 1904

Adams, Francis Alexandre
The Transgressors
Critic, 37:468, Nov 1900

Adams, Frederick Upham
The Kidnapped Millionaires
Dial, 31:33, 1 Jul 1901; 31:137, 1 Sep 1901
Literary World, 32:139, 1 Sep 1901

[Adams, Henry]
Democracy
Dial, 1:11-2, May 1880
Literary World, 13:373, 4 Nov 1882
Westminster Review, 118: 281, Oct 1882

Adams, Mary
Confessions of a Wife
Independent, 54:2593-4,

Adams, Mary (cont.)
30 Oct 1902; 54:2772, 20 Nov 1902
Literary World, 33:193, 1 Dec 1902
An Honorable Surrender
Independent, 35:11, 17 May 1883
Literary World, 14:91, 24 Mar 1883

Adams, Oscar Fay
The Archbishop's Unguarded Moment, and Other Stories
Literary World, 30:295, 16 Sep 1899
Dear Old Story-Tellers
Chautauquan, 11:127, Apr 1890

Adams, Samuel Hopkins
The Flying Death
Independent, 64:974, 30 Apr 1908
See also White, Stewart Edward, and Samuel Hopkins Adams.

[Adams, William Taylor]
All Taut
By Oliver Optic [pseud.].
Critic, NS 6:249, 20 Nov 1886
Brother Against Brother
By Oliver Optic [pseud.].
Chautauquan, 20:762, Mar 1895
Living Too Fast
By Oliver Optic [pseud.].
Independent, 28:8, 16 Nov 1876
A Millionaire at Sixteen
By Oliver Optic [pseud.].
Critic, NS 18:31, 16 Jul 1892
Taken by the Enemy
By Oliver Optic [pseud.].
Chautauquan, 9:189, Dec 1888
Independent, 41:1122, 29 Aug 1889
An Undivided Union
By Oliver Optic [pseud.].
Chautauquan, 30:330, Dec 1899
Up the River
By Oliver Optic [pseud.].
Independent, 34:11, 12 Jan 1882
Within the Enemy's Lines
By Oliver Optic [pseud.].
Chautauquan, 10:378, Dec 1889

Ade, George
Artie
Critic, NS 26:259, 31 Oct 1896
Independent, 49:91, 21 Jan 1897
Breaking into Society
Literary World, 35:111, Apr 1904
Doc' Horne
Independent, 51:2628-9, 28 Sep 1899
Fables in Slang
Dial, 27:370, 16 Nov 1899
In Babel
Critic, 44:379, Apr 1904
Literary World, 34:349, Dec 1903
More Fables
Dial, 32:207, 16 Mar 1902
Literary World, 32:75, 1 May 1901
People You Know
Critic, 43:474, Nov 1903
Literary World, 34:138, Jun 1903
Pink Marsh
Independent, 49:882, 8 Jul 1897
True Bills
Literary World, 35:380, Dec 1904

Adee, David Graham
No. 19 State Street
Critic, NS 9:317, 30 Jun 1888

Adeler, Max [pseud.].
See Clark, Charles Heber.

Adler, Cyrus
Told in the Coffee-House

Literary World, 29:155, 14 May 1898

The Affair at the Inn
By Kate Douglas Wiggin, Mary Findlater, Jane Helen Findlater, and Allan McAulay.
Catholic World, 80:262, Nov 1904
Chautauquan, 40:592, Feb 1905
Critic, 45:578, Dec 1904
Dial, 37:212, 1 Oct 1904
Independent, 57:865, 13 Oct 1904
Literary World, 35:283, Oct 1904

Afterem, George [pseud.].
See Williams, Harold.

Alcott, Louisa May
Aunt Jo's Scrap-Book
Catholic World, 17:142-3, Apr 1873
Eight Cousins
Catholic World, 22:431-2, Dec 1875
Literary World, 6:68-9, 1 Oct 1875
Jo's Boys
Catholic World, 44:412, Dec 1886
Chautauquan, 7:128, Nov 1886
Critic, NS 6:196, 23 Oct 1886
Kitty's Class-Day
Independent, 28:9, 15 Jun 1876
Little Men
Chautauquan, 34:333-4, Dec 1901
Literary World, 2:6-7, 1 Jun 1871
Westminster Review, 103:129, Jan 1875
Little Women
Westminster Review, 103:129, Jan 1875
Lulu's Library
Independent, 39:1458, 10 Nov 1887
A Modern Mephistopheles
Critic, NS 11:282, 8 Jun 1889
Literary World, 8:8, 1 Jun 1877; 20:159, 11 May 1889
An Old-Fashioned Girl
Galaxy, 9:710, May 1870
An Old-Fashioned Thanksgiving, and Other Stories
Independent, 34:11, 26 Oct 1882
Proverb Stories
Critic, 2:326, 2 Dec 1882
Rose in Bloom
Chautauquan, 40:592, Feb 1905
Literary World, 7:104, 1 Dec 1876
Westminster Review, 107:140, Jan 1877
Silver Pitchers, and Other Stories
Independent, 28:9, 15 Jun 1876
Literary World, 7:9, 1 Jun 1876

Alden, Mrs. G. R.
See Alden, Isabella (Macdonald).

Alden, Isabella (Macdonald)
As in a Mirror
Chautauquan, 29:510, Aug 1899
Links in Rebecca's Life
By Pansy [pseud.].
Chautauquan, 7:254, Jun 1887
Making Fate
Chautauquan, 24:127, Oct 1896
Twenty Minutes Late
By Pansy [pseud.].
Chautauquan, 17:762, Sep 1893
Why They Couldn't
Chautauquan, 22:639, Feb 1896
Wanted
By Pansy [pseud.].

Alden, Isabela (cont.)
Chautauquan, 20:511, Jan 1895
Yesterday Framed in To-Day
Chautauquan, 29:510, Aug 1899

Alden, William Livingston
The Adventures of Jimmy Brown
Critic, NS 3:245, 23 May 1885
Among the Freaks
Critic, NS 25:443, 20 Jun 1896
Jimmy Brown Trying To Find Europe
Critic, 47:381, Oct 1905
A New Robinson Crusoe
Critic, NS 9:281, 9 Jun 1888
Harper's, 76:Literary Notes, 1-2, May 1888
Told by the Colonel
Chautauquan, 19:126, Apr 1894
Critic, NS 20:412, 23 Dec 1893
Literary World, 24:423-4, 2 Dec 1893

Aldrich, Anne Reeve
The Feet of Love
Catholic World, 51:407-8, Jun 1890
Literary World, 21:155, 10 May 1890

Aldrich, Thomas Bailey
Marjorie Daw, and Other People
Critic, 1:97, 9 Apr 1881
Galaxy, 16:858, Dec 1873
Independent, 25:1354, 30 Oct 1873
Prudence Palfrey
Independent, 26:9, 25 Jun 1874
The Queen of Sheba
Literary World, 8:149, 1 Jan 1878
Westminster Review, 124 (NS 68):304-5, Jul 1885
A Sea Turn and Other Matters
Critic, 41:579, Dec 1902
Independent, 54:2717, 13 Nov 1902
Literary World, 33:196, 1 Dec 1902
Westminster Review, 158:716, Dec 1902
The Sisters' Tragedy
Critic, NS 20:298, 11 Nov 1893
The Stillwater Tragedy
Catholic World, 32:284, Nov 1880
Dial, 1:91-2, Sep 1880
Independent, 32:12, 16 Sep 1880
Literary World, 11:311, 11 Sep 1880
Westminster Review, 126 (NS 70):567, Oct 1886
The Story of a Bad Boy
Chautauquan, 9:189, Dec 1888
Critic, NS 22:428, 22 Dec 1894
Two Bites at a Cherry, with Other Tales
Dial, 15:343-4, 1 Dec 1893
Independent, 45:1653, 7 Dec 1893
Literary World, 24:351, 21 Oct 1893
Westminster Review, 140:693, Dec 1893
See also Oliphant, Margaret Oliphant (Wilson), and Thomas Bailey Aldrich, Jr.

Alger, Abby L.
In Indian Tents
Independent, 49:1624, 9 Dec 1897
Tales Told by Penobscot, Passamaquoddy and Micmac Indians to Abby L. Alger
Critic, NS 28:381, 18 Dec 1897

Allen, James Lane
Aftermath
Harper's, 92:Literary

Notes, 3-4, Feb 1896
Independent, 47:1727, 19 Dec 1895
Literary World, 27:77, 7 Mar 1896

The Bride of the Mistletoe
Independent, 67:250-1, 29 Jul 1909; 67:1153, 18 Nov 1909

The Choir Invisible
Chautauquan, 25:430, Jul 1897; 28:421, Jan 1899
Critic, NS 27:368, 29 May 1897
Dial, 22:310, 16 May 1897
Independent, 49:620, 13 May 1897
Literary World, 28:155, 15 May 1897

Flute and Violin, and Other Kentucky Tales and Romances
Critic, NS 16:1-2, 4 Jul 1891
Harper's, 83:Literary Notes, 2, Jun 1891
Independent, 43:1219, 13 Aug 1891
Westminster Review, 137:708-9, Jun 1892

John Gray
Critic, NS 19:200, 1 Apr 1893
Independent, 45:1154, 24 Aug 1893
Literary World, 24:148, 6 May 1893

A Kentucky Cardinal
Critic, NS 23:121-2, 16 Feb 1895
Harper's, 90:Literary Notes, 2, Jan 1895
Literary World, 26:59, 23 Feb 1895

The Mettle of the Pasture
Chautauquan, 41:96, Mar 1905
Dial, 35:154-5 [218-9], 1 Oct 1903
Independent, 55:1808-9, 30 Jul 1903; 55:2742, 19 Nov 1903

The Reign of Law
Chautauquan, 31:530, Aug 1900
Dial, 29:21-2, 1 Jul 1900
Independent, 52:2803, 22 Nov 1900
Literary World, 31:135, 1 Jul 1900

Summer in Arcady
Chautauquan, 23:493, Jul 1896
Critic, NS 25:424, 13 Jun 1896
Dial, 21:19-20, 1 Jul 1896
Independent, 48:1006-7, 23 Jul 1896

Allen, John W. [pseud.].
See Lesley, J. Peter.

Allen, Richard
Miss Eaton's Romance
Critic, NS 14:165, 4 Oct 1890
Literary World, 21:238, 19 Jul 1890

Allen, Willis Boyd
Cloud and Cliff
Chautauquan, 10:379, Dec 1889
Critic, NS 12:64, 10 Aug 1889

The Head of Pasht
Literary World, 31:269, 1 Dec 1900

Kelp
Critic, NS 10:125, 15 Sep 1888

The Lion City of Africa
Chautauquan, 12:423, Dec 1890

A Son of Liberty
Independent, 49:56, 14 Jan 1897

Altsheler, Joseph Alexander
Before the Dawn
Critic, 43:378, Oct 1903
Dial, 34:372, 1 Jun 1903
Independent, 55:1037, 30

Altsheler, J. (cont.)
Apr 1903
Literary World, 34:83, Apr 1903
The Candidate
Dial, 38:391, 1 Jun 1905
Guthrie of the 'Times'
Dial, 38:15, 1 Jan 1905
A Herald of the West
Dial, 26:124-5, 16 Feb 1899
Literary World, 29:456, 24 Dec 1898
The Hidden Mine
Literary World, 30:7, 7 Jan 1899
In Circling Camps
Critic, 37:278, Sep 1900
Dial, 29:307, 1 Nov 1900
In Hostile Red
Dial, 30:110, 16 Feb 1901
Independent, 52:2695-6, 8 Nov 1900
The Last Rebel
Independent, 52:2521, 18 Oct 1900
My Captive
Critic, 41:373, Oct 1902
Dial, 33:66, 1 Aug 1902
Literary World, 33:123, 1 Aug 1902
The Rainbow of Gold
Literary World, 30:7, 7 Jan 1899
A Soldier of Manhattan and His Adventures at Ticonderoga and Quebec
Dial, 23:285, 16 Nov 1897
Literary World, 28:479, 25 Dec 1897
Literature, 2:621, 28 May 1898
The Sun of Saratoga
Critic, NS 27:425, 19 Jun 1897
Literary World, 28:210, 26 Jun 1897
The Wilderness Road
Dial, 31:135, 1 Sep 1901
Independent, 53:1929, 15 Aug 1901

American Coin
Catholic World, 50:124-6, Oct 1889
Critic, NS 12:42, 27 Jul 1889

Ames, Lucia True
See Mead, Lucia True (Ames).

Ames, Mary (Clemmer)
Eirene
Literary World, 2:65, 1 Oct 1871

Anderson, Nellie V.
See Gordon, Helen (Van Metre) Van-Anderson.

[Anderson, Olive Santa Louie]
An American Girl and Her Four Years in a Boys' College
By Sola [pseud.].
Literary World, 8:194, 1 Apr 1878

Andrews, Charlton
A Parfit Gentil Knight
Dial, 32:88-9, 1 Feb 1902

[Andrews, Eliza Frances]
A Mere Adventurer
By Elzey Hay [pseud.].
Independent, 31:9, 12 Jun 1879
Literary World, 10:183, 7 Jun 1879
Prince Hal
Critic, 2:238, 9 Sep 1882
Literary World, 13:253, 29 Jul 1882

Andrews, Jessie Agnes
Eteocles
Critic, NS 14:153, 27 Sep 1890

Andrews, Mary Raymond (Shipman)
A Kidnapped Colony

Independent, 56:676, 24 Mar 1904
Literary World, 35:50, Feb 1904

Anthony, Geraldine
Four in Hand
Critic, 44:188, Feb 1904
A Victim of Circumstances
Dial, 31:28, 1 Jul 1901
Independent, 53:2053, 29 Aug 1901
Literary World, 32:124, 1 Aug 1901

Antrobus, Suzanne
See Robinson, Suzanne (Antrobus).

Archer, William
See The Broken Shaft.

Aristocracy
Catholic World, 48:399-401, Dec 1888
Literary World, 19:359, 27 Oct 1888

[Arkell, William J.]
Napoleon Smith
Literary World, 19:234, 21 Jul 1888

Armstrong, LeRoy
Dan Gunn
Literary World, 30:167, 27 May 1899
An Indiana Man
Independent, 43:457, 26 Mar 1891
The Outlaws
Critic, 41:478, Nov 1902

Armstrong, Minnie L.
The Social Crime
Literary World, 27:477, 26 Dec 1896

Armstrong, William
An American Nobleman
Critic, NS 27:285, 24 Apr 1897
Independent, 45:53, 12 Jan 1893
Literary World, 28:127, 17 Apr 1897
Cleopatra's Daughter
Critic, NS 13:155, 29 Mar 1890
Thekla
Critic, NS 8:128, 10 Sep 1887
Dial, 8:147, Nov 1887
Independent, 39:1269, 6 Oct 1887
Literary World, 18:370, 29 Oct 1887

Arnold, Birch [pseud.].
See Bartlett, Alice Elinor (Bowen).

Astor, John Jacob
A Journey in Other Worlds
Critic, NS 21:320-1, 12 May 1897
Literary World, 25:149, 19 May 1894

Astor, William Waldorf
Sforza
Chautauquan, 10:633, Feb 1890
Critic, NS 12:238, 16 Nov 1889
Independent, 41:1576, 28 Nov 1889
Literary World, 20:475-6, 21 Dec 1889
Valentino
Chautauquan, 6:365, Mar 1886
Critic, NS 5:30, 16 Jan 1886
Dial, 6:302, Mar 1886

Atherton, Gertrude Franklin (Horn)
American Wives and English Husbands
Critic, NS 29:328-9, 14 May 1898
Dial, 25:75-6, 1 Aug 1898

Atherton, G. (cont.)
Literary World, 29:401, 26 Nov 1898
Ancestors
Dial, 43:317-8, 16 Nov 1907
Independent, 63:1375, 5 Dec 1907
The Aristocrats
Critic, 39:262, Sep 1901
Before the Gringo Came
Chautauquan, 20:254, Nov 1894
Critic, NS 22:330, 17 Nov 1894
Dial, 17:333, 1 Dec 1894
Literary World, 25:352, 20 Oct 1894
The Bell in the Fog
Catholic World, 81:129, Apr 1905
Critic, 46:477, May 1905
The Californians
Critic, NS 30:394-5, Nov 1898
Dial, 25:306, 1 Nov 1898
Independent, 50:1275, 3 Nov 1898; 65:211-2, 23 Jul 1908
Literary World, 29:401, 26 Nov 1898
Literature, 3:328, 8 Oct 1898
Los Cerritos
Critic, NS 13:269, 31 May 1890
Independent, 42:967, 10 Jul 1890
Literary World, 21:238, 19 Jul 1890
Westminster Review, 135:707-8, Jun 1891
The Conqueror
Critic, 40:568-9, Jun 1902
Dial, 32:385, 1 Jun 1902
Independent, 54:2771, 20 Nov 1902
Literary World, 33:86, 1 Jun 1902
A Daughter of the Vine
Critic, NS 32:648, Jul 1899
Independent, 51:2230-1, 17 Aug 1899
Literary World, 30:235, 22 Jul 1899
The Doomswoman
Critic, NS 20:86, 5 Aug 1893
Literary World, 24:193, 17 Jun 1893
His Fortunate Grace
Critic, NS 27:425, 19 Jun 1897
Independent, 49:722, 3 Jun 1897
Literature, 2:511, 30 Apr 1898
Patience Sparhawk and Her Times
Critic, NS 27:283, 24 Apr 1897
Literary World, 28:342, 2 Oct 1897
A Question of Time
Critic, NS 16:182, 10 Oct 1891
Rulers of Kings
Critic, 44:471-2, May 1904
Dial, 37:40, 16 Jul 1904
Independent, 57:453, 25 Aug 1904
Literary World, 35:164, Jun 1904
Senator North
Dial, 29:126, 1 Sep 1900
The Splendid Idle Forties
Independent, 54:2902, 4 Dec 1902
Tower of Ivory
Catholic World, 91:392, Jun 1910
Dial, 48:243-4, 1 Apr 1910
Independent, 68:984-5, 5 May 1910
The Travelling Third
Critic, 47:510-1, Dec 1905
The Valiant Runaways
Chautauquan, 29:606, Sep 1899
Independent, 51:635, 2 Mar 1899
What Dreams May Come By Frank Lin [pseud.].

Critic, NS 11:4, 5 Jan 1889
A Whirl Asunder
Critic, NS 25:234, 4 Apr 1896

Austin, Jane (Goodwin)
Betty Alden
Independent, 43:1882, 17 Dec 1891
David Alden's Daughter, and Other Stories
Chautauquan, 16:382, Dec 1892
Critic, NS 19:60, 4 Feb 1893
Independent, 44:1834, 22 Dec 1892
Literary World, 23:408, 19 Nov 1892
The Desmond Hundred
Catholic World, 49:407-10, Jun 1889
Critic, 2:191, 15 Jul 1882
Dial, 3:60, Jul 1882
Independent, 34:11, 3 Aug 1882
Dr. LeBaron and His Daughters
Chautauquan, 13:685, Aug 1891
Critic, NS 15:167, 28 Mar 1891
Independent, 43:164, 29 Jan 1891; 43:236, 12 Feb 1891; 43:421, 19 Mar 1891
Dora Darling
Independent, 44:1599, 10 Nov 1892
Mrs. Beauchamp Brown
Dial, 1:13, May 1880
Literary World, 11:154, 8 May 1880
A Nameless Nobleman
Catholic World, 33:719, Aug 1881
Dial, 2:18, May 1881
Critic, 1:107-8, 23 Apr 1881
Literary World, 12:200, 4 Jun 1881
Nantucket Scraps
Independent, 35:12, 4 Jan 1883
Literary World, 14:20, 27 Jan 1883
Standish of Standish
Chautauquan, 10:633, Feb 1890; 22:380, Dec 1895
Critic, NS 13:319, 28 Jun 1890
Dial, 11:12-3, May 1890
Independent, 41:1577, 28 Nov 1889; 47:1542, 14 Nov 1895
Literary World, 20:453, 7 Dec 1889

Austin, Martha W.
Veronica
Chautauquan, 38:93-4, Sep 1903
Critic, 43:284, Sep 1903
Dial, 34:242, 1 Apr 1903
Independent, 55:1099, 7 May 1903
Literary World, 34:122, May 1903

Austin, Mary
Isidro
Independent, 59:210, 27 Jul 1905; 59:1154, 16 Nov 1905
Lost Borders
Independent, 68:368, 17 Feb 1910
Santa Lucia
Independent, 65:154-5, 16 Jul 1908

Austin, Maude Mason
'Cension
Critic, NS 25:234, 4 Apr 1896
Harper's, 92:Literary Notes, 4, Feb 1896
Literary World, 27:46, 8 Feb 1896

Avary, Myrta Locket
A Virginia Girl in the Civil War
Independent, 55:568-9, 5 Mar 1903

Babcock, Bernie (Smade)
Justice to the Woman
Critic, 39:574, Dec 1901

[Babcock, John Martin Luther]
The Dawning
Critic, NS 5:216, 1 May 1886

Babcock, William Henry
The Brides of the Tiger
Literary World, 24:57, 25 Feb 1893
Cian of the Chariots
Independent, 51:281, 26 Jan 1899
Literary World, 30:23, 21 Jan 1899
Cypress Beach
Independent, 42:1277, 11 Sep 1890
Kent Fort Manor
Dial, 34:377, 1 Jun 1903
Independent, 55:860-1, 9 Apr 1903
Literary World, 34:83, Apr 1903
The Tower of Wye
Critic, 39:181, Aug 1901
Dial, 31:31, 1 Jul 1901
Literary World, 32:107-8, 1 Jul 1901

Bacheller, Irving
Darrel of the Blessed Isles
Critic, 43:75, Jul 1903
Dial, 34:375, 1 Jun 1903
Independent, 55:1271-2, 28 May 1903
Literary World, 34:152, Jun 1903
D'ri and I
Catholic World, 74:395-6, Dec 1901
Chautauquan, 34:324, Dec 1901
Dial, 31:135-6, 1 Sep 1901
Independent, 53:2117-8, 5 Sep 1901
Literary World, 32:135, 1 Sep 1901
Eben Holden
Critic, 37:550, Dec 1900
Literary World, 31:267, 1 Dec 1900
Eben Holden's Last Day a-Fishing
Independent, 64:313, 6 Feb 1908
The Hand-Made Gentleman
Independent, 66:1343, 17 Jun 1909
The Master of Silence
Chautauquan, 15:774, Sep 1892
Critic, NS 18:104, 27 Aug 1892
Independent, 44:1329, 22 Sep 1892; 68:367, 17 Feb 1910
Literary World, 23:261, 30 Jul 1892
Silas Strong
Critic, 48:571, Jun 1906
Westminster Review, 166:592-3, Nov 1906
Vergilius
Catholic World, 80:124, Oct 1904
Critic, 45:542, Dec 1904
Dial, 37:314, 16 Nov 1904
Independent, 57:680, 22 Sep 1904
Literary World, 35:283, Oct 1904

Bacon, Dolores Marbourg
See Bacon, Mary Schell (Hoke).

Bacon, Eugenia (Jones)
Lyddy
Literary World, 30:54, 18 Feb 1899

Bacon, Josephine Dodge (Daskam)
The Biography of a Boy
Catholic World, 91:681-2, Aug 1910
Independent, 68:1296, 9 Jun 1910
The Domestic Adventurers
Independent, 64:312,

6 Feb 1908
Her Fiancé
Literary World, 35:381, Dec 1904
An Idyll of All Fools' Day
Independent, 65:1464, 17 Dec 1908
The Imp and the Angel
Critic, 39:575, Dec 1901
The Madness of Philip
Dial, 32:391, 1 Jun 1902
Memoirs of a Baby
Critic, 44:561, Jun 1904
Middle-Aged Love Stories
Critic, 43:187, Aug 1903
Dial, 34:376, 1 Jun 1903
Independent, 55:1406, 4 Jun 1903
Literary World, 34:151, Jun 1903
Smith College Stories
Critic, 36:573, Jun 1900
Literary World, 31:90, 1 Apr 1900
Whom the Gods Destroyed
Chautauquan, 37:102, Apr 1903
Critic, 41:580-1, Dec 1902
Dial, 33:332, 16 Nov 1902
Independent, 55:44-5, 1 Jan 1903

[Bacon, Mary Schell (Hoke)]
The Diary of a Musician
Ed. Dolores Marbourg Bacon [pseud.].
Critic, 46:285, Mar 1905
In High Places
By Dolores Bacon [pseud.].
Independent, 64:156-7, 16 Jan 1908
See also Eggleston, George Cary, and Dolores Marbourg [pseud.].

[Badcock, Winnifred (Eaton)]
Daughters of Nijo
By Onoto Watanna [pseud.].
Critic, 45:191, Aug 1904
Independent, 56:1445-6, 23 Jun 1904
The Heart of Hyacinth
By Onoto Watanna [pseud.].
Critic, 43:580-1, Dec 1903
A Japanese Nightingale
By Onoto Watanna [pseud.].
Critic, 39:578, Dec 1901
Literary World, 33:4-5, 1 Jan 1902
The Love of Azalea
By Onoto Watanna [pseud.].
Critic, 45:578, Dec 1904
Independent, 57:1332-3, 8 Dec 1904
The Wooing of Wistaria
By Onoto Watanna [pseud.].
Critic, 41:585, Dec 1902
Independent, 54:2537, 23 Oct 1902
Literary World, 33:194, 1 Dec 1902

Bagby, Albert Morris
"Miss Träumerei"
Dial, 19:384, 16 Dec 1895
Literary World, 26:250-1, 10 Aug 1895

[Bagby, George William]
The Old Virginia Gentleman
Independent, 69:1094-5, 17 Nov 1910

Bailey, Alice (Ward)
Mark Heffron
Harper's, 93:Literary Notes, 1-2, Jul 1896
Independent, 48:1007, 23 Jul 1896
Literary World, 27:329, 3 Oct 1896
The Sage Brush Parson
By A. B. Ward [pseud.].
Dial, 40:262-3, 16 Apr 1906
Independent, 60:1224, 24 May 1906

Bailey, James Montgomery
The Danbury Boom! . . .
Independent, 32:10, 16 Dec 1880

Bailey, James Montgomery (cont.)
Literary World, 11:412-3, 20 Nov 1880
Life in Danbury
Galaxy, 16:279, Aug 1873
Mr. Phillips' Goneness
Literary World, 10:310, 27 Sep 1879
They All Do It
Galaxy, 24:717-8, Nov 1877

Bailey, Thomas Loyd
An Entire Stranger
Chautauquan, 14:761, Mar 1892
Critic, NS 16:215, 10 Oct 1891

Baker, George Augustus
Mrs. Hephaestus, and Other Short Stories
Critic, NS 7:241, 14 May 1887

Baker, George Melville
Running to Waste
Literary World, 5:76, 1 Oct 1874

Baker, Julie Keim (Wetherill)
Wings
Independent, 30:12, 18 Jul 1878
Literary World, 9:47, 1 Aug 1878

Baker, William Mumford
Blessed Saint Certainty
Critic, 1:148, 4 Jan 1881
Dial, 2:42, Jun 1881
Literary World, 12:181-2, 21 May 1881
Carter Quarterman
Independent, 28:10, 23 Mar 1876
Literary World, 6:158-9, 1 Apr 1876
Colonel Dunwoddie, Millionaire
Independent, 30:12, 8 Aug 1878
His Majesty, Myself
Catholic World, 31:431, Jun 1880
Literary World, 11:58, 14 Feb 1880
The Making of a Man
Literary World, 16:46, 7 Feb 1885
Mose Evans
Independent, 26:10, 4 Jun 1874
The New Timothy
Galaxy, 10:561, Oct 1870
A Year Worth Living
Literary World, 9:13, 1 Jun 1878

[Balch, Elizabeth]
Mustard Leaves
By D. T. S. [pseud.].
Literary World, 16:405, 14 Nov 1885
Zorah
Critic, NS 9:5, 7 Jan 1888
Independent, 40:145, 2 Feb 1888
Literary World, 18:460, 10 Dec 1887
Westminster Review, 127 (NS 71):271, Jan 1887

Balch, Frederick Homer
The Bridge of the Gods
Dial, 11:241, Dec 1890
Independent, 43:456, 26 Mar 1891

Balch, William Stevens
A Peculiar People
Dial, 2:220-1, Jan 1882
Independent, 34:11, 9 Feb 1882

Baldwin, Eugene Francis, and Maurice Eisenberg
Doctor Cavallo
Independent, 48:255, 20 Feb 1896

Baldwin, Lydia Wood
A Yankee School Teacher in Virginia

Independent, 37:396, 26 Mar 1885

Baldy, Alice Montgomery
The Romance of a Spanish Nun
Critic, NS 16:63, 8 Aug 1891
Independent, 43:607, 23 Apr 1891

Balestier, Charles Wolcott
The Average Woman
Chautauquan, 16:383, Dec 1892
Critic, NS 18:190, 8 Oct 1892
Independent, 44:1329, 22 Sep 1892
Literary World, 23:258, 30 Jul 1892
Benefits Forgot
Chautauquan, 19:381, Jun 1894
Critic, NS 21:374, 2 Jun 1894
Dial, 16:366, 16 Jun 1894
Literary World, 25:90, 24 Mar 1894
A Fair Device
Critic, NS 2:5, 5 Jul 1884
Independent, 36:1131, 4 Sep 1884
A Victorious Defeat
Critic, NS 5:271, 29 May 1886
Dial, 7:66, Jul 1886
Harper's, 73:Literary Notes, 1-2, Jul 1886
Independent, 38:756, 17 Jun 1886
Literary World, 17:278, 21 Aug 1886

________, and Rudyard Kipling
The Naulahka
By Rudyard Kipling and Wolcott Balestier.
Catholic World, 56:137-8, Oct 1892
Dial, 13:104, Aug 1892
Independent, 44:1229, 1 Sep 1892
Literary World, 23:258, 30 Jul 1892
Westminster Review, 138:568-9, Nov 1892

Ballou, William Hosea
The Bachelor Girl
Independent, 42:1206, 28 Aug 1890

Bamford, Mary Ellen
Jessie's Three Resolutions
Critic, NS 23:158, 2 Mar 1895

Bangs, John Kendrick
The Bicyclers, and Three Other Farces
Independent, 48:628, 7 May 1896
Literary World, 27:350, 17 Oct 1896
The Booming of Acre Hill
Chautauquan, 31:533-4, Aug 1900
Critic, 37:279, Sep 1900
Literary World, 31:121, 1 Jun 1900
The Dreamers
Critic, NS 32:1056, Nov 1899
Independent, 51:2162-3, 10 Aug 1899
Literary World, 30:220, 8 Jul 1899
The Enchanted Type-Writer
Independent, 51:3300, 7 Dec 1899
Literary World, 30:405, 25 Nov 1899
Ghosts I Have Met, and Some Others
Harper's, 96:Literary Notes, 3, May 1898
Independent, 50:264, 28 Jul 1898
Half-Hours with Jimmieboy
Critic, NS 21:166, 10 Mar 1894
A House-Boat on the Styx
Chautauquan, 26:239, Nov 1897
Critic, NS 24:444, 28

Bangs, John Kendrick (cont.)
Dec 1895
Harper's, 92:Literary Notes, 4, Jan 1896

The Idiot
Critic, NS 23:439, 15 Jun 1895
Harper's, 91:Literary Notes, 3, Jun 1895
Independent, 47:874, 27 Jun 1895
Literary World, 26:124, 20 Apr 1895

The Idiot at Home
Independent, 52:3112, 27 Dec 1900
Literary World, 31:268, 1 Dec 1900

The Inventions of the Idiot
Critic, 45:380, Oct 1904

Mr. Bonaparte of Corsica
Critic, NS 23:437, 15 Jun 1895
Harper's, 91:Literary Notes, 4, Jul 1895

Mr. Munchausen . . .
Chautauquan, 34:328, Dec 1901
Critic, 39:574, Dec 1901
Literary World, 33:55, 1 Apr 1902

Mrs. Raffles
Critic, 47:577, Dec 1905

Olympian Nights
Critic, 41:276-7, Sep 1902
Literary World, 33:126, 1 Aug 1902

Over the Plum-Pudding
Critic, 39:574, Dec 1901

Paste Jewels
Harper's, 95:Literary Notes, 4, Nov 1897
Independent, 49:1548, 25 Nov 1897
Literary World, 29:183, 11 Jun 1898

Peeps at People
Independent, 51:634, 2 Mar 1899

The Pursuit of the House-Boat
Chautauquan, 26:239, Nov 1897
Critic, NS 27:423, 19 Jun 1897
Harper's, 95:Literary Notes, 1, Jul 1897
Independent, 49:882, 8 Jul 1897
Literary World, 28:262, 7 Aug 1897

R. Holmes & Co.
Critic, 49:284, Sep 1906

A Rebellious Heroine
Critic, NS 27:253, 10 Apr 1897
Harper's, 94:Literary Notes, 3, Jan 1897
Independent, 48:1693, 10 Dec 1896
Literary World, 28:13, 9 Jan 1897

Roger Camerden
Literary World, 18:139, 30 Apr 1887

Three Weeks in Politics
Harper's, 89:Literary Notes, 4, Sep 1894
Literary World, 25:234, 28 Jul 1894

Toppleton's Client
Critic, NS 22:38, 21 Jul 1894
Dial, 15:94, 16 Aug 1893
Independent, 45:1453, 26 Oct 1893
Literary World, 24:226, 15 Jul 1893

The Water Ghost, and Others
Critic, NS 23:258, 6 Apr 1895
Dial, 17:334, 1 Dec 1894
Harper's, 89:Literary Notes, 4, Aug 1894
Literary World, 25:301-2, 22 Sep 1894

_______, and Frank Dempster Sherman

New Waggings of Old Tales By Two Wags.
Catholic World, 46:704-6, Feb 1888
Critic, NS 8:312, 17 Dec 1887

Banks, Nancy (Huston)
The Little Hills
Critic, 47:284, Sep 1905
Independent, 59:200, 27 Jul 1905; 59:1154, 16 Nov 1905
Oldfield
Catholic World, 76:841-2, Mar 1903
Critic, 41:277, Sep 1902; 42:183, Feb 1903
Dial, 33:64, 1 Aug 1902
Independent, 54:1965-6, 14 Aug 1902
Literary World, 33:138, 1 Sep 1902; 34:35, Feb 1903
Round Anvil Rock
Dial, 35:69, 1 Aug 1903
Independent, 55:1815-6, 30 Jul 1903

[Barber, Harriet Boomer]
Wrecked, but Not Lost
By Faith Templeton [pseud.].
Literary World, 11:112, 27 Mar 1880

Barbour, Mrs. Anna Maynard
At the Time Appointed
Dial, 34:375-6, 1 Jun 1903
Breakers Ahead
Dial, 41:38-9, 16 Jul 1906
Independent, 61:213, 26 Jul 1906
Told in the Rockies
Literary World, 29:102, 2 Apr 1898

Barbour, Ralph Henry
The Golden Heart
Independent, 69:1248, 8 Dec 1910
The Land of Joy
Critic, 43:378, Oct 1903
Literary World, 34:178, Jul 1903
A Maid in Arcady
Independent, 62:157, 17 Jan 1907
My Lady of the Fog
Independent, 65:1463, 17 Dec 1908

Bardeen, Charles William
Commissioner Hume
Literary World, 30:107, 1 Apr 1899
Roderick Hume
Chautauquan, 22:127, Oct 1895

Barlow, Columbus
Day-Dreams of a Doctor
Independent, 50:552, 28 Apr 1898

Barnard, Charles
Camilla, A Tale of a Violin
Literary World, 5:91, 1 Nov 1874

Barnard, Edna A.
Maple Range
Dial, 3:141, Nov 1882
Independent, 35:12, 18 Jan 1883

Barnes, Annie Maria
Little Betty Blew
Chautauquan, 41:284, May 1905

Barnes, James
The Clutch of Circumstance
Independent, 64:1037-8, 7 May 1908
For King or Country
Harper's, 93:Literary Notes, 3, Jun 1896
A Loyal Traitor
Critic, NS 27:438, 26 Jun 1897
Dial, 23:286, 16 Nov 1897
Harper's, 93:Literary Notes, 1-2, Jul 1897
Independent, 49:722, 3 Jun 1897
A Princetonian
Independent, 49:155, 4 Feb 1897
Literary World, 28:164, 15 May 1897

Barnett, Evelyn Scott (Snead)
The Dragnet
Chautauquan, 57:467, Feb 1910

Barns, Charles Edward
A Venetian Study in Black and White
Dial, 10:58-9, Jul 1889

Barr, Amelia Edith (Huddleston)
The Beads of Tasmer
Critic, NS 16:64, 8 Aug 1891
Independent, 48:255, 20 Feb 1896
Literary World, 23:43, 30 Jan 1892
Bernicia
Independent, 47:1690, 12 Dec 1895
Literary World, 27:19, 25 Jan 1896
Between Two Loves
Critic, NS 7:17, 8 Jan 1887; NS 11:258, 25 May 1889
The Black Shilling
Critic, 44:92, Jan 1904
Literary World, 34:307, Nov 1903
A Border Shepherdess
Critic, NS 8:296, 3 Dec 1887
Independent, 39:1392-3, 27 Oct 1887
Literary World, 18:369, 29 Oct 1887
The Bow of Orange Ribbon
Chautauquan, 18:382, Dec 1893
Critic, NS 6:249, 20 Nov 1886
Independent, 38:1520, 25 Nov 1886
Literary World, 18:11-2, 8 Jan 1887
Cecilia's Lovers
Westminster Review, 165:711, Jun 1906
Christopher, and Other Stories
Critic, NS 9:257, 26 May 1888
Independent, 40:753, 14 Jun 1888
A Daughter of Fife
Critic, NS 5:194, 17 Apr 1886
Independent, 38:756, 17 Jun 1886
Literary World, 17:196, 12 Jun 1886
Feet of Clay
Catholic World, 50:833-4, Mar 1890
Chautauquan, 10:633, Feb 1890
Critic, NS 12:255, 23 Nov 1889
Independent, 41:1473, 7 Nov 1889
Literary World, 20:418, 23 Nov 1889
The Flower of Gala Water
Critic, NS 23:47, 19 Jan 1895
Friend Olivia
Critic, NS 15:26, 17 Jan 1891
Independent, 42:1760, 11 Dec 1890
Girls of a Feather
Literary World, 25:5, 13 Jan 1894
The Hallam Succession
Chautauquan, 5:556, Jun 1885
Critic, NS 3:125, 14 Mar 1885
Independent, 37:554-5, 30 Apr 1885; 37:1167, 10 Sep 1885
The Hands of Compulsion
Independent, 67:40, 1 Jul 1909
The Household of McNeil
Critic, NS 14:235, 8 Nov 1890
Independent, 42:1842, 25 Dec 1890
Literary World, 21:439, 22 Nov 1890
I, Thou, and the Other One
Literary World, 30:166, 27 May 1899

Jan Vedder's Wife
Critic, NS 3:197, 25 Apr 1885
Independent, 37:815-6, 25 Jun 1885
Literary World, 16:199, 13 Jun 1885

The King's Highway
Critic, NS 29:165, 5 Mar 1898
Literary World, 28:464, 11 Dec 1897

A Knight of the Nets
Literary World, 27:445, 12 Dec 1896
Literature, 2:116, 29 Jan 1898

The Last of the Macallisters
Critic, NS 5:181, 10 Apr 1886
Independent, 38:495, 22 Apr 1886
Literary World, 20:178, 25 May 1889

The Lion's Whelp
Independent, 53:2717, 14 Nov 1901
Literary World, 33:8, 1 Jan 1902

The Lone House
Chautauquan, 19:486, Jul 1894
Critic, NS 21:408, 16 Jun 1894
Literary World, 25:171, 2 Jun 1894

The Lost Silver of Briffault
Critic, NS 5:129, 13 Mar 1886
Independent, 38:75, 21 Jan 1886

Love for an Hour Is Love Forever
Critic, NS 18:43, 23 Jul 1892
Independent, 44:1261, 8 Sep 1892
Literary World, 23:181, 21 May 1892

The Maid of Maiden Lane
Catholic World, 72:129, Oct 1900
Critic, 37:466, Nov 1900

Master of His Fate
Catholic World, 47:416, Jun 1888
Critic, NS 9:257, 26 May 1888
Independent, 40:817, 28 Jun 1888
Literary World, 19:154, 12 May 1888; 23:88, 12 Mar 1892

Paul and Christina
Critic, NS 9:4, 7 Jan 1888
Literary World, 19:11, 7 Jan 1888

The Preacher's Daughter
Independent, 44:1599, 10 Nov 1892

Prisoners of Conscience
Chautauquan, 26:344, Dec 1897
Critic, NS 27:336, 15 May 1897
Independent, 49:851, 1 Jul 1897
Literary World, 28:173, 29 May 1897

A Reconstructed Marriage
Independent, 69:1090-1, 17 Nov 1910

Remember the Alamo
Catholic World, 48:267, Nov 1888
Critic, NS 10:219, 3 Nov 1888
Dial, 9:162, Nov 1888
Independent, 40:1644, 20 Dec 1888
Literary World, 19:294-5, 15 Sep 1888

Romances and Realities
Galaxy, 22:568, Oct 1876
Independent, 28:9, 9 Mar 1876

A Rose of a Hundred Leaves
Critic, NS 17:100, 13 Feb 1892
Independent, 43:1921, 24 Dec 1891
Literary World, 23:14, 2 Jan 1892

She Loved a Sailor
Catholic World, 53:443-4,

Barr, Amelia Edith (cont.)
Jun 1891
Critic, NS 16:64, 8 Aug 1891
Independent, 43:1219, 13 Aug 1891
A Singer from the Sea
Chautauquan, 18:254, Nov 1893
Critic, NS 20:100, 12 Aug 1893
Literary World, 24:210, 1 Jul 1893
A Sister to Esau
Critic, NS 17:35, 16 Jan 1892
Independent, 43:1844, 10 Dec 1891
Westminster Review, 138:223, Aug 1892
A Song of a Single Note
Critic, 42:283, Mar 1903
Literary World, 33:195, 1 Dec 1902
The Squire of Sandal-Side
Critic, NS 7:101-2, 26 Feb 1887
Independent, 39:398, 31 Mar 1887
Literary World, 18:73, 8 Mar 1887
Thyra Varrick
Critic, 43:187, Aug 1903
Dial, 35:158 [222], 1 Oct 1903
Independent, 55:1465, 18 Jun 1903
Trinity Bells
Independent, 52:73, 4 Jan 1900
Literary World, 30:434-5, 9 Dec 1899
Was It Right To Forgive?
Independent, 52:2874, 29 Nov 1900

Barr, Granville Walter
Shacklett
Independent, 53:3090, 26 Dec 1901

Barr, Robert
See Crane, Stephen, and Robert Barr.

Barrett, Wilson
The Sign of the Cross
Chautauquan, 25:576, Aug 1897
Literary World, 28:90, 20 Mar 1897

________, and Elwyn Alfred Barron
In Old New York
Dial, 28:86, 1 Feb 1900
Literary World, 31:70-1, 3 Mar 1900

Barron, Elwyn Alfred
Manders
Dial, 26:124, 16 Feb 1899
See also Barrett, Wilson, and Elwyn Alfred Barron.

Barrow, Elizabeth N.
The Fortune of War
Chautauquan, 31:314, Jun 1900

Barry, John Daniel
The Congressman's Wife
Critic, 43:576, Dec 1903
A Daughter of Thespis
Independent, 55:1521, 25 Jun 1905
Literary World, 34:141, Jun 1903
The Intriguers
Literary World, 28:127, 17 Apr 1897
Mademoiselle Blanche
Critic, 36:374, Apr 1900
Literary World, 28:146, 1 May 1897; 30:71, 3 Mar 1900
Our Best Society
Critic, 48:92, Jan 1906

Barry, Richard
The Events Man
Independent, 63:943, 17 Oct 1907
Sandy from the Sierras
Dial, 41:116, 1 Sep 1906

Independent, 61:699-700, 20 Sep 1906

Barry, William Francis
Arden Massiter
Chautauquan, 31:534, Aug 1900
Dial, 29:24, 1 Jul 1900
Literary World, 31:156, 1 Aug 1900
The Dayspring
Critic, 44:560, Jun 1904
Literary World, 35:205, Jul 1904
The Place of Dreams
Catholic World, 74:404, Dec 1901
The Wizard's Knot
Dial, 31:30, 1 Jul 1901
Independent, 53:1323-4, 6 Jun 1901

[Bartlett, Alice Elinor (Bowen)]
A New Aristocracy
By "Birch Arnold" [pseud.].
Independent, 43:1283, 27 Aug 1891
Literary World, 29:11, 8 Jan 1898
Until the Day Break
By Mrs. J. M. D. Bartlett
Literary World, 8:181, 1 Mar 1878

Bartlett, Frederick Orin
Joan of the Alley
Catholic World, 79:127, Apr 1904
Critic, 45:279, Sep 1904
Literary World, 35:106, Apr 1904
The Web of the Golden Spider
Independent, 66:763, 8 Apr 1909

Bartlett, George Herbert
A Commercial Trip with an Uncommercial Ending
Literary World, 15:194, 14 Jun 1884
Water Tramps
Independent, 47:1075, 8 Aug 1895

Bartlett, Mrs. J. M. D.
See Bartlett, Alice Elinor (Bowen).

Bartlett, Theodore
Heart Stories
Literary World, 20:288, 31 Aug 1889

Bartlett, William Chambers
An Idyl of War-Times
Chautauquan, 13:805-6, Sep 1891
Critic, NS 15:109, 28 Feb 1891

Barton, Lee [pseud.]
See Lewis, William H.

Barton, William Eleazar
A Hero in Homespun
Critic, NS 29:39, 15 Jan 1898
Independent, 49:1660, 16 Dec 1897
Sim Galloway's Daughter-in-Law
Independent, 50:222, 17 Feb 1898
Literary World, 29:76, 5 Mar 1898
When Boston Braved the King
Literary World, 31:90, 1 Apr 1900

Baskett, James Newton
"At You-All's House"
Chautauquan, 27:573, Aug 1898
Critic, NS 30:530, Dec 1898
Independent, 50:123-4, 14 Jul 1898
Literary World, 29:189, 11 Jun 1898
Literature, 3:256, 17 Sep 1898
Westminster Review, 150:475, Oct 1898

Bassett, George
Hippolyte, and Golden-Beak
Critic, NS 23:458, 22

Bassett, George (cont.)
Jun 1895
Dial, 19:95, 16 Aug 1895

Bassett, Mary E. (Stone)
A Fair Plebian
Dial, 4:42, Jun 1883
Independent, 35:11, 2 Aug 1883
Literary World, 14:211, 30 Jun 1883
Judith's Garden
Independent, 54:1727, 17 Jul 1902
Literary World, 33:123, 1 Aug 1902
A Riddle of Luck
Critic, NS 21:145, 3 Mar 1894
Independent, 45:1018, 27 Jul 1893

Bates, Arlo
Albrecht
Critic, NS 13:19-20, 11 Jan 1890
Dial, 11:13, May 1890
Independent, 42:493, 10 Apr 1890
Literary World, 21:70, 1 Mar 1890
A Book o' Nine Tales
Chautauquan, 13:552, Jul 1891
Critic, NS 15:309, 13 Jun 1891
Independent, 43:1283, 27 Aug 1891
The Diary of a Saint
Chautauquan, 36:448, Jan 1903
Critic, 42:283, Mar 1903
Dial, 33:329-30, 16 Nov 1902
Independent, 54:2898, 4 Dec 1902
Literary World, 34:11, 1 Jan 1903
In the Bundle of Time
Independent, 45:1154, 24 Aug 1893
Literary World, 24:89, 25 Mar 1893
A Lad's Love
Critic, NS 8:78, 13 Aug 1887
Independent, 39:1269, 6 Oct 1887
Literary World, 18:211-2, 9 Jul 1887
Love in a Cloud
Independent, 52:2935, 6 Dec 1900
Literary World, 31:172, 1 Sep 1900
Mr. Jacobs
Critic, 3:232, 19 May 1883
The Pagans
Independent, 36:651, 22 May 1884
Literary World, 15:78-9, 8 Mar 1884
Patty's Perversities
Critic, 1:219, 13 Aug 1881
Dial, 2:101, Sep 1881
Literary World, 12:296, 27 Aug 1881
The Philistines
Literary World, 20:13, 5 Jan 1889
The Puritans
Chautauquan, 28:629-30, Mar 1899
Critic, NS 31:165, Feb 1899
Dial, 25:306, 1 Nov 1898
Independent, 50:1123-4, 20 Oct 1898
Literary World, 29:335, 15 Oct 1898
The Romance of a Ritualist
Literary World, 30:166-7, 27 May 1899
A Wheel of Fire
Critic, NS 4:158, 3 Oct 1885
Independent, 37:1454, 12 Nov 1885
Literary World, 16:474, 12 Dec 1885

Bates, E. Katharine
Nile Days
Independent, 31:11, 7

Aug 1879

[Bates, Harriet Leonora (Vose)]
A Woodland Wooing
By Eleanor Putnam [pseud.].
Critic, NS 11:299, 15 Jun 1889
Literary World, 20:241, 20 Jul 1889

Bates, Josephine (White)
A Blind Lead
Critic, NS 10:125, 15 Sep 1888
Independent, 40:753, 14 Jun 1883
Literary World, 19:154, 12 May 1888
Bunch-Grass Stories
By Mrs. Lindon W. Bates.
Dial, 19:385, 16 Dec 1895
Independent, 47:1204, 5 Sep 1895
Literary World, 26:459, 14 Dec 1895
A Nameless Wrestler
Critic, NS 12:161-2, 5 Oct 1889
Literary World, 20:387, 9 Nov 1889

Bates, Katharine Lee
Hermit Island
Independent, 42:1414, 9 Oct 1890

Bates, Mrs. Lindon W.
See Bates, Josephine (White).

[Bates, Margret Holmes (Ernsperger)]
The Chamber over the Gate
By Margret Holmes [pseud.].
Critic, NS 6:137, 18 Sep 1886
Literary World, 17:309-10, 18 Sep 1886
Jasper Fairfax
By Margret Holmes [pseud.].
Literary World, 29:51, 19 Feb 1898

Bates, Morgan
Martin Brook
Critic, 38:566, Jun 1901
Dial, 31:27, 1 Jul 1901
Independent, 53:1505, 4 Jul 1901
Literary World, 32:103, 1 Jul 1901

Bates, Oric
A Madcap Cruise
Dial, 39:115-6, 1 Sep 1905

Bateson, Carleton
The Man in the Camlet Cloak
Literary World, 34:234, Sep 1903

Battershall, Fletcher Williams
A Daughter of This World
Critic, NS 21:271, 21 Apr 1894
Dial, 16:146, 1 Mar 1894
Mists
Literary World, 26:25, 26 Jan 1895

Baylor, Frances Courtenay
Behind the Blue Ridge
Critic, NS 8:52, 23 Jul 1887
Independent, 39:1133, 8 Sep 1887
Literary World, 18:218, 9 Jul 1887
Claudia Hyde
Critic, NS 23:27, 12 Jan 1895
Dial, 17:123, 1 Sep 1894
Literary World, 25:218, 14 Jul 1894
A Georgian Bungalow
Critic, 37:468, Nov 1900
Juan and Juanita
Chautauquan, 8:198, Dec 1887
Independent, 39:1458, 10 Nov 1887

Baylor, Frances Courtenay (cont.)
The Ladder of Fortune
Critic, NS 32:844, Sep 1899
Dial, 27:175, 16 Sep 1899
Independent, 51:1440, 25 May 1899
Literary World, 30:141, 29 Apr 1899
Miss Nina Barrow
Critic, NS 29:180, 12 Mar 1898
On Both Sides
Catholic World, 43:278, May 1886
Critic, NS 5:5, 2 Jan 1886
Independent, 37:1565, 3 Dec 1885
Literary World, 17:166-7, 15 May 1886
Westminster Review, 127 (NS 71):264, Jan 1887
A Shocking Example
Critic, NS 11:129, 16 Mar 1889
Literary World, 20:113, 30 Mar 1889

[Beach, Rebecca (Gibbons)]
The Puritan and the Quaker
Independent, 31:10, 19 Jun 1879
Literary World, 10:183, 7 Jun 1879

Beach, Rex
The Barrier
Dial, 44:350, 1 Jun 1908
Independent, 64:866, 16 Apr 1908
The Silver Horde
Dial, 48:20, 1 Jan 1910
Independent, 67:1152, 18 Nov 1909; 67:1262, 2 Dec 1909
The Spoilers
Critic, 48:571, Jun 1906
Dial, 40:364, 1 Jun 1906
Independent, 60:1547, 21 Jun 1906; 61:1158-60, 15 Nov 1906

Beale, Charles Willing
The Ghost of Guir House
Literary World, 28:377, 30 Oct 1897
The Secret of the Earth
Literary World, 30:167, 27 May 1899

Beale, Maria (Taylor)
Jack O'Doon
Critic, NS 23:438-9, 15 Jun 1895
Independent, 47:737, 30 May 1895

Bean, Fannie
Putney and Walp
Independent, 43:1386, 17 Sep 1891
Ruth Marsh
Independent, 44:1599, 10 Nov 1892
Literary World, 23:408, 19 Nov 1892

[Bean, Mrs. Helen Marr]
The Widow Wyse
Critic, NS 3:17, 10 Jan 1885
Literary World, 16:45-6, 7 Feb 1885

Beard, Daniel Carter
Moonblight, and Six Feet of Romance
Chautauquan, 15:653, Aug 1892
Critic, NS 18:67, 6 Aug 1892
Independent, 44:1130, 11 Aug 1892

Beard, Oliver Thomas
Bristling with Thorns
Literary World, 15:147, 3 May 1884

Beard, Wolcott Le Cléar
Sand and Cactus
Independent, 51:2900, 19 Oct 1899
Literary World, 30:365, 28 Oct 1899

Beattie, Hans Stevenson
Joshua Wray
Catholic World, 56:277-8, Nov 1892
Literary World, 24:44, 11 Feb 1893

Beatty, John
The Belle o' Becket's Lane
Independent, 35:11, 19 Apr 1883

Beckett, Charles Henry
Who Is John Norman?
Critic, NS 7:282, 4 Jun 1887
Literary World, 18:219, 9 Jul 1887

[Beebe, Charles Washington]
Edmund Dawn
By Ravenswood [pseud.].
Literary World, 4:76, Oct 1873

Beers, Henry Augustin
A Suburban Pastoral, and Other Tales
Literary World, 25:219, 14 Jul 1894

Belden, Jessie Perry (Van Zile)
Antonia
Critic, 39:373, Oct 1901
Dial, 31:33, 1 Jul 1901
Independent, 53:2182, 12 Sep 1901
Literary World, 32:133-4, 1 Sep 1901
Fate at the Door
Literary World, 26:246, 10 Aug 1895; 26:253, 10 Aug 1895

[Bell, John Keble]
The Smiths
By Keble Howard [pseud.].
Independent, 63:343-4, 8 Aug 1907

Bell, Lilian Lida
Abroad with the Jimmies
Literary World, 33:101, 1 Jul 1902
At Home with the Jardines
Literary World, 35:283, Oct 1904
A Book of Girls
Literary World, 34:306-7, Nov 1903
The Dowager Countess and the American Girl
Critic, 43:284, Sep 1903
Dial, 35:67, 1 Aug 1903
Independent, 55:2181, 10 Sep 1903
Literary World, 34:208-9, Aug 1903
The Expatriates
Critic, 38:84, Jan 1901
Literary World, 31:215, 1 Nov 1900
Hope Loring
Literary World, 34:36, Feb 1903
The Instinct of Step-Fatherhood
Harper's, 98:Literary Notes, 2-3, Dec 1898
Literary World, 29:435, 10 Dec 1898
The Interference of Patricia
Literary World, 34:208, Aug 1903
A Little Sister to the Wilderness
Dial, 18:270, 1 May 1895
Independent, 47:1170, 29 Aug 1895; 47:1579, 21 Nov 1895
Literary World, 26:170, 1 Jun 1895
The Love Affairs of an Old Maid
Critic, NS 20:394-5, 16 Dec 1893
Dial, 15:93-4, 16 Aug 1893
Harper's, 87:Literary Notes, 3, Jun 1893
Love Letters of a Worldly Woman
Literary World, 24:242, 29 Jul 1893
Sir John and the American

Bell, Lilian Lida (cont.)
Girl
Critic, 39:277, Sep 1901
Independent, 53:2184, 12 Sep 1901
Literary World, 32:126, 1 Aug 1901
The Under Side of Things
Chautauquan, 24:630, Feb 1897
Critic, NS 25:459, 27 Jun 1896
Dial, 21:94-5, 16 Aug 1896
Harper's, 93:Literary Notes, 3-4, Jul 1896
Independent, 48:976, 16 Jul 1896
Literary World, 27:285, 5 Sep 1896

Bellamy, Charles Joseph
The Breton Mills
Independent, 31:11, 7 Aug 1879
Literary World, 10:251, 2 Aug 1879
An Experiment in Marriage
Critic, NS 13:154, 29 Mar 1890
Literary World, 21:41, 1 Feb 1890
The Way Out
Independent, 37:1104, 27 Aug 1885
Were They Sinners?
Critic, NS 14:95, 23 Aug 1890

Bellamy, Edward
The Blindman's World, and Other Stories
Chautauquan, 29:605, Sep 1899
Independent, 50:1346, 10 Nov 1898
Literary World, 29:434, 10 Dec 1898
Dr. Heidenhoff's Process
Literary World, 11:280, 14 Aug 1880
The Duke of Stockbridge
Critic, 37:571, Dec 1900
Dial, 31:31, 1 Jul 1901
Independent, 53:1563-4, 4 Jul 1901
Literary World, 32:71, 1 May 1901
Equality
Catholic World, 65:844, Sep 1897
Chautauquan, 25:575, Aug 1897
Critic, NS 28:19-20, 10 Jul 1897
Dial, 23:49-50, 1 Jul 1897
Independent, 49:1243, 23 Sep 1897
Literary World, 28:251-2, 7 Aug 1897
Looking Backward, 2000-1887
Catholic World, 46:855-6, Mar 1888
Critic, NS 9:90, 25 Feb 1888; NS 11:322-3, 29 Jun 1889
Independent, 40:400, 29 Mar 1888
Literary World, 19:85-6, 17 Mar 1888
Miss Ludington's Sister
Critic, NS 2:40, 26 Jul 1884
Independent, 36:1163, 11 Sep 1884
Literary World, 15:255, 9 Aug 1884
Westminster Review, 123 (NS 67):292, Jan 1885
Six to One
Critic, NS 13:154, 29 Mar 1890
Independent, 30:12, 29 Aug 1878
Literary World, 9:57, 1 Sep 1878

[Bellamy, Elizabeth Whitfield (Croom)]
The Little Joanna
By Kamba Thorpe [pseud.].
Literary World, 6:131, 1 Feb 1876

Belt, Harriett Pennawell
Marjorie Huntingdon
Independent, 37:396, 26 Mar 1885
A Mirage of Promise
Literary World, 18:41, 5 Feb 1887

Benedict, Frank Lee
John Worthington's Name
Independent, 26:9-10, 14 May 1874
Literary World, 5:4-5, 1 Jun 1874
Miss Dorothy's Charge
Galaxy, 17:286-7, Feb 1874
Independent, 25:1256-7, 9 Oct 1873
Literary World, 4:81, Nov 1873
Westminster Review, 100:246, Oct 1873
Miss Van Kortland
Galaxy, 10:561-2, Oct 1870
Literary World, 1:8, 1 Jun 1870
Mr. Vaughan's Heir
Galaxy, 20:139-41, Jul 1875
Independent, 27:10, 29 Apr 1875
Literary World, 5:181-2, 1 May 1875
The Price She Paid
Dial, 4:138, Oct 1883
Independent, 35:11, 4 Oct 1883
Literary World, 14:351, 20 Oct 1883
St. Simon's Niece
Literary World, 6:52, 1 Sep 1875

Benham, Charles
The Fourth Napoleon
Dial, 23:391, 16 Dec 1897
Literary World, 29:11, 8 Jan 1898
Literature, 2:179, 12 Feb 1898

[Benham, George Chittenden]
A Year of Wreck
Dial, 1:136, Nov 1880
Independent, 32:11, 28 Oct 1880
Literary World, 11:389, 6 Nov 1880

[Benjamin, Charles A.]
The Strike in the B---- Mill
Critic, NS 7:241, 14 May 1887
Literary World, 18:139, 30 Apr 1887

Benjamin, Lewis
What Was It?
Critic, NS 12:99-100, 31 Aug 1889

[Bennett, Mary E.]
The Gentle Art of Pleasing
By Elizabeth Glover [pseud.].
Literary World, 30:123, 15 Apr 1899
Jefferson Wildrider
By Elizabeth Glover [pseud.].
Literary World, 30:7, 7 Jan 1899

Benson, Blackwood Ketchum
Bayard's Courier
Dial, 33:332, 16 Nov 1902
Literary World, 34:12, 1 Jan 1903
A Friend with the Countersign
Catholic World, 74:261, Nov 1901
Dial, 31:371, 16 Nov 1901
Literary World, 33:44, 1 Mar 1902
Old Squire
Chautauquan, 38:308, Nov 1903
Dial, 34:375, 1 Jun 1903
Independent, 55:1691, 16 Jul 1903

Benson, Blackwood Ketchum (cont.)
Literary World, 34:151-2, Jun 1903
Who Goes There?
Dial, 30:110, 16 Feb 1901
Literary World, 32:103, 1 Jul 1901

Bentley, Charles S., and Frank Kimball Scribner
The Fifth of November
Dial, 26:245, 1 Apr 1899

Bentley, Thomas
False Honor
Literary World, 10:214, 5 Jul 1879

Benton, Kate A.
Geber
Critic, 37:374, Oct 1900

Bergengren, Anna (Farquhar)
The Devil's Plough
Critic, 39:374, Oct 1901
Dial, 31:32, 1 Jul 1901
Independent, 53:1500, 27 Jun 1901
Literary World, 32:103, 1 Jul 1901
An Evans of Suffolk
Critic, 45:283, Sep 1904
Independent, 56:1087, 12 May 1904
Literary World, 35:73, Mar 1904
Her Washington Experiences
Independent, 53:2715, 14 Nov 1901
The Professor's Daughter
Independent, 51:2569, 21 Sep 1899
Literary World, 30:182-3, 10 Jun 1899
A Singer's Heart
Chautauquan, 25:575, Aug 1897
Literary World, 28:227, 10 Jun 1897

Berkeley, August
A Modern Quixote
Critic, NS 3:5, 3 Jan 1885
Independent, 37:75, 15 Jan 1885

Bernstein, Herman
Contrite Hearts
Critic, 48:571, Jun 1906
Dial, 40:20, 1 Jan 1906
Independent, 61:579-80, 6 Sep 1906
In the Gates of Israel
Critic, 41:579-80, Dec 1902
Independent, 54:2081-2, 28 Aug 1902
Dial, 33:331, 16 Nov 1902

Berringer, Mrs. Oscar
The New Virtue
Literary World, 27:121, 18 Apr 1896

Berry, Edward Payson
Leah of Jerusalem
Chautauquan, 12:286, Nov 1890
Critic, NS 13:319, 28 Jun 1890
Independent, 42:1205, 28 Aug 1890
Literary World, 21:358-9, 11 Oct 1890

Bertron, Mrs. Ottilie
Edith
Critic, NS 10:244, 17 Nov 1888

Bickford, Luther H.
A Hopeless Case
Critic, NS 12:42, 27 Jul 1889

________, and Richard Stillman Powell
Phyllis in Bohemia
Independent, 49:1548, 25 Nov 1897
Literary World, 28:436, 27 Nov 1897

Bien, Herman M.
Ben Beor
Independent, 43:1844, 10 Dec 1891

Bierce, Ambrose
Can Such Things Be?
Literary World, 25:58, 24 Feb 1894
Fantastic Fables
Literary World, 30:252, 5 Aug 1899
In the Midst of Life
Critic, NS 29:266, 16 Apr 1898
Independent, 50:693, 29 May 1898
Literary World, 29:205, 25 Jun 1898
Tales of Soldiers and Civilians
Critic, NS 17:167, 19 Mar 1892
Independent, 47:1170, 29 Aug 1895
Literary World, 26:283, 7 Sep 1895

________, and Gustav Adolph Danziger
The Monk and the Hangman's Daughter
Dial, 14:22-3, 1 Jan 1893

Bigelow, Edith Evelyn (Jaffray)
Diplomatic Disenchantments
Critic, NS 24:195-6, 28 Sep 1895
Dial, 19:93-4, 16 Aug 1895
Harper's, 91:Literary Notes, 4, Sep 1895
Independent, 47:1170, 29 Aug 1895
The Middle Course
By Mrs. Poultney Bigelow.
Critic, 43:474, Nov 1903

Bigelow, Mrs. Poultney
See Bigelow, Edith Evelyn (Jaffray).

Bingham, Joel Foote
The Twin Sisters of Martigny
Literary World, 30:6, 7 Jan 1899

[Bird, Frederic Mayer]
An Alien from the Commonwealth
By Robert Timsol [pseud.].
Critic, NS 12:5, 6 Jul 1889
Dial, 10:58, Jul 1889
Independent, 41:1153, 5 Sep 1889
Romance of an Odd Young Man
By Robert Timsol [pseud.].
Literary World, 20:258, 3 Aug 1889

Bishop, Putnam Peter
The Psychologist
Literary World, 17:466, 11 Dec 1886

Bishop, R. F.
Camerton Slope
Chautauquan, 18:255, Nov 1893

Bishop, William Henry (1843-?)
The Garden of Eden, U.S.A.
Independent, 47:1107, 15 Aug 1895; 47:1579, 21 Nov 1895
Literary World, 26:218, 13 Jul 1895

Bishop, William Henry (1847-1928)
The Brown Stone Boy, and Other Queer People
Critic, NS 10:30, 21 Jul 1888
Independent, 40:817, 28 Jun 1888
Literary World, 19:234, 21 Jul 1888
Choy Susan, and Other Stories
Critic, NS 2:305, 27 Dec 1884

Bishop, William Henry (1847-1928) (cont.)
Independent, 36:1546, 4 Dec 1884
Literary World, 15:453, 13 Dec 1884
Detmold
Literary World, 10:203, 21 Jun 1879; 10:296-7, 13 Sep 1879
The Golden Justice
Catholic World, 44:850-3, Mar 1887
Critic, NS 7:228, 7 May 1887
Independent, 39:782, 23 Jun 1887
Literary World, 18:41, 5 Feb 1887
The House of a Merchant Prince
Critic, 3:79, 24 Feb 1883
Independent, 35:11, 1 Mar 1883
Literary World, 14:39, 10 Feb 1883
A Pound of Cure
Literary World, 25:266, 25 Aug 1894
Writing to Rosina
Literary World, 25:393, 17 Nov 1894
The Yellow Snake
Critic, NS 17:52, 23 Jan 1892
Dial, 12:277, Dec 1891

Bisland, Elizabeth
See Wetmore, Elizabeth Bisland.

Black, Alexander
A Capital Courtship
Chautauquan, 26:687, Mar 1898
Independent, 50:224, 17 Feb 1898
Richard Gordon
Independent, 54:2900, 4 Dec 1902
Critic, 42:83, Jan 1903

Black, Margaret Horton (Potter)
The Castle of Twilight
Critic, 43:579, Dec 1903
Dial, 35:263, 16 Oct 1903
Independent, 55:2347-8, 1 Oct 1903
The Fire of Spring
Critic, 46:564, Jun 1905
The Flame-Gatherers
Critic, 45:191, Aug 1904
Dial, 37:40, 16 Jul 1904
The Genius
Critic, 48:573, Jun 1906
Dial, 40:366, 1 Jun 1906
The Golden Ladder
Dial, 45:91, 16 Aug 1908
Independent, 65:156-7, 16 Jul 1908
The House of de Mailly
Critic, 39:158, Aug 1901
Dial, 31:29, 1 Jul 1901
Independent, 53:2124, 5 Sep 1901
Istar of Babylon
Critic, 41:583, Dec 1902
Independent, 54:3100, 25 Dec 1902
Literary World, 34:36, Feb 1903
The Princess
Dial, 42:315, 16 May 1907
The Twilight Castle
Literary World, 34:261, Oct 1903
Uncanonized
Dial, 29:306-7, 1 Nov 1900
Independent, 53:161-2, 17 Jan 1901
Literary World, 32:38-9, 1 Mar 1901

Blackall, Emily (Lucas)
Superior to Circumstances
Chautauquan, 11:126-7, Apr 1890
Won and Not One
Chautauquan, 14:761, Mar 1892
Independent, 44:413, 24 Mar 1892

Blackwell, Antoinette Louisa (Brown)
The Island Neighbors
Literary World, 2:36-7, 1 Aug 1871

Blair, Eliza (Nelson)
Lisbeth Wilson
Chautauquan, 22:127, Oct 1895
Independent, 47:1406, 17 Oct 1895
Literary World, 26:170, 1 Jun 1895

Blaisdell, Albert Franklin
Stories from the Civil War
Independent, 42:1641, 20 Nov 1890

Blaisdell, Elijah Whittier
The Hidden Record
Critic, 2:355, 30 Dec 1882

Blake, Lillie (Devereux) Umsted
A Daring Experiment, and Other Stories
Critic, NS 21:324, 12 May 1894
Fettered for Life
Independent, 26:10, 23 Apr 1874
Literary World, 4:178-9, 1 May 1874

Blanchard, Amy Ella
Because of Conscience
Critic, 40:569, Jun 1902
Literary World, 33:8, 1 Jan 1902
Her Very Best
Critic, 38:278, Mar 1901
A Heroine of 1812
Literary World, 32:181, 1 Nov 1901
An Independent Daughter
Literary World, 29:371, 12 Nov 1898
A Revolutionary Maid
Independent, 51:3297, 7 Dec 1899

Blanchard, Evangeline B.
The Devil's Dream
Independent, 42:154, 30 Jan 1890

Blanche Seymour
Westminster Review, 95:275, Apr 1871

Bliss, William Root
The Old Colony Town and Other Sketches
Critic, NS 20:337-8, 25 Nov 1893

Blodgett, Mabel Louise (Fuller)
At the Queen's Mercy
Critic, NS 29:216, 26 Mar 1898
Literary World, 28:244, 24 Jul 1897

[Bloede, Gertrude]
The Story of Two Lives
By Stuart Sterne [pseud.].
Critic, NS 16:53, 1 Aug 1891

Bloomfield-Moore, Clara Sophia (Jessup)
On Dangerous Ground
Independent, 28:10, 23 Mar 1876
Literary World, 6:165, 1 Apr 1876

Bloomingdale, Charles
A Failure
Dial, 36:372, 1 Jun 1904
Mr., Miss, and Mrs.
Literary World, 30:140, 29 Apr 1899

Blossom, Henry Martyn
Checkers
Independent, 48:1462, 29 Oct 1896
The Documents in Evidence
Critic, NS 22:136, 1 Sep 1894

Blum, Edgar C.
Bertha Laycourt

Blum, Edgar C. (cont.)
Critic, NS 12:42, 27 Jul 1889
Satan's Realm
Literary World, 31:76, 3 Mar 1900

Bob Dean
Independent, 34:11, 2 Feb 1882

Boisgilbert, Edmund [pseud.]
See Donnelly, Ignatius Loyola.

Boit, Robert Apthorp
Eustis
Critic, NS 2:5, 5 Jul 1884
Literary World, 15:183, 31 May 1884

Bolton, Sarah (Knowles)
A Country Idyl
Literary World, 29:342, 15 Oct 1898

Bonner, Geraldine
Hard-Pan
Critic, 38:84, Jan 1901
Literary World, 32:71, 1 May 1901
The Pioneer
Critic, 46:477, May 1905
To-morrow's Tangle
Critic, 43:577, Dec 1903
Independent, 55:2634, 5 Nov 1903

Bonner, Sherwood [pseud.]
See McDowell, Katherine Sherwood (Bonner).

Bouton, John Bell
The Enchanted
Dial, 12:49-50, Jun 1891
Independent, 43:1219, 13 Aug 1891

Bouvé, Edward Tracy
Centuries Apart
Literary World, 25:392, 17 Nov 1894

Bouvé, Pauline Carrington (Rust)
Their Shadows Before
Literary World, 31:157, 1 Aug 1900

Bowles, John
The Stormy Petrel
Independent, 45:1250, 14 Sep 1893

Boyce, Neith
See Hapgood, Neith (Boyce).

Boyesen, Hjalmar Hjorth
Against Heavy Odds
Chautauquan, 12:423, Dec 1890
Critic, NS 14:233, 8 Nov 1890
Independent, 42:1644, 20 Nov 1890
A Daughter of the Philistines
Dial, 3:280, Apr 1883
Independent, 35:11, 17 May 1883
Literary World, 14:107, 7 Apr 1883
Falconberg
Independent, 31:10, 29 May 1879
The Golden Calf
Critic, NS 19:19, 14 Jan 1893
Gunnar
Independent, 26:10, 8 Oct 1874
Literary World, 5:76, 1 Oct 1874
Ilka on the Hill-Top, and Other Stories
Critic, 1:7, 29 Jan 1881
Dial, 1:218, Feb 1881
Literary World, 12:146, 23 Apr 1881
The Light of Her Countenance
Critic, NS 12:135, 21 Sep 1889
Literary World, 20:299, 14 Sep 1889
The Mammon of

Unrighteousness
Chautauquan, 14:255, Nov 1891
Critic, NS 16:106, 29 Aug 1891
Dial, 12:276-7, Dec 1891
The Modern Vikings
Chautauquan, 8:198, Dec 1887
Critic, NS 8:314, 17 Dec 1887
Norseland Tales
Critic, NS 23:159, 2 Mar 1895
Westminster Review, 144:708-9, Dec 1895
A Norseman's Pilgrimage
Galaxy, 20:286-7, Aug 1875
Literary World, 6:19, 1 Jul 1875
Queen Titania
Critic, 1:291, 22 Oct 1881
Dial, 2:151, Nov 1881
Literary World, 12:398, 5 Nov 1881
Social Strugglers
Dial, 14:339, 1 Jun 1893
Independent, 45:1314, 28 Sep 1893
Literary World, 24:194, 17 Jun 1893
Tales from Two Hemispheres
Galaxy, 23:427-8, Mar 1877
Literary World, 7:103, 1 Dec 1876
Vagabond Tales
Chautauquan, 9:564, Jun 1889
Critic, NS 12:17, 13 Jul 1889
Dial, 10:58, Jul 1889

Boyle, Virginia (Frazer)
Brockenburne
Independent, 50:224, 17 Feb 1898
Devil Tales
Critic, 38:278, Mar 1901
Serena
Critic, 47:284, Sep 1905
Independent, 59:210, 27 Jul 1905

Boyle, Zola M.
A Master of Life
Critic, 37:466, Nov 1900

Boyleston, Peter [pseud.]
See Curtis, George Ticknor.

Brace, Benjamin [pseud.]
See McCutcheon, Ben Frederick.

Bradford, Gamaliel
Between Two Masters
Independent, 60:1487, 21 Jun 1906
The Private Tutor
Catholic World, 80:406, Dec 1904
Dial, 38:128, 16 Feb 1905
Independent, 59:394, 17 Aug 1905
Literary World, 35:331, Nov 1904

Bradley, Mary Emily (Neely)
Friends for Good
Chautauquan, 24:751, Mar 1897

Bradshaw, William Richard
The Goddess of Atvatabar
Critic, NS 18:44, 23 Jul 1892
Independent, 44:1130, 11 Aug 1892

Brady, Cyrus Townsend
The Bishop
Critic, 43:379, Oct 1903
Dial, 34:375, 1 Jun 1903
Literary World, 34:150, Jun 1903
A Doctor of Philosophy
Critic, 44:279-80, Mar 1904
For Love of Country
Chautauquan, 27:333, Jun 1898
Critic, NS 29:329-30, 14

Brady, Cyrus Townsend (cont.)
May 1898; 37:9-10, Jul 1900
Dial, 24:296, 1 May 1898
Independent, 50:659, 12 May 1898
For the Freedom of the Sea
Dial, 28:86, 1 Feb 1900
The Grip of Honor
Dial, 29:307, 1 Nov 1900
Independent, 52:2813, 22 Nov 1900
Hohenzollern
Chautauquan, 35:620, Sep 1902
Critic, 41:277, Sep 1902
Dial, 32:391, 1 Jun 1902
Independent, 54:1611, 3 Jul 1902
Literary World, 33:106, 1 Jul 1902
In the Wasp's Nest
Chautauquan, 37:214, May 1903
The Island of Regeneration
Independent, 67:1507, 30 Dec 1909
A Little Traitor to the South
Critic, 44:561, Jun 1904
Independent, 56:1088, 12 May 1904
The Patriots
Dial, 40:263, 16 Apr 1906
Independent, 60:1219, 24 May 1906
The Quiberon Touch
Independent, 53:2905, 5 Dec 1901
Literary World, 33:61, 1 Apr 1902
The Southerners
Critic, 43:379, Oct 1903
Dial, 34:372, 1 Jun 1903
Independent, 55:981, 23 Apr 1903
Literary World, 34:152, Jun 1903
The Two Captains
Dial, 38:391-2, 1 Jun 1905
Independent, 59:582, 7 Sep 1905
Under Tops'ls and Tents
Independent, 53:1686, 18 Jul 1901
When Blades Are Out and Love's Afield
Catholic World, 73:246-7, May 1901
Critic, 39:85, Jul 1901
Independent, 53:1084-5, 9 May 1901
Woven with the Ship
Critic, 42:284, Mar 1903
Dial, 33:330, 16 Nov 1902

Braendle, Rose Ann
Only a Waif
Catholic World, 31:720, Aug 1880

Brainerd, Eleanor (Hoyt)
In Vanity Fair
Critic, 49:93, Jul 1906
Independent, 61:582, 6 Sep 1906

Branch, Edward Payson
Plain People
Independent, 44:1229, 1 Sep 1892

Brearley, William Henry
Wanted, a Copyist
Critic, NS 22:329, 17 Nov 1894
Literary World, 25:249, 11 Aug 1894
See also Kelley, Adelaide (Skeel), and William H. Brearley.

[Brewer, Willis]
The Children of Issachar
Independent, 40:785, 21 Jun 1888
Literary World, 15:355-6, 18 Oct 1884

[Bridge, James Howard]
A Fortnight in Heaven
By Harold Brydges [pseud.].
Critic, NS 8:138, 17 Sep 1887

Bridgman, Raymond Landon
Loyal Traitors
Dial, 34:243-4, 1 Apr 1903

[Brinton, Mrs. Bulah]
Man Is Love
By One Who Knows.
Independent, 25:236, 20 Feb 1873
Literary World, 3:139, 1 Feb 1873

Briscoe, Margaret Sutton
See Hopkins, Margaret Sutton (Briscoe).

Brodhead, Eva Wilder (McGlasson)
Bound in Shallows
Harper's, 93:Literary Notes, 4, Nov 1896
Independent, 49:916, 15 Jul 1897
Literary World, 28:227, 10 Jun 1897
Diana's Livery
Critic, NS 15:108, 28 Feb 1891
Harper's, 82:Literary Notes, 4, Jan 1891
Independent, 43:164, 29 Jan 1891
An Earthly Paragon
Critic, NS 19:19, 14 Jan 1893
Dial, 14:114, 16 Feb 1893
Harper's, 86:Literary Notes, 2, Feb 1893
Independent, 45:53, 12 Jan 1893
Literary World, 23:496-7, 31 Dec 1892
Ministers of Grace
Harper's, 90:Literary Notes, 2, Jan 1895
Independent, 47:737, 30 May 1895
Literary World, 26:58-9, 23 Feb 1895
One of the Visconti
Critic, NS 27:218, 27 Mar 1897
Literary World, 27:457, 12 Dec 1896

The Broken Shaft
Tales by F. Marion Crawford, R. Louis Stevenson, F. Anstey, W. H. Pollock, William Archer, and others.
Dial, 6:301, Mar 1886

Brooks, Elbridge Streeter
A Son of Issachar
Catholic World, 52:448-9, Dec 1890
Critic, NS 14:58, 2 Aug 1890
Independent, 42:1164, 21 Aug 1890
Literary World, 21:239, 19 Jul 1890
Stories of the Old Bay State
Independent, 51:2230, 17 Aug 1899

Brooks, Henry Stanford
A Catastrophe in Bohemia
Critic, NS 20:100, 12 Aug 1893
Independent, 45:1453, 26 Oct 1893

Brooks, Hildegard
The Master of Caxton
Critic, 41:277, Sep 1902
Dial, 32:390, 1 Jun 1902
Independent, 54:1550, 26 Jun 1902

Brooks, Lilian
See Camp, Walter Chauncey, and Lilian Brooks.

Brooks, Noah
Tales of the Maine Coast
Critic, NS 22:328-9, 17 Nov 1894
Literary World, 25:231, 28 Jul 1894

Brooks, Sarah (Warner)
My Fire Opal, and Other Tales

Brooks, Sarah (Warner) (cont.)
Independent, 48:1038, 30 Jul 1896
Poverty Knob
Literary World, 32:75, 1 May 1901

Brown, Abby Whitney
Can She Atone?
Independent, 32:12, 4 Nov 1880
Literary World, 11:436, 4 Dec 1800

Brown, Alice
Country Neighbors
Independent, 69:363, 18 Aug 1910
The Country Road
Independent, 62:443, 21 Feb 1907
The Court of Love
Dial, 41:39, 16 Jul 1906
Independent, 61:214, 26 Jul 1906
The Day of His Youth
Critic, NS 27:317, 8 May 1897
Independent, 49:719, 3 Jun 1897; 49:851, 1 Jul 1897
Literary World, 28:195, 12 Jun 1897
Fools of Nature
Critic, NS 8:244, 12 Nov 1887
Independent, 39:1586, 8 Dec 1887
Literary World, 18:387, 12 Nov 1887
High Noon
Critic, 45:474, Nov 1904
Independent, 57:40-1, 7 Jul 1904
Literary World, 35:146, May 1904
John Winterbourne's Family
Independent, 69:1092, 17 Nov 1910
Judgment
Critic, 43:577, Dec 1903
Dial, 35:264, 16 Oct 1903
Independent, 55:2872-3, 3 Dec 1903
Literary World, 34:306, Nov 1903
King's End
Chautauquan, 33:544, Aug 1901
Critic, 38:469, May 1901
Dial, 31:30, 1 Jul 1901
Independent, 53:1625, 11 Jul 1901
Literary World, 32:71, 1 May 1901
The Mannerings
Dial, 34:374, 1 Jun 1903
Independent, 56:1633-4, 9 Jul 1903
Margaret Warrener
Critic, 40:374, Apr 1902
Independent, 54:581, 6 Mar 1902
Literary World, 33:74, 1 May 1902
Meadow-Grass
Chautauquan, 22:380, Dec 1895
Critic, NS 24:178, 21 Sep 1895
Independent, 47:1690, 12 Nov 1895
Literary World, 26:251, 10 Aug 1895
Paradise
Critic, 48:380, Apr 1906
Rose McLeod
Independent, 65:378-9, 13 Aug 1908
The Story of Thyrza
Dial, 46:372, 1 Jun 1909
Independent, 66:812-3, 15 Apr 1909
Stratford-by-the-Sea
Literary World, 15:143-4, 3 May 1884
Tiverton Tales
Chautauquan, 29:388, Jul 1899
Critic, NS 32:757, Aug 1899
Independent, 51:2163, 10 Aug 1899
Literary World, 30:203, 24 Jun 1899

Brown, Anna Robeson
See Burr, Anna Robeson (Brown).

Brown, Caroline [pseud.]
See Krout, Caroline Virginia.

Brown, Demetra, and Kenneth Brown
The Duke's Price
Independent, 69:362, 18 Aug 1910
The First Secretary
Independent, 64:756, 2 Apr 1908

Brown, Helen Dawes
The Petrie Estate
Dial, 15:342, 1 Dec 1893
Literary World, 24:332, 7 Oct 1893
Two College Girls
Critic, NS 5:105, 27 Feb 1886; NS 10:114, 8 Sep 1888
Independent, 38:463, 15 Apr 1886
Literary World, 17:112, 3 Apr 1886

Brown, Katherine Holland
White Roses
Independent, 69:1092, 17 Nov 1910

Brown, Kenneth
See Brown, Demetra, and Kenneth Brown.

Brown, William Garrott
A Gentleman of the South
Independent, 55:1576-7, 2 Jul 1903
Literary World, 34:180-1, Jul 1903

Brown, William Horace
The Glory Seekers
Critic, 49:190, Aug 1906
Dial, 40:393-4, 16 Jun 1906
A Southern Heritage
Literary World, 24:243, 29 Jul 1893

Brown, William Perry
A Sea-Island Romance
Critic, NS 10:204, 27 Oct 1888

Brownell, Gertrude (Hall)
April's Sowing
Critic, 38:279, Mar 1901
Literary World, 32:71, 1 May 1901
Far from To-Day
Critic, NS 18:118, 3 Sep 1892
Independent, 44:1329, 22 Sep 1892
Foam of the Sea, and Other Tales
Chautauquan, 22:379, Dec 1895
Critic, NS 24:381-2, 30 Nov 1895
Independent, 47:1075, 8 Aug 1895
Literary World, 26:199, 29 Jun 1895
The Hundred, and Other Stories
Critic, NS 30:194-5, Sep 1898
Independent, 50:422, 11 Aug 1898
Literary World, 29:343, 15 Oct 1898

Brun, Samuel Jacques
Tales of Lanquedoc
Critic, NS 27:58, 23 Jan 1897

[Brush, Christine (Chaplin)]
The Colonel's Opera Cloak
Critic, NS 9:306, 23 Jun 1888
Literary World, 10:203, 21 Jun 1879
Inside Our Gate
Chautauquan, 11:511, Jul 1890
Critic, NS 11:299, 15 Jun 1889; NS 12:17, 13 Jul 1889

Bryan, Mary (Edwards)
Wild Work
Dial, 2:122, Oct 1881
Independent, 34:11, 9 Mar 1882
Literary World, 12:321, 24 Sep 1881

Bryce, Lloyd Stephens
Friends in Exile
Critic, NS 20:183, 16 Sep 1893
Literary World, 24:227, 15 Jul 1893; 31:268, 1 Dec 1900
Lady Blanche's Salon
Critic, 37:466, Nov 1900
Literary World, 31:7, 6 Jan 1900

Brydges, Harold [pseud.]
See Bridge, James Howard.

Bryn Mawr Stories
Ed. Margaretta Morris and Louise Buffum Congdon.
Independent, 53:2657, 7 Nov 1901
Literary World, 32:126, 1 Aug 1901

Buchanan, Rachel
See Longstreet, Rachel Abigail (Buchanan).

Buck, Francis Tillou
A Fiancé on Trial
Critic, NS 28:47, 24 Jul 1897
Literary World, 28:211, 26 Jun 1897
A Man of Two Minds
Chautauquan, 23:654-5, Aug 1896

Buckingham, Emma May
A Self-Made Woman
Literary World, 4:140, 1 Feb 1874

[Buckner, Alice Morris]
Towards the Gulf
Catholic World, 44:564, Jan 1887
Critic, NS 7:26-7, 15 Jan 1887
Harper's, 74:Literary Notes, 4, Dec 1886; 74:Literary Notes, 4, Jan 1887
Independent, 38:1665, 23 Dec 1886
Literary World, 17:454, 11 Dec 1886

Buffington, Thomas Patrick
Green Valley
Literary World, 32:138, 1 Sep 1901

Bugg, Lelia Hardin
The Prodigal's Daughter
Literary World, 29:205, 25 Jun 1898

Bunce, Oliver Bell
The Adventures of Timias Terrystone
Critic, NS 3:222, 9 May 1885
Dial, 6:123, Sep 1885
Independent, 37:815, 25 Jun 1885
Literary World, 16:158, 2 May 1885
The Story of Happinolande
Critic, NS 11:208, 27 Apr 1889
Independent, 41:929, 18 Jul 1889
Literary World, 20:258, 3 Aug 1889

Bunner, Henry Cuyler
Jersey Street and Jersey Lane
Critic, NS 26:358, 5 Dec 1896
Independent, 48:1037, 30 Jul 1896
Love in Old Cloathes, and Other Stories
Chautauquan, 24:376, Dec 1896
Critic, NS 26:358, 5 Dec

1896
Dial, 21:289, 16 Nov 1896
Independent, 48:1462, 29 Oct 1896
"Made in France"
Critic, NS 20:299, 11 Nov 1893
The Midge
Critic, NS 5:271, 29 May 1886
Dial, 7:68, Jul 1886
Independent, 38:788, 24 Jun 1886
Literary World, 17:253 24 Jul 1886
More "Short Sixes"
Critic, NS 23:123, 16 Feb 1895
The Runaway Browns
Critic, NS 18:275, 19 Nov 1892
Westminster Review, 139:218, Feb 1893
"Short Sixes"
Critic, NS 14:333, 20 Dec 1890
The Story of a New York House
Catholic World, 45:557-9, Jul 1887
Critic, NS 7:306, 18 Jun 1887
Dial, 8:68, Jul 1887
Independent, 39:1102, 1 Sep 1887
Literary World, 18:179, 11 Jun 1887
A Woman of Honor
Independent, 36:11, 3 Jan 1884
Literary World, 14:369, 3 Nov 1883
Zadoc Pine, and Other Stories
Catholic World, 53:439, Jun 1891
Critic, NS 15:249, 9 May 1891
Dial, 12:50, Jun 1891
Independent, 43:1218, 13 Aug 1891
See also Matthews, Brander, and Henry Cuyler Bunner, In Partnership and With My Friends.

Burdette, Robert Jones
Chimes from a Jester's Bells
Chautauquan, 26:463, Jan 1898

Burgess, Gelett
A Little Sister of Destiny
Independent, 60:1286, 31 May 1906
Vivette
Independent, 49:1626, 9 Dec 1897
Literary World, 29:11, 8 Jan 1898
The White Cat
Independent, 62:736, 28 Mar 1907

______, and Will Irwin
Picaroons
Critic, 45:94, Jul 1904
Literary World, 35:169, Jun 1904
The Reign of Queen Isyl
Critic, 44:561, Jun 1904
Literary World, 35:15, Jan 1904

Burnett, Frances Eliza (Hodgson) Townsend
The Captain's Youngest, and Other Tales
Westminster Review, 143:472, Apr 1895
Children I Have Known, and Giovanni and the Other
Westminster Review, 137:349, Mar 1892
The Dawn of To-morrow
Critic, 48:474, May 1906
Independent, 60:1487, 21 Jun 1906
Dolly (also published as Vagabondia)
Critic, NS 12:64, 10 Aug 1889
Literary World, 8:193, 1 Apr 1878; 20:226, 6 Jul 1889

Burnett, Frances Eliza (Hodgson) Townsend (cont.)
Earlier Stories
Critic, NS 16:106, 29 Aug 1891
Independent, 43:1024, 9 Jul 1891
A Fair Barbarian
Critic, 1:79, 26 Mar 1881
Dial, 1:264, Apr 1881
Literary World, 12:146, 23 Apr 1881
Giovanni and the Other
Independent, 44:1599, 10 Nov 1892
Haworth's
Independent, 31:11, 18 Sep 1879
Literary World, 10:310, 27 Sep 1879
His Grace of Osmonde
Chautauquan, 27:222, May 1898
Critic, NS 28:299, 20 Nov 1897
Independent, 49:1662, 16 Dec 1897
Literary World, 28:463, 11 Dec 1897
Literature, 2:17, 8 Jan 1898
In Connection with the De Willoughby Claim
Critic, 36:169-70, Feb 1900
Independent, 52:66-7, 4 Jan 1900
Literary World, 31:93, 1 Apr 1900
In the Closed Room
Critic, 45:576, Dec 1904
Kathleen
Literary World, 8:193, 1 Apr 1878
A Lady of Quality
Catholic World, 63:271-2, May 1896
Chautauquan, 23:654, Aug 1896
Critic, NS 25:212, 28 Mar 1896
Dial, 21:20, 1 Jul 1896
Independent, 48:769, 4 Jun 1896; 48:770, 4 Jun 1896
Literary World, 27:121, 18 Apr 1896
Lindsay's Luck
Independent, 35:11, 19 Jul 1883
Little Lord Fauntleroy
Chautauquan, 7:191, Dec 1886
Critic, NS 6:195, 23 Oct 1886
Independent, 38:1452, 11 Nov 1886
Little Saint Elizabeth, and Other Stories
Catholic World, 51:267-9, May 1890
Chautauquan, 11:650, Aug 1890
Independent, 42:788, 5 Jun 1890
Literary World, 21:174, 24 May 1890
Louisiana
Dial, 1:13, May 1880
Literary World, 11:153-4, 8 May 1880
The Methods of Lady Walderhurst
Critic, 41:89, Jul 1902
Dial, 32:391, 1 Jun 1902
Miss Crespigny
Literary World, 20:193, 8 Jun 1889
Miss Defarge
Critic, NS 10:78, 18 Aug 1888
The Pretty Sister of José
Chautauquan, 9:564, Jun 1889
Critic, NS 11:282, 8 Jun 1889
Independent, 41:929, 18 Jul 1889
Literary World, 20:178, 25 May 1889
A Quiet Life, and The Tide on the Moaning Bar
Literary World, 9:91, 1 Nov 1878
Sara Crewe
Catholic World, 47:410-2,

Jun 1888
Critic, NS 9:114, 10 Mar 1888
Independent, 40:401, 29 Nov 1888

The Shuttle
Dial, 43:318, 16 Nov 1907
Independent, 64:158-9, 16 Jan 1908

Surly Tim, and Other Stories
Catholic World, 26:574, Jan 1878
Literary World, 8:99, 1 Nov 1877

That Lass o'Lowrie's
Literary World, 7:189, 1 May 1877

"Theo"
Literary World, 8:99, 1 Nov 1877; 10:28, 18 Jan 1879

Through One Administration
Chautauquan, 3:480, May 1883
Critic, 3:229, 19 May 1883
Dial, 4:40, Jun 1883
Westminster Review, 120:279, Oct 1883

Two Little Pilgrims' Progress
Westminster Review, 145:233-4, Feb 1896

Burnham, Clara Louise (Root)

Dearly Bought
Critic, NS 13:180-1, 12 Apr 1890
Literary World, 15:258-9, 9 Aug 1884

Dr. Latimer
Independent, 45:1018, 27 Jul 1893
Literary World, 24:210, 1 Jul 1893

A Great Love
Independent, 50:1510, 24 Nov 1898

Jewel
Critic, 43:577, Dec 1903
Independent, 55:2876, 3 Dec 1903
Literary World, 34:308, Nov 1903

Miss Archer Archer
Chautauquan, 26:240, Nov 1897
Critic, NS 28:73, 7 Aug 1897
Literary World, 28:211, 26 Jun 1897

Miss Bagg's Secretary
Critic, NS 17:224-5, 16 Apr 1892
Dial, 12:425, Apr 1892
Independent, 44:313, 3 Mar 1892
Literary World, 23:88, 12 Mar 1892

Miss Pritchard's Wedding Trip
Critic, 39:374, Oct 1901
Independent, 53:1747, 25 Jul 1901
Literary World, 32:107, 1 Jul 1901

The Mistress of Beech Knoll
Catholic World, 52:285-6, Nov 1890
Chautauquan, 11:384, Jun 1890
Critic, NS 13:169, 5 Apr 1890; NS 14:17, 12 Jul 1890
Literary World, 21:187, 7 Jun 1890

Next Door
Critic, NS 5:271, 29 May 1886
Literary World, 17:218-9, 26 Jun 1886

'No Gentlemen"
Critic, 1:135-6, 21 May 1881; NS 13:154, 29 Mar 1890
Dial, 2:42, Jun 1881
Literary World, 12:245, 16 Jul 1881

The Right Princess
Critic, 42:283-4, Mar 1903
Independent, 54:2598, 30 Oct 1902
Literary World, 33:195,

Burnham, Clara Louise (Root) (cont.)
1 Dec 1902
A Sane Lunatic
Critic, NS 13:180-1, 12 Apr 1890
Dial, 3:60, Jul 1882
Sweet Clover
Critic, NS 23:458, 22 Jun 1895
Literary World, 25:371, 3 Nov 1894
We, Von Arldens
By Edith Douglas [pseud.].
Literary World, 12:454, 3 Dec 1881
The Wise Woman
Catholic World, 62:276, Nov 1895
Chautauquan, 23:783, Sep 1896
Critic, NS 25:424, 13 Jun 1896
Independent, 47:1543, 14 Nov 1895
Literary World, 26:428, 30 Nov 1895
Young Maids and Old
Catholic World, 48:402, Dec 1888
Critic, NS 11:52, 2 Feb 1889
Literary World, 19:388, 10 Nov 1888

Burr, Anna Robeson (Brown)
The Black Lamb
Independent, 48:255, 20 Feb 1896
A Cosmopolitan Comedy
Literary World, 30:250, 5 Aug 1899
The Immortal Garland
Critic, 36:573, Jun 1900
The Jessop Bequest
Dial, 44:44, 16 Jan 1908
Independent, 64:156, 16 Jan 1908
The Millionaire's Son
Critic, 44:92, Jan 1904
Dial, 35:262-3, 16 Oct 1903
Independent, 55:2353, 1 Oct 1903
Sir Mark
Chautauquan, 24:752, Mar 1897
Critic, NS 26:117, 22 Aug 1896
Literary World, 28:12, 9 Jan 1897
Truth and a Woman
Critic, 44:188, Feb 1904
Literary World, 34:179, Jul 1903
The Wine Press
Dial, 38:392, 1 Jun 1905
Independent, 59:208, 27 Jul 1905

Burr, Enoch Fitch
Aleph, the Chaldean
Chautauquan, 13:685, Aug 1891
Independent, 43:645, 30 Apr 1891
Fabius, the Roman
Chautauquan, 26:687-8, Mar 1898
Independent, 49:1662, 16 Dec 1897
Literary World, 28:463, 11 Dec 1897

Burwell, Letitia MacCreary
A Girl's Life in Virginia Before the War
Critic, NS 24:232, 12 Oct 1895

Butler, Ellis Parker
Kilo
Independent, 64:159, 16 Jan 1908

Butler, William Allen
Domesticus
Critic, NS 5:104, 27 Feb 1886
Literary World, 17:101-2, 20 Mar 1886
Mrs. Limber's Raffle
Literary World, 6:131, 1 Feb 1876; 25:282, 8 Sep 1894

Butterworth, Hezekiah
The Boys of Greenway Court
Chautauquan, 19:247, May 1894
In Old New England
Independent, 47:1204, 5 Sep 1895
Literary World, 26:282-3, 7 Sep 1895
The Patriot Schoolmaster
Chautauquan, 20:511, Jan 1895
Up from the Cape
Dial, 4:138, Oct 1883
Independent, 35:11, 13 Sep 1883
Literary World, 14:246, 28 Jul 1883

Bynner, Edwin Lassetter
Agnes Surriage
Critic, NS 6:318, 25 Dec 1886; NS 11:238, 11 May 1889
Independent, 38:1665, 23 Dec 1886
Literary World, 18:12, 8 Jan 1887
The Begum's Daughter
Critic, NS 11:238, 11 May 1889; NS 14:22, 12 Jul 1890; NS 14:30, 19 Jul 1890
Dial, 11:93, Aug 1890
Independent, 41:1277, 11 Sep 1890
Literary World, 21:199, 21 Jun 1890
Damen's Ghost
Catholic World, 46:559, Jan 1888
Critic, 1:277, 8 Oct 1881
Dial, 2:122, Oct 1881
Literary World, 12:319, 24 Sep 1881
Nimport
Literary World, 8:45, 1 Aug 1877
Penelope's Suitors
Critic, NS 8:128, 10 Sep 1887
Independent, 39:1392, 27 Oct 1887
Tritons
Independent, 30:12, 5 Sep 1878
Zachary Phips
Critic, NS 18:273-4, 19 Nov 1892
Dial, 14:114, 16 Feb 1893
Independent, 44:1599, 10 Nov 1892
Literary World, 23:390, 5 Nov 1892
See also Hale, Lucretia Peabody, and Edwin Lassetter Bynner.

C., H. W.
See Chaplin, Heman White.

C., P. H.
See Cowan, Pamela H.

C. & C.
See Cabot, Arthur Winslow, and Howard Coghill.

Cabell, James Branch
Chivalry
Dial, 47:520-1, 16 Dec 1909
The Eagle's Shadow
Critic, 45:576, Dec 1904
Dial, 37:314, 16 Nov 1904
Independent, 57:1095, 10 Nov 1904
The Line of Love
Critic, 48:92, Jan 1906

Cable, George Washington
Bonaventure
Chautauquan, 8:514, May 1888
Critic, NS 9:257, 26 May 1888
Dial, 9:67-8, Jul 1888
Literary World, 19:115, 14 Apr 1888
Bylow Hill
Critic, 41:580, Dec 1902
Dial, 33:63, 1 Aug 1902
Independent, 54:1488-9, 19 Jun 1902
The Cavalier

Cable, George Washington (cont.)
Catholic World, 74:260-1, Nov 1901
Chautauquan, 34:323, Dec 1901
Critic, 40:66, Jan 1902
Dial, 32:87, 1 Feb 1902
Independent, 53:3089-90, 26 Dec 1901; 54:2771, 20 Nov 1902
Literary World, 33:8, 1 Jan 1902
Dr. Sevier
Critic, NS 2:217, 8 Nov 1884; NS 31:252, Mar 1899
Dial, 5:204, Dec 1884
Independent, 36:1419, 6 Nov 1884
Literary World, 15:350-1, 18 Oct 1884
Westminster Review, 123 (NS 67):293, Jan 1885
The Grandissimes
Critic, 1:270-1, 8 Oct 1881; NS 31:252, Mar 1899
Dial, 1:115-6, Oct 1880; 1:240, Mar 1881
Independent, 32:11, 30 Sep 1880; 63:1471-2, 19 Dec 1907
Literary World, 11:347, 9 Oct 1880
John March, Southerner
Critic, NS 23:137-8, 16 Feb 1895; NS 31:252-3, Mar 1899
Dial, 18:51-2, 16 Jan 1895
Independent, 47:54, 10 Jan 1895
Literary World, 25:466, 29 Dec 1894
Kincaid's Battery
Dial, 46:87, 1 Feb 1909
Independent, 66:700, 1 Apr 1909
Madame Delphine
Critic, 1:190, 16 Jul 1881
Dial, 2:86, Aug 1881
Literary World, 27:154-5, 16 May 1896
Westminster Review, 128:784, Sep 1887
Old Creole Days
Chautauquan, 26:463, Jan 1898
Critic, NS 31:250-3, Mar 1899
Independent, 31:9, 12 Jun 1879; 35:11, 7 Jun 1883
Literary World, 10:234, 19 Jul 1879
Westminster Review, 120:144, Jul 1883
Strong Hearts
Chautauquan, 29:310-1, Jun 1899
Critic, NS 31:564-5, Jun 1899
Dial, 27:76, 1 Aug 1899
Independent, 51:2441-2, 7 Sep 1899
Literary World, 30:124, 15 Apr 1899
Writings (5 vols)
Critic, NS 20:354, 2 Dec 1893

Cabot, Arthur Winslow, and Howard Coghill
Two Gentlemen of Gotham
By C. & C.
Critic, NS 7:192, 16 Apr 1887; NS 7:256, 21 May 1887
Literary World, 18:138, 30 Apr 1887

Cabot, Elizabeth Lyman
In Plain Air
Critic, NS 27:424, 19 Jun 1897
Independent, 49:820, 24 Jun 1897
Literary World, 28:195, 12 Jun 1897

Cahan, Abraham
The Imported Bridegroom
Critic, NS 29:387, 11 Jun 1898
Independent, 50:727, 2 Jun

1898
The White Terror and the Red
Critic, 46:560-1, Jun 1905
Independent, 58:502-3, 2 Mar 1905
Yekl
Chautauquan, 24:512, Jan 1897
Critic, NS 26:53, 25 Jul 1896
Literary World, 27:349, 17 Oct 1896

Calder, Alma
See Johnston, Alma (Calder)

Calkins, Franklin Welles
The Cougar-Tamer, and Other Stories of Adventure
Independent, 51:2163-4, 10 Aug 1899

Camera, Cara [pseud.]
Society Rapids
By "One in the Swim."
Critic, NS 10:91, 25 Aug 1888
Literary World, 19:221, 7 Jul 1888

Cameron, Margaret
The Involuntary Chaperon
Independent, 68:581, 17 Mar 1910

Camp, Walter Chauncey, and Lilian Brooks
Drives and Puts
Literary World, 30:365, 28 Oct 1899

Campbell, Helen (Stuart)
Ballantyne
Critic, 39:181, Aug 1901
His Grandmothers
Literary World, 8:99, 1 Nov 1877
Miss Melinda's Opportunity
Critic, NS 6:101-2, 28 Aug 1886
Literary World, 17:351, 16 Oct 1886
Mrs. Herndon's Income
Chautauquan, 6:485, May 1886
Critic, NS 5:164, 3 Apr 1886
Literary World, 17:11, 9 Jan 1886
Roger Berkeley's Probation
Critic, NS 10:78, 18 Aug 1888
Literary World, 19:198, 23 Jun 1888
Six Sinners, or School Days in Bantam Valley
By Campbell Wheaton [pseud.].
Galaxy, 24:858-9, Dec 1877
Some Passages in the Practice of Dr. Martha Scarborough
Chautauquan, 18:254-5, Nov 1893
Critic, NS 19:363, 3 Jun 1893
Independent, 45:1154, 24 Aug 1893
Literary World, 24:147, 6 May 1893
Under Green Apple Boughs
Independent, 34:11, 23 Nov 1882
Literary World, 13:461, 16 Dec 1882
Unto the Third and Fourth Generation
Literary World, 11:199, 5 Jun 1880

Candee, Helen (Churchill)
An Oklahoma Romance
Critic, 39:575, Dec 1901
Dial, 31:371, 16 Nov 1901

Canfield, Dorothy
Gunhild
Independent, 63:1377, 5 Dec 1907

Canfield, Henry Spofford
Fergy the Guide

Canfield, Henry Spofford (cont.)
Critic, 45:576, Dec 1904
A Maid of the Frontier
Literary World, 29:403, 26 Nov 1898
A Paladin in Khaki
Literary World, 33:139, 1 Sep 1902

Carleton, Will.
See Carleton, William McKendree.

[Carleton, William McKendree]
City Legends
By Will Carleton.
Harper's, 79:Literary Notes, 4, Nov 1889
The Old Infant, and Similar Stories
By Will Carleton.
Harper's, 93:Literary Notes, 3, Nov 1896
Independent, 48:1462, 29 Oct 1896
Literary World, 27:365, 31 Oct 1896

Carpenter, Edith
Your Money or Your Life
Independent, 48:805, 11 Jun 1896
Literary World, 27:204, 27 Jun 1896

Carpenter, Edmund Janes
A Woman of Shawmut
Independent, 43:1762, 26 Nov 1891

Carpenter, Edward Childs
See Kauffman, Reginald Wright, and Edward Childs Carpenter.

Carpenter, Esther Bernon
South-County Neighbors
Critic, NS 8:257, 19 Nov 1887
Literary World, 19:26, 21 Jan 1888

Carr, Clark Ezra
The Illini
Independent, 58:844, 13 Apr 1905

Carr, Sarah (Pratt)
The Iron Way
Dial, 42:316, 16 May 1907
Independent, 62:1526, 27 Jun 1907

[Carrington, Kate]
Aschenbroedel
Critic, 2:175, 1 Jul 1882
Independent, 34:11, 3 Aug 1882

Carruth, Fred Hayden
The Adventures of Jones
Critic, NS 23:439, 15 Jun 1895
Harper's, 90:Literary Notes, 4, May 1895
Independent, 47:737, 30 May 1895
Literary World, 26:106, 6 Apr 1895
Mr. Milo Bush and Other Worthies
Harper's, 99:Literary Notes, 3-4, Sep 1899
Independent, 51:2629, 28 Sep 1899
The Voyage of the Rattletrap
Harper's, 95:Literary Notes, 2, Jun 1897
Independent, 49:980, 29 Jul 1897

Carryl, Charles Edward
The River Syndicate, and Other Stories
Harper's, 98:Literary Notes, 4, May 1899
Independent, 51:2442, 7 Sep 1899

Carryl, Guy Wetmore
Fables for the Frivolous
Harper's, 97:Literary Notes, 4, Sep 1898
Far from the Maddening Girls

Critic, 46:477, May 1905
The Lieutenant Governor
Critic, 43:187, Aug 1903
Dial, 35:69, 1 Aug 1903
Literary World, 34:75, Apr 1903
The Transgression of Andrew Vane
Critic, 45:474-5, Nov 1904
Dial, 37:210-1, 1 Oct 1904
Literary World, 35:162-3, Jan 1904
Zut and Other Parisians
Critic, 43:474, Nov 1903
Dial, 35:158[222], 1 Oct 1903

Carson, William Henry
The Fool
Dial, 33:68, 1 Aug 1902

Carus, Paul
The Chief's Daughter
Catholic World, 75:268, May 1902
Chautauquan, 34:336, Dec 1901
The Crown of Thorns
Catholic World, 75:268, May 1902
Chautauquan, 34:342, Dec 1901
Truth in Fiction
Critic, NS 19:364, 3 Jun 1893
Literary World, 24:89-90, 25 Mar 1893

Case, William Scoville
Forward House
Critic, NS 24:407, 14 Dec 1895
Independent, 47:1170, 29 Aug 1895

Caskoden, Edwin [pseud.]
See Major, Charles.

Castledon, D. R. [pseud.]
See Derby, Caroline Rosine.

Cather, Willa Sibert
The Troll Garden
Critic, 47:476, Nov 1905
Dial, 38:394, 1 Jun 1905
Independent, 58:1482-3, 29 Jun 1905

Catherwood, Mary (Hartwell)
The Chase of Saint-Castin
Critic, NS 22:347, 24 Nov 1894
Dial, 17:333, 1 Dec 1894
Literary World, 25:351, 20 Oct 1894
Craque-o'-Doom
Literary World, 12:454, 3 Dec 1881
The Days of Jeanne d'Arc
Chautauquan, 26:347, Dec 1897
Critic, NS 28:300, 20 Nov 1897
Literary World, 28:455, 11 Dec 1897
The Lady of Fort St. John
Catholic World, 54:604-5, Jan 1892
Critic, NS 16:347, 19 Dec 1891
Independent, 43:1921, 24 Dec 1891
Lazarre
Catholic World, 74:541, Dec 1901
Chautauquan, 34:322, Dec 1901
Critic, 39:474, Nov 1901
Dial, 31:365-6, 16 Nov 1901
Literary World, 32:210, 1 Dec 1901
Mackinac and Lake Stories
Critic, 36:91, Jan 1900
Harper's, 99:Literary Notes, 4, Nov 1899
Independent, 51:3172, 23 Nov 1899
Old Kaskaskia
Chautauquan, 17:761, Sep 1893
Critic, NS 20:87, 5 Aug 1893
Dial, 15:94, 16 Aug 1893

Catherwood, Mary (Hartwell) (cont.)
Literary World, 24:178, 3 Jun 1893
The Queen of the Swamp and Other Plain Americans
Chautauquan, 29:389, Jul 1899
Critic, NS 32:845-6, Sep 1899
Independent, 51:2163, 10 Aug 1899
Literary World, 30:237, 22 Jul 1899
Rocky Fork
Independent, 34:11, 3 Aug 1882
The Romance of Dollard
Chautauquan, 10:376, Dec 1889
Critic, NS 12:279-80, 7 Dec 1889
Dial, 10:215, Dec 1889
Independent, 41:1399, 24 Oct 1889
Literary World, 20:388, 9 Nov 1889
Spanish Peggy
Critic, 36:183, Feb 1900
Independent, 52:261, 25 Jan 1900
The Spirit of an Illinois Town and The Little Renault
Critic, NS 27:247-8, 10 Apr 1897
Independent, 49:719, 3 Jun 1897; 49:980, 29 Jul 1897
Literary World, 28:146, 1 May 1897
The Story of Tonty
Chautauquan, 11:383, Jun 1890
Critic, NS 13:103-4, 1 Mar 1890
Dial, 11:12, May 1890
Independent, 42:257, 20 Feb 1890
Literary World, 21:58, 15 Feb 1890
The White Islander
Critic, NS 21:144, 3 Mar 1894
Dial, 15:342-3, 1 Dec 1893
Literary World, 24:367, 4 Nov 1893
Yellow Pine Basin
Literary World, 28:194, 12 Jun 1897

Cavazza, Elisabeth
See Pullen, Elisabeth (Jones) Cavazza.

Cervus, G. I. [pseud.]
See Roe, William James.

Chadwick, J. H.
The Whole Truth
Critic, NS 7:164, 2 Apr 1887

Chamberlain, Henry Richardson
6,000 Tons of Gold
Critic, NS 23:122, 16 Feb 1895
Independent, 47:737, 30 May 1895
Literary World, 26:57, 23 Feb 1895

Chamberlain, Nathan Henry
The Sphinx in Aubrey Parish
Literary World, 20:193, 8 Jun 1889

[Chamberlain, William Mellen]
Manuela Parédes
Critic, 1:152, 4 Jun 1881
Dial, 2:41-2, Jun 1881
Literary World, 12:175, 21 May 1881

Chambers, Julius
The Destiny of Doris
Critic, 41:89, Jul 1902
On a Margin
Critic, NS 2:33, 15 Nov 1884
Independent, 36:1646, 25 Dec 1884
Literary World, 16:63, 21 Feb 1885

Chambers, Robert William
Ailsa Paige
Dial, 49:288-9, 16 Oct 1910
Ashes of Empire
Dial, 26:123-4, 16 Feb 1899
Independent, 51:426, 9 Feb 1899
Literary World, 30:23, 21 Jan 1899
The Cambric Mask
Critic, 37:86, Jul 1900
Dial, 29:22, 1 Jul 1900
Cardigan
Chautauquan, 34:324, Dec 1901
Critic, 39:474, Nov 1901
Dial, 31:366-7, 16 Nov 1901
Independent, 53:2479-80, 17 Oct 1901; 53:2778, 21 Nov 1901
Literary World, 32:212-3, 1 Dec 1901
The Conspirators
Critic, 37:374, Oct 1900
Dial, 29:22-3, 1 Jul 1900
Independent, 37:374, Oct 1900
The Danger Mark
Independent, 68:318, 10 Feb 1910
The Fighting Chance
Dial, 41:243, 16 Oct 1906
Independent, 61:756, 27 Sep 1906; 61:877-8, 11 Oct 1906; 61:1158-60, 15 Nov 1906
The Firing Line
Dial, 45:214, 1 Oct 1908
Independent, 65:553-4, 3 Sep 1908
In Search of the Unknown
Critic, 46:93, Jan 1905
Dial, 37:39, 16 Jul 1904
In the Quarter
Critic, NS 23:379-80, 25 May 1895
Iole
Independent, 59:395, 17 Aug 1905
A King and a Few Dukes
Chautauquan, 24:380, Dec 1896
Critic, NS 25:426, 13 Jun 1896
Dial, 20:337, 1 Jun 1896
Independent, 48:805, 11 Jun 1896
Literary World, 27:252, 8 Aug 1896
The King in Yellow
Chautauquan, 21:492, Jul 1895
Critic, NS 23:379, 25 May 1895
Independent, 54:2139, 4 Sep 1902
Literary World, 33:126-7, 1 Aug 1902
Lorraine
Dial, 24:80-1, 1 Feb 1898
Harper's, 96:Literary Notes, 3-4, Feb 1898
Independent, 49:1660, 16 Dec 1897
Literary World, 29:28, 22 Jan 1898
Literature, 2:620-1, 28 May 1898
The Maid-at-Arms
Dial, 32:243, 16 Oct 1902
Literary World, 33:180, 1 Nov 1902
The Maids of Paradise
Dial, 35:261-2, 16 Oct 1903
Independent, 55:2579-80, 29 Oct 1903; 55:2741, 19 Nov 1903
The Maker of Moons
Critic, NS 27:337, 15 May 1897
Dial, 22:23, 1 Jan 1897
Independent, 49:57, 14 Jan 1897
Literary World, 28:43, 6 Feb 1897
The Mystery of Choice
Dial, 24:81-2, 1 Feb 1898
Literary World, 29:60, 19 Feb 1898
Literature, 1:212, 4 Dec 1897

Chambers, Robert William (cont.)
Outsiders
Critic, NS 32:1056-7, Nov 1899
The Reckoning
Dial, 39:309, 16 Nov 1905
The Red Republic
Dial, 20:337, 1 Jun 1896
Special Messenger
Independent, 66:765, 8 Apr 1909
The Tracer of Lost Persons
Critic, 49:284, Sep 1906
A Young Man in a Hurry, and Other Stories
Critic, 46:188, Feb 1905
The Younger Set
Dial, 43:252-3, 16 Oct 1907
Independent, 63:756-7, 26 Sep 1907; 63:1226-8, 21 Nov 1907

Champney, Elizabeth J. (Williams)
A Daughter of the Huguenots
Chautauquan, 34:322, Dec 1901
Great Grandmother's Girls in New Mexico
Independent, 40:1504-5, 22 Nov 1888
Margarita
Independent, 54:2537-8, 23 Oct 1902
Patience, a Daughter of the Mayflower
Independent, 52:2520, 18 Oct 1900
Rosemary and Rue
Critic, 1:323, 19 Nov 1881
Literary World, 12:389, 5 Nov 1881
Three Vassar Girls Abroad
Independent, 34:9, 30 Nov 1882
Three Vassar Girls at Home
Critic, NS 8:258, 19 Nov 1887
Three Vassar Girls in Russia and Turkey
Critic, NS 12:255-6, 23 Nov 1889
Three Vassar Girls in the Tyrol
Independent, 43:1805, 3 Dec 1891
Witch Winnie's Studio
Chautauquan, 18:638-9, Feb 1894

Chandler, Bessie
A Woman Who Failed, and Other Stories
Critic, NS 20:100, 12 Aug 1893
Independent, 45:1453, 26 Oct 1893
Literary World, 24:242, 29 Jul 1893

Chandler, Mrs. G. W.
See Chandler, Izora Cecilia.

Chandler, Izora Cecilia
Anthè
Critic, NS 3:125, 14 Mar 1885
Independent, 57:1167, 10 Sep 1885

Channing, Grace Ellery
See Stetson, Grace Ellery (Channing).

Chapin, Anna Alice
Discords
Critic, 43:91, Jul 1903
The Story of the Rhinegold
Independent, 49:1546, 25 Nov 1897

[Chaplin, Heman White]
Five Hundred Dollars, and Other Stories of New England Life
By C. H. W.
Critic, NS 9:267-8, 2 Jun 1888
Independent, 40:241, 23 Feb 1888
Literary World, 19:59-60, 18 Feb 1888

Chapple, Joseph Mitchell
Boss Burt, Politician
Independent, 49:250, 25 Feb 1897

Charles, Frances (Asa)
The Awakening of the Duchess
Literary World, 35:15, Jan 1904
In the Country God Forgot
Critic, 41:478, Nov 1902
Dial, 32:390, 1 Jun 1902
Independent, 54:1784, 24 Jul 1902
Literary World, 33:94, 1 Jun 1902
The Siege of Youth
Dial, 35:69, 1 Aug 1903
Independent, 55:1692, 16 Jul 1903

Chase, Herbert E.
A Double Life
Independent, 36:1163, 11 Sep 1884
Literary World, 15:257-8, 9 Aug 1884

Chatfield-Taylor, Hobart Chatfield
An American Peeress
Dial, 16:19-20, 1 Jan 1894
The Crimson Wing
Dial, 32:386-7, 1 Jun 1902
Literary World, 33:76, 1 May 1902
Fame's Pathway
Dial, 47:47-8, 16 Jul 1909
Two Women & a Fool
Critic, NS 23:454-5, 22 Jun 1895
Dial, 18:271, 1 May 1895
The Vice of Fools
Critic, NS 29:164, 5 Mar 1898
Dial, 23:286, 16 Nov 1897
Literary World, 29:28, 22 Jan 1898
With Edge Tools
Critic, NS 17:154-5, 12 Mar 1892

Cheever, Harriet Anna
Links of Gold
Independent, 49:1695, 23 Dec 1897

Chellis, Mary Dwinell
Miss Belinda's Friends
Critic, NS 5:145, 20 Mar 1886

Cheney, Ednah Dow (Littlehale)
Nora's Return
Chautauquan, 11:383, Jun 1890
Critic, NS 13:160, 29 Mar 1890; NS 14:56, 2 Aug 1890
Independent, 42:788, 5 Jun 1890

Cheney, John Vance
The Old Doctor
Critic, NS 4:186, 17 Oct 1885
Literary World, 16:343, 3 Oct 1885

Cheney, Warren
The Challenge
Critic, 48:572, Jun 1906
The Way of the North
Independent, 59:335, 10 Aug 1905

Chesnutt, Charles Waddell
The Colonel's Dream
Independent, 59:816-7, 5 Oct 1905
The Conjure Woman
Critic, NS 32:650, Jul 1899
Independent, 51:2569-70, 21 Sep 1899
Literary World, 30:204, 24 Jun 1899
The House Behind the Cedars
Chautauquan, 32:334, Dec 1900
Critic, 37:571, Dec 1900
Literary World, 32:12, 1 Jan 1901

Chesnutt, Charles Waddell (cont.)
The Marrow of Tradition
Chautauquan, 34:327-8, Dec 1901
Independent, 54:582, 6 Mar 1902
Literary World, 33:22, 1 Feb 1902
The Wife of His Youth, and Other Stories of the Color Line
Critic, 36:182, Feb 1900
Literary World, 31:55, 17 Feb 1900

Chester, George Randolph
The Early Bird
Independent, 69:364, 18 Aug 1910
The Making of Bobby Burnit
Dial, 47:49, 16 Jul 1909
Independent, 67:550, 2 Sep 1909
Young Wallingford
Independent, 69:1091, 17 Nov 1910

Chester, John
Ruth, the Christian Scientist
Independent, 41:80-1, 17 Jan 1889
Literary World, 20:58-9, 16 Feb 1889

Child, Frank Samuel
A Colonial Witch
Critic, NS 29:74-5, 29 Jan 1898
Independent, 50:224, 17 Feb 1898
Literary World, 28:479-80, 25 Dec 1897; 30:6, 7 Jan 1899
Friend or Foe
Literary World, 32:38, 1 Mar 1901

Childs, Carrie Goldsmith
Lost Lineage
Independent, 49:916, 15 Jun 1897

[Childs, Eleanor Stuart (Patterson)]
Averages
By Eleanor Stuart [pseud.]
Literary World, 31:71, 3 Mar 1900
Stonepastures
By Eleanor Stuart [pseud.].
Independent, 48:770, 4 Jun 1896

Chisholm, Mrs. Belle V.
In Search of a Home
Independent, 43:500, 2 Apr 1891

Chopin, Kate (O'Flaherty)
The Awakening
Dial, 27:75, 1 Aug 1899
Bayou Folk
Critic, NS 21:299-300, 5 May 1894
Literary World, 25:121, 21 Apr 1894
A Night in Arcadie
Critic, NS 29:266, 16 Apr 1898
Independent, 49:1662, 16 Dec 1897

Church, Samuel Harden
John Marmaduke
Dial, 23:284, 16 Nov 1897
Literary World, 29:75, 5 Mar 1898

Churchill, Winston
The Celebrity
Critic, NS 29:250, 9 Apr 1898
Dial, 24:355, 1 Jun 1898
Independent, 50:629, 12 May 1898
Literary World, 29:140, 30 Apr 1898
Literature, 2:511, 30 Apr 1898
Coniston
Catholic World, 84:115-6, Oct 1906
Critic, 49:284-5, Sep 1906

Dial, 41:116, 1 Sep 1906
Independent, 61:96-7, 12 Jul 1906; 61:1158-60, 15 Nov 1906

The Crisis
Catholic World, 73:531-2, Jul 1901
Critic, 39:75-6, Jul 1901
Dial, 31:25-6, 1 Jul 1901
Independent, 53:1435-6, 20 Jun 1901; 53:2778, 21 Nov 1901
Literary World, 32:99, 1 Jul 1901

The Crossing
Catholic World, 80:405-6, Dec 1904
Critic, 45:187-8, Aug 1904
Dial, 37:38-9, 16 Jul 1904
Independent, 57:41-2, 7 Jul 1904; 57:1137, 17 Nov 1904

Mr. Crewe's Career
Dial, 44:349, 1 Jun 1908
Independent, 64:1400-1, 18 Jun 1908

A Modern Chronicle
Catholic World, 91:391, Jun 1910
Dial, 48:395-6, 1 Jun 1910
Independent, 68:1037-8, 12 May 1910

Richard Carvel
Catholic World, 70:132, Oct 1899
Chautauquan, 29:388-9, Jul 1899
Critic, NS 32:759, Aug 1899
Dial, 27:74, 1 Aug 1899
Literary World, 30:243, 5 Aug 1899
Westminster Review, 153:112, Jan 1900

Churton, Henry [pseud.]
See Tourgée, Albion Winegar.

Claflin, Mary Bucklin (Davenport)

Brampton Sketches
Independent, 42:1723, 4 Dec 1890

Clagett, Sue Harry

Her Lovers
Literary World, 8:76, 1 Oct 1877

Clark, Arnold

Beneath the Dome
Critic, NS 21:324, 12 May 1894

[Clark, Charles Heber]

Captain Bluitt
By Max Adeler [pseud.].
Independent, 54:816, 3 Apr 1902
Literary World, 33:44, 1 Mar 1902

Elbow Room
By Max Adeler [pseud.].
Independent, 28:8, 7 Dec 1876

The Fortunate Island, and Other Stories
By Max Adeler [pseud.].
Dial, 2:221, Jan 1882
Independent, 34:12, 5 Jan 1882

In Happy Hollow
By Max Adeler [pseud.].
Critic, 44:187-8, Feb 1904
Independent, 56:99, 14 Jan 1904

The Quakeress
By Max Adeler [pseud.].
Dial, 38:393, 1 Jun 1905
Independent, 58:1420, 22 Jun 1905

Random Shots
By Max Adeler
Independent, 31:10, 3 Jul 1879

[Clark, Charlotte (Moon)]

Baby Rue
Literary World, 12:258, 30 Jul 1881

The Modern Hagar
By Charles M. Clay [pseud.].

[Clark, Charlotte (Moon)] (cont.)
Critic, 2:322, 2 Dec 1882
Independent, 35:12, 18 Jan 1883
Literary World, 14:28, 27 Jan 1883

Clark, Felicia (Buttz)
The Cripple of Nuremberg
Chautauquan, 34:323, Dec 1901
Schwester Anna
Chautauquan, 27:429, Jul 1898
The Sword of Garibaldi
Literary World, 35:18, Jan 1905

Clark, Frederick Thickstun
In the Valley of Havilah
Independent, 42:1344, 25 Sep 1890
A Mexican Girl
By Frederick Thickstun [pseud.].
Catholic World, 48:119-23, Oct 1888
Critic, NS 10:102, 1 Sep 1888
Literary World, 19:284, 1 Sep 1888
The Mistress of the Ranch
Harper's, 94:Literary Notes, 2-3, May 1897
Independent, 49:650, 20 May 1897
Literary World, 28:194, 12 Jan 1897
On Cloud Mountain
Critic, NS 23:203, 16 Mar 1895
Harper's, 90:Literary Notes, 4, Mar 1895
Literary World, 25:352, 20 Oct 1894

Clark, Helen F.
The Lady of the Lily Feet, and Other Stories of Chinatown
Literary World, 32:27, 1 Feb 1901

Clark, Imogen
God's Puppets
Critic, 38:566, Jun 1901
Independent, 53:1624, 11 Jul 1901
The Las' Day
Chautauquan, 16:509, Jan 1893
The Victory of Ezry Gardner
Chautauquan, 24:127, Oct 1896
We Four and Two More
Independent, 67:1366, 16 Dec 1909

Clark, Kate Elizabeth
The Dominant Seventh
Independent, 42:788, 5 Jun 1890
Literary World, 21:125, 12 Apr 1890

Clark, Kate (Upson)
That Mary Ann
Literary World, 24:226, 15 Jul 1893
Up the Witch Brook Road
Critic, 42:284, Mar 1903
Dial, 33:333, 16 Nov 1902
Independent, 54:2536, 23 Oct 1902
White Butterflies, and Other Stories
Literary World, 32:55, 1 Apr 1901

Clark, Susie Champney
Lorita, an Alaskan Maiden
Independent, 43:1762, 26 Nov 1891

[Clarke, Rebecca Sophia]
Pauline Wyman
By Sophie May [pseud.].
Literary World, 29:455, 24 Dec 1898

Clarkson, L.
See Whitelock, Louise (Clarkson).

Clay, Charles M. [pseud.]
See Clark, Charlotte (Moon).

Claytor, Graham
Pleasant Waters
Critic, NS 9:152, 31 Mar 1888
Literary World, 19:123, 14 Apr 1888
Wheat and Tares
Critic, NS 12:42, 27 Jul 1889

[Clemens, Samuel Langhorne]
The Adventures of Huckleberry Finn
by Mark Twain [pseud.].
Harper's, 93:Literary Notes, 1-2, Sep 1896
Independent, 48:1007, 23 Jul 1896
Westminster Review, 123 (NS 67):596-7, Apr 1885
The Adventures of Tom Sawyer
By Mark Twain [pseud.].
Westminster Review, 106:279, Oct 1876
The American Claimant, and Other Stories and Sketches
By Mark Twain [pseud.].
Harper's, 94:Literary Notes, 2, May 1897
Independent, 49:650, 20 May 1897
A Connecticut Yankee in King Arthur's Court
By Mark Twain [pseud.].
Critic, NS 13:90, 22 Feb 1890
Harper's, 93:Literary Notes, 2, Sep 1896
Independent, 48:1008, 23 Jul 1896
Literary World, 21:52-3, 15 Feb 1890
A Double-Barrelled Detective Story
By Mark Twain [pseud.].
Critic, 41:479, Nov 1902
Dial, 32:390, 1 Jun 1902
Independent, 54:1431-32, 12 Jun 1902
Literary World, 33:76, 1 May 1902
Eve's Diary
By Mark Twain [pseud.].
Critic, 49:288, Sep 1906
Independent, 61:397, 16 Aug 1906
A Horse's Tale
By Mark Twain [pseud.].
Independent, 63:1377, 5 Dec 1907
The Man That Corrupted Hadleyburg, and Other Stories and Essays
By Mark Twain [pseud.].
Critic, 37:413-5, Nov 1900; 37:468, Nov 1900
Merry Tales
By Mark Twain [pseud.].
Independent, 44:776, 2 Jun 1892
Personal Recollections of Joan of Arc
By the Sieur Louis de Conte [pseud.].
Critic, NS 25:350-1, 16 May 1896
Independent, 48:769, 4 Jun 1896
Literary World, 27:163, 30 May 1896
The Prince and the Pauper
By Mark Twain [pseud.].
Critic, 1:368, 31 Dec 1881
Harper's, 93:Literary Notes, 2, Sep 1896
Westminster Review, 117:279, Apr 1882
The Stolen White Elephant, etc.
By Mark Twain [pseud.].
Dial, 3:78, Aug 1882
Independent, 34:11, 3 Aug 1882
Westminster Review, 118:278-9, Oct 1882
Tom Sawyer Abroad; Tom Sawyer, Detective; and Other Stories
By Mark Twain [pseud.].

[Clemens, Samuel Langhorne] (cont.)
Harper's, 94:Literary Notes, 2, May 1897
The Tragedy of Pudd'nhead Wilson
By Mark Twain [pseud.].
Critic, NS 23:338-9, 11 May 1895
A Tramp Abroad
Westminster Review, 114:139, Jul 1880

______, and Charles Dudley Warner
The Gilded Age
Galaxy, 17:428, Mar 1874
Independent, 26:1642, 1 Jan 1874

Clemens, William Montgomery
The Depew Story Book
Independent, 51:212, 19 Jan 1899
The Gilded Lady
Dial, 35:68-9, 1 Aug 1903

Clement, Clara (Erskine)
See Waters, Clara (Erskine) Clement.

Clews, James Blanchard
Fortunes
Independent, 50:990, 6 Oct 1898

Clodfelter, Noah J.
Snatched from the Poor-House
Critic, NS 9:152, 31 Mar 1888

Cobb, Sylvanus
Bion, the Wanderer
Independent, 44:313, 3 Mar 1892
Karmel the Scout
Literary World, 19:315, 29 Sep 1888
[Stories]
Critic, NS 9:281, 9 Jun 1888

Cocke, James R.
Blind Leaders of the Blind
Independent, 48:1037, 30 Jul 1896
Literary World, 27:365, 31 Oct 1896

Cody, Sherwin
In the Heart of the Hills
Literary World, 27:235, 25 Jul 1896

Coffin, Charles Carleton
Caleb Krinkle
Catholic World, 21:144, Apr 1875
Independent, 27:10, 28 Jan 1875
Literary World, 5:124, 1 Jan 1875
Dan of Millbrook
Literary World, 26:6-7, 12 Jan 1895
Daughters of the Revolution and Their Times
Critic, NS 24:89, 10 Aug 1895
Independent, 47:1074, 8 Aug 1895
Literary World, 26:154, 18 May 1895
Winning His Way
Independent, 34:10, 14 Dec 1882

Coffin, Roland Folger
An Old Sailor's Yarns
Literary World, 16:202, 13 Jun 1885

Coghill, Howard
See Cabot, Arthur Winslow, and Howard Coghill.

Cogswell, Frederick Hull
The Regicides
Critic, NS 27:425, 19 Jun 1897
Dial, 21:288, 16 Nov 1896
Independent, 48:1463, 29 Oct 1896

[Cohen, Alfred J.]
A Girl Who Wrote
By Alan Dale [pseud.].
Critic, 41:580, Dec 1902
Miss Innocence
By Alan Dale [pseud.].
Critic, NS 16:262, 14 Nov 1891
Wanted: A Cook
By Alan Dale [pseud.].
Independent, 58:210, 26 Jan 1905

Colburn, Frona Eunice Wait (Smith)
Yermah the Dorado
By Frona Wait [pseud.].
Literary World, 28:479, 25 Dec 1897

Colby, Frederic Myron
The Daughter of Pharaoh
Independent, 39:1038, 18 Aug 1887

[Cole, William Morse]
An Old Man's Romance
By Christopher Craigie [pseud.].
Critic, NS 24:179, 21 Sep 1895

Collingwood, Herbert Winslow
Andersonville Violets
Chautauquan, 10:252, Nov 1889
Independent, 41:402, 28 Mar 1889

Collins, Percy
See McVickar, Henry Goelet.

Colter, Hattie E.
In the Heart of the Hills
Independent, 51:2163, 10 Aug 1899

Colton, Arthur Willis
The Belted Seas
Critic, 47:382, Oct 1905
Dial, 38:394, 1 Jun 1905
Independent, 58:1250, 1 Jun 1905
The Cruise of the Violetta
Independent, 62:563, 7 Mar 1907
The Debatable Land
Critic, 40:471, May 1902
Dial, 32:87, 1 Feb 1902
Literary World, 33:45, 1 Mar 1902
The Delectable Mountains
Critic, 39:374, Oct 1901
Port Argent
Critic, 45:91, Jul 1904
Dial, 36:369, 1 Jun 1904
Literary World, 35:203, Jul 1904
Tioba, and Other Tales
Critic, 43:577, Dec 1903
Dial, 35:69, 1 Aug 1903
Literary World, 34:122, May 1903

Comer, Cornelia Atwood (Pratt)
A Book of Martyrs
Independent, 48:1693, 10 Dec 1896
Literary World, 27:381, 31 Oct 1896
The Daughter of a Stoic
Critic, NS 25:441, 20 Jun 1896
Independent, 48:976, 16 Jul 1896
See also Slee, Richard, and Cornelia Atwood Pratt.

Comfort, Will Levington
Routledge Rides Alone
Dial, 49:40, 16 Jul 1910
Trooper Tales
Literary World, 30:456, 23 Dec 1899

Comstock, Harriet Theresa (Nichols)
Janet of the Dunes
Independent, 64:694, 26 Mar 1908
Tower or Throne
Critic, 42:83-4, Jan 1903

Connelly, Emma Mary
Tilting at Windmills
Critic, NS 9:317, 30 Jun

Connelly, Emma Mary (cont.)
1888
Independent, 40:817, 28 Jun 1888

Connelly, James B. H.
Jeb Hutton
Independent, 54:2482, 16 Oct 1902

Conrad, Stephen [pseud.]
See Stimtz, Stephen Conrad.

Converse, Clarence Conyers
Mr. Isolate of Lonelyville
Chautauquan, 31:533, Aug 1900

Converse, Florence
The Burden of Christopher
Chautauquan, 31:531, Aug 1900
Diana Victrix
Independent, 49:1548, 25 Nov 1897
Literary World, 29:10, 8 Jan 1898
Long Will
Dial, 36:119-20, 16 Feb 1904
Independent, 56:445, 25 Feb 1904

Conway, Katherine Eleanor
The Way of the World, and Other Ways
Catholic World, 72:538-9, Jan 1901
The Woman Who Never Did Wrong
Catholic World, 90:546, Jan 1910

Conway, Moncure Daniel
Pine and Palm
Dial, 8:268, Mar 1888
Literary World, 19:25, 21 Jan 1888
Westminster Review, 129:536, Apr 1888
Prisons of Air
Chautauquan, 15:387, Jun 1892
Independent, 44:313, 3 Mar 1892
Literary World, 23:127, 9 Apr 1892

Conyngham, Dane [pseud.]
See Curran, Mrs. L. P. M.

Conyngham, David Power
Rose Parnell, the Flowers of Avondale
Catholic World, 38:286-7, Nov 1883
Sarsfield
Catholic World, 13:143, Apr 1871

Cook, George Cram
Roderick Taliaferro
Chautauquan, 38:518, Jan 1904
Critic, 43:76-7, Jul 1903
Dial, 34:372, 1 Jun 1903
Independent, 55:1038, 30 Apr 1903

Cook, Grace Louise
Wellesley Stories
Dial, 37:42, 16 Jul 1904

Cook, Mrs. James C.
See Cook, Mary Louise (Redd).

Cook, Mary Louise (Redd)
A Woman's Perils
Literary World, 13:253, 29 Jul 1881

Cooke, Grace (McGowan)
The Grapple
Dial, 39:307, 16 Nov 1905

________, and Alice McGowan
Huldah
Literary World, 35:165, Jun 1904

_______, and Annie Booth McKinney
Mistress Joy
Critic, 39:525, Dec 1901
Independent, 54:228, 23 Jan 1902

Cooke, John Esten
Bonnybel Vane
Independent, 36:651, 22 May 1884
Canolles
Galaxy, 24:285-6, Aug 1877
Doctor Vandyke
Literary World, 3:55, 1 Sep 1872
Fanchette
Critic, 3:183, 21 Apr 1883
Dial, 3:280, Apr 1883
Independent, 35:11, 19 Apr 1883
Literary World, 14:107, 7 Apr 1883
Her Majesty, the Queen
Independent, 25:985, 7 Aug 1873
Justin Harley
Independent, 26:10, 8 Oct 1874
Literary World, 5:75, 1 Oct 1874
The Maurice Mystery
Literary World, 16:342, 3 Oct 1885
My Lady Pokahontas
By Anas Todkill [pseud.].
Independent, 37:459, 9 Apr 1885
Literary World, 16:113, 4 Apr 1885
Pretty Mrs. Gaston, and Other Stories
Galaxy, 17:858, Jun 1874
Independent, 26:10, 9 Apr 1875
Professor Pressensee, Materialist and Inventor
Independent, 30:12, 26 Sep 1878
Stories of the Old Dominion
Independent, 31:10, 5 Jun 1879
The Virginia Bohemians
Literary World, 11:207-8, 19 Jun 1880
The Virginia Comedians
Critic, NS 1:76, 16 Feb 1884

Cooke, Rose Terry
The Deacon's Week
Independent, 37:75, 15 Jan 1885
Happy Dodd
Critic, NS 7:124, 12 Mar 1887
Literary World, 18:59, 19 Feb 1887
Huckleberries Gathered from New England Hills
Chautauquan, 14:761, Mar 1892
Critic, NS 17:20, 9 Jan 1892
Independent, 43:1844, 10 Dec 1891
Root Bound
Independent, 38:1237, 30 Sep 1886
Somebody's Neighbors
Dial, 1:265, Apr 1881
Literary World, 12:146-7, 23 Apr 1881
The Sphynx's Children and Other People's
Catholic World, 43:853-5, Sep 1886
Chautauquan, 6:547, Jun 1886
Critic, NS 5:194, 17 Apr 1886
Independent, 38:463, 15 Apr 1886
Literary World, 17:146, 1 May 1886
Steadfast
Chautauquan, 9:564, Jun 1889
Critic, NS 11:117, 9 Mar 1889
Independent, 41:769, 13 Jun 1889; 41:1658, 12 Dec 1889
Literary World, 20:71,

Cooke, Rose Terry (cont.)
2 Mar 1889

Cooley, Alice Kingsbury
Asaph
Critic, NS 15:250, 9 May 1891

Cooley, Ellen Hodges
The Boom of a Western City
Literary World, 29:456, 24 Dec 1898

Cooley, William Forbes
Emmanuel
Catholic World, 50:697-8, Feb 1890
Independent, 42:221, 13 Feb 1890

Coolidge, Susan [pseud.]
See Woolsey, Sarah Chauncey.

[Coombs, Anne (Sheldon)]
As Common Mortals
Critic, NS 6:75, 14 Aug 1886
Literary World, 17:278, 21 Aug 1886
A Game of Chance
Critic, NS 8:76-7, 13 Aug 1887
Literary World, 18:267, 20 Aug 1887
The Garden of Armida
Critic, NS 14:31, 19 Jul 1890
Literary World, 21:187, 7 Jun 1890

Cooper, Samuel Williams
Three Days
Critic, NS 12:63, 10 Aug 1889
Literary World, 20:324-5, 28 Sep 1889

Corbin, Caroline Elizabeth (Fairfield)
His Marriage Vow
Literary World, 4:86-7, Nov 1873
Rebecca
Literary World, 8:181, 1 Mar 1878

Corbin, John
The Cave Man
Independent, 63:339, 8 Aug 1907

Cornwall, C. M. [pseud.]
See Roe, Mary Abigail.

Cornwallis, Kinahan
Adrift with a Vengeance
Galaxy, 11:145, Jan 1871
Literary World, 1:105, 1 Dec 1870

Coryell, John Russell
Diego Pinzon, and the Fearful Voyages He Took into the Unknown Ocean
Harper's, 85:Literary Notes, 4, Oct 1892

Costello, Frederick Hankerson
Under the Rattlesnake Flag
Independent, 51:426, 9 Feb 1899

[Coulson, George James Atkinson]
Flesh & Spirit
Independent, 28:9, 15 Jun 1876
The Ghost of Redbrook
Literary World, 10:183, 7 Jun 1879
Harwood
Literary World, 6:37, 1 Aug 1875
The Lacy Diamonds
Literary World, 6:59-60, 1 Oct 1875
The Odd Trump
Independent, 27:9, 17 Jun 1875
Literary World, 6:20, 1 Jul 1875

Coulter, James W.
The Larger Faith

Literary World, 31:26, 20 Jan 1900

Coulter, John
Mr. Desmond, U. S. A.
Critic, NS 6:102, 28 Aug 1886
Dial, 7:68, Jul 1886
Independent, 38:1236, 30 Sep 1886
Literary World, 17:316, 18 Sep 1886

Coventry, John [pseud.]
See Palmer, John Williamson.

Cowan, James
Daybreak
Literary World, 27:366, 31 Oct 1896

Cowan, John Franklin
Endeavor Doin's Down to the Corners
Chautauquan, 18:254, Nov 1893
Independent, 45:1453, 26 Oct 1893
Literary World, 24:258, 12 Aug 1893
The Mother of the King's Children
Chautauquan, 17:486, Jul 1893

[Cowan, Pamela H.]
Aimée's Marriage
By P. H. C.
Chautauquan, 12:825, Mar 1891
Independent, 42:1842, 25 Dec 1890

[Cowley, Mrs. Winifred Jennings]
Lorin Mooruck, and Other Indian Stories
By George Truman Kercheval [pseud.].
Chautauquan, 9:624, Jul 1889
Critic, NS 11:40, 26 Jan 1889

Cox, Maria (McIntosh)
Jack Brereton's Three Months' Service
Chautauquan, 16:128, Oct 1892

Cozzens, Samuel Woodworth
The Marvellous Country
Critic, NS 14:336, 27 Dec 1890
Nobody's Husband
Literary World, 9:56, 1 Sep 1878

Crabtrie, N. Warrington [pseud.]
See James, Samuel Humphreys.

Craddock, Charles Egbert [pseud.]
See Murfree, Mary Noailles.

Craigie, Christopher [pseud.]
See Cole, William Morse.

Cram, George F.
Minette
Literary World, 33:61, 1 Apr 1902

Cram, Ralph Adams
Black Spirits & White
Dial, 20:339, 1 Jun 1896
Independent, 48:526, 16 Apr 1896
Literary World, 27:47, 8 Feb 1896

Crane, Anne Moncure
See Seemüller, Mrs. Anne Moncure (Crane).

Crane, James Lyons
The Two Circuits
Literary World, 8:180-1, 1 Mar 1878

Crane, Stephen
Active Service
Critic, 36:91, Jan 1900

Crane, Stephen (cont.)
Dial, 27:491, 16 Dec 1899
Independent, 51:3172, 23 Nov 1899; 51:3300, 7 Dec 1899
Literary World, 31:43, 3 Feb 1900
George's Mother
Critic, NS 25:421, 13 Jun 1896
Independent, 48:870, 25 Jun 1896
The Little Regiment, and Other Episodes of the American Civil War
Independent, 48:1801, 31 Dec 1896
Literary World, 27:477, 26 Dec 1896
Maggie, a Girl of the Streets By Johnston Smith [pseud.].
Chautauquan, 23:783, Sep 1896
Critic, NS 25:421, 13 Jun 1896
Literary World, 27:253, 8 Aug 1896
The Monster, and Other Stories
Critic, 36:182, Feb 1900
Independent, 52:324, 1 Feb 1900
Literary World, 31:157, 1 Aug 1900
The Open Boat, and Other Tales of Adventure
Chautauquan, 27:428, Jul 1898
Independent, 50:727, 2 Jun 1898; 50:1424, 17 Nov 1898
Literary World, 29:187, 11 Jun 1898
Literature, 2:535-6, 7 May 1898
The Red Badge of Courage
Chautauquan, 22:380, Dec 1895
Critic, NS 24:363, 30 Nov 1895
Dial, 20:80, 1 Feb 1896
Independent, 47:1474, 31 Oct 1895; 47:1579, 21 Nov 1895
Literary World, 26:458, 14 Dec 1895
The Third Violet
Critic, NS 27:438, 26 Jun 1897
Literary World, 28:280, 21 Aug 1897
Whilomville Stories
Critic, 37:374, Oct 1900

________, and Robert Barr
The O'Ruddy
Dial, 36:121, 16 Feb 1904
Independent, 56:273, 4 Feb 1904

Crawford, Francis Marion
Adam Johnstone's Son
Catholic World, 63:408, Jun 1896
Chautauquan, 23:492, Jul 1896
Critic, NS 25:269, 18 Apr 1896
Dial, 20:336-7, 1 Jun 1896
Literary World, 27:251, 8 Aug 1896
Westminster Review, 146:234-5, Aug 1896
An American Politician
Catholic World, 40:573, Jan 1885
Critic, NS 2:306, 27 Dec 1884
Dial, 5:205, Dec 1884
Independent, 36:1546, 4 Dec 1884
Literary World, 15:452-3, 13 Dec 1884
Arethusa
Independent, 64:421-2, 20 Feb 1908
Ave Roma Immortalis
Critic, NS 30:519-20, Dec 1898
Casa Braccio
Chautauquan, 22:509, Jan 1896
Critic, NS 24:382, 30

Nov 1895
Dial, 19:384, 16 Dec 1895
Independent, 47:1727, 19 Dec 1895
Literary World, 27:76, 7 Mar 1896

Cecilia
Dial, 34:88, 1 Feb 1903
Independent, 55:157, 15 Jan 1903
Literary World, 33:209, 1 Dec 1902
Westminster Review, 158:715, Dec 1902

The Children of the King
Catholic World, 57:127-32, Apr 1893
Critic, NS 19:91-2, 18 Feb 1893
Literary World, 24:70, 11 Mar 1893

A Cigarette-Maker's Romance
Catholic World, 52:442-3, Dec 1890
Critic, NS 14:333, 27 Dec 1890
Dial, 11:241, Dec 1890
Literary World, 21:468-9, 6 Dec 1890
Westminster Review, 135:589, May 1891

Corleone
Catholic World, 66:562-4, Jan 1898
Chautauquan, 26:573, Feb 1898
Critic, NS 28:298, 20 Nov 1897
Dial, 23:284-5, 16 Nov 1897
Independent, 49:1543, 25 Nov 1897
Literary World, 29:5-6, 8 Jan 1898
Literature, 1:178-9, 27 Nov 1897
Westminster Review, 150:713, Dec 1898

The Diva's Ruby
Dial, 45:457, 16 Dec 1908
Independent, 65:1183, 19 Nov 1908
Westminster Review, 170:713-4, Dec 1908

Doctor Claudius
Critic, 3:282, 16 Jun 1883
Independent, 35:11, 21 Jun 1883
Literary World, 14:187-8, 16 Jun 1883

Don Orsina
Catholic World, 57:127-32, Apr 1893
Critic, NS 19:215, 8 Apr 1893
Dial, 14:113, 16 Feb 1893
Independent, 45:22, 5 Jan 1893
Literary World, 23:401, 19 Nov 1892
Westminster Review, 139:90-1, Jan 1893

Fair Margaret
Catholic World, 82:837-8, Mar 1906
Independent, 60:111, 11 Jan 1906

Greifenstein
Catholic World, 49:544-7, Jul 1889
Critic, NS 12:213, 2 Nov 1889
Dial, 10:57, Jul 1889
Independent, 41:1025, 8 Aug 1889
Literary World, 20:173, 25 May 1889

The Heart of Rome
Catholic World, 78:689, Feb 1904
Critic, 44:380, Apr 1904
Dial, 36:18, 1 Jan 1904
Independent, 55:3072, 24 Dec 1903

In the Palace of the King
Catholic World, 73:673, Aug 1901
Critic, 38:85, Jan 1901
Independent, 52:2871-2, 29 Nov 1900; 53:2778, 21 Nov 1901
Literary World, 32:12,

Crawford, Francis Marion (cont.)
1 Jan 1901
Katharine Lauderdale
Catholic World, 62:274-5, Nov 1895
Chautauquan, 19:381, Jun 1894
Critic, NS 21:232, 31 Mar 1894
Dial, 16:366, 16 Jun 1894
Literary World, 25:104, 7 Apr 1894; 26:387-8, 16 Nov 1895
Westminster Review, 141:703-4, Jun 1894
Khaled
Catholic World, 53:607-8, Jul 1891
Critic, NS 16:73, 15 Aug 1891
Independent, 43:1142, 30 Jul 1891
Westminster Review, 136:229, Aug 1891
A Lady of Rome
Dial, 42:15, 1 Jan 1907
Independent, 62:501-2, 28 Feb 1907
Westminster Review, 167:111, Jan 1907
The Little City of Hope
Independent, 63:1405-6, 19 Dec 1907
Love in Idleness
Critic, NS 22:253-4, 20 Oct 1894
Literary World, 26:76, 9 Mar 1895
Westminster Review, 142:715, Dec 1894
Marietta, a Maid of Venice
Critic, 40:178, Feb 1902
Dial, 32:88, 1 Feb 1902
Independent, 54:463, 20 Feb 1902
Literary World, 33:28, 1 Feb 1902
Westminster Review, 157:112, Jan 1902
Marion Darche
Chautauquan, 18:761, Mar 1894
Dial, 15:341, 1 Dec 1893
Independent, 45:1653, 7 Dec 1893
Literary World, 24:423, 2 Dec 1893
Westminster Review, 141:110, Jan 1894
Marzio's Crucifix
Catholic World, 46:556-7, Jan 1888
Chautauquan, 8:635, Jul 1888
Critic, NS 8:323, 24 Dec 1887
Dial, 8:267, Mar 1888
Independent, 39:1586, 8 Dec 1887
Literary World, 18:458, 10 Dec 1887
Westminster Review, 128:1181-2, Dec 1887
Mr. Isaacs
Critic, 2:353, 30 Dec 1882
Dial, 3:234, Feb 1883
Literary World, 14:6-7, 13 Jan 1883
Paul Patoff
Catholic World, 46:837-9, Mar 1888
Critic, NS 8:323, 24 Dec 1887
Dial, 8:267, Mar 1888
Independent, 39:1693, 29 Dec 1887
Westminster Review, 129:265, Feb 1888
Pietro Ghisleri
Catholic World, 57:875-6, Sep 1893
Chautauquan, 17:761-2, Sep 1893
Critic, NS 20:50, 22 Jul 1893
Dial, 15:93, 16 Aug 1893
Literary World, 24:239, 29 Jul 1893
The Primadonna
Independent, 65:101, 9 Jul 1908
Westminster Review, 169:604, May 1908

The Ralstons
Catholic World, 70:422-3, Dec 1899
Chautauquan, 21:124, Apr 1895
Critic, NS 23:141, 16 Feb 1895
Dial, 18:272, 1 May 1895
Independent, 47:317, 7 Mar 1895; 47:1579, 21 Nov 1895
Literary World, 26:41, 9 Feb 1895

A Roman Singer
Catholic World, 39:714-5, Aug 1884; 57:127-32, Apr 1893
Chautauquan, 17:125, Apr 1893
Critic, NS 1:267, 7 Jun 1884
Dial, 5:64-5, Jul 1884
Independent, 36:747, 12 Jun 1884
Literary World, 15:183-4, 31 May 1884

A Rose of Yesterday
Catholic World, 65:844, Sep 1897
Chautauquan, 25:575, Aug 1897
Critic, NS 28:33, 17 Jul 1897
Dial, 23:18, 1 Jul 1897
Literary World, 28:287, 4 Sep 1897
Westminster Review, 148:356, Sep 1897

Sant' Ilario
Catholic World, 50:123, Oct 1889
Critic, NS 12:147-8, 28 Sep 1889
Independent, 41:1354-5, 17 Oct 1889
Literary World, 20:321, 28 Sep 1889

Saracinesca
Catholic World, 44:702-3, Feb 1887; 45:425-7, Jun 1887
Critic, NS 7:266, 28 May 1887; 36:182, Feb 1900
Dial, 8:66, Jul 1887
Independent, 39:686, 2 Jun 1887
Literary World, 18:165-6, 28 May 1887
Westminster Review, 128:516-7, Jul 1887

Stradella
Catholic World, 90:694, Feb 1910
Independent, 67:1453, 23 Dec 1909

A Tale of a Lonely Parish
Catholic World, 43:274, May 1886
Dial, 7:15, May 1886
Independent, 38:398, 1 Apr 1886
Literary World, 17:111, 3 Apr 1886

Taquisara
Chautauquan, 24:376, Dec 1896
Critic, NS 26:381, 5 Dec 1896
Dial, 22:22, 1 Jan 1897
Independent, 48:1693, 10 Dec 1896
Literary World, 28:12, 9 Jan 1897
Westminster Review, 146:710, Dec 1896

The Three Fates
Catholic World, 55:285-6, May 1892
Critic, NS 18:43, 23 Jul 1893
Independent, 44:664, 12 May 1892
Literary World, 23:159, 7 May 1892
Westminster Review, 138:221-2, Aug 1892

To Leeward
Dial, 4:229, Jan 1884
Independent, 36:75, 17 Jan 1884
Literary World, 14:481, 29 Dec 1883

The Undesirable Governess
Catholic World, 91:391-2, Jun 1910
Independent, 68:1139, 26

Crawford, Francis Marion (cont.)
May 1910
The Upper Berth
Chautauquan, 19:486, Jul 1894
Critic, NS 21:374, 2 Jun 1894
Via Crucis
Catholic World, 70:420-22, Dec 1899
Dial, 28:85-6, 1 Feb 1900
Independent, 51:3499, 28 Dec 1899
Literary World, 30:455, 23 Dec 1899
The White Sister
Catholic World, 89:690, Aug 1909
Dial, 47:181, 16 Sep 1909
Independent, 66:982, 6 May 1909
Westminster Review, 172:472, Oct 1909
Whosoever Shall Offend
Catholic World, 80:403-5, Dec 1904
Critic, 46:477, May 1905
Dial, 38:16, 1 Jan 1905
Independent, 58:1133, 18 May 1905
The Witch of Prague
Catholic World, 54:296-7, Nov 1891
Critic, NS 17:154, 12 Mar 1892
Dial, 12:276, Dec 1891
Independent, 43:1570, 22 Oct 1891
Westminster Review, 136:461, Oct 1891
With the Immortals
Critic, NS 10:78, 18 Aug 1888
Dial, 9:161, Nov 1888
Independent, 40:1644, 20 Dec 1888
Literary World, 19:260, 18 Aug 1888
Zoroaster
Critic, NS 3:291, 20 Jun 1885
Dial, 6:122, Sep 1885
Independent, 37:815, 25 Jun 1885
Literary World, 16:244, 11 Jul 1885
Westminster Review, 124 (NS 68):302-1, Jul 1885
See also The Broken Shaft.

Creelman, James
Eagle Blood
Critic, 41:580, Dec 1902
Independent, 54:3099, 25 Dec 1902
Literary World, 34:12, 1 Jan 1903

Crim, Martha Jane
Adventures of a Fair Rebel
By Matt Crim [pseud.].
Chautauquan, 15:652-3, Aug 1892
Critic, NS 17:69, 30 Jan 1892
Independent, 44:21, 7 Jan 1892
Elizabeth, Christian Scientist
By Matt Crim [pseud.].
Chautauquan, 17:637, Aug 1893
Critic, NS 19:400, 17 Jun 1893
Independent, 45:1154, 24 Aug 1893
Literary World, 24:194, 17 Jun 1893
In Beaver Cove and Elsewhere
Chautauquan, 15:774, Sep 1892
Critic, NS 17:314, 4 Jun 1892
Independent, 44:664, 12 May 1892
Literary World, 23:151, 23 Apr 1892

Crim, Matt
See Crim, Martha Jane.

Crinkle, Nym [pseud.]
See Wheeler, Andrew Carpenter.

Crosby, Ernest Howard
Captain Jinks, Hero
Critic, 41:373, Oct 1902

Crosby, Margaret
A Violin Obligato, and Other Stories
Critic, NS 16:16, 11 Jul 1891
Chautauquan, 13:552, Jul 1891
Independent, 43:1283, 27 Aug 1891

Crowley, Mary Catherine
The Heroine of the Strait
Catholic World, 75:547-8, Jul 1902
Dial, 32:391, 1 Jun 1902
Independent, 54:1728, 17 Jul 1902
Literary World, 33:122, 1 Aug 1902
In Treaty with Honor
Catholic World, 85:104-5, Apr 1907
Love Thrives in War
Critic, 44:380, Apr 1904
Dial, 35:65, 1 Aug 1903

Crowninshield, Mary (Bradford)
The Archbishop and the Lady
By Mrs. Schuyler Crowninshield.
Chautauquan, 33:108, Apr 1901
Critic, 38:371, Apr 1901
Independent, 53:964, 25 Apr 1901
Latitude 19°
Critic, NS 30:527, Dec 1898
Dial, 27:20, 1 Jul 1899
San Isidro
Critic, 36:90, Jan 1900
Literary World, 31:68, 3 Mar 1900
Valencia's Garden
Critic, 39:181, Aug 1901
Dial, 31:32, 1 Jul 1901
Independent, 53:1747, 25 Jul 1901
Literary World, 32:142, 1 Sep 1901
Where the Trade-Wind Blows
Chautauquan, 27:333, Jun 1898
Critic, NS 29:181, 12 Mar 1898
Independent, 50:521, 21 Apr 1898
Literary World, 29:141, 30 Apr 1898

Crowninshield, Mrs. Schuyler
See Crowninshield, Mary (Bradford).

Crozier, Robert Haskins
Fiery Trials
Independent, 36:299, 6 Mar 1884

[Cruger, Julie Grinnell (Storrow)]
A Diplomat's Diary
By Julien Gordon [pseud.].
Critic, NS 14:151, 27 Sep 1890
Independent, 42:1459, 16 Oct 1890; 43:456, 26 Mar 1891
Eat Not Thy Heart
By Julien Gordon [pseud.].
Independent, 50:224, 17 Feb 1898
Literary World, 28:479, 25 Dec 1897
His Letters
By Julien Gordon [pseud.].
Independent, 45:1282, 21 Sep 1893
Literary World, 24:193-4, 17 Jun 1893; 28:297, 4 Sep 1897
Mademoiselle Résèda
By Julien Gordon [pseud.].
Critic, NS 17:153, 12 Mar 1892
Independent, 43:1882, 17 Dec 1891
Marionettes

[Cruger, Julie Grinnell (Storrow)] (cont.)
By Julien Gordon [pseud.].
Catholic World, 57:876, Sep 1893
Dial, 13:102, Aug 1892
Independent, 44:1260, 8 Sep 1892
Literary World, 23:198, 4 Jun 1892

Mrs. Clyde
By Julien Gordon [pseud.].
Critic, 38:370, Apr 1901
Literary World, 32:103, 1 Jul 1901

Poppaea
By Julien Gordon [pseud.].
Critic, NS 23:440, 15 Jun 1895
Dial, 18:272, 1 May 1895
Literary World, 25:470, 29 Dec 1894

A Puritan Pagan
By Julien Gordon [pseud.].
Critic, NS 16:149-50, 26 Sep 1891
Dial, 12:277, Dec 1891
Independent, 43:1386, 17 Sep 1891

A Successful Man
By Julien Gordon [pseud.].
Critic, NS 15:51, 31 Jan 1891

Vampires
By Julien Gordon [pseud.].
Critic, NS 17:153, 12 Mar 1892
Independent, 43:1882, 17 Dec 1891

The Wage of Character
By Julien Gordon [pseud.].
Critic, 39:575, Dec 1901
Independent, 54:285, 30 Jan 1902
Literary World, 33:171-2, 1 Nov 1902

A Wedding, and Other Stories
By Julien Gordon [pseud.].
Critic, NS 24:406, 14 Dec 1895
Dial, 19:385, 16 Dec 1895
Independent, 47:1728, 19 Dec 1895
Literary World, 27:188, 13 Jun 1896

World's People
By Julien Gordon [pseud.].
Independent, 54:2139-40, 4 Sep 1902
Literary World, 33:139, 1 Sep 1902

Cruger, Mary
A Den of Thieves
Literary World, 17:279, 21 Aug 1886

Hyperaesthesia
Chautauquan, 6:425, Apr 1886
Literary World, 17:102, 20 Mar 1886

The Vanderheyde Manor-House
Critic, NS 9:17, 14 Jan 1888

Cummings, Arthur M.
The Hercules Brand
Critic, NS 3:280, 13 Jan 1885

Cunningham, Mrs. B. Sim
In Sancho Panza's Pit
Independent, 35:11, 1 Mar 1883

Curran, John Elliott
Miss Frances Merley
Literary World, 19:284, 1 Sep 1888

[Curran, Mrs. L. P. M.]
Eunice Quince
By Dane Conyngham [pseud.].
Literary World, 27:75, 7 Mar 1896

[Curtis, Caroline Gardiner (Cary)]
From Madge to Margaret
By Carroll Winchester [pseud.].
Literary World, 11:264, 31 Jul 1880

The Love of a Lifetime
By Carroll Winchester [pseud.].
Literary World, 15:327, 4 Oct 1884

Curtis, David A.
Stand Pat
Critic, 49:285, Sep 1906

Curtis, Emma Ghent
The Administratrix
Critic, NS 15:263, 16 May 1891

[Curtis, George Ticknor]
John Charáxes
By Peter Boyleston [pseud.].
Critic, NS 11:307, 22 Jun 1889; NS 12:71, 10 Aug 1889

Curtis, George William
Prue and I
Harper's, 86:Literary Notes, 1, Dec 1892

Curtis, Georgina Pell
Trammelings
Catholic World, 91:260, May 1910

Curtis, Wardon Allan
The Strange Adventures of Mr. Middleton
Dial, 36:18-9, 1 Jan 1904

Cushing, Frank Hamilton
Zuni Folk Tales
Independent, 54:1375, 5 Jun 1902
Literary World, 33:95, 1 Apr 1902

Cushing, Paul [pseud.]
See Wood-Seys, Roland Alexander.

Cutler, Mary C.
Philip
Critic, NS 13:319, 28 Jun 1890
Independent, 42:1028, 24 Jul 1890
Literary World, 21:253-4, 2 Aug 1890

Cutting, Mary Stewart (Doubleday)
Heart of Lynn
Independent, 57:213-4, 28 Jul 1904
Little Stories of Married Life
Critic, 42:84, Jan 1903
The Suburban Whirl
Independent, 64:312, 6 Feb 1908
The Wayfarers
Independent, 65:550, 3 Sep 1908

Czeika [pseud.]
See Furniss, Louise E.

Dabney, Virginius
Gold That Did Not Glitter
Chautauquan, 10:252, Nov 1889
Critic, NS 12:214, 2 Nov 1889
Independent, 41:1659, 12 Dec 1889
Literary World, 20:371, 26 Oct 1889
The Story of Don Miff
Critic, NS 5:316, 26 Jun 1886
Independent, 39:590, 12 May 1887
Literary World, 17:293, 4 Sep 1886

Daggett, Mrs. Charles Stewart
See Daggett, Mary (Stewart).

Daggett, Mary (Stewart)
Mariposilla
Critic, NS 25:93, 8 Feb 1896
Literary World, 27:220, 11 Jul 1896

Dahlgren, Madeleine (Vinton)
Chim, His Washington Winter

Dahlgren, Madeleine (Vinton) (cont.)
Catholic World, 56:576-7, Jan 1893
Chautauquan, 17:383, Jun 1893
Critic, NS 19:45, 28 Jan 1893
Independent, 45:507, 13 Apr 1893

Lights and Shadows of a Life
Catholic World, 45:698-700, Aug 1887
Critic, NS 7:307, 18 Jun 1887

The Lost Name
Catholic World, 43:421, Jun 1886
Critic, NS 5:217, 1 May 1886
Literary World, 17:350, 16 Oct 1886

South Mountain Magic
Critic, 2:188, 15 Jul 1882

A Washington Winter
Catholic World, 38:142-3, Oct 1883
Dial, 4:113, Sep 1883
Literary World, 14:268-9, 25 Aug 1883

Daintrey, Laura
Eros
Critic, NS 10:102, 1 Sep 1888

Fedor
Critic, NS 12:186, 19 Oct 1889

Dale, Alan [pseud.]
See Cohen, Alfred J.

Dale, Annan [pseud.]
See Johnston, James Wesley.

Dallas, Mary (Kyle)
The Devil's Anvil
Independent, 42:1164, 21 Aug 1890

Dallas, Richard [pseud.]
See Williams, Nathan Winslow.

Dalton, Edith Leverett
A Slight Romance
Independent, 49:219, 18 Feb 1897
Literary World, 28:210, 26 Jun 1897

Damon, Sophie M. (Buckman)
Old New-England Days
Critic, NS 8:336, 31 Dec 1887
Independent, 39:1458, 10 Nov 1887
Literary World, 18:387, 12 Nov 1887

Dana, Francis
The Decoy
Independent, 54:1076-7, 1 May 1902
Literary World, 33:77, 1 May 1902

Leonora of the Yawmish
Critic, NS 29:76, 29 Jan 1898
Harper's, 95:Literary Notes, 2, Jul 1897
Independent, 49:916, 15 Jul 1897
Literary World, 28:262, 7 Aug 1897

Dana, Katharine Floyd
Our Phil, and Other Stories
Critic, NS 11:28, 19 Jan 1889
Independent, 40:1610-1, 13 Dec 1888
Literary World, 20:6, 5 Jan 1889

Dana, Marion
A Puritan Witch
Literary World, 34:151, Jun 1903

Daniel, Charles S.
AI: A Social Vision
Independent, 45:258, 23 Feb 1893

Literary World, 24:242, 29 Jul 1893

Daniels, Cora Linn (Morrison)
The Bronze Buddha
Independent, 52:2874, 29 Nov 1902
Literary World, 31:71, 3 Mar 1900
Sardia
Critic, NS 15:237, 2 May 1891

Daniels, Gertrude Potter
The Warners
Literary World, 32:87, 1 Jun 1901

Danziger, Gustav Adolph
See Bierce, Ambrose, and Gustav Adolph Danziger.

Darby, John [pseud.]
See Garretson, James Edward.

Darrow, Clarence Seward
An Eye for an Eye
Independent, 59:1052, 2 Nov 1905
Farmington
Critic, 46:93, Jan 1905

Daskam, Josephine Dodge
See Bacon, Josephine Dodge (Daskam).

Daugé, Henri [pseud.]
See Hammond, Henrietta (Hardy).

Daughters of Aesculapius
Literary World, 28:281, 21 Aug 1897

Davidson, George Trimble
The Moderns
Critic, 39:277-8, Sep 1901

Davis, Arline E.
The Romance of Guardamonte
Literary World, 27:330, 3 Oct 1896

Davis, Charles Belmont
The Lodger Overhead, and Others
Independent, 67:551, 2 Sep 1909

Davis, Edith (Smith)
Whether White or Black, A Man
Chautauquan, 27:428, Jul 1898

Davis, Ethel
When Love Is Done
Independent, 47:1240, 12 Sep 1895

Davis, Harriet Riddle
Gilbert Elgar's Son
Catholic World, 52:291-2, Nov 1890
Critic, NS 14:321, 20 Dec 1890
Independent, 42:1644, 20 Nov 1890
In Sight of the Goddess
Independent, 48:976, 16 Jul 1896
Literary World, 27:235, 25 Jul 1896

Davis, Leela B.
Modern Argonaut
Literary World, 27:252, 8 Aug 1896

Davis, Lemuel Clarke
A Stranded Ship
Literary World, 11:214, 19 Jun 1880

Davis, Mary Evelyn (Moore)
An Elephant's Track, and Other Stories
Critic, NS 27:251, 10 Apr 1897
Harper's, 93:Literary Notes, 3, Nov 1896
Independent, 48:1771, 24 Dec 1896
Literary World, 28:58,

Davis, Mary Evelyn (Moore) (cont.)
20 Feb 1897
In War Times at La Rose Blanche
Chautauquan, 9:125, Nov 1888
Critic, NS 10:138, 22 Sep 1888
Independent, 41:865, 4 Jul 1889
Jaconetta
Critic, 39:575, Dec 1901
Independent, 53:2786, 21 Nov 1901
The Little Chevalier
Critic, 44:92-3, Jan 1904
Independent, 56:675, 24 Mar 1904
The Prince of Silence
Dial, 42:380, 16 Jun 1907
The Wire Cutters
Independent, 51:968, 6 Apr 1899
Literary World, 30:92, 18 Mar 1899

Davis, Rebecca (Harding)
Dr. Warrick's Daughters
Dial, 21:20, 1 Jul 1896
Harper's, 92:Literary Notes, 3, Apr 1896
Independent, 48:496, 9 Apr 1896
Literary World, 27:154, 16 May 1896
Frances Waldeaux
Critic, NS 27:251, 10 Apr 1897
Dial, 22:312, 16 May 1897
Harper's, 94:Literary Notes, 3, Apr 1897
Literary World, 28:27, 23 Jan 1897
John Andross
Galaxy, 17:858-9, Jun 1874
Kent Hampden
Critic, NS 19:61, 4 Feb 1893
Independent, 44:1712A, 1 Dec 1892
Natasqua
Critic, NS 5:217, 1 May 1886
Independent, 38:690, 3 Jun 1886
Silhouettes of American Life
Critic, NS 19:61, 4 Feb 1893
Independent, 44:1563, 3 Nov 1892
Literary World, 23:375, 22 Oct 1892

Davis, Richard Harding
Captain Macklin
Critic, 42:68, Jan 1903
Dial, 33:326-7, 16 Nov 1902
Independent, 54:2479, 16 Oct 1902; 54:2772, 20 Nov 1902
Literary World, 33:195, 1 Dec 1902
Cinderella, and Other Stories
Catholic World, 63:409, Jun 1896
Chautauquan, 23:654, Aug 1896
Critic, NS 25:352, 16 May 1896
Dial, 20:338-9, 1 Jun 1896
The Exiles, and Other Stories
Critic, NS 22:20, 14 Jul 1894
Dial, 16:368, 16 Jun 1894
Harper's, 89:Literary Notes, 3-4, Jul 1894
Literary World, 25:199, 30 Jun 1894
Gallegher, and Other Stories
Catholic World, 53:438-9, Jun 1891
Critic, NS 15:286, 16 May 1891
In the Fog
Critic, 41:478, Nov 1902
The King's Jackal
Chautauquan, 27:573, Aug 1898

Critic, NS 30:396, Nov 1898
Dial, 25:75, 1 Aug 1898
Independent, 50:263, 28 Jul 1898; 50:1424, 17 Nov 1898
Literary World, 29:261, 20 Aug 1898
Literature, 3:352, 15 Oct 1898

The Lion and the Unicorn
Critic, 36:28-30, Jan 1900
Critic, 36:28-9, Jan 1900
Independent, 51:2830, 19 Oct 1899; 51:3171, 23 Nov 1899

Once Upon a Time
Independent, 69:1089-90, 17 Nov 1910

The Princess Aline
Chautauquan, 21:492, Jul 1895
Critic, NS 23:292-3, 20 Apr 1895
Dial, 18:273, 1 May 1895
Harper's, 90:Literary Notes, 3-4, May 1895
Independent, 47:874, 27 Jun 1895; 47:1579, 21 Nov 1895
Literary World, 26:121, 20 Apr 1895

Ranson's Folly, and Other Stories
Dial, 33:64, 1 Aug 1902
Independent, 54:2140, 4 Sep 1902
Literary World, 33:142, 1 Sep 1902

The Scarlet Car
Independent, 63:761, 26 Sep 1907

Soldiers of Fortune
Chautauquan, 25:430-1, Jul 1897
Critic, NS 27:387, 5 Jun 1897
Dial, 23:18-9, 1 Jul 1897
Independent, 49:819, 24 Jun 1897; 49:1505, 18 Nov 1897
Literary World, 28:239, 24 Jul 1897

Van Bibber, and Others
Critic, NS 18:162, 24 Sep 1892; NS 22:38, 21 Jul 1894
Dial, 13:103, Aug 1892
Harper's, 84:Literary Notes, 4, May 1892
Independent, 44:664, 12 May 1892
Literary World, 23:181, 21 May 1892; 25:267, 25 Aug 1894
Westminster Review, 138:569, Nov 1892

The White Mice
Dial, 47:48, 16 Jul 1909
Independent, 67:423, 19 Aug 1909

[Davis, Robert S.]
As It May Happen
By Trebor [pseud.].
Independent, 31:12, 6 Mar 1879
Literary World, 10:54, 15 Feb 1879

Davis, Varina Anne Jefferson
A Romance of Summer Seas
Critic, NS 30:104-5, Jul-Aug 1898
Dial, 25:305, 1 Nov 1898
Independent, 50:421, 11 Aug 1898
Harper's, 97:Literary Notes, 1-2, Sep 1898
Literary World, 29:279, 3 Sep 1898

The Veiled Doctor
Critic, NS 24:103, 17 Aug 1895
Harper's, 91:Literary Notes, 3, Oct 1895
Literary World, 26:243, 10 Aug 1895

Davis, William M.
Nimrod of the Sea
Galaxy, 18:858, Dec 1874

Davis, William Stearns
Belshazzar

Davis, William Stearns (cont.)
Dial, 33:67, 1 Aug 1902
Independent, 54:2480, 16 Oct 1902
Literary World, 33:180, 1 Nov 1902
Falaise of the Blessed Voice
Independent, 57:1329-30, 8 Dec 1904
A Friend of Caesar
Critic, 37:468, Nov 1900
God Wills It
Catholic World, 74:821-3, Mar 1902
Dial, 32:88, 1 Feb 1902
Independent, 54:934-5, 17 Apr 1902
Literary World, 33:60, 1 Apr 1902

The Dawn of the World
Ed. C. Hart Merriam.
Independent, 69:826, 13 Oct 1910

Dawson, Emma Frances
An Itinerant House, and Other Stories
Independent, 49:948, 22 Jul 1897
Literary World, 28:145-6, 1 May 1897

Dawson, William James
A Prophet in Babylon
Independent, 64:370-1, 13 Feb 1908
The Redemption of Edward Strahan
Literary World, 23:14, 2 Jan 1892
Thro' Lattice-Windows
Chautauquan, 26:573, Feb 1898

Day, Holman Francis
King Spruce
Dial, 44:349-50, 1 Jun 1908

Dean, Frederic Alva
The Heroines of Petoséga
Critic, NS 12:99, 31 Aug 1889

DeForest, John William
The Bloody Chasm
Catholic World, 34:576, Jan 1882
Critic, 1:259, 24 Sep 1881
Dial, 2:150, Nov 1881
Literary World, 12:365-6, 22 Oct 1881
Honest John Vane
Independent, 27:10, 28 Jan 1875
Justine's Lovers
Literary World, 9:13, 1 Jun 1878
Kate Beaumont
Galaxy, 13:713-4, May 1872
Literary World, 2:156, 1 Mar 1872
A Lover's Revolt
Literary World, 30:235, 22 Jul 1899
Literature, 3:578-9, 17 Dec 1898
Overland
Galaxy, 12:869-71, Dec 1871
Playing the Mischief
Literary World, 6:37, 1 Aug 1875
The Wetherel Affair
Galaxy, 18:853-4, Dec 1874
Independent, 26:9, 26 Feb 1874

De Jeans, Elizabeth
The Heart of Desire
Independent, 69:138, 21 Jul 1910

De Kay, Charles
The Bohemian
Independent, 31:11, 27 Feb 1879
Literary World, 10:28, 18 Jan 1879

De Koven, Anna (Farwell)
By the Waters of Babylon
Critic, 39:182, Aug 1901
A Sawdust Doll
Critic, NS 23:454, 22 Jun 1895
Dial, 18:270-1, 1 May 1895
Independent, 47:737, 30 May 1895
Literary World, 26:137, 4 May 1895

De Koven, Mrs. Reginald
See De Koven, Anna (Farwell).

Deland, Ellen Douglas
Alan Ransford
Harper's, 96:Literary Notes, 2, Feb 1898
In the Old Herrick House, and Other Stories
Harper's, 94:Literary Notes, 4, Apr 1897
Independent, 49:447, 8 Apr 1897
Oakleigh
Harper's, 91:Literary Notes, 2, Nov 1895

Deland, Margaret Wade (Campbell)
The Awakening of Helena Ritchie
Dial, 41:115, 1 Sep 1906
Independent, 61:336-8, 9 Aug 1906; 61:1158-60, 15 Nov 1906
Dr. Lavendar's People
Critic, 44:186, Feb 1904
Dial, 36:23, 1 Jan 1904
An Encore
Independent, 63:1473, 19 Dec 1907
John Ward, Preacher
Catholic World, 47:559-61, Jul 1888
Critic, NS 10:54, 4 Aug 1888
Dial, 9:67, Jul 1888
Independent, 40:1008, 9 Aug 1888
Literary World, 19:153, 12 May 1888
Mr. Tommy Dove, and Other Stories
Critic, NS 20:86-7, 5 Aug 1893
Dial, 15:94, 16 Aug 1893
Independent, 45:889, 29 Jun 1893
Literary World, 24:178, 3 Jun 1893
Old Chester Tales
Critic, NS 31:261, Mar 1899
Harper's, 98:Literary Notes, 2-3, Mar 1899
Independent, 51:281, 26 Jan 1899
Literary World, 29:431, 10 Dec 1898
Philip and His Wife
Chautauquan, 21:126, Apr 1895
Critic, NS 22:325, 17 Nov 1894
Dial, 18:272, 1 May 1895
Literary World, 25:445, 15 Dec 1894
Sidney
Catholic World, 52:443-6, Dec 1890
Chautauquan, 12:421, Dec 1890
Critic, NS 14:256, 22 Nov 1890
Dial, 11:240, Dec 1890
Literary World, 21:393-4, 8 Nov 1890
The Story of a Child
Critic, NS 19:126-7, 4 Mar 1893
Independent, 45:53, 12 Jan 1893
Literary World, 23:497, 31 Dec 1892
The Wisdom of Fools
Critic, NS 27:422-3, 19 Jun 1897

De Leon, Thomas Cooper
John Holden, Unionist
Independent, 45:1018, 27 Jul 1893

De Leon, Thomas Cooper (cont.)
The Pride of the Mercers
Literary World, 29:140-1, 30 Apr 1898

De Mille, James
The Lily and the Cross
Catholic World, 21:143, Apr 1875

Deming, Philander
Tompkins, and Other Folk
Critic, NS 3:18, 10 Jan 1885
Independent, 37:75, 15 Jan 1885
Literary World, 16:16, 10 Jan 1885

Denison, Mary (Andrews)
Captain Molly
Literary World, 28:195, 12 Jun 1897
Cracker Joe
Critic, NS 8:101, 27 Aug 1887
Independent, 39:943, 28 Jul 1887
Literary World, 18:186, 11 Jun 1887
An Every-Day Heroine
Chautauquan, 25:111, Apr 1897
His Triumph
Independent, 35:10, 27 Dec 1883
Literary World, 14:292, 8 Sep 1883
Mr. Peter Crewitt
Literary World, 9:56, 1 Sep 1878
Old Slip Warehouse
Independent, 30:12, 3 Oct 1878
Rothmell
Independent, 30:13, 11 Jul 1878
That Husband of Mine
Literary World, 8:64, 1 Sep 1877
Victor Norman, Rector
Independent, 25:236, 20 Feb 1873

[Denison, Thomas Stewart]
An Iron Crown
Chautauquan, 6:426, Apr 1886
Critic, NS 5:104, 27 Feb 1886
Literary World, 17:130, 17 Apr 1886
The Man Behind
Catholic World, 47:125-7, Apr 1888
Critic, NS 9:152, 31 Mar 1888
Literary World, 19:153-4, 12 May 1888

Denton, Lyman W.
Under the Magnolias
Critic, NS 11:130, 16 Mar 1889
Literary World, 20:113, 30 Mar 1889

Derby, Aleck
Ida Goldwin
Galaxy, 21:715, May 1876

[Derby, Caroline Rosina]
Salem
By D. R. Castleton [pseud.].
Independent, 26:10, 8 Oct 1874
Literary World, 5:91, 1 Nov 1874

Despard, Matilda (Pratt)
Kilrogan Cottage
Independent, 30:12, 22 Aug 1878

Despotism and Democracy
Dial, 35:261, 16 Oct 1903
Literary World, 34:179, Jul 1903

Despot's Champion
By "A Southern."
Critic, NS 13:16, 11 Jan 1890

Dessar, Leo Charles
A Royal Enchantress
Critic, 37:279, Sep 1900

De Vallière, George [pseud.]
See Duysters, George F.

Devereux, Mary
From Kingdom to Colony
Independent, 53:451, 21 Feb 1901
Literary World, 31:74, 3 Mar 1900
Lafitte of Louisiana
Dial, 33:67-8, 1 Aug 1902
Literary World, 33:138-9, 1 Sep 1902
Up and Down the Sands of Gold
Critic, 41:183, Aug 1902
Dial, 31:373, 16 Nov 1901

Devoore, Ann
Oliver Iverson
Literary World, 30:234-5, 22 Jul 1899

Dick, Herbert G. [pseud.]
See Morgan, Carrie A.

Dickinson, Mrs. Ellen E.
The King's Daughters
Independent, 49:219, 18 Feb 1897

Dickinson, Mary (Lowe)
Among the Thorns
Independent, 32:10, 1 Jul 1880; 32:12, 23 Sep 1880
From Hollow to Hilltop
Literary World, 27:365, 31 Oct 1896
Three Times and Out
Chautauquan, 21:255, May 1895

Dickson, Harris
The Black Wolf's Breed
Critic, 36:355, Apr 1900
Gabrielle, Transgressor
Independent, 62:674, 21 Mar 1907
The Ravanels
Critic, 47:93, Jul 1905
Dial, 39:208-9, 1 Oct 1905
Independent, 58:1423, 22 Jun 1905
The Siege of Lady Resolute
Dial, 32:386, 1 Jun 1902
Independent, 54:1189-90, 15 May 1902
Literary World, 33:138, 1 Sep 1902

Dillingham, Lucy
The Missing Chord
Critic, NS 23:459, 22 Jun 1895

Dillon, Mary C. (Johnson)
In Old Bellaire
Independent, 60:1219-20, 24 May 1906
The Leader
Dial, 42:17, 1 Jan 1907
Independent, 61:939-40, 18 Oct 1906
A Rose of Old St. Louis
Critic, 45:475, Nov 1904
Dial, 37:212, 1 Oct 1904
Literary World, 35:259, Sep 1904

Diltz, Hanson Penn
The Duchess Undine
Literary World, 14:40, 10 Feb 1883

Dix, Beulah Marie
Blount of Breckenhow
Critic, 44:300, Apr 1904
The Fair Maid of Greystones
Catholic World, 82:563-4, Jan 1906
Dial, 40:155, 1 Mar 1906
Independent, 59:1345-6, 7 Dec 1905
A Little Captive Lad
Critic, 42:563, Jun 1903
The Making of Christopher Ferringham
Catholic World, 73:110-1,

Dix, Beulah Marie (cont.)
Apr 1901
Critic, 39:374, Oct 1901
Dial, 31:28-9, 1 Jul 1901
Independent, 53:1501, 27 Jun 1901
Literary World, 32:71, 1 May 1901

Merrylips
Independent, 62:275-6, 31 Jan 1907

Soldier Rigdale
Independent, 52:501, 22 Feb 1900

_______, and Carrie A. Harper

The Beau's Comedy
Critic, 41:581, Dec 1902
Independent, 54:1843, 31 Jul 1902
Literary World, 33:106, 1 Jul 1902

Dix, Edwin Asa

Deacon Bradbury
Chautauquan, 31:532, Aug 1900
Critic, 36:355, Apr 1900

Old Bowen's Legacy
Critic, 38:560, Jun 1901
Dial, 31:34, 1 Jul 1901
Independent, 53:1686, 18 Jul 1901

Prophet's Landing
Independent, 63:339, 7 Aug 1907

Dix, Gertrude

The Girl from the Farm
Independent, 47:1075, 8 Aug 1895
Literary World, 26:243, 10 Aug 1895

The Image Breakers
Critic, 38:181, Feb 1901

Dixon, Ella Hepworth

The Story of a Modern Woman
Critic, NS 23:178, 9 Mar 1895

Dixon, Thomas

The Clansman
Critic, 46:277-8, Mar 1905
Independent, 58:325-6, 9 Feb 1905

The Leopard's Spots
Chautauquan, 35:622, Sep 1902
Critic, 42:84, Jan 1903
Dial, 32:389, 1 Jun 1902
Independent, 54:1548-9, 26 Jun 1902; 54:2771, 20 Nov 1902

The One Woman
Independent, 55:2117-9, 3 Sep 1903; 57:1149, 17 Nov 1904
Literary World, 34:228, Sep 1903

The Traitor
Independent, 63:762, 26 Sep 1907

Dod, Samuel Bayard

A Hillside Parish
Independent, 45:1653, 7 Dec 1893
Literary World, 24:452, 16 Dec 1893

Stubble or Wheat?
Catholic World, 47:701-2, Aug 1888
Critic, NS 11:209, 27 Apr 1889
Independent, 41:865, 4 Jul 1889

Dodd, Anna Bowman (Blake)

The American Husband in Paris
Independent, 53:1625, 11 Jul 1901
Literary World, 32:107, 1 Jul 1901

Glorinda
Literary World, 19:365, 27 Oct 1888

On the Knees of the Gods
Independent, 65:209, 23 Jul 1908

Struthers, and the Comedy of the Masked Musicians
Critic, NS 22:186, 22

Sep 1894
Literary World, 25:234, 28 Jul 1894

[Dodge, Louise Preston]
A Question of Identity
Independent, 39:270, 3 Mar 1887
Literary World, 18:27, 22 Jan 1887
See also Preston, Harriet Waters, and Louise Preston Dodge.

[Dodge, Mary Abigail]
First Love Is Best
By Gail Hamilton [pseud.].
Galaxy, 24:285, Aug 1877
Literary World, 8:30, 1 Jul 1877

Dodge, Mary Elizabeth (Mapes)
Hans Brinker; or, the Silver Skates
Galaxy, 17:284-5, Feb 1874
Theophilus and Others
Galaxy, 22:568, Oct 1876
Independent, 28:9, 29 Jun 1876

[Doissy, Louise]
A Drama in Dutch
By Z. Z. [pseud.].
Critic, NS 23:47, 19 Jan 1895

Dole, Edmund Pearson
The Stand-By
Critic, NS 27:249-50, 10 Apr 1897
Dial, 23:284, 16 Nov 1897
Independent, 49:851, 1 Jul 1897
Literary World, 28:187, 12 Jun 1897

Dole, Nathan Haskell
Not Angels Quite
Critic, NS 20:395, 16 Dec 1893
Dial, 15:227, 16 Oct 1893
Literary World, 24:286, 9 Sep 1893
Omar, the Tentmaker
Dial, 26:245-6, 1 Apr 1899
Literary World, 30:38-9, 4 Feb 1899
On the Point
Critic, NS 26:57, 25 Jul 1896
Independent, 47:1203, 5 Sep 1895
Literary World, 26:266, 24 Aug 1895

Dollarocracy
Independent, 44:881, 23 Jun 1892

Donaldson, A. L.
A Millbrook Romance, and Other Tales
Independent, 45:507, 13 Apr 1893

Donnell, Annie (Hamilton)
Rebecca Mary
Chautauquan, 43:192, Apr 1906
Independent, 59:1347, 7 Dec 1905

Donnelly, Eleanor Cecilia
A Klondike Picnic
Catholic World, 68:704-5, Feb 1899

Donnelly, Eleanor, and Mary Kilpatrick
Miss Varney's Experience, and Other Stories
Catholic World, 75:263, May 1902

Donnelly, Ignatius Loyola
Caesar's Columns
By Edmund Boisgilbert [pseud.].
Catholic World, 51:269-70, May 1890
Chautauquan, 11:649, Aug 1890
Critic, NS 13:258, 24

Donnelly, Ignatius Loyola (cont.)
May 1890
Independent, 42:788, 5 Jun 1890
Doctor Huguet
Critic, NS 16:165, 3 Oct 1891
Independent, 43:1762, 26 Nov 1891

Donnelly, Joseph Gordon
Jesus Delaney
Critic, NS 32:843, Sep 1899
Literary World, 30:183, 10 Jun 1899

Doran, James
In the Depths of the First Degree
Literary World, 29:155, 14 May 1898

Dorr, Julia Caroline (Ripley)
Expiation
Independent, 25:236, 20 Feb 1873
In King's Houses
Dial, 25:76, 1 Aug 1898
Independent, 50:124, 14 Jul 1898
Literary World, 29:204, 25 Jun 1898
Sibyl Huntington
Independent, 25:586, 8 May 1873

Dorr, Louise Snow
The Mills of the Gods
Literary World, 32:55, 1 Apr 1901

Dorsey, Anna Hanson (McKenney)
The Flemmings
Catholic World, 11:431, Jun 1870

[Dorsey, Sarah Anne (Ellis)]
Athalie
Literary World, 2:183-4, 1 May 1872

Doubleday, Roman [pseud.]
See Long, Lily Augusta.

Dougall, Lily
A Question of Faith
Dial, 20:80-1, 1 Feb 1896
The Mormon Prophet
Literary World, 30:141, 29 Apr 1899

Douglas, Amanda Minnie
Bertha Wray's New Name
Independent, 45:1453, 26 Oct 1893
Literary World, 24:243, 29 Jul 1893
Drifted Asunder
Independent, 28:11, 3 Feb 1876
Foes of Her Household
Critic, NS 7:124, 12 Mar 1887
Literary World, 18:139, 30 Apr 1887
The Fortunes of the Faradays
Critic, NS 9:5, 7 Jan 1888
From Hand to Mouth
Literary World, 8:181, 1 Mar 1878
Hannah Ann
Literary World, 29:154, 14 May 1898
The Heirs of Bradley House
Critic, NS 16:348, 19 Dec 1891
Independent, 43:1606, 29 Oct 1891
Her Place in the World
Literary World, 29:102, 2 Apr 1898
Hope Mills
Literary World, 11:58, 14 Feb 1880
In the King's Country
Critic, NS 21:374, 2 Jun 1894
In Wild Rose Time
Independent, 47:971, 18 Jul 1895
Literary World, 26:90,

23 Mar 1895
Larry
Literary World, 24:210, 1 Jul 1893
Lost in a Great City
Critic, NS 9:306, 23 Jun 1888
Lyndell Sherburne
Literary World, 24:451, 16 Dec 1893
A Modern Adam and Eve in a Garden
Critic, NS 10:219, 3 Nov 1888
Independent, 40:1314, 11 Oct 1888
Literary World, 19:388, 10 Nov 1888
Nelly Kinnard's Kingdom
Independent, 28:8, 16 Nov 1876
Literary World, 7:102, 1 Dec 1876
Osborne of Arrochar
Critic, NS 13:28, 18 Jan 1890; 16:165, 3 Oct 1891
Literary World, 20:426, 23 Nov 1889
Out of the Wreck
Critic, NS 3:5, 3 Jan 1885
Independent, 37:75, 15 Jan 1885
Literary World, 16:210, 13 Jun 1885
A Question of Silence
Independent, 53:1625-6, 11 Jul 1901
A Romance at the Antipodes
Literary World, 21:207, 21 Jun 1890
Sherburne House
Critic, NS 19:144, 11 Mar 1893
Independent, 44:1834, 22 Dec 1892
Literary World, 24:58, 25 Feb 1893
A Sherburne Inheritance
Independent, 54:820, 3 Apr 1902
A Sherburne Romance
Independent, 47:1650, 5 Dec 1895; 47:1690, 12 Dec 1895
Whom Katie Married
Independent, 35:11, 19 Jul 1883
Literary World, 14:179-80, 2 Jun 1883
A Woman's Inheritance
Critic, NS 5:145, 20 Mar 1886

Douglas, Edith [pseud.]
See Burnham, Clara Louise (Root).

[Douglas, Sarah E.]
Mahaly Sawyer
Critic, NS 9:139-40, 24 Mar 1888

Dowling, George Thomas
The Wreckers
Critic, NS 6:112, 4 Sep 1886
Literary World, 17:252, 24 Jul 1886

[Downs, Sarah Elizabeth (Forbush)]
Wedded by Fate
By Mrs. Georgie Sheldon [pseud.].
Critic, NS 19:44, 28 Jan 1893

Drake, Jeanie
In Old St. Stephen's
Catholic World, 56:272, Nov 1892
Critic, NS 18:275, 19 Nov 1892
Independent, 44:1599, 10 Nov 1892
Literary World, 23:368, 22 Oct 1892
The Metropolitans
Catholic World, 65:701-2, Aug 1897
Critic, NS 27:425, 19 Jun 1897
Dial, 22:23, 1 Jan 1897
Literary World, 27:477,

Drake, Jeanie (cont.)
26 Dec 1896

Drake, Samuel Adams
Captain Nelson
Literary World, 10:86, 15 Mar 1879
The Watch Fires of '76
Critic, NS 25:335, 9 May 1896

Driscoll, Clara
In the Shadow of the Alamo
Critic, 49:286, Sep 1906

Dromgoole, Will Allen
Cinch, and Other Stories
Literary World, 29:434, 10 Dec 1898
The Heart of Old Hickory, and Other Stories of Tennessee
Independent, 47:1728, 19 Dec 1895
A Moonshiner's Son
Literary World, 30:7, 7 Jan 1899
The Valley Path
Independent, 50:726-7, 2 Jun 1898
Literary World, 29:189, 11 Jun 1898

Drysdale, William
The Mystery of Abel Forefinger
Harper's, 88:Literary Notes, 2-3, Apr 1894

Du Bois, Constance Goddard
Columbus and Beatriz
Catholic World, 55:449, Jun 1892
Critic, NS 18:106, 27 Aug 1892
Dial, 12:425, Apr 1892
Independent, 44:776, 2 Jun 1892
Literary World, 23:390, 5 Nov 1892
Martha Corey
Critic, NS 15:27, 17 Jan 1891
Dial, 11:241, Dec 1890
A Modern Pagan
Chautauquan, 21:775, Sep 1895
Critic, NS 25:59, 25 Jan 1896
Literary World, 26:202, 29 Jun 1895
The Shield of the Fleur de Lis
Literary World, 27:163, 30 May 1896
A Soul in Bronze
Critic, 37:468, Nov 1900

Duer, Catherine King
Unconscious Comedians
Critic, 40:374, Apr 1902
Independent, 53:3091, 26 Dec 1901

Duffy, James Oscar Greeley
Glass and Gold
Dial, 31:370, 16 Nov 1901

Dunbar, Alice
See Nelson, Alice Ruth (Moore) Dunbar.

Dunbar, Paul Lawrence
The Fanatics
Critic, 38:567, Jun 1901
Folks from Dixie
Critic, NS 29:413, 25 Jun 1898
Independent, 50:726, 2 Jun 1898
Literary World, 29:204, 25 Jun 1898
The Heart of Happy Hollow
Critic, 46:477-8, May 1905
In Old Plantation Days
Critic, 44:476, May 1904
The Love of Landry
Critic, 38:278, Mar 1901
Independent, 53:789, 4 Apr 1901
The Sport of the Gods
Critic, 42:380, Apr 1903
Dial, 32:390, 1 Jun 1902
The Strength of Gideon, and Other Stories

Independent, 52:1508, 21 Jun 1900
Literary World, 31:157, 1 Aug 1900
The Uncalled
Chautauquan, 28:421, Jan 1899
Independent, 50:1704, 8 Dec 1898
Literary World, 29:437, 10 Dec 1898

Duncan, Norman
The Cruise of the Shining Light
Independent, 63:101-2, 11 Jul 1907
Dr. Grenfell's Parish
Critic, 46:472, May 1905
Dr. Luke of the Labrador
Critic, 45:473, Nov 1904
Independent, 58:210, 26 Jan 1905
Every Man for Himself
Independent, 65:1305-6, 3 Dec 1908
The Mother
Critic, 59:577, Dec 1905
Independent, 59:986, 26 Oct 1905
The Soul of the Street
Critic, 38:278-9, Mar 1901
Independent, 53:1500, 27 Jun 1901
Literary World, 32:75, 1 May 1901
The Way of the Sea
Independent, 55:2580-1, 29 Oct 1903

Dunham, Curtis
The Casino Girl in London
Literary World, 29:437, 10 Dec 1898

Dunn, Martha (Baker)
'Lias's Wife
Dial, 31:372, 16 Nov 1901

Dunning, Mrs. Annie Ketchum
What To Do
Independent, 35:13, 5 Jul 1883

Dunning, Charlotte [pseud.]
See Wood, Charlotte Dunning.

Durham, Robert Lee
The Call of the South
Dial, 45:90-1, 16 Aug 1908

[Duysters, George F.]
Opals from a Mexican Mine By George De Valliére [pseud.].
Literary World, 27:457, 12 Dec 1896

Dyar, C. W.
See Montague, Charles Howard, and C. W. Dyar.

Earle, Alice (Morse)
Colonial Days in Old New York
Chautauquan, 24:510, Jan 1897
In Old Narragansett
Independent, 50:765, 9 Jun 1898

Earle, Anne Richardson
Her Great Ambition
Chautauquan, 14:383, Dec 1891
Critic, NS 16:128, 12 Sep 1891
Independent, 42:1644, 20 Nov 1890

Earle, Mary Tracy
The Man Who Worked for Collister
Literary World, 29:455, 24 Dec 1898
The Wonderful Wheel
Chautauquan, 24:631, Feb 1897
Critic, NS 26:260, 31 Oct 1896
Independent, 49:122, 28 Jan 1897

Eastman, Charles A.
Red Hunters and the Animal People
Critic, 46:478, May 1905

Eastman, Elaine (Goodale)
Little Brother o' Dreams
Independent, 68:987, 5 May 1910

Eastman, Julia Arabella
Striking for the Right
Independent, 25:331, 13 Mar 1873

[Eaton, Frances U.]
A Fearless Investigator
Independent, 48:1770, 24 Dec 1896

Eckstrom, Fannie Hardy
The Penobscot Man
Critic, 45:190, Aug 1904
Dial, 37:43, 16 Jul 1904
Literary World, 35:224, Aug 1904

Edwards, George Wharton
P'tit Martinic' and Other Monotones
Literary World, 25:456, 15 Dec 1894

Edwards, Harry Stillwell
His Defense, and Other Stories
Independent, 52:196, 18 Jan 1900
The Marbeau Cousins
Literary World, 29:188, 11 Jun 1898
Sons and Fathers
Critic, NS 27:213-4, 27 Mar 1897
Literary World, 28:27, 23 Jan 1897
Two Runaways, and Other Stories
Chautauquan, 10:376, Dec 1889
Critic, NS 12:268, 30 Nov 1889
Dial, 10:217, Dec 1889
Independent, 41:1399, 24 Oct 1889
Literary World, 20:387, 9 Nov 1889

Egan, Lavinia Hartwell
A Bundle of Fagots
Literary World, 27:234, 25 Jul 1896

Egan, Maurice Francis
The Chatelaine of the Roses
Catholic World, 66:844-5, Mar 1898
From the Land of St. Lawrence
Independent, 50:264, 28 Jul 1898
The Life Around Us
Catholic World, 53:300-1, May 1891
Independent, 37:1199, 17 Sep 1885
A Marriage of Reason
Catholic World, 57:876-7, Sep 1893
Independent, 45:1282, 21 Sep 1893
The Vocation of Edward Conway
Catholic World, 64:263, Nov 1896
Critic, NS 27:76, 30 Jan 1897

Eggleston, Edward
The Circuit Rider
Galaxy, 17:859, Jun 1874
Independent, 26:8, 21 May 1874
Literary World, 4:188, 1 May 1874
Duffels
Chautauquan, 18:382, Dec 1893
Independent, 45:1653, 7 Dec 1893
Literary World, 24:386, 18 Nov 1893
The End of the World
Literary World, 3:87, 1 Nov 1872
The Faith Doctor

Critic, NS 17:6-7, 2 Jan 1892
Dial, 12:278, Dec 1891
Independent, 43:1762, 26 Nov 1891

The Graysons
Critic, NS 10:231, 10 Nov 1888
Dial, 9:161-2, Nov 1888
Literary World, 19:388, 10 Nov 1888

The Hoosier Schoolmaster
Independent, 44:1601, 10 Nov 1892
Literary World, 2:131-2, 1 Feb 1872

The Mystery of Metropolisville
Independent, 25:616, 15 May 1873
Literary World, 3:188, 1 May 1873

Roxy
Literary World, 9:91, 1 Nov 1878

Eggleston, George Cary

A Captain in the Ranks
Critic, 46:478, May 1905

A Carolina Cavalier
Critic, 38:567, Jun 1901
Dial, 31:33, 1 Jul 1901
Independent, 53:1564, 4 Jul 1901
Literary World, 32:103, 1 Jul 1901

A Daughter of the South
Dial, 39:208, 1 Oct 1905
Independent, 59:987, 26 Oct 1905

Dorothy South
Critic, 41:278, Sep 1902
Dial, 32:390, 1 Jun 1902
Independent, 54:1312, 29 May 1902
Literary World, 33:91, 1 Jun 1902

Evelyn Bird
Dial, 37:43, 16 Jul 1904
Independent, 57:395, 18 Aug 1904
Literary World, 35:203-4, Jul 1904

Irene of the Mountains
Dial, 48:244-5, 1 Apr 1910
Independent, 67:828, 7 Oct 1909

A Man of Honor
Galaxy, 17:285-6, Feb 1874

The Master of Warlock
Literary World, 34:83, Apr 1903

Southern Soldier Stories
Independent, 50:629, 12 May 1898
Literary World, 29:155, 14 May 1898
Literature, 2:542, 7 May 1898

Two Gentlemen of Virginia
Dial, 45:457, 16 Dec 1908
Independent, 65:785, 1 Oct 1908

The Wreck of the "Red Bird"
Independent, 34:11, 26 Oct 1882

________, and Dolores Marbourg

Juggernaut
Critic, NS 15:236, 2 May 1891
Independent, 43:645, 30 Apr 1891

Eisenberg, Maurice
See Baldwin, Eugene Francis, and Maurice Eisenberg.

Elbon, Barbara [pseud.]
See Halsted, Lenora B.

[Elder, Mrs. D. H.]

Mahetible Hopkins on Her Travels
Literary World, 15:233, 12 Jul 1884

Eleven Possible Cases
Critic, NS 16:182, 10 Oct 1891

Eliot, Annie [pseud.]
See Trumbull, Annie Eliot.

Ellerton, Edward
A Fatal Resemblance
Critic, NS 5:117, 6 Mar 1886
Literary World, 17:219, 26 Jun 1886

Ellicott, John M.
Justified
Critic, NS 16:153, 26 Sep 1891

Elliott, Henry Rutherford
The Bassett Claim
Critic, NS 3:5, 3 Jan 1885
Independent, 36:1513, 27 Nov 1884
The Common Chord
Critic, NS 7:175, 9 Apr 1887
Independent, 39:398, 31 Mar 1887

Elliott, Maud (Howe)
Atalanta in the South
Critic, NS 5:142, 20 Mar 1886
Independent, 38:495, 22 Apr 1886
Literary World, 17:182, 29 May 1886
Honor
Independent, 45:1453, 26 Oct 1893
Literary World, 23:291, 9 Sep 1893
A Newport Aquarelle
Dial, 4:113, Sep 1883
Independent, 35:11, 4 Oct 1883
Literary World, 14:283-4, 8 Sep 1883
Phillida
Critic, NS 17:35-6, 16 Jan 1892
The San Rosario Ranch
Critic, NS 1:290, 21 Jun 1884
Dial, 5:67, Jul 1884
Independent, 36:1067, 21 Aug 1884
Literary World, 15:191, 14 Jun 1884

Elliott, Mrs. Sarah Barnwell
The Durket Sperret
Independent, 50:729, 2 Jun 1898
Literary World, 29:236, 23 Jul 1898
Literature, 3:17, 9 Jul 1898
The Felmeres
Catholic World, 43:418-21, Jun 1886
Critic, NS 5:244, 15 May 1886
Independent, 31:11, 7 Aug 1879; 39:590, 12 May 1887
Literary World, 10:214, 5 Jul 1879
An Incident, and Other Happenings
Harper's, 98:Literary Notes, 3-4, Apr 1899
Independent, 51:2442, 7 Sep 1899
Literary World, 30:124, 15 Apr 1899
Jerry
Catholic World, 53:606-7, Jul 1891
Critic, NS 15:287, 16 May 1891
Independent, 43:1218, 13 Aug 1891
John Paget
Critic, NS 20:98, 12 Aug 1893
Dial, 15:93, 16 Aug 1893
Independent, 45:1018, 27 Jul 1893
Literary World, 24:172, 3 Jun 1893
The Making of Jane
Critic, 40:280, Mar 1902
Independent, 54:285, 30 Jan 1902
A Simple Heart
Critic, NS 7:192, 16 Apr 1887

Ellis, Edward Sylvester
Cowmen and Rustlers
Independent, 51:284, 26 Jan 1899

Ellis, John Breckenridge
Arkinsaw Cousins
Independent, 64:1452, 25 Jun 1908
Garcilaso
Dial, 31:32, 1 Jul 1901
The Holland Wolves
Critic, 42:183, Feb 1903
Dial, 33:327, 16 Nov 1902

Embree, Charles Fleming
A Dream of a Throne
Literary World, 31:268, 1 Dec 1900
For the Love of Tonita, & Other Tales of the Mesas
Independent, 49:1544, 25 Nov 1897
Literary World, 28:436, 27 Nov 1897
A Heart of Flame
Dial, 31:34, 1 Jul 1901

[Emerson, Mary S.]
Among the Chosen
Critic, NS 2:77, 16 Aug 1884
Independent, 36:1159, 2 Oct 1884
Literary World, 15:242, 26 Jul 1884

Emerson, Willis George
Buell Hampton
Dial, 32:392, 1 Jun 1902
Independent, 54:1966, 14 Aug 1902

Emery, Sarah Anna
My Generation
Literary World, 26:106, 6 Apr 1895
Three Generations
Literary World, 3:4-5, 1 Jun 1872

Emory, A. M. [pseud.]
See Watrous, Charles.

[English, Thomas Dunn]
Jacob Schuyler's Millions
Critic, NS 5:117, 6 Mar 1886
Independent, 38:234, 25 Feb 1886
Literary World, 17:166, 15 May 1886

Ervin, Mable Clare
As Told by the Typewriter Girl
Literary World, 30:124, 15 Apr 1899

Evans, Elizabeth Edson (Gibson)
Laura, an American Girl
Literary World, 15:37-8, 9 Feb 1884

Evans, Florence (Wilkinson)
The Lady of the Flag-Flowers
Dial, 27:75, 1 Aug 1899
Independent, 51:2570-1, 21 Sep 1899
The Strength of the Hills
Dial, 32:19, 1 Jan 1902
Independent, 53:3025, 19 Dec 1901
Literary World, 32:218, 1 Dec 1901

Everett, Edith Townsend
A Duel with Destiny, and Other Stories
Independent, 50:729, 2 Jun 1898
Literary World, 29:269, 20 Aug 1898

Everett, William
Thine, Not Mine
Chautauquan, 13:407, Jun 1891

Ewell, Alice Maude
A White Guard to Satan
Critic, 38:567, Jun 1901

Ewell, Alice Maude (cont.)
Literary World, 32:87, 1 Jun 1901

Expatriation
Critic, NS 14:152, 27 Sep 1890
Literary World, 21:266-7, 16 Aug 1890

Eyster, Nellie (Blessing)
A Chinese Quaker
Literary World, 33:172, 1 Nov 1902
A Colonial Boy
Chautauquan, 11:127, Apr 1890

Faber, Christine [pseud.]
See Smith, Mary E.

Fadette [pseud.]
See Reeves, Marian Calhoun Legaré.

Fair Harvard
Catholic World, 10:858, Mar 1870
Galaxy, 9:138, Jan 1870

Fall, Mrs. Anna Christy
The Tragedy of a Widow's Third
Independent, 50:1058, 13 Oct 1898

Farmer, James Eugene
Brinton Eliot
Dial, 33:65-6, 1 Aug 1902
Literary World, 33:132, 1 Sep 1902
The Grand Mademoiselle
Dial, 28:86, 1 Feb 1900
Literary World, 31:156, 1 Aug 1900
The Grenadier
Dial, 25:306-7, 1 Nov 1898
Literary World, 29:456, 24 Dec 1898

Farmer, Lydia (Hoyt)
Aunt Belindy's Points of View, and A Modern Mrs. Malaprop
Chautauquan, 23:655, Aug 1896
The Doom of the Holy City
Critic, NS 25:93, 8 Feb 1896

Farquhar, Anna
See Bergengren, Anna (Farquhar).

Farrar, Charles Alden John
Up the North Branch
Independent, 40:1314, 11 Oct 1888

Farrington, Margaret Vere
See Livingston, Margaret Vere (Farrington).

Fawcett, Edgar
The Adopted Daughter
Independent, 44:1835, 22 Dec 1892
The Adventures of a Widow
Critic, NS 9:192, 21 Apr 1888
Dial, 5:205-6, Dec 1884
Independent, 36:1419, 6 Nov 1884
Literary World, 15:304-5, 20 Sep 1884
An Ambitious Woman
Catholic World, 38:720, Feb 1884
Critic, NS 15:335, 27 Jun 1891
Dial, 4:228-9, Jan 1884
Independent, 36:299, 6 Mar 1884
Literary World, 15:11-2, 12 Jan 1884
The Confessions of Claud
Independent, 39:943, 28 Jul 1887
Literary World, 18:185-6, 11 Jun 1887
A Demoralizing Marriage
Critic, NS 11:167, 6 Apr 1889
Literary World, 20:131, 13 Apr 1889

Divided Lives
Critic, NS 11:40, 26 Jan 1889
Ellen Story
Galaxy, 22:282-4, Aug 1876
Independent, 28:9, 29 Jun 1876
Literary World, 7:123, 1 Jan 1877
The Evil That Men Do
Literary World, 21:71, 1 Mar 1890
Fabian Dimitry
Literary World, 21:267, 16 Aug 1890
A Gentleman of Leisure
Critic, 1:174-5, 2 Jul 1881
Dial, 2:65, Jul 1881
Literary World, 12:257-8, 30 Jul 1881
An Heir to Millions
Independent, 44:1599, 10 Nov 1892
Her Fair Fame
Critic, NS 23:203, 16 Mar 1895
A Hopeless Case
Dial, 1:59-60, Jul 1880
Literary World, 11:214-5, 19 Jun 1880
The House at High Bridge
Dial, 7:189-90, Dec 1886
Literary World, 17:363-4, 30 Oct 1886
A Man's Will
Chautauquan, 8:635, Jul 1888
Critic, NS 10:125, 12 Sep 1888
Independent, 40:817, 28 Jun 1888
Literary World, 19:198, 23 Jun 1888
Miriam Balestier
Critic, NS 11:142, 23 Mar 1889
New York
Independent, 51:280-1, 26 Jan 1899
A New York Family
Catholic World, 55:599-600, Jul 1892
Independent, 43:1283, 27 Aug 1891; 44:1130, 11 Aug 1892
Olivia Delaplaine
Catholic World, 47:700-1, Aug 1888
Independent, 40:817, 28 Jun 1888
Literary World, 19:187, 9 Jun 1888
Purple and Fine Linen
Galaxy, 16:427-8, Sep 1873
Independent, 25:984, 7 Aug 1873
A Romance of Old New York
Critic, NS 28:58, 31 Jul 1897
Independent, 49:948, 22 Jul 1897
Literary World, 28:99, 3 Apr 1897
Rutherford
Dial, 5:206, Dec 1884
Independent, 36:1324, 16 Oct 1884
Literary World, 15:328, 4 Oct 1884
Social Silhouettes
Independent, 37:1488, 19 Nov 1885
Literary World, 16:474-5, 12 Dec 1885
Tinkling Cymbals
Dial, 5:66, Jul 1884
Independent, 36:1131, 4 Sep 1884
Literary World, 15:223-4, 12 Jul 1884
The Vulgarians
Literary World, 34:210, Aug 1903
Women Must Weep
Literary World, 23:150, 23 Apr 1892

Fearing, Lilian Blanche
Roberta
Chautauquan, 22:639, Feb 1896

Fenollosa, Mary (McNeil)
The Dragon Painter
Independent, 61:1494, 20 Dec 1906

Fernald, Chester Bailey
The Cat and the Cherub, and Other Stories
Independent, 48:1801, 31 Dec 1896
Literary World, 28:74, 6 Mar 1897
John Kendry's Idea
Dial, 43:252, 16 Oct 1907
Under the Jack-Staff
Critic, 44:380-1, Apr 1904

Fessenden, Laura (Dayton)
A Puritan Lover
Literary World, 18:369-70, 29 Oct 1887

Field, Alice Durand
Palermo
Dial, 7:190, Dec 1886
Literary World, 16:464, 12 Dec 1885

[Field, Caroline C. (Alden)]
Two Gentlemen of Boston
Critic, NS 7:192, 16 Apr 1887
Literary World, 18:102, 2 Apr 1887

[Field, Caroline Leslie (Whitney)]
High-Lights
Critic, NS 5:56, 30 Jan 1886
Literary World, 16:474, 12 Dec 1885

Field, Charles Kellogg, and Will H. Irwin
Stanford Stories
Chautauquan, 31:534, Aug 1900

Field, Eugene
The Holy Cross, and Other Tales
Literary World, 25:106, 7 Apr 1894
A Little Book of Profitable Tales
Literary World, 27:47, 8 Feb 1896

Field, Roswell Martin
The Bondage of Ballinger
Critic, 43:577-8, Dec 1903
Dial, 35:265, 16 Oct 1903
In Sunflower Land
Dial, 14:114-5, 16 Feb 1893
Independent, 45:53, 12 Jan 1893
The Romance of an Old Fool
Dial, 33:331, 16 Nov 1902

Figaro Fiction
Independent, 45:507, 13 Apr 1893

Findlater, Jane Helen
See The Affair at the Inn.

Findlater, Mary
See The Affair at the Inn.

Finley, Martha
Christmas with Grandma Elsie
Independent, 41:865, 4 Jul 1889
Elsie's Motherhood
Galaxy, 23:285, Feb 1877
Mildred and Elsie
Critic, 1:291, 22 Oct 1881
Mildred at Home
Critic, NS 3:5, 3 Jan 1885
Signing the Contract and What It Cost
Literary World, 10:119, 12 Apr 1879
The Tragedy of Wild River Valley

Independent, 45:1018, 27 Jul 1893
Wanted--A Pedigree
Literary World, 2:172, 1 Apr 1872

Fisguill, Richard [pseud.]
See Wilson, Richard Henry.

Fish, Williston
Short Rations
Dial, 27:76, 1 Aug 1899
Harper's, 98:Literary Notes, 2-3, Feb 1899
Literary World, 30:106, 1 Apr 1899

[Fish, Williston]
Won at West Point
By Fush [pseud.].
Literary World, 15:91, 22 Mar 1884

Fisher, George P., Jr.
Out of the Woods
Independent, 48:1462, 29 Oct 1896

Fiske, Amos Kidder
Beyond the Bourn
Critic, NS 16:17, 11 Jul 1891
Independent, 43:1219, 13 Aug 1891

Fiske, Stephen Ryder
Holiday Stories
Catholic World, 54:771, Feb 1892

Fitch, Clyde
Some Correspondence and Six Conversations
Critic, NS 27:58-9, 23 Jan 1897
Independent, 48:1462, 29 Oct 1896
Literary World, 27:314, 19 Sep 1896

Flagg, Elizabeth E.
Holden with Cords
Independent, 35:11, 19 Jul 1883

Flagg, William Joseph
Wall Street and the Woods
Critic, NS 10:204, 27 Oct 1888
Independent, 37:1199, 17 Sep 1885

Flandrau, Charles Macomb
The Diary of a Freshman
Critic, 39:374, Oct 1901
Independent, 53:2053, 29 Aug 1901
Harvard Episodes
Literary World, 29:11, 22 Jan 1898

The Flaw in the Marble
Independent, 48:1462, 29 Oct 1896

Fleckenstein, Alfred C.
The Prince of Gravas
Literary World, 30:106, 1 Apr 1899

Fleming, George [pseud.]
See Fletcher, Julia Constance.

Fleming, Mary Agnes (Early)
A Terrible Secret
Literary World, 5:107-8, 1 Dec 1874

Flemming, Harford [pseud.]
See McClellan, Harriet (Hare).

Fletcher, Coyne
The Bachelor's Baby
Critic, NS 16:248, 7 Nov 1891

[Fletcher, Julia Constance]
Andromeda
By George Fleming [pseud.].
Critic, NS 4:162, 3 Oct 1885
Dial, 6:179, Nov 1885
Independent, 37:1154, 12 Nov 1885

[Fletcher, Julia Constance] (cont.)
Literary World, 16:340, 3 Oct 1885
The Head of Medusa
By George Fleming [pseud.].
Dial, 1:195, Jan 1881
Kismet
Literary World, 7:138, 1 Feb 1877
Mirage
Literary World, 8:194, 1 Apr 1878
The Truth About Clement Ker
By George Fleming [pseud.].
Catholic World, 49:271-2, May 1889
Chautauquan, 9:625, Jul 1889
Critic, NS 11:129, 16 Mar 1889
Literary World, 20:95, 16 Mar 1889
Vestigia
By George Fleming [pseud.].
Critic, NS 1:124, 15 Mar 1884
Independent, 36:523, 24 Apr 1886
Literary World, 15:78, 8 Mar 1884

Fletcher, Robert Howe
A Blind Bargain
Literary World, 21:126, 12 Apr 1890
The Johnstown Stage, and Other Stories
Critic, NS 17:36, 16 Jan 1892
Independent, 43:1844, 10 Dec 1891

Flint, Annie
A Girl of Ideas
Dial, 34:377, 1 Jun 1903
Independent, 55:976-7, 23 Apr 1903
Literary World, 34:153, Jun 1903

Flisch, Julia A.
Ashes of Hopes
Critic, NS 5:181, 10 Apr 1886
Literary World, 17:234, 10 Jul 1886

Flower, Elliott
Delightful Dodd
Literary World, 35:379, Dec 1904
Policeman Flynn
Dial, 32:390, 1 Jun 1902
Literary World, 33:91, 1 Jun 1902
Slaves of Success
Independent, 59:451-2, 24 Aug 1905
The Spoilsmen
Independent, 55:2059, 27 Aug 1903
Literary World, 34:74-5, Apr 1903

Flynt, Josiah [pseud.]
See Willard, Josiah Flynt.

Foote, Mary (Hallock)
The Chosen Valley
Critic, NS 19:379, 10 Jun 1893
Dial, 14:114, 16 Feb 1893
Independent, 45:617, 4 May 1893
Literary World, 24:11, 14 Jan 1893
Coeur d'Alene
Critic, NS 22:327, 17 Nov 1894
Dial, 18:271-2, 1 May 1895
Literary World, 25:372, 3 Nov 1894
The Cup of Trembling, and Other Stories
Critic, NS 25:92-3, 8 Feb 1892
Dial, 20:174, 16 Mar 1896
Independent, 47:1727, 19 Dec 1895
Literary World, 27:47, 8 Feb 1896

The Desert and the Sown
Critic, 41:278, Sep 1902
Dial, 33:327-8, 16 Nov 1902
Independent, 54:1610, 3 Jul 1902
In Exile, and Other Stories
Catholic World, 59:134, Apr 1894
Critic, NS 21:374, 2 Jun 1894
Dial, 16:368, 16 Jun 1894
Literary World, 25:139, 5 May 1894
John Bodewin's Testimony
Literary World, 17:252, 24 Jul 1886
The Last Assembly Ball, and The Fate of a Voice
Critic, NS 12:293-4, 14 Dec 1889
Independent, 41:1576, 28 Nov 1889
Literary World, 20:414, 23 Nov 1889
The Led-Horse Claim
Critic, 3:206, 5 May 1883
Independent, 35:12, 10 May 1883
Literary World, 14:164, 19 May 1883
The Little Fig-Tree Stories
Literary World, 31:12, 6 Jan 1900
The Prodigal
Critic, 38:279, Mar 1901
Independent, 53:789, 4 Apr 1901
Literary World, 32:54, 1 Apr 1901
A Touch of Sun, and Other Stories
Critic, 44:93, Jan 1904; 44:381, Apr 1904
Dial, 36:22-3, 1 Jan 1904
Independent, 56:675-6, 24 Mar 1904
Literary World, 35:19, Jan 1905

Ford, Harriet
Me an' Methuselar, and Other Episodes
Critic, NS 25:234, 4 Apr 1896
Independent, 48:57, 9 Jan 1896

Ford, James Lauren
Bohemia Invaded, and Other Stories
Chautauquan, 23:493-4, Jul 1896
Literary World, 27:187, 13 Jun 1896
Cupid and the Footlights
Independent, 51:3501, 28 Dec 1899
Dr. Dodd's School
Independent, 45:53, 12 Jan 1893
Dolly Dillenbeck
Critic, NS 24:406, 14 Dec 1895
Dial, 20:80, 1 Feb 1896
Literary World, 27:60, 22 Feb 1896
Hypnotic Tales and Other Stories
Critic, NS 21:358, 26 May 1894
The Wooing of Folly
Independent, 61:1352, 6 Dec 1906

Ford, Paul Leicester
The Great K. & A. Train Robbery
Critic, NS 27:354, 22 May 1897
Dial, 22:311, 16 May 1897
Literary World, 28:255, 7 Aug 1897
The Honorable Peter Stirling and What People Thought of Him
Chautauquan, 25:430, Jul 1897
Critic, NS 23:179, 9 Mar 1895
Dial, 18:52, 16 Jan 1895
Literary World, 25:469, 29 Dec 1894
Literature, 2:542, 7 May

Ford, Paul Leicester (cont.)
1898
A House Party
Critic, 41:89, Jul 1902
Janice Meredith
Catholic World, 70:423, Dec 1899
Chautauquan, 30:319, Dec 1899
Critic, 36:27-8, Jan 1900
Dial, 27:490-1, 16 Dec 1899
Independent, 51:3094-5, 16 Nov 1899; 51:3171, 23 Nov 1899
Literary World, 30:347-8, 14 Oct 1899
The Story of an Untold Love
Chautauquan, 27:222, May 1898
Critic, NS 28:246, 16 Oct 1897
Dial, 23:285, 16 Nov 1897
Literature, 3:230, 10 Sep 1898
Tattle-Tales of Cupid
Independent, 51:209, 19 Jan 1899
Literary World, 29:438, 10 Dec 1898
Wanted--A Chaperon
Critic, 41:581, Dec 1902
Wanted--A Match Maker
Independent, 52:2813, 22 Nov 1900
Literary World, 32:71, 1 May 1901

Forman, Justus Miles
Bianca's Daughter
Independent, 68:1139-40, 26 May 1910
Buchanan's Wife
Dial, 41:242-3, 16 Oct 1906
Independent, 61:939, 18 Oct. 1906
The Garden of Lies
Dial, 34:87-8, 1 Feb 1903
Jason
Catholic World, 90:101-2, Oct 1909
Dial, 47:387, 16 Nov 1909
Journey's End
Critic, 43:187-8, Aug 1903
Literary World, 34:83, Apr 1903
Monsigny
Dial, 35:156 [220], 1 Oct 1903
Independent, 55:2469, 15 Oct 1903
A Stumbling Block
Independent, 63:761, 26 Sep 1907

Forney, John Wien
The New Mobility
Critic, 1:48, 26 Feb 1881
Dial, 1:263-4, Apr 1881
Literary World, 12:115, 26 Mar 1881

Forsslund, Mary Louise [pseud.]
The Ship of Dreams
Dial, 33:330, 16 Nov 1902
Literary World, 33:195, 1 Dec 1902

Fosdick, Gertrude Christian
Out of Bohemia
Critic, NS 21:357, 26 May 1894
Literary World, 25:352, 20 Oct 1894

Fosdick, James William
The Honor of the Braxtons
Independent, 54:1728, 17 Jul 1902

Foster, Mabel G.
The Heart of the Doctor
Critic, 42:380, Apr 1903
Literary World, 34:60, Mar 1903

Foster, Mary Farrington
Doty Dontcare
Independent, 47:1204, 5 Sep 1895

[Foster, Theodosia Maria (Toll)]
The Boynton Neighborhood
By Faye Huntington [pseud.].
Literary World, 27:251, 8 Aug 1896
His First Charge
By Faye Huntington [pseud.].
Literary World, 29:219, 9 Jul 1898
St. Paul's Problem
By Faye Huntington [pseud.].
Critic, NS 8:78-9, 13 Aug 1887
Transformed
By Faye Huntington [pseud.].
Critic, NS 5:128, 13 Mar 1886
What Fide Remembers
By Faye Huntington [pseud.].
Critic, NS 2:161, 4 Oct 1884

Fowler, Sada (Bailey)
Irene
Critic, NS 6:317, 25 Dec 1886

[Fox, Mrs. Emily]
Gemini
Literary World, 8:217, 1 May 1878
Off the Rocks
By Toler King [pseud.].
Critic, 2:226-7, 26 Aug 1882
Rose O'Connor
By Toler King [pseud.].
Catholic World, 32:286-7, Nov 1880

Fox, John William, Jr.
Blue Grass and Rhododendron
Independent, 54:286, 30 Jan 1902
Christmas Eve on Lonesome, and Other Stories
Critic, 45:576, Dec 1904
Independent, 57:1455, 22 Dec 1904
Literary World, 35:331, Nov 1904
Crittenden
Critic, 38:164, Feb 1901
Dial, 30:110, 16 Feb 1901
Independent, 53:964, 25 Apr 1901
Literary World, 32:87, 1 Jun 1901
A Cumberland Vendetta, and Other Stories
Critic, NS 25:233, 4 Apr 1896
Independent, 47:1690, 12 Dec 1895
Dial, 20:173, 16 Mar 1896
Harper's, 91:Literary Notes, 2, Nov 1895
Literary World, 26:427-8, 30 Nov 1895; 31:122, 1 Jun 1900
"Hell-fer-Sartain," and Other Stories
Critic, NS 28:139, 11 Sep 1897
Harper's, 95:Literary Notes, 1, Sep 1897
Independent, 49:1085, 19 Aug 1897
Literary World, 28:260, 7 Aug 1897
The Kentuckians
Critic, NS 29:6, 1 Jan 1898
Dial, 24:80, 1 Feb 1898
Harper's, 96:Literary Notes, 2, Jan 1898
Independent, 49:1660, 16 Dec 1897
Literary World, 29:83, 19 Mar 1898
The Little Shepherd of Kingdom Come
Dial, 35:262, 16 Oct 1903
Independent, 55:2466-7, 15 Oct 1903
Literary World, 34:260-1, Oct 1903
A Mountain Europa
Harper's, 100:Literary Notes, 3-4, Dec 1899
Independent, 51:3171-2, 23 Nov 1899
The Trail of the Lonesome Pine

Fox, John William, Jr. (cont.)
Dial, 45:457, 16 Dec 1908
Independent, 65:1121-2, 12 Nov 1908; 65:1182-3, 19 Nov 1908

France, Lewis Browne
Mr. Dide, His Vacation in Colorado, and Other Sketches
Independent, 42:1313, 18 Sep 1890
Pine Valley
Chautauquan, 15:653, Aug 1892
Critic, NS 18:43, 23 Jul 1892
Literary World, 23:150, 23 Apr 1892; 28:260, 7 Aug 1897

Frances, Mary [pseud.]
See Mason, Fanny Witherspoon.

Francis, Mary C.
Dalrymple
Dial, 36:368, 1 Jun 1904

Frankel, A. H.
In Gold We Trust
Literary World, 29:268, 20 Aug 1898

Frederic, Harold
The Copperhead
Critic, NS 21:145, 3 Mar 1894
Dial, 15:341, 1 Dec 1893
Independent, 45:1692, 14 Dec 1893
Literary World, 24:423, 2 Dec 1893
The Damnation of Theron Ware
Chautauquan, 25:430, Jul 1897
Critic, NS 25:309-10, 2 May 1896; 26:156, 12 Sep 1896
Dial, 20:336, 1 Jun 1896
Harper's, 93:Literary Notes, 3-4, Sep 1896
Independent, 48:769, 4 Jun 1896; 48:770, 4 Jun 1896
The Deserter, and Other Stories
Chautauquan, 29:509-10, Aug 1899
Independent, 51:284, 26 Jan 1899
Literary World, 30:295, 16 Sep 1899
Gloria Mundi
Dial, 25:459, 16 Dec 1898
Independent, 50:1869-70, 22 Dec 1898
Literary World, 30:684, Mar 1899
Literature, 3:449, 12 Nov 1898
In the Valley
Chautauquan, 12:421, Dec 1890
Critic, NS 16:28, 18 Jul 1891
Dial, 11:239-40, Dec 1890
Independent, 42:1720, 4 Dec 1890
Literary World, 21:473, 6 Dec 1890
Westminster Review, 135:95, Jan 1891
The Lawton Girl
Catholic World, 51:402-3, Jun 1890
Chautauquan, 16:383, Dec 1892
Critic, NS 14:191-2, 18 Oct 1890
Dial, 11:93, Aug 1890
Independent, 42:966, 10 Jul 1890
Literary World, 21:174, 24 May 1890
March Hares
Chautauquan, 24:380, Dec 1896
Critic, NS 26:269, 10 Oct 1896
Dial, 21:288-9, 16 Nov 1896

Independent, 48:1462, 29 Oct 1896
Literary World, 27:477, 26 Dec 1896

The Market-Place
Critic, NS 32:649, Jul 1899
Dial, 27:21-2, 1 Jul 1899
Independent, 51:2164, 10 Aug 1899

Marsena, and Other Stories of the Wartime
Critic, NS 23:27, 12 Jan 1895
Dial, 17:333, 1 Dec 1894
Literary World, 25:302, 22 Sep 1894

The Return of the O'Mahony
Critic, NS 18:275-6, 19 Nov 1892
Dial, 14:21, 1 Jan 1893

Seth's Brother's Wife
Catholic World, 46:558-9, Jan 1888
Chautauquan, 8:445, Apr 1888
Critic, NS 9:54, 4 Feb 1888
Independent, 39:1586-7, 8 Dec 1887
Literary World, 18:460, 10 Dec 1887
Westminster Review, 129:394-5, Mar 1888

See also Tales of Our Coast.

Freeman, Mary Eleanor (Wilkins)

By the Light of the Soul
Independent, 62:443, 21 Feb 1907

Comfort Pease and Her Gold Ring
Chautauquan, 22:382, Dec 1895

The Debtor
Independent, 59:1340, 7 Dec 1905; 61:1158-60, 15 Nov 1906

"Doc." Gordon
Independent, 62:159, 17 Jan 1907

Evelina's Garden
Literary World, 31:55, 17 Feb 1900

The Fair Lavinia and Others
Independent, 64:312-3, 6 Feb 1908

A Far-away Melody, and Other Stories
Westminster Review, 134:215-6, Aug 1890

The Givers
Critic, 45:475, Nov 1904
Dial, 37:41, 16 Jul 1904
Independent, 57:455, 25 Aug 1904
Literary World, 35:223, Aug 1904

The Heart's Highway
Chautauquan, 31:644, Sep 1900
Critic, 37:276, Sep 1900

A Humble Romance, and Other Stories
Critic, NS 8:30, 16 Jul 1887; 14:169, 4 Oct 1890
Harper's, 75:Literary Notes, 3, Jun 1887
Independent, 39:1166, 15 Sep 1887
Literary World, 18:203, 25 Jun 1887

The Jamesons
Chautauquan, 29:389, Jul 1899
Critic, NS 32:745-6, Aug 1899
Literary World, 30:187, 10 Jun 1899

Jane Field
Catholic World, 57:280-1, May 1893
Chautauquan, 17:382, Jun 1893
Critic, NS 19:126, 4 Mar 1893
Harper's, 86:Literary Notes, 1, Feb 1893
Independent, 45:157, 2 Feb 1893
Literary World, 24:3-4, 14 Jan 1893

Jerome, A Poor Man
Critic, NS 28:153-4, 18

Freeman, Mary Eleanor (Wilkins) (cont.)
Sep 1897
Dial, 24:79-80, 1 Feb 1898
Harper's, 95:Literary Notes, 1-2, Sep 1897
Independent, 49:1505, 18 Nov 1897; 49:1547, 25 Nov 1897
Literary World, 28:351, 16 Oct 1897
Literature, 1:19-20, 23 Oct 1897

The Love of Parson Lord, and Other Stories
Critic, 36:547-8, Jun 1900
Literary World, 31:140, 1 Jul 1900

Madelon
Chautauquan, 23:782-3, Sep 1896
Critic, NS 25:367, 23 May 1896
Dial, 21:94, 16 Aug 1896
Harper's, 93:Literary Notes, 1, Jul 1896
Independent, 48:769, 4 Jun 1896; 48:1006, 23 Jul 1896
Literary World, 27:172-3, 30 May 1896

A New England Nun, and Other Stories
Catholic World, 53:298-9, May 1891
Critic, NS 15:286, 16 May 1891
Harper's, 82:Literary Notes, 2, Apr 1891
Independent, 43:607, 23 Apr 1891
Westminster Review, 136:107-8, Jul 1891

Pembroke
Critic, NS 22:35-6, 21 Jul 1894
Harper's, 89:Literary Notes, 3-4, Jun 1894
Literary World, 25:147-8, 19 May 1894

The People of Our Neighborhood
Chautauquan, 29:206, May 1899
Independent, 50:1129, 20 Oct 1898

The Portion of Labor
Critic, 40:180, Feb 1902
Independent, 54:345-6, 6 Feb 1902; 54:2772, 20 Nov 1902
Literary World, 33:91, 1 Jun 1902

The Pot of Gold, and Other Stories
Catholic World, 55:135, Apr 1892

The Shoulders of Atlas
Independent, 65:554, 3 Sep 1908

Silence, and Other Stories
Critic, NS 31:261-2, Mar 1899
Harper's, 97:Literary Notes, 2, Jul 1898
Independent, 50:264, 28 Jul 1898
Literature, 3:18-9, 9 Jul 1898

Six Trees
Critic, 43:185, Aug 1903
Independent, 55:686, 19 Mar 1903
Literary World, 34:183, Apr 1903

Some of Our Neighbors
Literature, 3:524, 3 Dec 1898

Understudies
Critic, 39:86, Jul 1901
Independent, 53:1501, 27 Jun 1901

The Wind in the Rose-Bush
Critic, 43:185, Aug 1903
Dial, 34:376, 1 Jun 1903
Independent, 55:1212-3, 21 May 1903
Literary World, 34:124, May 1903
Westminster Review, 160:231, Aug 1903

Young Lucretia, and Other Stories
Critic, NS 18:231-2, 29

Oct 1892
Harper's, 85:Literary Notes, 2, Oct 1892
Independent, 44:1229, 1 Sep 1892
Literary World, 23:274-5, 13 Aug 1892

[French, Alice]
A Book of True Lovers
By Octave Thanet [pseud.].
Dial, 24:81, 1 Feb 1898
Independent, 50:123, 27 Jan 1898
By Inheritance
By Octave Thanet [pseud.].
Catholic World, 92:102-3, Oct 1910
Dial, 48:244, 1 Apr 1910
Independent, 68:985-6, 5 May 1910
Expiation
By Octave Thanet [pseud.].
Catholic World, 51:403, Jun 1890
Chautauquan, 11:384, Jun 1890
Critic, NS 14:184, 4 Oct 1890
Dial, 11:13, May 1890
Independent, 42:855, 19 Jun 1890
Literary World, 21:152, 10 May 1890
The Heart of Toil
By Octave Thanet [pseud.].
Independent, 50:1276, 3 Nov 1898
Literary World, 29:401, 26 Nov 1898
Knitters in the Sun
By Octave Thanet [pseud.].
Critic, NS 9:53, 4 Feb 1888
Dial, 8:148, Nov 1887
Independent, 40:145, 2 Feb 1888
The Lion's Share
By Octave Thanet [pseud.].
Dial, 44:44, 16 Jan 1908
Independent, 64:472, 27 Feb 1908
The Man of the Hour
By Octave Thanet [pseud.].
Dial, 39:307-8, 16 Nov 1905
Independent, 59:581, 7 Sep 1905
The Missionary Sheriff
By Octave Thanet [pseud.].
Critic, NS 27:437, 26 Jun 1897
Harper's, 95:Literary Notes, 3-4, Jun 1897
Independent, 49:1085, 19 Aug 1897
Literary World, 28:180, 29 May 1897
Literature, 2:118, 29 Jan 1898
Otto the Knight, and Other Trans-Mississippi Stories
By Octave Thanet [pseud.].
Chautauquan, 13:552, Jul 1891
Critic, NS 16:16, 11 Jul 1891
Dial, 12:51, Jun 1891
Independent, 43:1283, 27 Aug 1891
A Slave to Duty, & Other Women
By Octave Thanet [pseud.].
Independent, 50:1792, 15 Dec 1898
Literary World, 29:456, 24 Dec 1898
Stories of a Western Town
By Octave Thanet [pseud.].
Critic, NS 19:404, 17 Jun 1893
Dial, 14:340-1, 1 Jun 1893
Independent, 45:1154, 24 Aug 1893
Literary World, 24:178-9, 3 Jun 1893
We All
By Octave Thanet [pseud.].
Independent, 43:1605, 29 Oct 1891

French, Allen
The Barrier
Dial, 37:39, 16 Jul 1904
The Colonials

French, Allen (cont.)
Critic, 41:279, Sep 1902
Dial, 32:246, 1 Apr 1902
Literary World, 33:123, 1 Aug 1902

French, Anne (Warner)
The Diary of a Bride
Independent, 59:1046, 2 Nov 1905
In a Mysterious Way
Catholic World, 89:689-90, Aug 1909
Just Between Themselves
Independent, 69:139, 21 Jul 1910
The Panther
Independent, 65:1463-4, 17 Dec 1908
Susan Clegg and Her Friend Mrs. Lathrop
Chautauquan, 40:592, Feb 1905
Critic, 45:577-8, Dec 1904
Independent, 57:1510-1, 29 Dec 1904
Literary World, 35:329, Nov 1904
Susan Clegg and a Man in the House
Independent, 64:313, 6 Feb 1908
A Woman's Will
Literary World, 35:168, Jun 1904

French, Harry W. [pseud.]
See French, Henry Willard.

[French, Henry Willard]
Ego
By Harry W. French [pseud.].
Literary World, 11:468, 18 Dec 1880
The Only One
By Harry W. French [pseud.].
Literary World, 15:266, 9 Aug 1884

Friedman, Isaac Kahn
The Autobiography of a Beggar
Literary World, 34:139, Jun 1903
By Bread Alone
Critic, 40:281, Mar 1902
Dial, 32:388, 1 Jun 1902
Independent, 54:754, 27 Mar 1902
Literary World, 33:8, 1 Jan 1902
The Lucky Number
Critic, NS 27:219, 27 Mar 1897
Dial, 22:24, 1 Jan 1897
Independent, 49:57, 14 Jan 1897
Literary World, 28:58, 20 Feb 1897
Poor People
Critic, 37:86, Jul 1900
Independent, 52:896, 12 Apr 1900
The Radical
Dial, 43:318, 16 Nov 1907

Frothingham, Eugenia Brooks
The Evasion
Critic, 48:572, Jun 1906
The Turn of the Road
Critic, 38:377, Apr 1901
Independent, 53:1323, 6 Jun 1901
Literary World, 32:124, 1 Aug 1901

Frye, James Albert
From Headquarters
Literary World, 24:114, 8 Apr 1893

Fuller, Anna
Katherine Day
Critic, 39:278, Sep 1901; 40:346, Apr 1902
Dial, 31:371, 16 Nov 1901
Independent, 53:2304, 26 Sep 1901
Literary World, 32:181, 1 Nov 1901
A Literary Courtship
Chautauquan, 17:636, Aug

1893
Literary World, 24:210, 1 Jul 1893
One of the Pilgrims
Critic, NS 31:165-6, Feb 1899
Literature, 3:603, 24 Dec 1898
Peak and Prairie
Critic, NS 23:27-8, 12 Jan 1895
Dial, 17:333, 1 Dec 1894
Literary World, 25:352, 20 Oct 1894
Pratt Portraits
Critic, NS 18:31, 16 Jul 1892
Literary World, 23:198, 4 Jun 1892
A Venetian June
Independent, 48:1038, 30 Jun 1896
Literary World, 27:330, 3 Oct 1896

Fuller, Caroline Macomber
Across the Campus
Independent, 51:2164, 10 Aug 1899
Brunhilde's Paying Guest
Catholic World, 86:820-1, Mar 1908
Independent, 64:49, 2 Jan 1908

Fuller, Edward
The Complaining Millions of Men
Dial, 15:227, 16 Oct 1893
Harper's, 87:Literary Notes, 2, Aug 1893
Independent, 45:1453, 26 Oct 1893
Literary World, 24:267, 26 Aug 1893
Fellow Travellers
Critic, NS 5:305, 19 Jun 1886
Dial, 7:67, Jul 1886
Literary World, 17:234, 10 Jul 1881
Forever and a Day
Critic, 2:238, 9 Sep 1882

John Malcolm
Independent, 55:45, 1 Jan 1903
Literary World, 34:35, Feb 1903

Fuller, Henry Blake
The Chatelaine of La Trinité
Catholic World, 56:275-6, Nov 1892
Critic, NS 18:248, 5 Nov 1892
Literary World, 23:407, 19 Nov 1892
The Chevalier of Pensieri-Vani
By Stanton Page [pseud.].
Catholic World, 53:921, Sep 1891
Critic, NS 15:179, 4 Apr 1891
Dial, 13:103, Aug 1892
Independent, 43:607, 23 Apr 1891; 44:664, 12 May 1892
Literary World, 23:165, 7 May 1892
The Cliff-Dwellers
Chautauquan, 18:381-2, Dec 1893
Critic, NS 20:221, 7 Oct 1893
Dial, 15:227-8, 16 Oct 1893
Harper's, 87:Literary Notes, 4, Oct 1893
Literary World, 24:309-10, 23 Sep 1893
From the Other Side
Critic, NS 29:345-6, 21 May 1898
Dial, 25:79, 1 Aug 1898
Literary World, 29:141, 30 Apr 1898
Literature, 2:758, 2 Jul 1898
The Last Refuge
Chautauquan, 33:539-40, Aug 1901
Critic, 37:570, Dec 1900
Dial, 30:109, 16 Feb 1901

Fuller, Henry Blake (cont.)
Independent, 53:850-1, 11 Apr 1901
Under the Skylights
Critic, 40:345, Apr 1902
Dial, 32:89-90, 1 Feb 1902
With the Procession
Critic, NS 23:453-4, 22 Jun 1895
Dial, 19:18-9, 1 Jul 1895
Harper's, 91:Literary Notes, 3-4, Jun 1895
Independent, 47:1170, 29 Aug 1895; 47:1579, 21 Nov 1895
Literary World, 26:148-9, 18 May 1895

Fuller, Hulbert
God's Rebel
Literary World, 31:75, 3 Mar 1900
Vivian of Virginia
Critic, NS 29:164, 5 Mar 1898
Dial, 24:295-6, 1 May 1898
Independent, 50:222, 17 Feb 1898
Literary World, 29:44, 5 Feb 1898
Westminster Review, 154:594-5, Nov 1900

Furman, Lucy S.
Stories of a Sanctified Town
Critic, NS 27:75, 30 Jan 1897
Dial, 22:23, 1 Jan 1897
Literary World, 28:4-5, 9 Jan 1897

[Furniss, Louise E.]
An Operetta in Profile By Czeika [pseud.].
Critic, NS 8:178, 8 Oct 1887
Independent, 39:1425, 3 Nov 1887

Fush [pseud.]
See Fish, Williston.

Futrelle, Jacques
Elusive Isabel
Independent, 67:425, 19 Aug 1909
The Thinking Machine on the Case
Independent, 64:1037-8, 7 May 1908

Gale, Zona
Friendship Village
Independent, 65:1248, 26 Nov 1908
The Loves of Pelleas and Etarre
Independent, 64:586, 12 Mar 1908
Romance Island
Dial, 42:227, 1 Apr 1907

Gallagher, George Washington
One Man's Struggle
Independent, 42:1414, 9 Oct 1890

Gardener, Helen Hamilton
See Smart, Helen Hamilton (Gardener).

Gardenhire, Samuel Major
The Long Arm
Critic, 48:475, May 1906
Lux Crucis
Critic, 44:470, May 1904
Literary World, 35:79, Mar 1904
Purple and Homespun
Dial, 45:90, 16 Aug 1908
Independent, 65:379, 13 Aug 1908
The Silence of Mrs. Harrold
Dial, 38:391, 1 Jun 1905

Gardner, Celia Emmeline
Tested
Literary World, 5:75, 1 Oct 1874

Gardner, Mrs. Sarah M. H.
Quaker Idyls
Critic, NS 22:428, 22 Dec 1894
Independent, 69:307, 11

Aug 1910
Literary World, 25:233, 28 Jul 1894

Garland, Hamlin

The Captain of the Gray-Horse Troop
Critic, 41:278, Sep 1902
Dial, 32:387, 1 Jun 1902
Independent, 54:1252, 22 May 1902
Literary World, 33:123, 1 Aug 1902

Cavanagh
Independent, 68:1138, 26 May 1910

The Eagle's Heart
Chautauquan, 32:333, Dec 1900
Dial, 30:109, 16 Feb 1901

Her Mountain Lover
Catholic World, 73:396-7, Jun 1901
Critic, 39:77-8, Jul 1901
Dial, 31:26-7, 1 Jul 1901
Independent, 53:1323, 6 Jun 1901
Literary World, 32:103, 1 Jul 1901

Hesper
Dial, 36:19, 1 Jan 1904
Independent, 55:3072, 24 Dec 1903

The Light of the Star
Critic, 45:475, Nov 1904
Dial, 37:41, 16 Jul 1904
Literary World, 35:165, Jun 1904

A Little Norsk
Chautauquan, 16:508, Jan 1893
Critic, NS 18:118, 3 Sep 1892
Independent, 44:1329, 22 Sep 1892
Literary World, 23:294, 27 Aug 1892

Main-Travelled Roads
Chautauquan, 30:326-7, Dec 1899

A Member of the Third House
Critic, NS 17:314, 4 Jun 1892
Dial, 13:102-3, Aug 1892
Independent, 44:664, 12 May 1892
Literary World, 23:166, 7 May 1892

Money Magic
Dial, 43:318-9, 16 Nov 1907
Independent, 63:1177, 14 Nov 1907

Other Main-Travelled Roads
Independent, 69:1092, 17 Nov 1910

Prairie Folks
Critic, 37:86, Jul 1900
Literary World, 24:113, 8 Apr 1893

Rose of Dutcher's Coolly
Chautauquan, 29:389, Jul 1899
Critic, NS 25:89, 8 Feb 1896
Dial, 20:80, 1 Feb 1896
Independent, 48:189, 6 Feb 1896
Literary World, 27:38, 8 Feb 1896

The Shadow World
Independent, 65:1183, 19 Nov 1908; 65:1245, 26 Nov 1908

The Spirit of Sweetwater
Chautauquan, 29:207, May 1899
Literature, 3:603, 24 Dec 1898

A Spoil of Office
Critic, NS 18:249, 5 Nov 1892
Dial, 14:114, 16 Feb 1893

The Tyranny of the Dark
Critic, 47:284, Sep 1905
Independent, 59:575, 7 Sep 1905

Wayside Courtships
Chautauquan, 26:573, Feb 1898

Works (Uniform Edition)
Critic, NS 29:213-4, 26 Mar 1898

[Garretson, James Edmund]
Brushland
By John Darby [pseud.].
Independent, 34:11, 3 Aug 1882

Garrett, Edmund Henry
Romance and Reality of the Puritan Coast
Independent, 49:1731, 30 Dec 1897

Gasch, Marie (Manning)
Judith of the Plains
Critic, 44:185-6, Feb 1904
Dial, 36:119, 16 Feb 1904
Lord Alingham, Bankrupt
Critic, 42:67-8, Jan 1903

[Gatchell, Charles]
Haschisch
By Thorold King [pseud.].
Catholic World, 47:269, May 1888
Critic, NS 5:305, 19 Jun 1886; NS 9:281, 9 Jun 1888
Dial, 7:15-6, May 1886
Independent, 38:789, 24 Jun 1886
Literary World, 17:315, 18 Sep 1886
What a Woman Did
Literary World, 31:267, 1 Dec 1900

Gates, Eleanor
The Biography of a Prairie Girl
Critic, 42:477, Apr 1903
Dial, 33:331, 16 Nov 1902
Literary World, 34:3, 1 Jan 1903
The Plow-Woman
Independent, 61:1570-1, 27 Dec 1906

[Gazzam, Anna Reading]
A Sketch in the Ideal
Independent, 43:1605, 29 Oct 1891

Genone, Hudor [pseud.]
See Roe, William James.

Geppert, Dora (Higbee)
In "God's Country"
Literary World, 29:11, 8 Jan 1898
The Scherzo in B Flat Minor
Critic, NS 23:436-7, 15 Jun 1895

Gestefeld, Ursula Newell
The Leprosy of Miriam
Literary World, 26:58, 23 Feb 1895
The Woman Who Dares
Catholic World, 56:580, Jan 1893
Literary World, 24:42, 11 Feb 1893

Gibbs, George
In Search of Mademoiselle
Dial, 31:31, 1 Jul 1901
Independent, 53:2054, 29 Aug 1901
The Love of Monsieur
Critic, 43:285, Sep 1903
Independent, 55:2354, 1 Oct 1903
The Medusa Emerald
Independent, 64:208-9, 23 Jan 1908

Gibson, Charles Donnel
My Lady and Allan Darke
Dial, 28:86, 1 Feb 1900
Independent, 52:196, 18 Jan 1900

[Gibson, Eva Katherine (Clapp)]
Her Bright Future
Literary World, 11:198, 5 Jun 1880
A Woman's Triumph
Literary World, 16:405, 14 Nov 1885

Gielow, Mrs. Henry G.
See Gielow, Martha (Sawyer).

Gielow, Martha (Sawyer)
Mammy's Reminiscences, and Other Sketches
Chautauquan, 34:344, Dec 1901

[Gilbert, Mrs. R. L.]
Thump's Client
By Charles D. Knight [pseud.].
Literary World, 11:468, 18 Dec 1880

Gilchrist, Annie (Somers)
Harcourt
Critic, NS 7:241, 14 May 1887
Literary World, 18:169, 28 May 1887

Gilder, Jeanette Leonard
The Autobiography of a Tomboy
Chautauquan, 34:336, Dec 1901
Taken by Siege
Independent, 39:270, 3 Mar 1887; 49:1548, 25 Nov 1897
Literary World, 18:203, 25 Jun 1887; 28:478, 25 Dec 1897
The Tomboy at Work
Independent, 58:786, 6 Apr 1905

Giles, Ella A.
See Ruddy, Mrs. Ella Augusta (Giles).

Gilliam, Edward Winslow
1791: A Tale of San Domingo
Catholic World, 51:549, Jul 1890

Gillman, Henry
Hassan, a Fellah
Chautauquan, 27:687, Sep 1898
Critic, NS 30:103, Jul-Aug 1898
Dial, 24:56, 1 Jun 1898
Independent, 50:763, 9 Jun 1898

Gilman, Bradley
Back to the Soil
Literary World, 32:139, 1 Sep 1901
Kibboo Ganey
By Walter Wentworth [pseud.].
Chautauquan, 11:127, Apr 1890
Ronald Carnaguay, A Commercial Clergyman
Chautauquan, 38:518, Jan 1904
Critic, 43:285, Sep 1903
Dial, 35:156[220], 1 Oct 1903
Literary World, 34:139-40, Jun 1903

Gilman, Charlotte (Perkins) Stetson
The Yellow Wall Paper
Independent, 51:2162, 10 Aug 1899

Gilman, Mrs. Stella Lucile
That Dakota Girl
Literary World, 23:295, 27 Aug 1892

Gilmore, Minnie L.
A Son of Esau
Critic, NS 18:118, 3 Sep 1892
Literary World, 23:310, 10 Sep 1892; 24:114, 8 Apr 1893
The Woman Who Stood Between
Critic, NS 19:61, 4 Feb 1893

Gilson, Roy Rolfe
The Flower of Youth
Literary World, 35:329, Nov 1904
In the Morning Glow
Dial, 33:332, 16 Nov 1902

Gilson, Roy Rolfe (cont.)
Katrina
Independent, 61:1499, 20 Dec 1906
When Love Is Young
Dial, 32:87, 1 Feb 1902
Independent, 54:756, 27 Mar 1902

Glasgow, Ellen Anderson Gholson
The Ancient Law
Dial, 44:134-5, 1 Mar 1908
Independent, 64:469-70, 27 Feb 1908
The Battle-Ground
Critic, 41:279, Sep 1902
Dial, 32:385, 1 Jun 1902
Independent, 54:1251, 22 May 1902
The Deliverance
Dial, 36:119, 16 Feb 1904
Independent, 56:442-3, 25 Feb 1904; 57:1137, 17 Nov 1904
Literary World, 35:48-9, Feb 1904
The Descendant
Critic, NS 27:352-3, 22 May 1897
Dial, 22:310-1, 16 May 1897
Independent, 49:980, 29 Jul 1897
Literary World, 28:164, 15 May 1897
Phases of an Inferior Planet
Critic, NS 30:512-3, Dec 1898
Dial, 25:172, 16 Sep 1898
Harper's, 97:Literary Notes, 3, Oct 1898
Independent, 50:1127-8, 20 Oct 1898
Literary World, 29:353-4, 29 Oct 1898
Literature, 3:524-5, 3 Dec 1898
The Romance of a Plain Man
Independent, 67:423, 19 Aug 1909
The Voice of the People
Dial, 29:23-4, 1 Jul 1900
Independent, 52:1267, 24 May 1900
The Wheel of Life
Critic, 48:435, May 1906
Dial, 40:156, 1 Mar 1906

Glaspell, Susan
The Glory of the Conquered
Dial, 47:183, 16 Sep 1909
Independent, 67:602-3, 9 Sep 1909

Glover, Elizabeth [pseud.]
See Bennett, Mary E.

Godfrey, Hollis
The Man Who Ended War
Dial, 45:458, 16 Dec 1908

Goff, Harriett Newell Kneeland
Who Cares?
Critic, NS 9:17, 14 Jan 1888

Gooch, Fani Pusey
Miss Mordeck's Father
Catholic World, 51:263-5, May 1890
Independent, 42:967, 10 Jul 1890
Literary World, 21:155, 10 May 1890

Goodloe, Abbie Carter
College Girls
Dial, 19:385, 16 Dec 1895

Goodrich, Arthur Frederick
The Balance of Power
Chautauquan, 47:235-6, Jul 1907

[Goodwin, Henry Leavitt]
Clare Duval
By Clement Wilkes [pseud.].
Critic, 37:467, Nov 1900

Goodwin, Mrs. H. B.
See Talcott, Hannah Elizabeth (Bradbury) Goodwin.

Goodwin, Maud (Wilder)
The Colonial Cavalier
Literary World, 27:12, 11 Jan 1896
Flint, His Faults, His Friendships, and His Fortunes
Literary World, 28:464-5, 11 Dec 1897
Four Roads to Paradise
Critic, 44:561-2, Jun 1904
Dial, 36:371, 1 Jun 1904
Literary World, 35:162, Jun 1904
The Head of a Hundred
Critic, NS 24:180, 21 Sep 1895; 38:85, Jan 1901
Dial, 19:94, 16 Aug 1895
Literary World, 26:201-2, 29 Jun 1895; 31:257, 1 Dec 1900
Sir Christopher
Critic, 38:567, Jun 1901
Literary World, 33:8-9, 1 Jan 1902
The Up-Grade
Catholic World, 91:259-60, May 1910
Independent, 69:824-5, 13 Oct 1910
White Aprons
Dial, 22:155-6, 1 Mar 1897
Independent, 48:1006, 23 Jul 1896
Literary World, 27:203, 27 Jun 1896

Gordon, Helen (Van Metre) Van-Anderson
The Right Knock
By Nellie V. Anderson.
Critic, NS 12:64, 10 Aug 1889

Gordon, Julien [pseud.]
See Cruger, Julie Grinnell (Storrow).

Goss, Charles Frederic
The Loom of Life
Independent, 55:392, 12 Feb 1903
The Redemption of David Corson
Independent, 52:1448-9, 14 Jun 1900

Goss, Warren Lee
Jack Alden
Chautauquan, 22:382, Dec 1895
Jed
Chautauquan, 10:378, Dec 1889
Independent, 41:1399, 24 Oct 1889

[Graham, Edwin Brown]
In the Coils
Independent, 34:11, 19 Oct 1882

Graham, Margaret (Collier)
Stories of the Foot-Hills
Literary World, 26:90, 23 Mar 1895
Critic, NS 23:433-4, 15 Jun 1895
The Wizard's Daughter
Critic, 48:475, May 1906

Grant, Robert
An Average Man
Critic, NS 1:291, 21 Jun 1884
Dial, 5:67, Jul 1884
Independent, 36:779-80, 19 Jan 1884
Literary World, 15:194, 14 Jun 1884
The Bachelor's Christmas, and Other Stories
Chautauquan, 22:379, Dec 1895
Dial, 20:173-4, 16 Mar 1896
Independent, 47:1728, 19 Dec 1895

Grant, Robert (cont.)
The Chippendales
Dial, 46:370-1, 1 Jun 1909
The Confessions of a Frivolous Girl
Dial, 1:37, Jun 1880
Face to Face
Critic, NS 5:306, 19 Jan 1886
Independent, 38:1204, 23 Sep 1886
Literary World, 17:316, 18 Sep 1886
Jack Hall
Critic, NS 8:285, 3 Dec 1887
Independent, 40:51, 12 Jan 1888
The Knave of Hearts
Critic, NS 5:145, 20 Mar 1886
Dial, 6:302, Mar 1886
Literary World, 17:131, 17 Apr 1886
The Law-Breakers
Critic, 49:93, Jul 1906
Independent, 60:1047, 3 May 1906
The Orchid
Critic, 47:91-2, Jul 1905
Independent, 58:1008, 4 May 1905
The Reflections of a Married Man
Catholic World, 55:598-9, Jul 1892
Critic, NS 18:4, 2 Jul 1892
Independent, 44:1130, 11 Aug 1892
Literary World, 23:230, 2 Jul 1892
A Romantic Young Lady
Critic, NS 6:170, 9 Oct 1886
Independent, 38:1336, 21 Oct 1886
The Undercurrent
Dial, 38:15, 9 Jan 1905
Independent, 58:1008, 4 May 1905
Literary World, 35:377, Dec 1904
Unleavened Bread
Dial, 29:125, 1 Sep 1900
Independent, 52:1321-2, 31 May 1900; 52:2803, 22 Nov 1900
Literary World, 31:115-6, 1 Jun 1900
See also The King's Men.

Gray, David
Gallops
Critic, NS 30:395, Nov 1898
Literary World, 29:354, 29 Oct 1898

[Gray, Isa E.]
Marjory Graham
Dial, 3:98, Sep 1882
Independent, 34:11, 3 Aug 1882

Gray, Robertson [pseud.]
See Raymond, Rossiter Worthington.

Grayson, Pauline
Kreutzer Sonata Bearing Fruit
Catholic World, 52:136, Oct 1890

Greaves, Richard [pseud.]
See McCutcheon, George Barr.

Green, Anna Katharine
See Rohlfs, Anna Katharine (Green).

Greene, Belle C.
Sec Greene, Isabel Catherine (Colton).

Greene, Homer
The Blind Brother
Catholic World, 46:703-4, Feb 1888
A Lincoln Conscript
Catholic World, 89:548-9, Jul 1909
Pickett's Gap

Chautauquan, 38:520, Jan 1904

Greene, Isabel Catherine (Colton)
A New England Conscience
Critic, NS 4:125, 12 Sep 1885
Independent, 37:1295, 8 Oct 1885
Literary World, 16:307, 5 Sep 1885

Greene, Sarah Pratt (McLean)
Cape Code Folks
Critic, 1:247, 10 Sep 1887; NS 11:102, 2 Mar 1889
Dial, 2:102, Sep 1881
Literary World, 12:255-6, 30 Jul 1881; 12:309, 10 Sep 1881
Deacon Lysander
Dial, 37:314, 16 Nov 1904
Flood Tide
Critic, 40:83-4, Jan 1902
Dial, 31:371, 16 Nov 1901
Independent, 53:2658, 7 Nov 1901
Literary World, 32:218, 1 Dec 1901
Lastchance Junction, Far, Far West
Catholic World, 48:847, Mar 1889
Literary World, 20:76, 2 Mar 1889
Leon Pontifex
Independent, 42:1720, 4 Dec 1890
Literary World, 21:398, 8 Nov 1890
The Moral Imbeciles
Dial, 25:172, 16 Sep 1898
Independent, 50:915, 29 Sep 1898
Literary World, 29:339, 15 Oct 1898
Power Lot
Independent, 61:756, 27 Sep 1906
Stuart and Bamboo
Critic, NS 28:340, 4 Dec 1897
Harper's, 96:Literary Notes, 4, Feb 1898
Independent, 50:224, 17 Feb 1898
Literary World, 28:479, 25 Dec 1897
Literature, 2:326, 19 Mar 1898
Towhead
Critic, 3:31-2, 27 Jan 1883
Literary World, 13:393, 18 Nov 1882
Vesty of the Basins
Critic, NS 18:66, 6 Aug 1892
Harper's, 85:Literary Notes, 1-2, Sep 1892
Independent, 44:1330, 22 Sep 1892
Literary World, 32:71, 1 May 1901
Winslow Plain
Critic, 42:284, Mar 1903

Greenough, Sarah Dana (Loring)
In Extremis
Literary World, 3:66-7, 1 Oct 1872
Treason at Home
Independent, 25:236, 20 Feb 1873

Greenwood, Grace [pseud.]
See Lippincott, Sara Jane (Clarke).

Grendel, M. R.
Contrasts
Critic, 1:177, 2 Jul 1881

[Griffen, Annie M.]
All Wrong
Literary World, 8:30-1, 1 Jul 1877

Griffin, La Roy Freese
The Abduction of Princess Chriemhild

Griffin, La Roy Freese (cont.)
Literary World, 29:205, 25 Jun 1898

Griffis, William Elliot
Honda the Samurai
Independent, 43:456, 26 Mar 1891
The Pathfinders of the Revolution
Dial, 30:109, 16 Feb 1901

Grinnell, George Bird
Blackfoot Lodge Tales
Critic, NS 19:179, 25 Mar 1893
Dial, 14:182-3, 16 Mar 1893
Independent, 45:1154, 24 Aug 1893
Literary World, 24:67, 11 Mar 1893
Pawnee Hero Stories and Folk-Tales
Independent, 42:257, 20 Feb 1890
Literary World, 21:36-7, 1 Feb 1890
The Punishment of the Stingy
Literary World, 33:27, 1 Feb 1902

Griswold, Harriet (Tyng)
Waiting on Destiny
Independent, 42:222, 13 Feb 1890

[Griswold, Lorenzo]
Priest and Puritan
Catholic World, 50:690-1, Feb 1890
Literary World, 21:289, 30 Aug 1890

Guernsey, Lucy Ellen
The Chevalier's Daughter
Independent, 32:12, 23 Sep 1880
Literary World, 11:468, 18 Dec 1880
The Hidden Treasure
Independent, 42:1842, 25 Dec 1890
Literary World, 21:439, 20 Nov 1890
Lady Betty's Governess
Independent, 25:586, 8 May 1873
Loveday's History
Literary World, 16:277, 8 Aug 1885
Oldham
Critic, NS 4:161, 3 Oct 1885

Guiney, Louise Imogen
Lovers' Saint Ruth's, and Three Other Tales
Catholic World, 62:698-9, Feb 1896
Critic, NS 25:272-3, 18 Apr 1896
Dial, 20:174, 16 Mar 1896
Literary World, 27:46, 8 Feb 1896

Gunsaulus, Frank Wakeley
Monk and Knight
Dial, 12:48-9, Jun 1891
Independent, 43:756, 21 May 1891

Gunter, Archibald Clavering
Her Senator
Westminster Review, 146:111-2, Jul 1896
Jack Curzon
Literary World, 30:107, 1 Apr 1899
Mr. Barnes of New York
Critic, NS 7:307, 18 Jun 1887
Mr. Potter of Texas
Catholic World, 47:268, May 1888
The Power of Woman
Catholic World, 66:414-5, Dec 1897
A Princess of Paris
Critic, NS 21:271, 21 Apr 1894

Habberton, John
All He Knew
Catholic World, 50:553-4, Jan 1890
Chautauquan, 12:421, Dec 1890
Independent, 42:1459, 16 Oct 1890
The Barton Experiment
Galaxy, 23:139, Jan 1877
Literary World, 7:124, 1 Jan 1877
The Bowsham Puzzle
Critic, NS 1:161, 5 Apr 1884
Independent, 36:716, 5 Jun 1884
Brueton's Bayou
Catholic World, 44:853, Mar 1887
Critic, NS 10:78, 18 Aug 1888
Caleb Wright
Dial, 31:373, 16 Nov 1901
Literary World, 33:44, 1 Mar 1902
The Chautauquans
Literary World, 23:59, 13 Feb 1892
Couldn't Say No
Literary World, 21:58, 15 Feb 1890
Country Luck
Catholic World, 46:702-3, Feb 1888
Critic, NS 9:54, 4 Feb 1888
Independent, 39:1425, 3 Nov 1887
Literary World, 18:460, 10 Dec 1887
The Crew of the "Sam Weller"
Independent, 30:11-2, 22 Aug 1878
Literary World, 9:57, 1 Sep 1878
Helen's Babies
Independent, 28:11, 3 Aug 1876
Literary World, 7:51, 1 Sep 1876
A Lucky Lover
Westminster Review, 139:461, Apr 1893
Mrs. Mayburn's Twins
Dial, 2:293, Apr 1882
Independent, 34:11, 22 Jun 1882; 43:608, 23 Apr 1891
Other People's Children
Galaxy, 24:574, Oct 1877
Out at Twinnett's
Critic, NS 16:216, 24 Oct 1891
Independent, 43:1571, 22 Oct 1891
The Worst Boy in Town
Independent, 32:12, 7 Oct 1880

Hadermann, Jeannette R.
See Walworth, Jeannette Ritchie (Hadermann).

Hague, Parthenia Antoinette (Vardaman)
A Blockhead Family
Catholic World, 48:694-5, Feb 1889

Hains, Thornton Jenkins
Bahama Bill
Independent, 65:45-6, 2 Jul 1908
The Cruise of the Petrel
Independent, 53:1624, 11 Jul 1901

Hale, Edward Everett
Christmas in Narragansett
Chautauquan, 8:198, Dec 1887
Critic, NS 3:53, 31 Jan 1885
Independent, 37:396, 26 Mar 1885
Literary World, 16:308, 5 Sep 1885
Crusoe in New York, and Other Tales
Dial, 1:94, Sep 1880
Literary World, 11:280, 14 Aug 1880
East and West
Catholic World, 56:273,

Hale, Edward Everett (cont.)
Nov 1892
Critic, NS 18:249, 5 Nov 1892
Independent, 44:1563, 3 Nov 1892
Literary World, 23:375, 22 Oct 1892

The Fortunes of Rachel
Dial, 5:67, Jul 1884
Independent, 36:1067, 21 Aug 1884
Literary World, 15:255-6, 9 Aug 1884

Four and Five
Chautauquan, 14:761, Mar 1892

G. T. T.; or, The Wonderful Adventures of a Pullman
Galaxy, 24:715-6, Nov 1877

His Level Best, and Other Stories
Galaxy, 16:137-8, Jul 1873
Literary World, 3:123, 1 Jan 1873

How They Lived in Hampton
Literary World, 19:254, 4 Aug 1888

In His Name
Chautauquan, 29:389, Jul 1899
Independent, 26:9, 26 Feb 1874
Literary World, 18:454, 10 Dec 1887

The Man Without a Country, and Other Stories
Chautauquan, 29:206-7, May 1899
Independent, 50:1275, 3 Nov 1898; 51:969, 6 Apr 1899
Literary World, 19:446, 8 Dec 1888

Mr. Tangier's Vacations
Critic, NS 10:114, 8 Sep 1888
Literary World, 19:220, 7 Jul 1888

Mrs. Merriam's Scholars
Literary World, 10:54, 15 Feb 1879

My Friend the Boss
Critic, NS 10:231, 10 Nov 1888

The New Ohio
Westminster Review, 138:691, Dec 1892

Our Christmas in a Palace
Chautauquan, 8:198, Dec 1887; 14:382, Dec 1891
Critic, NS 1:31, 19 Jan 1884
Independent, 36:43, 10 Jan 1884

Our New Crusade
Independent, 27:10, 28 Jan 1875
Literary World, 5:118, 1 Jan 1875

Philip Nolan's Friends
Catholic World, 25:719, Aug 1877
Independent, 28:8, 7 Dec 1876
Literary World, 7:115-6, 1 Jan 1877

Susan's Escort, and Others
Critic, NS 29:74, 29 Jan 1898
Dial, 23:287, 16 Nov 1897
Harper's, 95:Literary Notes, 2-3, Sep 1897
Independent, 49:1117, 26 Aug 1897
Literary World, 28:298, 4 Sep 1897

Sybil Knox
Independent, 44:665, 12 May 1892

Ten Times One Is Ten
Catholic World, 12:856-7, Mar 1871
Galaxy, 11:144-5, Jan 1871

Ups and Downs
Literary World, 4:9, 1 Jun 1873

Vanna
Critic, NS 24:407, 14 Dec 1895

See also Six of One, by Half

a Dozen of the Other.

_______, and Lucretia Peabody Hale
The New Harry and Lucy
Critic, NS 18:263, 12 Nov 1892
Independent, 44:1261, 8 Sep 1892
Literary World, 23:213-4, 18 Jun 1892

Hale, Lucretia Peabody
See Six of One, by Half a Dozen of the Other.

_______, and Edwin Lassetter Bynner
An Uncloseted Skeleton
Critic, 40:657, 24 May 1888; NS 19:281, 9 Jun 1888
Literary World, 19:153, 12 May 1888
See also Hale, Edward Everett, and Lucretia Peabody Hale.

Hale, Robert Beverly
Six Stories, and Some Verses
Critic, NS, 27:255, 10 Apr 1897

Hale, Susan
The Rejuvenation of Miss Semaphore
Literary World, 29:371, 12 Nov 1898

Hall, Alice C.
Miss Leighton's Perplexities
Independent, 34:13, 21 Dec 1882

Hall, Eliza Calvert [pseud.]
See Obenchain, Eliza Caroline (Calvert).

Hall, Gertrude
See Brownell, Gertrude (Hall).

Hall, Ruth
The Black Gown
Critic, 38:181, Feb 1901
Independent, 53:964-5, 25 Apr 1901
Literary World, 31:268, 1 Dec 1900
The Boys of Scrooby
Independent, 51:2828, 19 Oct 1899
A Downrenter's Son
Critic, 42:84, Jan 1903
Literary World, 33:181, 1 Nov 1902
The Golden Arrow
Critic, 40:374, Apr 1902
In the Brave Days of Old
Independent, 50:1346, 10 Nov 1898
The Pine Grove House
Catholic World, 79:692, Aug 1904
Critic, 43:578, Dec 1903
Literary World, 35:20, Jan 1905

Hall, Thomas Winthrop
An Experimental Wooing
Literary World, 30:107, 1 Apr 1899

Hall, Violette
Chanticleer
Literary World, 33:142, 1 Sep 1902

[Halsted, Leonora B.]
Bethesda
By Barbara Elbon [pseud.].
Critic, NS 1:196, 26 Apr 1884
Dial, 5:15-6, May 1884
Independent, 36:651, 22 May 1884
Literary World, 15:107-8, 5 Apr 1884

Hamblen, Herbert Elliott
The General Manager's Story
Chautauquan, 27:686-7, Sep 1898
Critic, NS 30:303, Oct 1898
Independent, 50:729, 2

Hamblen, Herbert Elliott (cont.)
Jun 1898
Literary World, 29:236, 23 Jul 1898
On Many Seas
By Frederick Benton Williams [pseud.].
Dial, 22:311, 16 May 1897
The Story of a Yankee Boy
Chautauquan, 28:526, Feb 1899
Tom Benton's Luck
Chautauquan, 29:605, Sep 1899
Independent, 51:210, 19 Jan 1899
We Win
Chautauquan, 30:329, Dec 1899

Hamilton, Alice King
Mildred's Cadet
Literary World, 12:280, 13 Aug 1881
One of the Duanes
Critic, NS 3:280, 13 Jun 1885; NS 8:18, 2 Jul 1887
Independent, 37:1103, 27 Aug 1885
Literary World, 16:209, 13 Jun 1885

Hamilton, Mrs. C. V.
See Jamison, Cecilia Viets (Dakin) Hamilton.

Hamilton, Gail [pseud.]
See Dodge, Mary Abigail.

Hamilton, George W.
Kit Caffrey's Grit
Independent, 48:494, 9 Apr 1890

Hamilton, Kate Waterman
The Parson's Proxy
Critic, NS 25:425, 13 Jun 1896
Literary World, 27:153-4, 16 May 1896
Rachel's Share of the Road
Critic, 2:297, 4 Nov 1882
Literary World, 13:461, 16 Dec 1882

Hamlin, Myra Louise (Sawyer)
A Politician's Daughter
Catholic World, 44:131-3, Oct 1886
Critic, NS 6:112-3, 4 Sep 1886
Literary World, 17:278, 21 Aug 1886

[Hammond, Henrietta (Hardy)]
A Fair Philosopher
By Henri Daugé [pseud.].
Critic, 2:237, 9 Sep 1882
The Georgians
Critic, 1:177-8, 2 Jul 1881
Dial, 2:85-6, Aug 1881
Literary World, 12:223, 2 Jul 1881

Hammond, William Alexander
Doctor Grattan
Independent, 37:555, 30 Apr 1885
Literary World, 16:25, 24 Jan 1885
Lal
Critic, NS 2:74-5, 16 Aug 1884; NS 3:53, 31 Jan 1885
Dial, 5:88, Aug 1884
Independent, 36:1163, 11 Sep 1884
Literary World, 15:259, 9 Aug 1884
Mr. Oldmixon
Critic, NS 3:280, 13 Jun 1885
Independent, 37:1103, 27 Aug 1885
Literary World, 16:184-5, 30 May 1885
On the Susquehanna
Independent, 39:494, 21 Apr 1887
Literary World, 18:120, 16 Apr 1887
The Son of Perdition

Independent, 51:634, 2 Mar 1899
Literary World, 30:7, 7 Jan 1899
A Strong-Minded Woman
Literary World, 16:474, 12 Dec 1885

_______, and Clara Hammond Lanza
Tales of Eccentric Life
Catholic World, 43:416, Jun 1886
Independent, 38:690, 3 Jun 1886

Hancock, Albert Elmer
Henry Bourland
Critic, 39:374, Oct 1901
Dial, 31:136, 1 Sep 1901

Hancock, Anson Uriel
The Genius of Galilee
Critic, NS 16:29, 18 Jul 1891

Hancock, Elizabeth H.
See Neale, Walter, and Elizabeth H. Hancock.

[Hanifin, John M.]
The Blind Man and the Devil
By Phineas [pseud.].
Critic, NS 14:129, 13 Sep 1890

Hanks, Beulah Downey
For the Honor of a Child
Literary World, 30:139, 29 Apr 1899

Hapgood, Mrs. Hutchins
See Hapgood, Neith (Boyce).

Hapgood, Neith (Boyce)
The Bond
By Neith Boyce.
Dial, 45:91, 16 Aug 1908
The Eternal Spring
By Neith Boyce.
Critic, 48:474, May 1906
Dial, 41:115, 1 Sep 1906
The Folly of Others
By Neith Boyce.
Critic, 45:474, Nov 1904

Harben, William Nathaniel
Abner Daniel
Dial, 33:65, 1 Aug 1902
Independent, 54:2481-2, 16 Oct 1902
Literary World, 33:126, 1 Aug 1902
Almost Persuaded
Critic, NS 16:64-5, 8 Aug 1891
Ann Boyd
Dial, 42:16, 1 Jan 1907
Independent, 62:211, 24 Jan 1907
Dixie Hart
Independent, 69:1095, 17 Nov 1910
The Georgians
Dial, 37:312, 16 Nov 1904
Independent, 57:798-9, 6 Oct 1904
Gilbert Neal
Independent, 65:1121-2, 12 Nov 1908
The Land of the Changing Sun
Chautauquan, 22:510, Jan 1896
Mam' Linda
Dial, 44:45, 16 Jan 1908
Independent, 63:1058-9, 31 Oct 1907; 63:1226-8, 21 Nov 1907
Northern Georgia Sketches
Critic, 38:85, Jan 1901
Pole Baker
Critic, 47:578, Dec 1905
Independent, 59:1154, 16 Nov 1905; 59:1228-9, 23 Nov 1905
The Redemption of Kenneth Galt
Catholic World, 91:113, Apr 1910
Independent, 68:101-2, 13 Jan 1910
The Substitute
Critic, 43:188, Aug 1903
Dial, 35:67, 1 Aug 1903
Independent, 55:2350-1, 1 Oct 1903
Literary World, 34:151,

Harben, William Nathaniel (cont.)
Jun 1903
Westerfelt
Dial, 31:367, 16 Nov 1901
Independent, 53:2243, 19 Sep 1901
Literary World, 32:142, 1 Sep 1901
White Marie
Critic, NS 13:16, 11 Jan 1890
A Woman Who Trusted
Critic, 39:182, Aug 1901
Literary World, 32:103, 1 Jul 1901

Harding, John William
The Gate of the Kiss
Catholic World, 75:678, Aug 1902
Dial, 32:393, 1 Jun 1902
Independent, 54:1967, 14 Aug 1902

Hardy, Arthur Sherburne
But Yet a Woman
Critic, 3:194-5, 28 Apr 1883; NS 4:5, 4 Jul 1885; NS 12:64, 10 Aug 1889
Dial, 4:41-2, Jun 1883
Independent, 35:12, 31 May 1883
Literary World, 14:139-40, 5 May 1883
His Daughter First
Critic, 43:188, Aug 1903
Dial, 34:372, 1 Jun 1903
Independent, 55:1344-5, 4 Jun 1903; 55:2740, 19 Nov 1903
Literary World, 34:153, Jun 1903
Passe Rose
Catholic World, 49:272, May 1889
Chautauquan, 9:625, Jul 1889
Critic, NS 11:232, 11 May 1889
Dial, 10:57, Jul 1889
Literary World, 20:126, 13 Apr 1889
The Wind of Destiny
Catholic World, 43:706-9, Aug 1886
Critic, NS 5:303-4, 19 Jun 1886
Dial, 7:68, Jul 1886
Independent, 38:789, 24 Jun 1886
Literary World, 17:195-6, 12 Jun 1886
Westminster Review, 126 (NS 70):564, Oct 1886

Harlan, Caleb
The Fate of Marcel
Independent, 35:10, 27 Dec 1883
Literary World, 14:350-1, 20 Oct 1883

Harland, Henry
As It Was Written
By Sidney Luska [pseud.].
Critic, NS 4:147, 26 Sep 1885
Dial, 6:182, Nov 1885
Independent, 37:1295, 8 Oct 1885
Literary World, 16:373-4, 17 Oct 1885
The Cardinal's Snuff-Box
Catholic World, 72:510-11, Mar 1901
Critic, 37:274-5, Sep 1900
Comedies and Errors
Dial, 25:79, 1 Aug 1898
Literary World, 29:236, 23 Jul 1898
Grandison Mather
Catholic World, 53:440, Jun 1891
Critic, NS 11:233, 11 May 1889
Literary World, 20:177, 25 May 1889
Gray Roses
Chautauquan, 22:127, Oct 1895
Dial, 19:95, 16 Aug 1895

Independent, 47:1075, 8 Aug 1895
Literary World, 26:203, 29 Jun 1895
Westminster Review, 144:233, Aug 1895

The Lady Paramount
Catholic World, 75:398-403, Jun 1902
Critic, 40:555-6, Jun 1902
Dial, 33:62, 1 Aug 1902
Independent, 54:1252, 22 May 1902; 54:2771, 20 Nov 1902
Literary World, 33:91, 1 Jun 1902

A Latin-Quarter Courtship, and Other Stories
Critic, NS 11:129, 16 Mar 1889
Literary World, 20:95, 16 Mar 1889

Mademoiselle Miss
Critic, NS 21:323-4, 12 May 1894
Dial, 16:147, 1 Mar 1894

Mea Culpa
Critic, NS 16:105-6, 29 Aug 1891
Westminster Review, 136:106, Jul 1891

Mrs. Peixada
By Sidney Luska [pseud.].
Catholic World, 43:565, Jul 1886
Critic, NS 5:180, 10 Apr 1886
Independent, 38:690, 3 Jun 1886
Literary World, 17:131, 17 Apr 1886

My Friend Prospero
Catholic World, 79:126-7, Apr 1904
Dial, 36:120-1, 16 Feb 1904
Independent, 56:212, 28 Jan 1904; 57:1138, 17 Nov 1904
Literary World, 35:49, Feb 1904

My Uncle Florimond
Critic, NS 10:204, 27 Oct 1888
Independent, 41:1659, 12 Dec 1889

The Royal End
Independent, 66:1083, 20 May 1909

Two Women or One?
Critic, NS 14:95, 23 Aug 1890
Independent, 42:1133, 14 Aug 1890
Literary World, 21:238, 19 Jul 1890

The Yoke of the Thorah
By Sidney Luska [pseud.].
Catholic World, 45:553-7, Jul 1887
Critic, NS 7:316, 25 Jun 1887
Literary World, 18:185, 11 Jun 1887

Harland, Marion [pseud.]
See Terhune, Mary Virginia (Hawes).

Harper, Carrie A.
See Dix, Beulah Marie, and Carrie A. Harper.

Harper, Frances Ellen (Watkins)

Iola Leroy
Independent, 45:21, 5 Jan 1893; 48:1463, 29 Oct 1896

Harriman, Karl Edwin

Ann Arbor Tales
Critic, 42:377-8, Apr 1903

The Homebuilders
Literary World, 35:77-8, Mar 1904

Harris, Frank

Elder Conklin, and Other Stories
Dial, 17:332-3, 1 Dec 1894
Literary World, 26:25, 26 Jan 1895

The Road to Ridgeby's

Harris, Frank (cont.)
Chautauquan, 34:329, Dec 1901
Critic, 39:262-3, Sep 1901
Dial, 31:370, 16 Nov 1901
Independent, 53:2123, 5 Sep 1901

Harris, Joel Chandler
Aaron in the Wildwoods
Independent, 49:1624, 9 Dec 1897
Balaam and His Master, and Other Sketches and Stories
Chautauquan, 13:552, Jul 1891
Critic, NS 16:29, 18 Jul 1891
Dial, 12:50-1, Jun 1891
Independent, 43:1283, 27 Aug 1891
Westminster Review, 136:229-30, Aug 1891
The Chronicles of Aunt Minervy Ann
Independent, 51:2964, 2 Nov 1899; 51:3171, 23 Nov 1899
Daddy Jake the Runaway, and Short Stories Told After Dark
Chautauquan, 10:380, Dec 1889; 24:383, Dec 1896
Critic, NS 12:212, 2 Nov 1889
Independent, 41:1577, 28 Nov 1889; 49:56, 14 Jan 1897
Literary World, 20:423, 23 Nov 1889; 27:456, 12 Dec 1896
Free Joe, and Other Georgian Sketches
Catholic World, 46:836-7, Mar 1888
Chautauquan, 8:327, Feb 1888
Critic, NS 9:17, 14 Jan 1888
Literary World, 19:26, 21 Jan 1888
Gabriel Tolliver
Critic, 41:581, Dec 1902
Dial, 34:243, 1 Apr 1903
Independent, 54:2903, 4 Dec 1902
A Little Union Scout
Critic, 45:94, Jul 1904
Independent, 57:216, 28 Jul 1904
Literary World, 35:229, Aug 1904
The Making of a Statesman, and Other Stories
Critic, 41:279, Sep 1902
Dial, 32:389, 1 Jun 1902
Mingo, and Other Sketches in Black and White
Critic, NS 2:51, 2 Aug 1884; NS 9:17, 14 Jan 1888
Independent, 36:1067, 21 Aug 1884
Literary World, 15:242, 26 Jul 1884
Westminster Review, 122:617, Oct 1884
Nights with Uncle Remus
Catholic World, 38:427-8, Dec 1883
Critic, NS 1:64, 9 Feb 1884
Dial, 4:195, Dec 1883
Independent, 35:11, 6 Dec 1883
On the Plantation
Chautauquan, 15:387, Jun 1892
Critic, NS 18:65, 6 Aug 1892
Independent, 44:664, 12 May 1892
On the Wing of Occasions
Chautauquan, 32:330-1, Dec 1900
Independent, 52:2874, 29 Nov 1900
Plantation Pageants
Independent, 51:3299, 7 Dec 1899
The Shadow Between His Shoulder-Blades
Independent, 67:1455, 23 Dec 1909
Sister Jane, Her Friends and Acquaintances

Critic, NS 26:417-8, 26 Dec 1896
Independent, 49:153, 4 Feb 1897
Literary World, 28:43, 6 Feb 1897

The Story of Aaron
Chautauquan, 24:379, Dec 1896
Literary World, 28:13, 9 Jan 1897

Tales of the Home Folks in Peace and War
Critic, NS 30:204-5, Sep 1898
Independent, 50:729, 2 Jun 1898

Uncle Remus
Chautauquan, 22:256, Nov 1895
Literary World, 27:203, 27 Jun 1896

Uncle Remus and His Friends
Critic, NS 18:372, 31 Dec 1892
Dial, 14:186, 16 Mar 1893
Literary World, 23:498, 31 Dec 1892

Uncle Remus and the Little Boy
Independent, 69:707, 29 Sep 1910

Uncle Remus, His Songs and His Sayings
Chautauquan, 4:612, Jul 1884
Dial, 1:183-5, Jan 1881

Harris, Miriam (Coles)

Missy
Critic, NS 4:5, 4 Jul 1885

A Perfect Adonis
Independent, 27:10, 6 May 1875

Phoebe
Catholic World, 39:856, Sep 1884
Independent, 36:971, 31 Jul 1884
Literary World, 15:261-2, 9 Aug 1884
Westminster Review, 123 (NS 67):291, Jan 1885

Richard Vandermarck
Galaxy, 13:277-8, Feb 1872
Literary World, 2:108, 1 Dec 1871

The Tents of Wickedness
Catholic World, 86:403-4, Dec 1907

An Utter Failure
Chautauquan, 14:761, Mar 1892
Critic, NS 16:347, 19 Dec 1891
Independent, 43:1844, 10 Dec 1891

Harrison, Mrs. Burton
See Harrison, Constance (Cary).

Harrison, Constance (Cary)

The Anglomaniacs
Catholic World, 52:291, Nov 1890
Critic, NS 14:187, 18 Oct 1890
Dial, 11:241, Dec 1890
Literary World, 21:399, 8 Nov 1890; 30:408, 25 Nov 1899

A Bachelor Maid
Critic, NS 23:25, 12 Jan 1895
Dial, 18:272, 1 May 1895
Literary World, 26:11, 12 Jan 1895
Westminster Review, 143:474, Apr 1895

Bar Harbor Days
Critic, NS 8:38, 23 Jul 1887
Harper's, 75:Literary Notes, 2, Aug 1887
Literary World, 18:236, 23 Jul 1887

Belhaven Tales/Crow's Nest/Una and King David
Critic, NS 18:339-40, 17 Dec 1892
Dial, 14:115, 16 Feb 1893
Independent, 44:1599, 10

Harrison, Constance (Cary) (cont.)
Nov 1892
Bric-a-Brac Stories
Chautauquan, 6:184, Dec 1885; 12:423, Dec 1890
Critic, NS 4:207, 31 Oct 1885
Independent, 37:1566, 3 Dec 1885
The Carcellini Emerald, with Other Tales
Dial, 27:76, 1 Aug 1899
Independent, 51:2024, 27 Jul 1899
Literary World, 30:235, 22 Jul 1899
The Carlyles
Critic, 48:190, Feb 1906
The Circle of a Century
Independent, 51:3297, 7 Dec 1899
Literary World, 31:70, 3 Mar 1900
A Daughter of the South, and Shorter Stories
Catholic World, 55:450, Jun 1892
Critic, NS 18:3, 2 Jul 1892
Independent, 44:1260, 8 Sep 1892
Literary World, 23:198, 4 Jun 1892
An Edelweiss of the Sierras/ Golden-Rod/and Other Tales
Harper's, 85:Literary Notes, 2, Sep 1892
Independent, 44:1130, 11 Aug 1892
Literary World, 23:213, 18 Jun 1892
An Errant Wooing
Chautauquan, 21:774-5, Sep 1895
Critic, NS 21:227, 31 Mar 1894; NS 24:197, 28 Sep 1895
Dial, 19:93, 16 Aug 1895
Literary World, 26:217, 13 Jul 1895
Flower de Hundred
Catholic World, 50:766, Aug 1892
Critic, NS 15:191, 11 Apr 1891
Independent, 43:164, 29 Jan 1891
Good Americans
Chautauquan, 28:216, Nov 1898
Dial, 25:305-6, 1 Nov 1898
Independent, 50:1429, 17 Nov 1898
Literary World, 29:353, 29 Oct 1898
Latter-Day Sweethearts
Westminster Review, 166:111, Jul 1906
The Mercy Maid of Arcady, His Lordship, and Other Stories
Critic, NS 27:337-8, 15 May 1897
Independent, 49:719, 3 Jun 1897; 49:851, 1 Jul 1897
A Princess of the Hills
Critic, 39:278, Sep 1901
Literary World, 32:143, 1 Sep 1901
A Son of the Old Dominion
Independent, 49:979, 29 Jul 1897
Literary World, 28:288-9, 4 Sep 1897
Sweet Bells Out of Tune
Chautauquan, 18:382, Dec 1893
Critic, NS 20:391-2, 16 Dec 1893
Dial, 15:342, 1 Dec 1893
Literary World, 24:348, 21 Oct 1893
Sylvia's Husband
Critic, 44:476, May 1904
Independent, 56:1034, 5 May 1904
Literary World, 35:79, Mar 1904
A Triple Entanglement
Independent, 51:2569, 21 Sep 1899
Westminster Review,

151:107, Jan 1899
The Unwelcome Mrs. Hatch
Dial, 35:67, 1 Aug 1903
Literary World, 34:209, Aug 1903
A Virginia Cousin & Bar Harbor Tales
Critic, NS 25:444, 20 Jun 1896
Literary World, 27:60, 22 Feb 1896

Harrison, Jennie [pseud.]
See Tomkins, Jane Harrison.

Harrison, Louis Reeves
Rothermal
Independent, 42:854, 19 Jun 1890

[Harsha, William Justin]
Ploughed Under
Critic, 1:46-7, 26 Feb 1881
Dial, 2:13, May 1881
Literary World, 12:146, 23 Apr 1881
A Timid Brave
Critic, NS 5:305, 19 Jun 1886

Hart, Jerome Alfred
A Vigilante Girl
Dial, 48:396, 1 Jun 1910
Independent, 69:825, 13 Oct 1910

Hart, Thomas W.
Robert Sanders
Literary World, 29:91, 19 Mar 1898

Harte, Bret
The Argonauts of North Liberty
Critic, NS 10:136-7, 22 Sep 1888
Dial, 9:68, Jul 1888
Literary World, 19:170, 26 May 1888
Barker's Luck, and Other Stories
Catholic World, 64:410-1, Dec 1896
Critic, NS 27:19-20, 9 Jan 1897
Dial, 22:23, 1 Jan 1897
The Bell-Ringer of Angel's, and Other Stories
Critic, NS 23:200, 16 Mar 1895
Dial, 17:333, 1 Dec 1894
By Shore and Sedge
Critic, NS 4:27, 18 Jul 1885
Dial, 6:124, Sep 1885
Literary World, 16:236-7, 11 Jul 1885
Clarence
Dial, 20:79, 1 Feb 1896
Literary World, 26:389, 16 Nov 1895
Colonel Starbottle's Client, and Some Other People
Dial, 13:103, Aug 1892
Condensed Novels
Critic, 41:581, Dec 1902
Literary World, 2:7, 1 Jun 1871
Condensed Novels, Second Series
Dial, 33:284, 1 Nov 1902
Independent, 54:2718, 13 Nov 1902
Literary World, 33:180-1, 1 Nov 1902
Cressy
Critic, NS 11:129, 16 Mar 1889
Dial, 9:292-3, Mar 1889
Literary World, 20:76, 2 Mar 1889
The Crusade of the Excelsior
Catholic World, 45:843, Sep 1887
Critic, NS 8:126-7, 10 Sep 1887
Dial, 8:147-8, Nov 1887
Independent, 39:1269, 6 Oct 1887
Literary World, 18:236, 23 Jul 1887
Drift from Two Shores
Independent, 30:12, 22 Aug 1878
A First Family of Tasajara

Harte, Bret (cont.)
Critic, NS 17:225, 16 Apr 1892
Dial, 12:424-5, Apr 1892
Independent, 44:313, 3 Mar 1892
Literary World, 23:67, 27 Feb 1892

Flip, and Found at Blazing Star
Critic, 2:266, 7 Oct 1882
Dial, 3:115-6, Oct 1882
Independent, 34:12, 26 Oct 1882
Literary World, 13:315, 23 Sep 1882

From Sand Hill to Pine
Critic, 37:278, Sep 1900
Literary World, 31:157-8, 1 Aug 1900

The Heritage of Dedlow Marsh, and Other Tales
Critic, NS 12:214, 2 Nov 1889
Dial, 10:217-8, Dec 1889
Independent, 41:1399, 24 Oct 1889
Literary World, 20:352-3, 12 Oct 1889

In a Hollow of the Hills
Catholic World, 62:566, Jan 1896
Dial, 20:79, 1 Feb 1896
Literary World, 27:59, 22 Feb 1896

In the Carquinez Woods
Critic, NS 1:280, 14 Jun 1884
Dial, 4:126-9, Oct 1883
Literary World, 14:301-2, 22 Sep 1883

The Luck of Roaring Camp, and Other Sketches
Galaxy, 9:850-1, Jun 1870
Literary World, 1:6, 1 Jun 1870

Maruja
Critic, NS 5:33, 16 Jan 1886
Dial, 6:180, Nov 1885
Independent, 37:1454, 12 Nov 1885
Literary World, 16:373, 3 Oct 1885

A Millionaire of Rough-and-Ready, and Devil's Ford
Catholic World, 44:132-4, Apr 1887
Critic, NS 7:124, 12 Mar 1887
Dial, 7:292, Apr 1887
Literary World, 18:73, 8 Mar 1885

Mr. Jack Hamlin's Meditation, and Other Stories
Dial, 28:87-8, 1 Feb 1900
Independent, 51:3172, 23 Nov 1899; 52:726, 22 Mar 1900

Mrs. Skaggs's Husbands, and Other Sketches
Literary World, 3:140, 1 Feb 1873

On the Frontier
Critic, NS 2:87-8, 23 Aug 1884
Dial, 5:110, Sep 1884; 5:206, Dec 1884
Literary World, 15:295, 6 Sep 1884

Openings in the Old Trail
Critic, 41:581-2, Dec 1902

A Phyllis of the Sierras, and A Drift from Redwood Camp
Critic, NS 9:90, 25 Feb 1888
Dial, 8:269, Mar 1888
Literary World, 19:51, 18 Feb 1888

A Protégée of Jack Hamlin's, and Other Stories
Critic, NS 21:237, 7 Apr 1894
Dial, 16:146-7, 1 Mar 1894
Literary World, 25:70, 10 Mar 1894

The Queen of Pirate Isle
Chautauquan, 7:442, Apr 1887
Critic, NS 6:291, 11 Dec 1886
Literary World, 17:462, 11 Dec 1886

Sally Dows, and Other Stories
Critic, NS 20:374-5, 9 Dec 1893
Dial, 14:341, 1 Jun 1893
Literary World, 24:194, 17 Jun 1893
A Sappho of Green Springs, and Other Stories
Critic, NS 15:85, 14 Feb 1891; 16:16, 11 Jul 1891
Dial, 12:50, Jun 1891
Independent, 43:500, 2 Apr 1891
Snow-bound at Eagle's
Catholic World, 43:283, May 1886
Critic, NS 5:181, 10 Apr 1886
Dial, 7:14, May 1886
Literary World, 17:146, 1 May 1886
Stories in Light and Shadow
Critic, NS 31:263, Mar 1899
Dial, 27:76, 1 Aug 1899
Literature, 3:574, 17 Dec 1898
The Story of a Mine
Literary World, 8:181, 1 Mar 1878
Susy
Dial, 14:113, 16 Feb 1893
Literary World, 24:41, 11 Feb 1893
Tales of Trail and Town
Critic, NS 29:265, 16 Apr 1898
Dial, 25:79, 1 Aug 1898
Literature, 2:511-2, 30 Apr 1898
Thankful Blossom
Literary World, 7:143, 1 Feb 1877
Three Partners
Dial, 23:284, 16 Nov 1897
Independent, 49:1586, 2 Dec 1897
Literary World, 28:453, 11 Dec 1897
Trent's Trust and Other Stories
Critic, 43:76, Jul 1903
Dial, 34:371-2, 1 Jun 1903
Literary World, 34:180, Jul 1903
Under the Redwoods
Independent, 53:1563, 4 Jul 1901
A Waif of the Plains
Catholic World, 51:832, Sep 1890
Chautauquan, 11:384, Jun 1890
Critic, NS 13:169, 5 Apr 1890; 14:17, 12 Jul 1890
Independent, 42:788, 5 Jun 1890
Literary World, 21:151, 10 May 1890
A Ward of the Golden Gate
Catholic World, 52:607-8, Jan 1891
Chautauquan, 12:826, Mar 1891
Critic, NS 15:54, 31 Jan 1891
Dial, 11:241-2, Dec 1890
Independent, 43:164, 29 Jan 1891

Harvey, James Clarence
See Lanza, Clara (Hammond), and James Clarence Harvey; also Wilson, Theodora B., and James Clarence Harvey.

Hastings, Elizabeth [pseud.]
See Sherwood, Margaret (Pollock).

Hatch, Mary R. (Platt)
The Bank Tragedy
Literary World, 21:290, 30 Aug 1890

Hatchett, Mamie Lamkin
Myra
Literary World, 15:265, 9 Aug 1884

Hawthorne, Hildegarde
A Country Interlude
Critic, 44:477, May 1904
Dial, 36:369, 1 Jun 1904
Independent, 56:794-5, 7 Apr 1904
The Fairest of the Fair
Critic, NS 23:26, 12 Jan 1895

Hawthorne, Julian
An American Penman
Critic, NS 9:53, 4 Feb 1888
Independent, 39:1587, 8 Dec 1887
Literary World, 19:123, 14 Apr 1888
Another's Crime
Critic, NS 11:52, 2 Feb 1889
Literary World, 19:388, 10 Nov 1888
Archibald Malmaison
Dial, 5:65-6, Jul 1884
Independent, 36:747, 12 Jun 1884
Literary World, 15:194, 14 Jun 1884; 31:77, 3 Mar 1900
Beatrix Randolph
Critic, NS 1:64, 9 Feb 1884; NS 9:80, 18 Feb 1888
Dial, 4:286, Mar 1884
Independent, 36:204, 14 Feb 1884
Literary World, 15:35-6, 9 Feb 1884
Bressant
Independent, 25:957, 31 Jul 1873
Westminster Review, 100:122-3, Jul 1873
Constance, and Calbot's Rival
Critic, NS 11:180, 13 Apr 1889
David Poindexter's Disappearance, and Other Tales
Critic, NS 9:258, 26 May 1888
Independent, 40:400, 29 Mar 1888
Literary World, 19:106, 31 Mar 1888
A Dream and a Forgetting
Critic, NS 10:17, 14 Jul 1888
Dust
Critic, 3:102, 10 Mar 1883
Independent, 35:11, 8 Mar 1883
Literary World, 14:79, 10 Mar 1883
A Fool of Nature
Critic, NS 25:426, 13 Jun 1896
Dial, 21:95, 16 Aug 1896
Independent, 48:629, 7 May 1896
Literary World, 27:235, 25 Jul 1896
Fortune's Fool
Dial, 5:66, Jul 1884
Literary World, 14:361, 3 Nov 1883
Garth
Literary World, 8:30, 1 Jul 1877
The Golden Fleece
Literary World, 28:43, 6 Feb 1897
The Great Bank Robbery
Catholic World, 46:415-6, Dec 1887
Critic, NS 8:174, 8 Oct 1887
Literary World, 18:298, 17 Sep 1887
Idolatry
Galaxy, 18:856-7, Dec 1874
Independent, 26:10, 8 Oct 1874
Literary World, 5:67-8, 1 Oct 1874
Westminster Review, 103:128, Jan 1875
John Parmelee's Curse
Critic, NS 6:137, 18 Sep 1886
Dial, 7:190, Dec 1886
Love Is a Spirit
Critic, NS 26:54, 25 Jul

1896
Harper's, 93:Literary Notes, 3-4, Aug 1896
Independent, 48:1463, 29 Oct 1896
Literary World, 27:324, 3 Oct 1896

Love--or a Name
Critic, NS 4:186, 17 Oct 1885
Dial, 6:181, Nov 1885
Independent, 37:1565, 3 Dec 1885
Literary World, 16:343, 3 Oct 1885

Mr. Dunton's Invention, and Other Stories
Literary World, 27:285, 5 Sep 1896

Noble Blood
Critic, NS 2:306, 27 Dec 1884
Dial, 5:331, Apr 1885
Independent, 37:75, 15 Jan 1885
Literary World, 15:453, 13 Dec 1884

One of Those Coincidences, and Ten Other Stories
Chautauquan, 30:327, Dec 1899

Prince Saroni's Wife, and The Pearl-Shell Necklace
Critic, NS 3:54, 31 Jan 1885

The Professor's Sister
Critic, NS 11:243, 18 May 1889

Sebastian Strome
Literary World, 11:72-3, 28 Feb 1880

Section 558
Critic, NS 9:152, 31 Mar 1888
Literary World, 19:105, 31 Mar 1888

Six Cent Sam's
Independent, 45:1251, 14 Sep 1893

A Tragic Mystery
Critic, NS 8:54, 30 Jul 1887
Literary World, 18:235-6, 23 Jul 1887

The Trial of Gideon, and Countess Almara's Murder
Critic, NS 7:27, 15 Jan 1887
Literary World, 18:41-2, 5 Feb 1887

Hawthorne, Nathaniel

Doctor Grimshawe's Secret
Literary World, 14:3-4, 13 Jan 1883
Westminster Review, 119:289, Apr 1883

Septimus Felton
Galaxy, 14:569-70, Oct 1872
Literary World, 3:35-6, 1 Aug 1872
Westminster Review, 98:263, Oct 1872

Hay, Elzey [pseud.]
See Andrews, Eliza Frances.

[Hay, John Milton]

The Bread-Winners
Critic, NS 1:7, 5 Jan 1884
Dial, 4:259, Feb 1884
Harper's, 89:Literary Notes, 1, Feb 1894
Independent, 36:299-300, 6 Mar 1884
Literary World, 15:27, 26 Jan 1884
Westminster Review, 122:307-8, Jul 1884

Hayes, Augustus Allen

The Jesuit's Ring
Critic, NS 7:240, 14 May 1887
Dial, 8:66-7, Jul 1887
Independent, 39:782, 23 Jun 1887
Literary World, 18:139, 30 Apr 1887

Hayes, Henry [pseud.]
See Kirk, Ellen Warner (Olney).

Haynes, Emory James
Dollars and Duty
Critic, NS 7:165, 2 Apr 1887
Independent, 40:785, 21 Jun 1888
Literary World, 18:41, 5 Feb 1887
A Farm-House Cobweb
Harper's, 90:Literary Notes, 4, May 1895
Independent, 47:737, 30 May 1895
Literary World, 26:106, 6 Apr 1895

Hays, Mrs. Helen
Aspirations
Literary World, 17:293-4, 4 Sep 1886
A Village Maid
Critic, NS 8:245, 12 Nov 1887
Independent, 39:1424, 3 Nov 1887
Literary World, 18:349, 15 Oct 1887

Heard, John, Jr.
A Charge for France, and Other Stories
Harper's, 85:Literary Notes, 1-2, Oct 1892
Literary World, 23:278, 13 Aug 1892

Hearn, Lafcadio
Chita
Catholic World, 51:127, Apr 1890
Critic, NS 12:214, 2 Nov 1889
Harper's, 79:Literary Notes, 3, Oct 1889
Literary World, 20:481, 21 Dec 1889
In Ghostly Japan
Chautauquan, 31:534, Aug 1900
A Japanese Miscellany
Literary World, 32:207-8, 1 Dec 1901
Kotto
Independent, 54:2839-40, 27 Nov 1902
Literary World, 33:196, 1 Dec 1902
Kwaidan
Chautauquan, 40:300, Nov 1904
Critic, 45:94, Jul 1904
Independent, 57:510, 1 Sep 1904
The Romance of the Milky Way, and Other Studies and Stories
Critic, 48:222, Mar 1906
Dial, 39:276, 1 Nov 1905
Shadowings
Dial, 30:19, 1 Jan 1901
Independent, 52:2812, 22 Nov 1900
Some Chinese Ghosts
Critic, NS 7:149, 26 Mar 1887
Independent, 39:621, 19 May 1887
Literary World, 18:85-6, 19 Mar 1887
Stray Leaves from Strange Literature
Critic, NS 2:52, 2 Aug 1884
Youma
Critic, NS 14:93, 23 Aug 1890
Harper's, 81:Literary Notes, 2-3, Jul 1890
Literary World, 21:206, 21 Jun 1890

[Heaton, Ellen Marvin]
The Octagon Club
Dial, 1:93, Sep 1880
Independent, 32:12, 19 Aug 1880
Literary World, 11:310-1, 11 Sep 1880

Heaven, Louise (Palmer)
Chata and Chinita
Critic, NS 12:214, 2 Nov 1889
Dial, 10:215-6, Dec 1889

Literary World, 20:349-50, 12 Oct 1889
An Idol of Bronze
Literary World, 33:73, 1 May 1902

Heckel, George B.
See Wall, George A., and George B. Heckel.

Heermans, Forbes
Thirteen Stories of the Far West
Critic, NS 8:128, 10 Sep 1887
Literary World, 18:244-5, 6 Aug 1887

Hegan, Alice Caldwell
See Rice, Alice Caldwell (Hegan).

Helmbold, Masson Pell
Althea St. John
Independent, 38:398, 1 Apr 1886

Hemenway, Crabtree [pseud.]
See Hemenway, Myles.

[Hemenway, Myles]
Doomsday
By Crabtree Hemenway [pseud.].
Literary World, 30:75, 4 Mar 1899

Hemstreet, Charles
The Flower of the Fort
Critic, 45:284, Sep 1904

Henderson, Charles Hanford
John Percyfield
Critic, 43:285, Sep 1903
Dial, 35:68, 1 Aug 1903
Literary World, 34:122, May 1903

Henderson, Isaac
Agatha Page
Catholic World, 47:852, Sep 1888
Critic, NS 9:305-6, 23 Jun 1888
Independent, 40:1008, 9 Aug 1888
Literary World, 19:153, 12 May 1888
The Prelate
Catholic World, 43:416-8, Jun 1886
Critic, NS 5:216, 1 May 1886
Dial, 7:16, May 1886
Independent, 38:756, 17 Jun 1886
Literary World, 17:218, 26 Jun 1886

Henderson, William James
Afloat with the Flag
Harper's, 91:Literary Notes, 3, Aug 1895
Literary World, 26:217, 13 Jul 1895

Henry, Arthur
The House in the Woods
Independent, 57:510, 1 Sep 1904
Literary World, 35:166, Jun 1904
An Island Cabin
Independent, 54:1250, 22 May 1902
Lodgings in Town
Dial, 40:19-20, 1 Jan 1906
Nicholas Blood, Candidate
Chautauquan, 12:421, Dec 1890
Independent, 42:1605, 13 Nov 1900; 44:1229, 1 Sep 1892
A Princess of Arcady
Catholic World, 72:539-40, Jan 1901
Critic, 37:569, Dec 1900
Literary World, 32:11, 1 Jan 1901
The Unwritten Law
Dial, 39:115, 1 Sep 1905

Henry, Edgar [pseud.]
See Tourgée, Albion Winegar.

Henry, O. [pseud.]
See Porter, William Sydney.

Hepworth, George Hughes
! ! !
Critic, 1:178, 2 Jul 1881
Literary World, 12:246, 16 Jul 1881
The Farmer and the Lord
Independent, 48:629, 7 May 1896
Literary World, 27:172, 30 May 1896
The Queerest Man Alive, and Other Stories
Literary World, 29:102, 2 Apr 1898
They Met in Heaven
Critic, NS 21:358, 26 May 1894

Her Crime
Critic, 2:296, 4 Nov 1882
Independent, 34:13, 21 Dec 1882
Literary World, 13:373, 4 Nov 1882

Herrick, Robert
The Common Lot
Critic, 45:576, Dec 1904
Dial, 37:311, 16 Nov 1904
Independent, 57:1137-8, 17 Nov 1904; 57:1210-1, 24 Nov 1904
The Gospel of Freedom
Dial, 24:354-5, 1 Jun 1898
Independent, 50:727, 2 Jun 1898
Literary World, 29:219, 9 Jul 1898
Literature, 2:758, 2 Jul 1898
A Life for a Life
Dial, 49:39-40, 16 Jul 1910
Independent, 69:877, 20 Oct 1910
Literary Love-Letters, and Other Stories
Dial, 24:82, 1 Feb 1898
Literary World, 29:60, 19 Feb 1898
Love's Dilemmas
Critic, NS 32:843-4, Sep 1899
Dial, 27:76, 1 Aug 1899
Independent, 51:2163, 10 Aug 1899
The Man Who Wins
Critic, NS 27:249, 10 Apr 1897
Dial, 22:311, 16 May 1897
Independent, 49:949, 22 Jul 1897
The Memoirs of an American Citizen
Dial, 39:114, 1 Sep 1905
Independent, 59:450-2, 24 Aug 1905; 59:1154, 16 Nov 1905
The Real World
Critic, 40:149, Feb 1902
Dial, 32:19-20, 1 Jan 1902
Independent, 54:284, 30 Jan 1902
Literary World, 33:91, 1 Jun 1902
Together
Dial, 45:213, 1 Oct 1908
Independent, 65:263-4, 30 Jul 1908
The Web of Life
Critic, 37:551-2, Dec 1900
Dial, 29:124, 1 Sep 1900
Literary World, 31:172, 1 Sep 1900
Westminster Review, 154:475, Oct 1900

Heywood, Joseph Converse
How Will It End?
Literary World, 2:153-4, 1 Mar 1872

Hibbard, George Abiah
The Governor, and Other Stories
Critic, NS 18:5, 2 Jul 1892

Dial, 13:103, Aug 1892
Independent, 44:664, 12 May 1892
Literary World, 23:165, 7 May 1892

Iduna, and Other Stories
Critic, NS 16:52, 1 Aug 1891
Harper's, 83:Literary Notes, 4, Aug 1891
Independent, 43:1605, 29 Oct 1891

Nowadays, and Other Stories
Critic, NS 20:255, 21 Oct 1893
Dial, 15:228, 16 Oct 1893
Harper's, 87:Literary Notes, 3-4, Oct 1893
Literary World, 24:335, 7 Oct 1893

Higbee, Dora
See Geppert, Dora (Higbee).

Higginson, Ella Rhoads

The Flower That Grew in the Sand, and Other Stories
Independent, 48:1801, 31 Dec 1896

A Forest Orchid, and Other Stories
Chautauquan, 26:688, Mar 1898
Critic, NS 28:381, 18 Dec 1897
Independent, 49:1623, 9 Dec 1897
Literary World, 29:205, 25 Jun 1898

From the Land of the Snow-Pearls
Chautauquan, 26:239, Nov 1897
Critic, NS 28:266, 16 Oct 1897
Independent, 49:1546, 25 Nov 1897
Literary World, 28:298, 4 Sep 1897

Mariella of Out West
Chautauquan, 38:95, Sep 1903
Dial, 34:241-2, 1 Apr 1903
Independent, 55:157, 15 Jan 1903
Literary World, 34:11, 1 Jan 1903

Higginson, Sara Jane (Hatfield)

A Princess of Java
Critic, NS 8:244, 12 Nov 1887
Dial, 8:146, Nov 1887
Independent, 39:1424, 3 Nov 1887
Literary World, 18:315, 1 Oct 1887

Higginson, Thomas Wentworth

The Monarch of Dreams
Chautauquan, 7:442, Apr 1887
Critic, NS 7:101, 26 Feb 1887

Oldport Days
Independent, 25:1449, 20 Nov 1873

Tales of the Enchanted Islands of the Atlantic
Independent, 51:284, 26 Jan 1899

Higham, Mrs. Mary R.

The Other House
Independent, 30:12, 3 Oct 1878

Hill, Beveridge

"The Story of a Cañon"
Independent, 47:737, 30 May 1895

Hill, Francis

The Outlaws of Horseshoe Hole
Independent, 53:2786, 21 Nov 1901

Hill, Frederick Trevor

The Accomplice
Dial, 39:114, 1 Sep 1905

The Case and Exceptions

Hill, Frederick Trevor (cont.)
Critic, 38:181, Feb 1901
The Minority
Critic, 41:279, Sep 1902
Dial, 33:65, 1 Aug 1902
The Web
Dial, 36:19-20, 1 Jan 1904
Independent, 56:620, 17 Mar 1904

Hill, Grace (Livingston)
Katharine's Yesterday, and Other Christian Endeavor Stories
Chautauquan, 22:510, Jan 1896

Hill, Grace Livingston
Lone Point
Literary World, 30:7, 7 Jan 1899
An Unwilling Guest
Literary World, 33:140, 1 Sep 1902

Hill, James A.
See The Railroad.

Hillyer, Shaler Granby
The Marable Family
Literary World, 10:326, 11 Oct 1879

Hinman, Walter N.
Under the Maples
Critic, NS 11:52-3, 2 Feb 1889

His Dear Little Wife
Independent, 30:13, 1 Aug 1878

Hodder, Alfred Le Roy
The New Americans
Critic, 40:150-1, Feb 1902
Independent, 53:2650-1, 7 Nov 1901
Literary World, 32:218-9, 1 Dec 1901

[Hoes, Robert R.]
Two Broken Hearts
Literary World, 17:102, 20 Mar 1886

Hoff, J. Wallace
Some Strange Stories
Independent, 49:219, 18 Feb 1897

Hogbin, Alfred C.
Elsa
Independent, 31:11, 7 Aug 1879

Holbrook, Elizabeth
Old 'Kaskia Days
Chautauquan, 19:127, Apr 1894
Independent, 45:1453, 26 Oct 1893

Holbrook, Richard Thayer
Boys and Men
Independent, 52:1018, 26 Apr 1900
Literary World, 31:90, 1 Apr 1900

Holcombe, William Henry
A Mystery of New Orleans Solved by New Methods
Critic, NS 15:28, 17 Jan 1891
Independent, 43:457, 26 Mar 1891

[Holden, E. Goodman]
A Famous Victory
Dial, 1:33-4, Jun 1880
Literary World, 11:263, 31 Jul 1880

Holden, Mrs. Martha Everts
A String of Amber Beads
Critic, NS 21:166, 10 Mar 1894

Holland, Josiah Gilbert
Arthur Bonnicastle
Galaxy, 16:858-9, Dec 1873
Independent, 25:1225-6, 2 Oct 1873

Literary World, 4:57-8, 1 Sep 1873
The Mistress of the Manse
Catholic World, 20:430, Dec 1874
Galaxy, 18:858-9, Dec 1874
Westminster Review, 103:129, Jan 1875
Nicholas Minturn
Catholic World, 26:575, Jan 1878
Literary World, 8:98-9, 1 Nov 1877
Westminster Review, 109:134-5, Jan 1878
Sevenoaks
Catholic World, 22:430, Dec 1875
Literary World, 6:82-3, 1 Nov 1875

Holley, Marietta
Miss Richards' Boy, and Other Stories
Independent, 35:12, 18 Jan 1883
Samantha Among the Brethren
Chautauquan, 12:559, Jan 1891
Critic, NS 15:28, 17 Jan 1891
Samantha at the St. Louis Exposition
By Josiah Allen's Wife.
Independent, 58:212, 26 Jan 1905
Samantha at the World's Fair
Chautauquan, 18:761, Mar 1894
Samantha in Europe
Chautauquan, 22:767, 7 Mar 1896
Samantha vs. Josiah
Critic, 49:286, Sep 1906
Sweet Cicely
Critic, NS 5:93, 20 Feb 1886
Literary World, 17:102-3, 20 Mar 1886

Hollister, Gideon Hiram
Kinley Hollow
Independent, 34:11, 12 Oct 1882
Literary World, 13:295, 9 Sep 1882

[Holloway, Mrs. Anna]
Kate Comerford
By Teresa A. Thornet [pseud.].
Literary World, 12:43, 29 Jan 1881

Holloway, Charlotte Molyneux
A Story of Five
Critic, NS 15:322, 20 Jun 1891
Independent, 43:457, 26 Mar 1891

Holloway, Laura
See Langford, Laura Carter (Holloway).

Holm, Saxe [pseud.]
See Jackson, Helen Maria (Fiske) Hunt.

Holmes, Margret [pseud.]
See Bates, Margret Holmes (Ernsperger).

Holmes, Mary Jane (Hawes)
Doctor Hathern's Daughter
Literary World, 26:262-3, 24 Aug 1895

Holmes, Mary Jane
Gretchen
Literary World, 18:350, 15 Oct 1887
West Lawn, and the Rector of St. Marks
Literary World, 5:92, 1 Nov 1874

Holmes, Oliver Wendell
A Mortal Antipathy
Chautauquan, 6:246, Jan 1886
Critic, NS 5:31, 16 Jan 1886

Holmes, Oliver Wendell (cont.)
Independent, 38:234, 25 Feb 1886
Literary World, 17:23, 23 Jan 1886

Holmes, Richard Sill
The Maid of Honor
Independent, 64:755, 2 Apr 1908
The Victor
Independent, 65:1311, 3 Dec 1908

Holt, Henry
Sturmsee
Independent, 59:451-2, 24 Aug 1905

Hooper, Cyrus Lauron
A Cloverdale Skeleton
Critic, NS 12:186, 19 Oct 1889

[Hooper, Lucy Hamilton (Jones)]
Those Pretty St. George Girls
Independent, 35:11, 19 Jul 1883
Literary World, 14:228-9, 14 Jul 1883
The Tsar's Window
Critic, 1:91-2, 9 Apr 1881
Dial, 2:18, May 1881
Under the Tricolor
Literary World, 11:112, 27 Mar 1880

Hoover, Francis Trout
Enemies in the Rear
Independent, 47:875, 27 Jun 1895

Hopkins, Herbert Müller
The Fighting Bishop
Critic, 41:279, Sep 1902
Dial, 32:390, 1 Jun 1902
Independent, 54:1249, 22 May 1902
The Mayor of Warwick
Critic, 49:191, Aug 1906
Dial, 40:365, 1 Jun 1906
Independent, 61:218, 26 Jul 1906
Priest and Pagan
Dial, 45:90, 16 Aug 1908
The Torch
Dial, 36:120, 16 Feb 1904
Independent, 56:384-5, 18 Feb 1904
Literary World, 34:350, Dec 1903

Hopkins, Margaret Sutton (Briscoe)
Jimty, and Others
Critic, NS 29:249, 9 Apr 1898
Harper's, 96:Literary Notes, 3-4, Mar 1898
Independent, 50:521, 21 Apr 1898
Literary World, 29:60, 19 Feb 1898
Links in a Chain
Chautauquan, 19:646, Aug 1894
Critic, NS 21:374, 2 Jun 1894
Literary World, 25:166, 2 Jun 1894
"Perchance to Dream," and Other Stories
Critic, NS 19:44, 28 Jan 1893
Independent, 45:507, 13 Apr 1893
Literary World, 24:57, 25 Feb 1893
The Sixth Sense, and Other Stories
Harper's, 99:Literary Notes, 3, Sep 1899
Independent, 51:1957-8, 20 Jul 1899
Literary World, 30:235, 22 Jul 1899

Hopkins, Mark
The World's Verdict
Critic, NS 9:114, 10 Mar 1888
Independent, 40:625, 17

May 1888
Literary World, 19:91, 17 Mar 1888

Hopkins, Pauline Bradford (Mackie)
Mademoiselle de Berny
Critic, NS 29:165, 5 Mar 1898
Independent, 50:222, 17 Feb 1898
Literary World, 29:27, 22 Jan 1898
The Voice in the Desert
Critic, 43:380, Oct 1903
Dial, 35:65-6, 1 Aug 1903
Literary World, 34:152-3, Jun 1903
The Washingtonians
Critic, 40:374, Apr 1902
Dial, 33:64, 1 Aug 1902
Literary World, 33:44, 1 Mar 1902
Ye Lyttle Salem Maide
Dial, 25:305, 1 Nov 1898
Independent, 50:422, 11 Aug 1898
Literary World, 29:403, 26 Nov 1898

Hoppin, Augustus
A Fashionable Sufferer
Critic, 3:254-5, 2 Jun 1883
Independent, 35:11, 19 Jul 1883
Literary World, 14:211, 30 Jun 1883
Two Compton Boys
Chautauquan, 5:181, Dec 1884
Independent, 36:1419, 6 Nov 1884

Hoppin, Emily Howland
From Out of the Past
Critic, NS 20:70, 29 Jul 1893
Dial, 15:93, 16 Aug 1893
Under the Corsican
Independent, 47:971, 18 Jul 1895
Literary World, 26:105, 6 Apr 1895

Horton, George
Constantine
Dial, 23:286-7, 16 Nov 1897
The Edge of Hazard
Critic, 48:475, May 1906
A Fair Brigand
Dial, 27:174, 16 Sep 1899
Independent, 51:2629-30, 28 Sep 1899
Literary World, 30:235, 22 Jul 1899
In Argolis
Critic, 41:582, Dec 1902
Like Another Helen
Critic, 38:438, May 1901
The Long Straight Road
Critic, 41:582, Dec 1902
Independent, 55:329-30, 5 Feb 1903
The Tempting of Father Anthony
Critic, 40:179, Feb 1902
Dial, 31:369, 16 Nov 1901
Literary World, 33:44, 1 Mar 1902

[Hosea, Lucy (Klinck) Rice]
Eastward
Critic, NS 14:233, 8 Nov 1890

Hosmer, George Washington
"As We Went Marching On"
Critic, NS 4:209, 31 Oct 1885
Independent, 37:1488, 19 Nov 1885
Literary World, 16:405, 14 Nov 1885

Hosmer, James Kendall
How Thankful Was Bewitched
Critic, NS 23:457, 22 Jun 1895
Independent, 47:53, 10 Jan 1895
Literary World, 26:6,

Hosmer, James Kendall (cont.)
12 Jan 1895

Hotchkiss, Chauncey Crafts
A Colonial Free-Lance
Critic, NS 24:229, 12 Oct 1895; NS 28:155, 18 Sep 1897
Dial, 23:285, 16 Nov 1897
Literary World, 28:464, 11 Dec 1897
For a Maiden Brave
Dial, 34:243, 1 Apr 1903
Independent, 55:628, 12 Mar 1903
In Defiance of the King
Independent, 47:1543, 14 Nov 1895; 47:1579, 21 Nov 1895
Literary World, 27:203, 27 Jun 1896
The Strength of the Weak
Dial, 32:246, 1 Apr 1902
Literary World, 33:91, 1 Jun 1902

Hough, Emerson
54-40 or Fight
Dial, 46:264, 16 Apr 1909
Independent, 66:374-5, 18 Feb 1909
Heart's Desire
Dial, 40:155, 1 Mar 1906
The Law of the Land
Critic, 45:577, Dec 1904
Dial, 38:128, 16 Feb 1905
Literary World, 35:380, Dec 1904
The Mississippi Bubble
Dial, 32:386, 1 Jun 1902
Independent, 54:1611, 3 Jul 1902
The Singing Mouse Stories
Critic, NS, 25:444, 20 Jun 1896
The Story of the Cowboy
Chautauquan, 26:347, Dec 1897
Independent, 49:1626, 9 Dec 1897

House, Edward Howard
The Midnight Warning, and Other Stories
Critic, NS 19:95, 18 Feb 1893
Harper's, 86:Literary Notes, 3, Feb 1893
Independent, 45:507, 13 Apr 1893
Yone Santo, a Child of Japan
Critic, NS 11:50, 2 Feb 1889

How He Reached the White House
Independent, 36:1546, 4 Dec 1884

How Is Your Man?
Literary World, 12:454, 3 Dec 1881

Howard, Blanche Willis
See Teuffel, Blanche Willis (Howard) von.

Howe, Edgar Watson
The Confession of John Whitlock
Critic, NS 16:247, 7 Nov 1891
A Man Story
Independent, 41:402, 28 Mar 1889
Literary World, 19:387, 10 Nov 1888
A Moonlight Boy
Catholic World, 43:853, Sep 1886
Critic, NS 6:14, 10 Jul 1886
Independent, 38:1204, 23 Sep 1886
Literary World, 17:234-5, 10 Jul 1886
The Mystery of the Locks
Critic, NS 3:86-7, 21 Feb 1885
Independent, 37:426-7, 2 Apr 1885
Literary World, 16:40, 7 Feb 1885

The Story of a Country Town
Critic, NS 2:158-9, 4 Oct 1884
Dial, 5:205, Dec 1884
Independent, 36:1419, 6 Nov 1884
Literary World, 15:352-3, 18 Oct 1884

Howe, Julia Ward
See A Week Away from Time.

Howe, Maud
See Elliott, Maud (Howe).

Howell, Jeanne M.
A Common Mistake
Literary World, 25:219, 14 Jul 1894

Howells, William Dean
Annie Kilburn
Chautauquan, 9:434, Apr 1889
Critic, NS 11:63-4, 9 Feb 1889
Harper's, 78:Literary Notes, 1-2, Jan 1889; 83:Literary Notes, 4, Jun 1891
Independent, 41:401, 28 Mar 1889; 43:645, 30 Apr 1891
Literary World, 20:35, 2 Feb 1889
April Hopes
Catholic World, 46:557, Jan 1888
Critic, NS 9:17, 14 Jan 1888
Dial, 8:267-8, Mar 1888
Harper's, 76:Literary Notes, 1-2, Dec 1887; 83:Literary Notes, 3, Aug 1891
Literary World, 19:20, 21 Jan 1888
Westminster Review, 129:124, Jan 1888
A Chance Acquaintance
Galaxy, 16:139-40, Jul 1873
Independent, 25:682, 29 May 1873
Literary World, 4:13, 1 Jun 1873
The Coast of Bohemia
Critic, NS 22:2, 7 Jul 1894
Dial, 15:340-1, 1 Dec 1893
Harper's, 88:Literary Notes, 4, Jan 1894
Literary World, 24:468, 30 Dec 1893
The Day of Their Wedding
Critic, NS 25:307, 2 May 1896
Dial, 20:335, 1 Jun 1896
Harper's, 92:Literary Notes, 1, Feb 1896
Independent, 48:422, 26 Mar 1896
Literary World, 27:154, 16 May 1896
Doctor Breen's Practice
Critic, 1:350-1, 17 Dec 1881
Dial, 2:214-6, Jan 1882
Literary World, 12:484, 17 Dec 1881
A Fearful Responsibility, and Other Stories
Critic, 1:191, 16 Jul 1881; NS 9:80, 18 Feb 1888
Dial, 2:85, Aug 1881
Literary World, 12:296, 27 Aug 1881
Fennel and Rue
Dial, 44:350-1, 1 Jun 1908
Independent, 64:925, 23 Apr 1908
The Flight of Pony Baker
Critic, 41:582, Dec 1902
A Foregone Conclusion
Independent, 26:7-8, 26 Nov 1874
A Hazard of New Fortunes
Catholic World, 51:119-22, Apr 1890
Critic, NS 13:13-4, 11 Jan 1890

Howells, William Dean (cont.)
Harper's, 80:Literary Notes, 1-2, Feb 1890; 83:Literary Notes, 4, Jun 1891
Independent, 42:257, 20 Feb 1890; 43:645, 30 Apr 1891
Literary World, 21:20-1, 18 Jan 1890
Westminster Review, 134:89-90, Jul 1890

An Imperative Duty
Critic, NS 17:34, 16 Jan 1892
Harper's, 83:Literary Notes, 2, Nov 1891
Independent, 43:1921, 24 Dec 1891
Westminster Review, 137:224, Jan 1892

Indian Summer
Catholic World, 43:130, Apr 1886
Chautauquan, 6:485, May 1886
Dial, 6:303, Mar 1886
Independent, 38:366, 25 Mar 1886
Westminster Review, 126 (NS 70):295, Oct 1886

The Kentons
Dial, 32:387-8, 1 Jun 1902
Independent, 54:1247-8, 22 May 1902; 54:2770, 20 Nov 1902
Literary World, 33:84, 1 Jun 1902

The Lady of the Aroostook
Independent, 31:10, 29 May 1879
Literary World, 10:86-7, 15 Mar 1879

The Landlord at Lion's Head
Critic, NS 27:420, 19 Jun 1897
Dial, 22:310, 16 May 1897
Harper's, 95:Literary Notes, 3, Jun 1897
Independent, 49:650, 20 May 1897; 49:719, 3 Jun 1897
Literary World, 28:262-3, 7 Aug 1897
Westminster Review, 147:714, Jun 1897

Letters Home
Dial, 35:263-4, 16 Oct 1903
Literary World, 34:307, Nov 1903

A Little Swiss Sojourn
Harper's, 86:Literary Notes, 3, Jan 1893

The Minister's Charge
Catholic World, 44:702-5, Feb 1887
Critic, NS 7:63, 5 Feb 1887
Independent, 39:270, 3 Mar 1887
Literary World, 18:4-5, 8 Jan 1887
Westminster Review, 128:262, May 1887

Miss Bellard's Inspiration
Critic, 47:452, Nov 1905
Dial, 39:115, 1 Sep 1905
Independent, 59:208, 27 Jul 1905; 59:1152, 16 Nov 1905

A Modern Instance
Critic, 2:278-9, 21 Oct 1882
Dial, 3:106-7, Oct 1882
Independent, 34:9, 30 Nov 1882
Literary World, 13:373, 4 Nov 1882
Westminster Review, 119:138, Jan 1883

An Open-Eyed Conspiracy
Dial, 23:284, 16 Nov 1897
Harper's, 95:Literary Notes, 2-3, Nov 1897
Independent, 49:1505, 18 Nov 1897; 49:1546, 25 Nov 1897; 50:1424, 17 Nov 1898
Literary World, 28:355, 16 Oct 1897
Westminster Review,

149:593, May 1898

A Pair of Patient Lovers

Critic, 39:182, Aug 1901
Independent, 53:1746, 25 Jul 1901
Literary World, 32:107, 1 Jul 1901

A Parting and a Meeting

Critic, NS 25:405, 6 Jun 1896
Dial, 20:335, 1 Jun 1896
Harper's, 93:Literary Notes, 3, Jul 1896
Independent, 48:805, 11 Jun 1896
Literary World, 27:204, 27 Jun 1896

Private Theatricals

Independent, 28:8-9, 18 May 1876

The Quality of Mercy

Critic, NS 17:262, 7 May 1892
Dial, 13:102, Aug 1892
Harper's, 85:Literary Notes, 2-3, Jun 1892
Independent, 44:664, 12 May 1892: 44:1599, 10 Nov 1892
Literary World, 23:149, 23 Apr 1892
Westminster Review, 137:464-5, Apr 1892

Questionable Shapes

Critic, 43:374-5, Oct 1903
Independent, 55:1932-3, 13 Aug 1903
Literary World, 34:168, Jul 1903

Ragged Lady

Dial, 27:20-1, 1 Jul 1899
Harper's, 98:Literary Notes, 1-2, Apr 1899
Independent, 51:2231, 17 Aug 1899; 51:3171, 23 Nov 1899
Literary World, 30:131, 29 Apr 1899

The Rise of Silas Lapham

Catholic World, 42:274-80, Nov 1885
Dial, 6:122, Sep 1885
Independent, 37:1294-5, 8 Oct 1885
Literary World, 16:299, 5 Sep 1885
Westminster Review, 125 (NS 69):303, Jan 1886

The Shadow of a Dream

Critic, NS 14:44, 26 Jul 1890
Dial, 11:93, Aug 1890
Harper's, 81:Literary Notes, 1, Jul 1890
Independent, 42:1133, 14 Aug 1890
Literary World, 21:221, 5 Jul 1890

The Son of Royal Langbrith

Critic, 46:184, Feb 1905
Dial, 37:310-1, 16 Nov 1904
Independent, 57:1136, 17 Nov 1904; 57:1270-1, 1 Dec 1904
Literary World, 35:378, Dec 1904

The Story of a Play

Dial, 25:21-2, 1 Jul 1898
Harper's, 97:Literary Notes, 1, Aug 1898
Independent, 50:262-3, 28 Jul 1898
Literary World, 29:243, 6 Aug 1898
Literature, 3:18, 9 Jul 1898

Their Silver Wedding Journey

Independent, 52:257-8, 25 Jan 1900
Literary World, 31:10, 6 Jan 1900

Their Wedding Journey

Critic, 2:213, 12 Aug 1882; NS 9:152, 31 Mar 1888
Galaxy, 13:426-8, Mar 1872
Literary World, 2:124, 1 Jan 1872; 19:73, 3 Mar 1888; 25:422, 1 Dec 1894
Westminster Review,

Howells, William Dean (cont.)
143:226-9, Feb 1895
Through the Eye of the Needle
Independent, 62:1207-8, 23 May 1907
A Traveler from Altruria
Critic, NS 21:434, 30 Jun 1894
Harper's, 89:Literary Notes, 1, Sep 1894
Literary World, 25:201, 30 Jun 1894
The Undiscovered Country
Dial, 1:52-3, Jul 1880
Independent, 32:12, 8 Jul 1880
Literary World, 11:274-5, 14 Aug 1880
A Woman's Reason
Critic, NS 9:4, 7 Jan 1888
Dial, 4:126-9, Oct 1883
Independent, 35:9-10, 6 Dec 1883
Literary World, 14:350, 20 Oct 1883
The World of Chance
Critic, NS 20:135-6, 26 Aug 1893
Dial, 14:339-40, 1 Jun 1893
Harper's, 86:Literary Notes, 1, May 1893
Independent, 45:1154, 24 Aug 1893
Literary World, 24:108, 8 Apr 1893
Westminster Review, 139:584, May 1893

[Howland, Frances Louise (Morse)]
Cliveden
By Kenyon West [pseud.].
Literary World, 34:152, Jun 1903

Hubbard, Elbert
No Enemy but Himself
Chautauquan, 20:253, Nov 1894
Literary World, 25:279, 8 Sep 1894
Time and Chance
Independent, 54:225-6, 23 Jan 1902
Literary World, 33:180, 1 Nov 1902

Hubbell, Walter
The Great Amherst Mystery
Catholic World, 47:268-9, May 1888
Critic, NS 9:192, 21 Apr 1888
Independent, 40:625, 17 May 1888
Literary World, 19:123, 14 Apr 1888

Hudson, William Cadwalader
An American Cavalier
Independent, 49:980, 25 Jul 1897
Literary World, 28:244, 24 Jul 1897
The Diamond Button
By Barclay North [pseud.].
Critic, NS 11:307, 22 Jun 1889
The Dugdale Millions
Critic, NS 20:6, 1 Jul 1893
The Man with a Thumb
Critic, NS 15:166-7, 28 Mar 1891
Vivier of Vivier, Longman & Company, Bankers
Critic, NS 14:95, 23 Aug 1890

[Hughes, Mrs. Reginald]
Oxley
By Lyndon [pseud.].
Independent, 25:492, 17 Apr 1873
Literary World, 3:185-6, 1 May 1873

Hughes, Rupert
The Real New York
Literary World, 35:284, Oct 1904
The Whirlwind
Dial, 34:89, 1 Feb 1903

Zal
Dial, 40:20, 1 Jan 1906

Hulbert, Archer Butler
The Queen of Quelparte
Chautauquan, 36:328-9, Dec 1902

Humphrey, Frances A.
The Children of Old Park's Tavern
Critic, NS 6:101, 28 Aug 1886
Harper's, 73:Literary Notes, 2-3, Sep 1886

Humphrey, Frank Pope
A New England Cactus, and Other Tales
Critic, NS 19:61, 4 Feb 1893
Independent, 44:1834, 22 Dec 1892
Literary World, 23:408, 19 Nov 1892
Westminster Review, 138:222-3, Aug 1892

Humphrey, Mrs. Frank Pope
Phoebe Tilson
Literary World, 29:455, 24 Dec 1898

Huneker, James Gibbons
Melomaniacs
Critic, 41:479, Nov 1902
Independent, 54:935, 17 Apr 1902
Visionaries
Critic, 48:381, Apr 1906

Huntington, Faye [pseud.]
See Foster, Theodosia Maria (Toll).

Huntley, Stanley
Mr. and Mrs. Spoopendyke
Literary World, 12:295-6, 27 Aug 1881
Spoopendyke Sketches
Independent, 51:2502-3, 14 Sep 1899

Hurd, Grace Marguerite
The Bennett Twins
Critic, 38:182, Feb 1901
Independent, 52:2639-40, 1 Nov 1900

Hurd, Marion Kent
See Stokely, Edith (Keeley), and Marion Kent Hurd.

Hurlbut, Ella Childs
Mrs. Clift-Crosby's Niece
Literary World, 24:258, 12 Aug 1893

Hutson, Charles Woodward
The Story of Beryl
Critic, NS 11:65, 9 Feb 1899
Literary World, 19:365, 27 Oct 1888

Hutton, Laurence
A Boy I Knew, Four Dogs, and Some More Dogs
Harper's, 97:Literary Notes, 1, Jul 1898

I., J. T.
See Irving, John Treat.

Inasmuch
Independent, 50:638, 1 Sep 1898

Ingersoll, Ernest
The Silver Caves
Independent, 42:1720, 4 Dec 1890

Ingersoll, Robert Green
For Her Daily Bread
Catholic World, 47:414, Jun 1888

Inman, Henry
The Old Santa Fe Trail
Literature, 2:322-3, 19 Mar 1898
The Ranch on the Oxhide
Chautauquan, 28:526, Feb 1899

Innsley, Owen [pseud.]
See Jennison, Lucy White.

Ireland, Mary Eliza (Haines)
Timothy
Critic, 2:269, 7 Oct 1882
What I Told Dorcas
Literary World, 27:47, 8 Feb 1896

[Irving, John Treat]
The Van Gelder Papers, and Other Sketches
Ed. J. T. I.
Literary World, 18:251-2, 6 Aug 1887
Westminster Review, 128:784, Sep 1887

Irwin, William Henry
See Burgess, Gelett, and Will Irwin; also Field, Charles Kellogg, and Will H. Irwin.

Isaacs, Abram Samuel
Stories from the Rabbis
Literary World, 24:179, 3 Jun 1893

Isham, Frederic Stewart
Black Friday
Independent, 57:1214, 24 Nov 1904
The Strollers
Independent, 54:1610, 3 Jul 1902
Under the Rose
Dial, 35:66, 1 Aug 1903

J. S. of Dale [pseud.]
See Stimson, Frederic Jesup.

[Jackson, Edward Payson]
A Demigod
Catholic World, 44:563-4, Jan 1887
Dial, 7:190, Dec 1886
Harper's, 73:Literary Notes, 2, Nov 1886; 74:Literary Notes, 3, Jan 1887
Independent, 39:270, 3 Mar 1887
Literary World, 18:11, 8 Jan 1887

Jackson, George Anson
The Son of a Prophet
Catholic World, 58:600, Jan 1894
Chautauquan, 18:761, Mar 1894
Dial, 15:341, 1 Dec 1893
Literary World, 24:451, 16 Dec 1893

Jackson, Helen Maria (Fiske) Hunt
Between Whiles
Chautauquan, 7:634, Jul 1887
Critic, NS 7:307, 18 Jun 1887
Dial, 8:46, Jun 1887
Literary World, 18:168, 28 May 1887
Hetty's Strange History
Literary World, 8:45-6, 1 Aug 1877
Mercy Philbrick's Choice
Independent, 28:9, 19 Oct 1876
Literary World, 7:79-80, 1 Nov 1876
Nelly's Silver Mine
Independent, 30:9, 21 Nov 1878
Ramona
Catholic World, 43:130-1, Apr 1886
Chautauquan, 5:369, Mar 1885; 32:328-9, Dec 1900
Critic, NS 2:291, 20 Dec 1884; 37:568, Dec 1900
Dial, 5:328, Apr 1885
Literary World, 15:448-9, 13 Dec 1884; 31:227, 1 Nov 1900
Saxe Holm's Stories
Catholic World, 18:574-5, Jan 1874
Critic, NS 4:170, 10 Oct

1885
Independent, 26:9-10, 19 Feb 1874
Literary World, 4:121, 1 Jan 1874
Saxe Holm's Stories, Second Series
Independent, 30:12, 8 Aug 1876
Literary World, 9:57, 1 Sep 1878
Zeph
Chautauquan, 6:485-6, May 1886
Critic, NS 5:67, 6 Feb 1886
Independent, 38:463, 15 Apr 1886
Literary World, 17:55, 20 Feb 1886
Westminster Review, 137:708, Jun 1892

Jackson, Margaret (Doyle)
The Horse-Leech's Daughters
Critic, 44:562, Jun 1904
Independent, 57:511, 1 Sep 1904

Jacobi, Mary (Putnam)
Found and Lost
Critic, NS 23:457, 22 Jun 1895
Stories and Sketches
Independent, 64:319, 6 Feb 1908

Jacobus, Russell P.
An Escape from Philistia
Critic, NS 20:69, 29 Jul 1893
Literary World, 24:193, 17 Jun 1893

James, Henry
The Ambassadors
Critic, 44:146-50, Feb 1904
Dial, 36:22, 1 Jan 1904
Literary World, 34:348, Dec 1903
The American
Galaxy, 24:135-8, Jul 1877
Literary World, 8:29-30, 1 Jul 1877
Westminster Review, 113:138, Jan 1880
The American Scene
Independent, 63:95-6, 11 Jul 1907
The Aspern Papers
Critic, NS 11:61-2, 9 Feb 1889
The Author of Beltraffio and others
Critic, NS 3:206, 2 May 1885
Independent, 37:459, 9 Apr 1885
Literary World, 16:102, 21 Mar 1885
The Awkward Age
Critic, NS 32:754-7, Aug 1889
Dial, 27:21, 1 Jul 1899
Harper's, 98:Literary Notes, 2, Apr 1899
Independent, 51:2163, 10 Aug 1899
Literary World, 30:227, 22 Jul 1899
The Better Sort
Dial, 34:374, 1 Jun 1903
Independent, 55:741, 26 Mar 1903; 55:2740, 19 Nov 1903
Literary World, 34:73, Apr 1903
The Bostonians
Catholic World, 43:560-1, Jul 1886
Critic, NS 5:191-2, 17 Apr 1886
Dial, 7:14-5, May 1886
Independent, 38:495, 22 Apr 1886
Literary World, 17:198, 12 Jun 1886
Confidence
Literary World, 11:119-20, 10 Apr 1880
Daisy Miller
Harper's, 86:Literary Notes, 1-2, Dec 1892
Embarrassments

James, Henry (cont.)
Chautauquan, 23:783, Sep 1896
Critic, NS 26:52, 25 Jul 1896
Independent, 48:1037, 30 Jul 1896

The Europeans
Independent, 30:9, 21 Nov 1878
Literary World, 10:28, 18 Jan 1879

The Finer Grain
Independent, 69:1091, 17 Nov 1910

The Golden Bowl
Independent, 58:153-4, 19 Jan 1905

In the Cage
Critic, NS 30:523, Dec 1898
Independent, 50:1424, 17 Nov 1898; 50:1791, 15 Dec 1898
Literature, 3:158-9, 20 Aug 1898

An International Episode
Harper's, 86:Literary Notes, 2, Dec 1892

Julia Bride
Independent, 68:51, 6 Jan 1910

The Lesson of the Master [and others]
Literary World, 23:110, 26 Mar 1892

A London Life, and Other Tales
Catholic World, 49:688-92, Aug 1889
Critic, NS 12:3, 6 Jul 1889
Independent, 41:1185, 12 Sep 1889
Literary World, 20:178-9, 25 May 1889

The Madonna of the Future, and Other Tales
Westminster Review, 113:138, Jan 1880

The Other House
Chautauquan, 24:630-1, Feb 1897
Critic, NS 26:335, 28 Nov 1896
Dial, 22:22, 1 Jan 1897
Independent, 48:1693, 10 Dec 1896
Literary World, 27:476-7, 26 Dec 1896

A Passionate Pilgrim, and Other Tales
Independent, 27:10, 25 Mar 1875
Literary World, 5:157, 1 Mar 1875

The Portrait of a Lady
Catholic World, 34:716-7, Feb 1882
Critic, 1:333-4, 3 Dec 1881; 3:27, 27 Jan 1883
Dial, 2:214-6, Jan 1882
Literary World, 12:473-4, 17 Dec 1881

The Princess Casamassima
Catholic World, 44:554-9, Jan 1887
Critic, NS 7:51, 29 Jan 1887
Dial, 7:189, Dec 1886
Independent, 38:1665, 23 Dec 1886
Literary World, 18:5, 8 Jan 1887
Westminster Review, 127 (NS 71):264-5, Jan 1887

The Private Life [and others]
Critic, NS 20:236, 14 Oct 1893
Harper's, 87:Literary Notes, 4, Sep 1893
Independent, 45:1453, 26 Oct 1893
Literary World, 24:291, 9 Sep 1893

The Real Thing, and Other Tales
Catholic World, 57:284, May 1893
Chautauquan, 17:485-6, Jul 1893
Critic, NS 19:230, 15 Apr 1893

Dial, 14:341, 1 Jun 1893
Independent, 45:1154, 24 Aug 1893
Literary World, 24:113, 8 Apr 1893

The Reverberator
Catholic World, 48:402-5, Dec 1888
Critic, NS 10:123, 15 Sep 1888
Independent, 40:1609, 13 Dec 1888
Literary World, 19:313, 29 Sep 1888
Westminster Review, 130:251, Aug 1888

Roderick Hudson
Westminster Review, 112:298, Oct 1879

The Sacred Fount
Critic, 38:368-70, Apr 1901
Independent, 53:619-20, 14 Mar 1901

The Siege of London [and others]
Critic, 3:91-2, 3 Mar 1883
Dial, 3:280, Apr 1883
Literary World, 14:90, 24 Mar 1883

The Soft Side
Catholic World, 73:249, May 1901
Independent, 52:2638, 1 Nov 1900; 52:2803-4, 22 Nov 1900

The Spoils of Poynton
Critic, NS 27:301, 1 May 1897
Dial, 22:311, 16 May 1897
Independent, 49:980, 29 Jul 1897
Literary World, 28:126-7, 17 Apr 1897

Tales of Three Cities
Critic, NS 2:304, 27 Dec 1884
Dial, 5:206-7, Dec 1884

Terminations
Critic, NS 24:67-8, 3 Aug 1895
Harper's, 91:Literary Notes, 3, Sep 1895
Independent, 47:1579, 21 Nov 1895
Literary World, 26:218, 13 Jul 1895

The Tragic Muse
Chautauquan, 11:649, Aug 1890
Critic, NS 13:250, 17 May 1890; NS 14:55, 2 Aug 1890
Dial, 11:92-3, Aug 1890
Literary World, 21:231-2, 19 Jul 1890

The Two Magics [and others]
Chautauquan, 28:630, Mar 1899
Critic, NS 30:523, Dec 1898
Independent, 51:73, 5 Jan 1899
Literary World, 29:367, 12 Nov 1898
Literature, 3:351, 15 Oct 1898

Washington Square
Dial, 1:195-6, Jan 1881
Harper's, 90:Literary Notes, 2-3, Apr 1895
Independent, 47:737, 30 May 1895
Literary World, 12:10, 1 Jan 1881

Watch and Ward
Independent, 30:13, 11 Jul 1878
Literary World, 9:47, 1 Aug 1878

What Maisie Knew
Critic, NS 29:21, 8 Jan 1898
Independent, 49:1660, 16 Dec 1897
Literary World, 28:454-5, 11 Dec 1897
Literature, 1:19, 23 Oct 1897

The Wheel of Time [and others]
Critic, NS 20:253, 21 Oct 1893
Dial, 15:344, 1 Dec 1893

James, Henry (cont.)
Harper's, 87:Literary Notes, 3, Oct 1893
Literary World, 24:367, 4 Nov 1893
The Wings of the Dove
Critic, 41:409-14, Nov 1902
Independent, 54:2711-2, 13 Nov 1902

[James, Samuel Humphreys]
A Prince of Good Fellows
Ed. N. Warrington Crabtrie [pseud.].
Critic, NS 15:287, 16 May 1891

Jamison, Cecilia Viets (Dakin) Hamilton
Lady Jane
Catholic World, 54:458-60, Dec 1891
Chautauquan, 14:383, Dec 1891
Something To Do
Literary World, 1:181-2, 1 May 1871
The Story of an Enthusiast
Critic, NS 9:4, 7 Jan 1888
Dial, 8:268, Mar 1888
Independent, 39:1692, 29 Dec 1887
Woven of Many Threads
Literary World, 1:135, 1 Feb 1871

Janney, Lucy N.
Alton-Thorpe
Literary World, 12:42-3, 29 Jan 1881

[Janvier, Margaret Thomson]
Clover Beach
By Margaret Vandergrift [pseud.].
Independent, 32:10, 16 Dec 1880
Ways and Means
By Margaret Vandergrift [pseud.].
Critic, NS 6:248, 20 Nov 1886
Literary World, 18:139, 30 Apr 1887

Janvier, Thomas Allibone
The Aztec Treasure-House
Dial, 11:241, Dec 1890
Harper's, 80:Literary Notes, 4, May 1890
Independent, 42:1414, 9 Oct 1890
Literary World, 21:268-9, 16 Aug 1890
Color Studies
Critic, NS 4:209, 31 Oct 1885; NS 16:105, 29 Aug 1891
Dial, 6:182, Nov 1885
Independent, 38:398, 1 Apr 1886
In Great Waters
Critic, 40:179, Feb 1902
Independent, 54:286, 30 Jan 1902
Literary World, 33:27, 1 Feb 1902
In Old New York
Critic, NS 22:441-2, 29 Dec 1894
Harper's, 89:Literary Notes, 4, Oct 1894
Literary World, 25:325, 6 Oct 1894
In the Sargasso Sea
Critic, NS 30:87-8, Jul-Aug 1898
Dial, 25:306, 1 Nov 1898
Harper's, 97:Literary Notes, 1, Sep 1898
Independent, 50:421, 11 Aug 1898; 67:1507, 30 Dec 1909
Literary World, 29:243, 6 Aug 1898
Literature, 3:207-8, 3 Sep 1898
Legends of Mexico
Independent, 69:482, 1 Sep 1910
The Passing of Thomas [and others]
Independent, 52:2397, 4 Oct 1900

Stories of Old New Spain
Chautauquan, 13:555, Jul 1891
Critic, NS 15:319-20, 20 Jun 1891
Dial, 12:51, Jun 1891
Independent, 43:1218, 13 Aug 1891
The Uncle of an Angel, and Other Stories
Critic, NS 16:152, 26 Sep 1891
Harper's, 83:Literary Notes, 3, Oct 1891

Jay, W. L. M. [pseud.]
See Woodruff, Julia Louisa Matilda (Curtiss).

Jefferson-Davis, Varina Ann
See Davis, Varina Anne Jefferson.

Jeffrey, Rosa Vertner (Griffith) Johnson
Marah
Independent, 36:523, 24 Apr 1884

[Jelley, Symmes M.]
Shadowed to Europe
By "Le Jemlys" [pseud.].
Literary World, 16:158-9, 2 May 1885

Jenkins, Katharine
Stories
Independent, 44:664, 12 May 1892

Jenkins, Stephen
A Princess and Another
Dial, 44:351, 1 Jun 1908

[Jennison, Lucy White]
Penelope's Web
By Owen Innsly [pseud.].
Literary World, 21:468, 6 Dec 1890

Jerome, Ferris
High-Water-Mark
Literary World, 10:251, 2 Aug 1879

Jessop, George Henry
Gerald Ffrench's Friends
Critic, NS 13:295, 14 Jun 1890
Dial, 10:217, Dec 1889
Literary World, 21:4, 4 Jan 1890

Jessup, George H.
See also Matthews, Brander, and George H. Jessup; and Matthews, Brander, With My Friends.

Jewett, Sarah Orne
Betty Leicester
Chautauquan, 11:126, Apr 1890
Literary World, 20:460, 7 Dec 1889
Country By-Ways
Critic, 1:304-5, 5 Nov 1881
Independent, 34:11, 30 Mar 1882
Literary World, 12:419-20, 19 Nov 1881
A Country Doctor
Critic, NS 2:16, 12 Jul 1884
Dial, 5:66, Jul 1884
Independent, 36:1164, 11 Sep 1884
Literary World, 15:211, 28 Jun 1884
The Country of the Pointed Firs
Critic, NS 27:110, 13 Feb 1897
Independent, 48:1651, 3 Dec 1896
Literary World, 27:457, 12 Dec 1896
Deephaven
Catholic World, 44:561-2, Jan 1887
Literary World, 8:9, 1 Jun 1877
The King of Folly Island, and Other People
Critic, NS 10:54, 4 Aug

Jewett, Sarah Orne (cont.)
1888
Independent, 40:817, 28 Jun 1888
Literary World, 19:365, 27 Oct 1888
The Life of Nancy
Chautauquan, 22:380, Dec 1895
Independent, 47:1689, 12 Dec 1895
Literary World, 26:388, 16 Nov 1895
A Marsh Island
Critic, NS 4:64, 8 Aug 1885
Dial, 6:123, Sep 1885
Independent, 37:1200, 17 Sep 1885
Literary World, 16:191-2, 30 May 1885
The Mate of the Daylight, and Friends Ashore
Dial, 4:230, Jan 1884
Independent, 35:11, 27 Dec 1883
Literary World, 15:12, 12 Jan 1884
A Native of Winby, and Other Tales
Critic, NS 21:165, 10 Mar 1894
Independent, 45:1653-4, 7 Dec 1893
Literary World, 24:423, 2 Dec 1893
Old Friends and New
Literary World, 10:381, 22 Nov 1879
The Queen's Twin, and Other Stories
Critic, 36:170, Feb 1900
Independent, 52:324, 1 Feb 1900
Literary World, 31:29, 20 Jan 1900
Strangers and Wayfarers
Catholic World, 53:613, Jul 1891
Chautauquan, 12:826, Mar 1891
Critic, NS 14:335, 27 Dec 1890
Independent, 43:164, 29 Jan 1891
Tales of New England
Chautauquan, 11:649, Aug 1890
Critic, NS 13:269, 31 May 1890
Independent, 42:1061, 31 Jul 1890
The Tory Lover
Chautauquan, 34:321, Dec 1901
Critic, 39:469-70, Nov 1901
Dial, 31:365, 16 Nov 1901
Independent, 53:2717, 14 Nov 1901
Literary World, 32:218, 1 Dec 1901
The White Heron, and Other Stories
Catholic World, 44:413-4, Dec 1886
Critic, NS 6:172, 9 Oct 1886
Literary World, 17:388, 13 Nov 1886

John Van Buren, Politician
Dial, 39:114-5, 1 Sep 1905

Johnes, Winifred Wallace (Tinker)
Memoirs of a Little Girl
Critic, NS 26:58, 25 Jul 1896

Johnson, Elizabeth Winthrop
Two Loyal Lovers
Critic, NS 15:322, 20 Jun 1891
Independent, 43:164, 29 Jan 1891
Yesterday
Literary World, 13:230, 15 Jul 1882

Johnson, Helen Louise (Kendrick)
Raleigh Westgate
Critic, NS 11:117, 9 Mar

1889
Dial, 9:293, Mar 1889
Independent, 41:401, 28 Mar 1889

Johnson, Owen McMahon
The Arrows of the Almighty
Critic, 38:438-9, May 1901
Dial, 31:26, 1 Jul 1901
Independent, 53:1260-1, 30 May 1901; 53:2777, 21 Nov 1901
Literary World, 32:91-2, 1 Jun 1901
The Humming Bird
Independent, 69:363, 18 Aug 1910
In the Name of Liberty
Chautauquan, 43:96, Mar 1906
Critic, 46:381, Apr 1905

Johnson, P. Demarest
Claudius, the Cowboy of Ramapo Valley
Critic, NS 23:158, 2 Mar 1895

Johnson, Virginia Wales
The Calderwood Secret
Literary World, 6:57-8, 1 Oct 1875
An English "Daisy Miller"
Independent, 34:12, 15 Jun 1882
The Fainalls of Tipton
Critic, NS 2:63, 9 Aug 1884
Dial, 5:110, Sep 1884
Independent, 36:1159, 2 Oct 1884; 38:1237, 30 Sep 1886
Literary World, 15:263-4, 9 Aug 1884
The House of the Musician
Catholic World, 45:836-7, Sep 1887
Literary World, 18:236, 23 Jul 1887
Joseph the Jew
Galaxy, 17:425-6, Mar 1874
Miss Nancy's Pilgrimage
Literary World, 8:46, 1 Aug 1877
The Neptune Vase
Critic, 1:234, 27 Aug 1881
Literary World, 12:311-2, 10 Sep 1881
Travels of an American Owl
Literary World, 1:101, 1 Dec 1870
The Treasure Tower
Critic, NS 14:30, 19 Jul 1890
Tulip Place
Catholic World, 43:424-5, Jun 1886
Critic, NS 5:216, 1 May 1886
Two Old Cats
Critic, 2:227, 26 Aug 1882
Literary World, 13:201, 17 Jun 1882

Johnson, William Henry
King or Knave, Which Wins?
Chautauquan, 29:389, Jul 1899
Dial, 27:174, 16 Sep 1899
Literary World, 30:203, 24 Jun 1899
The King's Henchman
Dial, 25:22, 1 Jul 1898
Literary World, 29:204, 25 Jun 1898

Johnston, Alma (Calder)
Miriam's Heritage
Independent, 30:12, 8 Aug 1878
Literary World, 9:47, 1 Aug 1878

Johnston, Annie (Fellows)
Asa Holmes at the Cross Roads
Literary World, 33:124, 1 Aug 1902
Joel: A Boy of Galilee
Independent, 47:1650, 5 Dec 1895

Johnston, Henry Phelps
Dr. Congalton's Legacy
Independent, 48:630, 7 May 1898

[Johnston, James Wesley]
Dwellers in Gotham
By Annan Dale [pseud.].
Literary World, 30:75, 4 Mar 1899

Johnston, Mary
Audrey
Catholic World, 75:410-1, Jun 1902
Critic, 40:260, Mar 1902
Dial, 32:246, 1 Apr 1902
Independent, 54:696-7, 20 Mar 1902; 54:2771, 20 Nov 1902
Literary World, 33:35-6, 1 Mar 1902
Lewis Rand
Catholic World, 88:259-60, Nov 1908
Dial, 45:294-5, 1 Nov 1908
Independent, 65:1182, 19 Nov 1908; 65:1464, 17 Dec 1908; 65:1563-4, 24 Dec 1908
Prisoners of Hope
Critic, NS 30:532, Dec 1898
Chautauquan, 28:421, Jan 1899
Dial, 25:304-5, 1 Nov 1898
Independent, 50:1942, 29 Dec 1898
Literary World, 29:353, 29 Oct 1898
Sir Mortimer
Critic, 45:94-5, Jul 1904
Dial, 36:368, 1 Jun 1904
Independent, 56:1143-4, 19 May 1904
Literary World, 35:145, May 1904
To Have and To Hold
Critic, 36:351-2, Apr 1900
Dial, 29:23, 1 Jul 1900
Independent, 52:667-8, 15 Mar 1900; 52:2803, 22 Nov 1900
Literary World, 31:69-70, 3 Mar 1900

Johnston, Richard Malcolm
The Chronicles of Mr. Bill Williams
Independent, 44:1229, 1 Sep 1892
Dukesborough Tales
By Philemon Perch [pseud.].
Literary World, 2:55-6, 1 Sep 1871
Little Ike Templin, and Other Stories
Chautauquan, 21:126, Apr 1895
Independent, 47:53, 10 Jan 1895
Mr. Absalom Billingslea, and Other Georgia Folks
Catholic World, 46:857, Mar 1888
Critic, NS 9:126, 17 Mar 1888
Harper's, 75:Literary Notes, 3, Nov 1887
Independent, 40:400, 29 Mar 1888
Literary World, 19:38-9, 4 Feb 1888
Mr. Billy Downs and His Likes
Chautauquan, 16:508, Jan 1893
Mr. Fortner's Marital Claims, and Other Stories
Catholic World, 56:271, Nov 1892
Chautauquan, 16:380, Dec 1892
Critic, NS 19:180-1, 25 Mar 1893
Independent, 44:1563, 3 Nov 1892
Literary World, 23:329-30, 24 Sep 1892
Ogeechee Cross-Firings
Critic, NS 12:185, 19 Oct 1889
Literary World, 20:353, 12 Oct 1889

Old Mark Langston
Independent, 36:523, 24 Apr 1884
Literary World, 15:217, 28 Jun 1884
Old Times in Middle Georgia
Chautauquan, 26:574, Feb 1898
Critic, NS 28:340-1, 4 Dec 1897
Dial, 23:287, 16 Nov 1897
Independent, 49:1585, 2 Dec 1897
Literary World, 28:377, 30 Oct 1897
Pearce Amerson's Will
Dial, 25:22, 1 Jul 1898
Independent, 50:192, 21 Jul 1898; 50:1424, 17 Nov 1898
The Primes and Their Neighbors
Chautauquan, 13:685, Aug 1891
Critic, NS 15:308, 13 Jun 1891
Dial, 12:50, Jun 1891
Independent, 43:607, 23 Apr 1891
Widow Guthrie
Chautauquan, 12:826, Mar 1891
Catholic World, 52:936-7, Mar 1891
Critic, NS 15:134, 14 Mar 1891
Independent, 43:164, 29 Jan 1891

Jones, Alice Ilgenfritz
Beatrice of Bayou Têche
Independent, 47:1689, 12 Dec 1895
Literary World, 26:458, 14 Dec 1895
Gabriel Praed's Castle
Dial, 37:314, 16 Nov 1904

Jones, Charles C., Jr.
Negro Myths from the Georgia Coast
Critic, NS 9:292, 16 Jun 1888
Dial, 9:47-8, Jun 1888
Literary World, 19:150, 12 May 1888

Jones, Charles Henry
Davault's Mills
Independent, 28:9, 6 Apr 1876

Jones, Ira Lafayette
Beoni the Sphinx
Independent, 50:565, 25 Aug 1898

Jones, M. P.
Rebekah
Critic, NS 12:161, 5 Oct 1889

Jones, Randolph
The Buccaneers
Literary World, 8:180-1, 1 Mar 1878

Jordan, David Starr
Matka and Kotik
Literary World, 28:297, 4 Sep 1897

Jordan, Elizabeth Garver
May Iverson
Literary World, 35:381, Dec 1904
Tales of Destiny
Critic, 41:279, Sep 1902
Dial, 33:67, 1 Aug 1902
Independent, 54:2139, 4 Sep 1902
Literary World, 33:127, 1 Aug 1902
Tales of the City Room
Critic, NS 29:265-6, 16 Apr 1898
Literary World, 29:141, 30 Apr 1898
Tales of the Cloister
Catholic World, 74:263, Nov 1901
Critic, 39:474, Nov 1901
Dial, 31:370, 16 Nov 1901
Independent, 53:2363, 3

Jordan, Elizabeth Garver (cont.)
Oct 1901
Literary World, 33:9, 1 Jan 1902

Jordan, Kate
A Circle in the Sand
Independent, 51:562-3, 23 Feb 1899
Literary World, 30:75, 4 Mar 1899
The Other House
Critic, NS 18:274, 19 Nov 1892
Literary World, 23:375, 22 Oct 1892
Time the Comedian
Critic, 47:188, Dec 1905

Julian, Harry
Love Ventures
Critic, NS 10:219, 3 Nov 1888

Justice, Maibelle Heicks (Monroe)
Love Affairs of a Worldly Man
Critic, NS 21:272, 21 Apr 1894

Kane, James Johnson
Ilian
Dial, 9:293, Mar 1889

Kaufman, Reginald Wright
Jarvis of Harvard
Literary World, 33:27, 1 Feb 1902
Miss Frances Baird, Detective
Independent, 61:697, 20 Sep 1906
The Things That Are Caesar's
Dial, 33:331, 16 Nov 1902

________, and Edward Childs Carpenter
The Chasm
Dial, 36:22, 1 Jan 1904

Keeler, Ralph
Vagabond Adventures
Literary World, 1:109, 1 Dec 1870

Keenan, Henry Francis
The Aliens
Catholic World, 43:276-7, May 1886
Critic, NS 5:181, 10 Apr 1886
Dial, 7:15, May 1886
Independent, 38:1013, 12 Aug 1886
Literary World, 17:131-2, 17 Apr 1886
The Iron Game
Catholic World, 53:610, Jul 1891
Chautauquan, 13:552, Jul 1891
Critic, NS 15:264, 16 May 1891
Independent, 43:1218, 13 Aug 1891
The Money-Makers
Catholic World, 40:142, Apr 1885
Dial, 5:330, Apr 1885
Independent, 37:459, 9 Apr 1885
Literary World, 16:55, 21 Feb 1885
Trajan
Critic, NS 3:148, 28 Mar 1885
Dial, 5:330, Apr 1885
Independent, 37:619, 14 May 1885
Literary World, 16:133, 18 Apr 1885

Keith, Alyn Yates [pseud.]
See Morris, Eugenia Laura (Tuttle).

Kelley, Adelaide (Skeel), and William H. Brearley
King Washington
Dial, 24:296, 1 May 1898
Independent, 49:1662, 16 Dec 1897
Literary World, 29:44-5,

5 Feb 1898

Kelley, James Douglas Jerrold
A Desperate Chance
Critic, NS 5:194, 17 Apr 1886
Literary World, 17:183, 29 May 1886

Kellogg, Elijah
The Elm Island Stories
Literary World, 1:25, 1 Jul 1870

Kellogg, Margaret Augusta
Leo Dayne
Literary World, 30:409, 25 Nov 1899

Kelly, Florence (Finch)
The Delafield Affair
Independent, 66:1032, 13 May 1909

Kelly, Myra
The Isle of Dreams
Independent, 62:1268, 30 May 1907
Little Citizens
Critic, 46:189, Feb 1905
Literary World, 35:327-8, Nov 1904

Kennedy, Sara Beaumont (Cannon)
Joscelyn Cheshire
Dial, 31:33, 1 Jul 1901

Kennedy, Walker
In the Dwellings of Science
Critic, NS 21:108, 17 Feb 1894
Dial, 16:20, 1 Jan 1894
Literary World, 25:54-5, 24 Feb 1894
Javan Ben Seir
Independent, 50:194, 21 Jul 1898

Kent, James
The Johnson Manor
Galaxy, 24:708-9, Nov 1877
Sibyl Spencer
Independent, 30:12, 26 Dec 1878

Kenyon, Ellen E.
See Warner, Ellen E. (Kenyon).

Ker, David
Into Unknown Seas
Harper's, 73:Literary Notes, 2, Oct 1886

Kerr, Alvah Milton
The Diamond Key
Independent, 62:1526, 27 Jun 1907
An Honest Lawyer
Independent, 44:881, 23 Jun 1892

Kerr, Orpheus C. [pseud.]
See Newell, Robert Henry.

Kester, Paul
Tales of the Real Gypsy
Independent, 49:1662, 16 Dec 1897
Literary World, 29:27-8, 22 Jan 1898

Kester, Vaughan
The Fortunes of the Landrays
Critic, 47:578, Dec 1905
Dial, 39:309, 16 Nov 1905
The Manager of the B. & A.
Critic, 39:278, Sep 1901
Independent, 53:2242, 19 Sep 1901
Literary World, 32:181, 1 Nov 1901

Keyser, Harriette A.
On the Borderland
Independent, 34:11, 3 Aug 1882
Literary World, 13:253, 29 Jul 1882
Westminster Review, 122:617, Oct 1884
Thorns in Your Side

Keyser, Harriette A. (cont.)
Independent, 36:779, 19 Jun 1884
Literary World, 15:264, 9 Aug 1884

Kildare, Owen Frawley
The Good of the Wicked
Independent, 57:1216, 24 Nov 1904
The Wisdom of the Simple
Critic, 48:381, Apr 1906

Kilpatrick, Mary
See Donnelly, Eleanor, and Mary Kilpatrick.

[Kimball, Annie Lydia (Mc-Phail)]
At Daybreak
By A. Stirling [pseud.].
Literary World, 15:265, 9 Aug 1884

Kimball, George Selwyn
Jay Gould Harmon
Independent, 59:1346, 7 Dec 1905

King, Anna (Eichberg)
See Lane, Anna (Eichberg) King.

King, Basil
See King, William Benjamin Basil.

King, Charles
An Apache Princess
Dial, 35:265, 16 Oct 1903
An Army Portia
Critic, NS 19:45, 28 Jan 1893
An Army Wife
Critic, NS 26:117, 22 Aug 1896
Independent, 48:1038, 30 Jul 1896
Between the Lines
Critic, NS 12:98, 31 Aug 1889
Harper's, 78:Literary Notes, 3-4, May 1889
Literary World, 20:241, 20 Jul 1889
By Land and by Sea
Ed. Charles King.
Critic, NS 16:182, 10 Oct 1891
Cadet Days
Critic, NS 22:38, 21 Jul 1894
Harper's, 88:Literary Notes, 3-4, May 1894
Literary World, 25:186, 16 Jun 1894
Campaigning with Crook, and Stories of Army Life
Harper's, 81:Literary Notes, 2-3, Sep 1890
Independent, 42:1760, 11 Dec 1890
Captain Blake
Critic, NS 16:182, 10 Oct 1891
Independent, 43:1142, 30 Jul 1891
Captain Close, and Sergeant Croesus
Literary World, 26:202, 29 Jun 1895
Captain Dreams, and Other Stories
Ed. Charles King.
Independent, 47:1076, 8 Aug 1895
The Colonel's Christmas Dinner
Ed. Charles King.
Critic, NS 15:167, 28 Mar 1891
Independent, 42:1760, 11 Dec 1890
The Colonel's Daughter
Dial, 3:256, Mar 1883
Independent, 35:11, 17 May 1883
Literary World, 14:90-1, 24 Mar 1883
A Daughter of the Sioux
Literary World, 34:123, May 1903
The Deserter, and From the Ranks
Critic, NS 10:6, 7 Jul 1888

Literary World, 19:220, 7 Jul 1888

Foes in Ambush
Critic, NS 22:38, 21 Jul 1894
Literary World, 24:239, 29 Jul 1893

From School to Battlefield
Independent, 50:1787, 15 Dec 1898

A Garrison Tangle
Independent, 48:1697, 10 Dec 1896; 49:1546, 25 Nov 1897

The General's Double
Critic, NS 29:164, 5 Mar 1898
Literary World, 29:10, 8 Jan 1898
Literature, 2:621, 28 May 1898

In Spite of Foes
Literary World, 32:143, 1 Sep 1901

An Initial Experience, and Other Stories
Ed. Charles King.
Chautauquan, 19:646, Aug 1894
Literary World, 25:267, 25 Aug 1894

The Iron Brigade
Critic, 41:582, Dec 1902

"Laramie"
Critic, NS 12:99, 31 Aug 1889
Literary World, 20:242, 20 Jul 1889

Marion's Faith
Critic, NS 5:306, 19 Jun 1886
Literary World, 17:316, 18 Sep 1886

Ray's Recruit
Independent, 50:729, 2 Jun 1898

A Soldier's Secret
Critic, NS 19:45, 28 Jan 1893

A Soldier's Trial
Catholic World, 84:116-7, Oct 1906
Independent, 59:1542, 28 Dec 1905

Starlight Ranch, and Other Stories
Independent, 42:561, 24 Apr 1890
Literary World, 21:105, 29 Mar 1890; 26:267, 24 Aug 1895

The Story of Fort Frayne
Literary World, 26:233, 27 Jul 1895

Sunset Pass
Critic, NS 16:128, 12 Sep 1891
Independent, 42:1842, 25 Dec 1890
Literary World, 27:477, 26 Dec 1896

A Tame Surrender
Critic, NS 27:426, 19 Jun 1897
Dial, 22:23, 1 Jan 1897

To the Front
Independent, 64:974, 30 Apr 1908

Trials of a Staff Officer
Independent, 43:1218, 13 Aug 1891

Trooper Ross and Signal Butte
Literary World, 26:459, 14 Dec 1895

Trumpeter Fred
Critic, NS 26:57, 25 Jul 1896
Literary World, 27:219-20, 11 Jul 1896

Two Soldiers, and Dunraven Ranch
Critic, NS 15:179, 4 Apr 1891
Independent, 43:607, 23 Apr 1891

Under Fire
Literary World, 26:76, 9 Mar 1895

Waring's Peril
Critic, NS 22:38, 21 Jul 1894
Literary World, 25:106, 7 Apr 1894

Warrior Gap
Literary World, 29:76, 5

King, Charles (cont.)
Mar 1898
A War-Time Wooing
Critic, NS 10:125, 15 Sep 1888
Independent, 40:1644, 20 Dec 1888
Literary World, 19:300, 15 Sep 1888
A Wounded Name
Independent, 50:192, 21 Jul 1898

King, Edward Smith
The Gentle Savage
Critic, 3:157, 7 Apr 1883
Literary World, 14:123-4, 21 Apr 1883
The Golden Spike
Critic, NS 5:31-2, 16 Jan 1886
Literary World, 17:167, 15 May 1886
Joseph Zalmonah
Literary World, 23:291, 9 Sep 1893
Kentucky's Love
Literary World, 3:139, 1 Feb 1873

King, Grace Elizabeth
Balcony Stories
Chautauquan, 18:382, Dec 1893
Critic, NS 20:316, 18 Nov 1893
Literary World, 24:369, 4 Nov 1893
Monsieur Motte
Independent, 40:1073, 23 Aug 1888
Literary World, 19:187, 9 Jun 1888
Tales of a Time and Place
Critic, NS 19:180, 25 Mar 1893
Harper's, 84:Literary Notes, 4, May 1892
Independent, 44:664, 12 May 1892
Literary World, 23:229, 2 Jul 1892

King, Stanton Henry
Dog-Watches at Sea
Critic, 38:567, Jun 1901

King, Thorold [pseud.]
See Gatchell, Charles.

King, Toler [pseud.]
See Fox, Mrs. Emily.

King, William Benjamin Basil
The Giant's Strength
Dial, 43:64, 1 Aug 1907
In the Garden of Charity
Literary World, 34:75-6, Apr 1903
Let Not Man Put Asunder
Dial, 32:19, 1 Jan 1902
Independent, 54:994, 24 Apr 1902
Literary World, 33:19, 1 Feb 1902
The Steps of Honor
Dial, 37:210, 1 Oct 1904
Independent, 57:569, 8 Sep 1904
Literary World, 35:166, Jun 1904

King, William Harvey
My Smoking-Room Companions
Literary World, 31:78, 3 Mar 1900

The King's Men
By Robert Grant, John Boyle O'Reilly, J. S. of Dale, and John T. Wheelwright.
Chautauquan, 5:121, Nov 1884
Critic, NS 2:135-6, 20 Sep 1884
Dial, 5:207, Dec 1884
Independent, 36:1159, 2 Oct 1884
Literary World, 15:287, 6 Sep 1884

Kingsley, Florence (Morse)
Lead, Kindly Light
Critic, 45:185, Aug 1904
The Needle's Eye

Literary World, 33:172, 1 Nov 1902
Paul, a Herald of the Cross
Independent, 49:1148, 2 Sep 1897
The Resurrection of Miss Cynthia
Independent, 59:1344, 7 Dec 1905
Stephen, a Soldier of the Cross
Critic, NS 26:259, 31 Oct 1896
Those Brewster Children
Independent, 68:767, 7 Apr 1910

Kinkead, Eleanor Talbot
The Courage of Blackburn Blair
Dial, 44:44, 16 Jan 1908
Florida Alexander, a Kentucky Girl
Literary World, 30:38, 4 Feb 1899
The Invisible Bond
Critic, 49:190, Aug 1906
Dial, 41:115-6, 1 Sep 1906
Independent, 61:213, 26 Jul 1906
Young Greer of Kentucky
Literary World, 26:453-4, 14 Dec 1895

Kinzie, Mrs. John H.
See Kinzie, Juliette Augusta (Magill).

Kinzie, Juliette Augusta (Magill)
Mark Logan
Critic, NS 8:138, 17 Sep 1887
Literary World, 18:369, 29 Oct 1887

Kip, William Fargo
Would You Have Left Her?
Literary World, 20:76, 2 Mar 1889

Kipling, Rudyard
See Balestier, Charles Wolcott, and Rudyard Kipling.

Kirk, Ellen Warner (Olney)
The Apology of Ayliffe
Independent, 57:1095, 10 Nov 1904
Better Times Stories
Critic, NS 11:40, 26 Jan 1889
Literary World, 20:12-3, 5 Jan 1889
Ciphers
Critic, NS 17:181, 26 Mar 1892
Independent, 43:1921, 24 Dec 1891
Clare and Bébé
Literary World, 10:214, 5 Jul 1879
A Daughter of Eve
Catholic World, 49:115, Apr 1889
Critic, NS 11:166, 6 Apr 1889
Independent, 41:706, 30 May 1889
Literary World, 20:109, 30 Mar 1889
Good-Bye, Proud World
Dial, 35:157[221], 1 Oct 1903
His Heart's Desire
Independent, 30:9, 14 Nov 1878
Literary World, 10:214, 5 Jul 1879
A Lesson in Love
Critic, 1:166, 18 Jun 1881
Dial, 2:41, Jun 1881
Love in Idleness
Galaxy, 23:711-2, May 1877
Literary World, 8:46, 1 Aug 1877
Marcia
Independent, 62:1268-9, 30 May 1907
A Midsummer Madness
Independent, 36:971, 31 Jul 1884

Kirk, Ellen Warner (Olney) (cont.)
Literary World, 15:226, 12 Jul 1884
Our Lady Vanity
Independent, 53:2596, 31 Oct 1901
Literary World, 33:8, 1 Jan 1902
Queen Money
Catholic World, 47:415-6, Jun 1888
Critic, NS 9:90, 25 Feb 1888
Independent, 40:400, 29 Mar 1888
Literary World, 19:59, 18 Feb 1888
A Remedy for Love
Critic, 42:381, Apr 1903
Independent, 54:2539, 23 Oct 1902
A Revolutionary Love-Story, and The High Steeple of St. Chrysostom's
Literary World, 29:342, 15 Oct 1898
Sons and Daughters
Critic, NS 7:306, 18 Jun 1887; NS 10:6, 7 Jul 1888
Literary World, 18:53, 19 Feb 1887
The Story of Lawrence Garthe
Critic, NS 23:437, 15 Jun 1895
The Story of Margaret Kent By Henry Hayes [pseud.].
Critic, NS 5:43, 23 Jan 1886
Independent, 38:234, 25 Feb 1886
Literary World, 17:39-40, 6 Feb 1886
Through Winding Ways
Literary World, 11:11, 3 Jan 1880
Walford
Critic, NS 14:240, 8 Nov 1890; NS 15:27, 17 Jan 1891
Independent, 43:164, 29 Jan 1891

Kirk, Hyland Clare
When Age Grows Young
Catholic World, 48:405-6, Dec 1888
Critic, NS 11:4, 5 Jan 1889

Kirkland, Joseph
The Captain of Company K
Critic, NS 16:261, 14 Nov 1891
The McVeys
Catholic World, 48:267-9, Nov 1888
Critic, NS 10:244, 17 Nov 1888
Dial, 9:161, Nov 1888
Independent, 41:177, 7 Feb 1889
Literary World, 19:382-3, 10 Nov 1888
Zury, the Meanest Man in Spring County
Critic, NS 7:254, 21 May 1887; NS 8:3, 2 Jul 1887
Dial, 8:67, Jul 1887
Independent, 39:1134, 8 Sep 1887
Literary World, 18:169, 28 May 1887

Kitchell, Eva Paine
See Wood, Frances Hartson, and Eva Paine Kitchell.

Kitchin, William Copeman
Paoli, the Last of the Missionaries
Critic, NS 14:335-6, 27 Dec 1890
The Story of Sodom
Critic, NS 17:52, 23 Jan 1892
Independent, 44:21, 7 Jan 1892

Knapp, Adeline
The Well in the Desert
Dial, 45:458, 16 Dec 1908

Knight, Charles D. [pseud.]
See Gilbert, Mrs. R. L.

Knowlton, J. A.
Txleama
Catholic World, 57:430-1, May 1893
Independent, 45:1018, 27 Jul 1893

Knox, Adeline (Trafton)
An American Girl Abroad
Literary World, 2:171, 1 Apr 1872
Dorothy's Experience
Critic, NS 15:109, 28 Feb 1891
His Inheritance
Independent, 30:13, 8 Aug 1878
Literary World, 9:31, 1 Jul 1878
Katherine Earle
Independent, 26:10, 8 Oct 1874
Literary World, 5:76, 1 Oct 1874

Knox, Thomas Wallace
John Boyd's Adventures
Chautauquan, 19:247, May 1894
The Lost Army
Chautauquan, 20:511, Jan 1895
The Voyage of the Vivian
Chautauquan, 5:182, Dec 1884
Critic, NS 2:136, 20 Sep 1884

[Kouns, Nathan Chapman]
Arius the Libyan
Chautauquan, 4:436, Apr 1884
Dial, 4:229-30, Jan 1884
Independent, 35:11, 22 Nov 1883
Literary World, 14:455, 15 Dec 1883
Dorcas, the Daughter of Faustina
Chautauquan, 5:369, Mar 1885
Independent, 37:75, 15 Jan 1885
Literary World, 15:453-4, 13 Dec 1884

Kramer, Harold Morton
The Castle of Dawn
Dial, 45:296, 1 Nov 1908
Independent, 64:974, 30 Apr 1908
The Chrysalis
Dial, 46:48-9, 16 Jul 1909

[Krausé, Lyda Farrington]
Christine's Inspiration
By Barbara Yechton [pseud.].
Critic, NS 17:340, 18 Jun 1892
Fortune's Boats
By Barbara Yechton [pseud.].
Chautauquan, 33:544, Aug 1901
Independent, 52:2934, 6 Dec 1900
Literary World, 31:268, 1 Dec 1900
A Little Turning Aside
By Barbara Yechton [pseud.].
Independent, 51:634-5, 2 Mar 1899
Literary World, 29:437, 10 Dec 1898
A Lovable Crank
By Barbara Yechton [pseud.].
Independent, 50:990, 6 Oct 1898
We Ten
By Barbara Yechton [pseud.].
Chautauquan, 25:111, Apr 1897
Literary World, 28:12, 9 Jan 1897

[Krout, Caroline Virginia]
Knights in Fustian
By Caroline Brown [pseud.].
Dial, 29:24, 1 Jul 1900
Independent, 52:1389, 7 Jun 1900
Literary World, 31:140, 1 Jul 1900

Lamb, Martha Joan Reade (Nash)
Spicy
Literary World, 3:121, 1 Jan 1873

Lancaster, Albert Edmund
See Vincent, Frank, and Albert Edmund Lancaster.

Lane, Anna (Eichberg) King
Brown's Retreat, and Other Stories
Critic, NS 22:136, 1 Sep 1894
Independent, 45:1453, 26 Oct 1893
Literary World, 24:209, 1 Jul 1893
Kitwyk Stories
Critic, NS 24:441, 28 Dec 1895
Dial, 19:385, 16 Dec 1895

Lane, Elinor (Macartney)
All for the Love of a Lady
Critic, 49:190-1, Aug 1906
Independent, 60:1377-8, 7 Jun 1906
Katrine
Independent, 66:760-1, 8 Apr 1909
Mills of God
Critic, 39:182, Aug 1901
Dial, 31:370, 16 Nov 1901
Independent, 53:1926-7, 15 Aug 1901
Literary World, 32:133, 1 Sep 1901
Nancy Stair
Critic, 45:190, Aug 1904
Independent, 57:509-10, 1 Sep 1904
Literary World, 35:201, Jul 1904

Langford, Laura Carter (Holloway)
The Woman's Story
Critic, NS 11:258, 25 May 1889

Lanza, Clara (Hammond)
Mr. Perkins' Daughter
Critic, 1:121-2, 7 May 1881
A Modern Marriage
Critic, NS 14:217-8, 1 Nov 1890
Independent, 42:1344, 25 Sep 1890
Westminster Review, 135:708, Jun 1891
A Righteous Apostate
Independent, 35:10, 27 Dec 1883
Literary World, 14:422, 1 Dec 1883
Tit for Tat
Independent, 32:12, 23 Sep 1880

_______, and James Clarence Harvey
Scarabaeus
Literary World, 24:41, 11 Feb 1893
See also Hammond, William A., and Clara Hammond Lanza.

Larned, Walter Cranston
Arnaud's Master-Piece
Dial, 23:286, 16 Nov 1897
Rembrandt
Dial, 26:246, 1 Apr 1899
Literary World, 30:75, 4 Mar 1899

Lathrop, George Parsons
Afterglow
Literary World, 8:30, 1 Jul 1877
An Echo of Passion
Critic, 2:201, 29 Jul 1882
Dial, 3:38, Jun 1882
Independent, 37:396, 26 Mar 1885
Literary World, 13:164, 20 May 1882
Westminster Review, 123

(NS 67):292, Jan 1885

Gold of Pleasure

Critic, NS 16:53, 1 Aug 1891; 19:60, 4 Feb 1893

Independent, 44:1835, 22 Dec 1892

In the Distance

Critic, NS 3:208, 2 May 1885

Dial, 2:293, Apr 1882

Independent, 34:11, 6 Apr 1882; 37:751, 11 Jun 1885

Literary World, 13:111, 8 Apr 1882

Newport

Critic, NS 1:134, 12 Mar 1884

Independent, 36:523, 24 Apr 1884

Literary World, 15:87-8, 22 Mar 1884

Somebody Else

Independent, 30:12, 22 Aug 1878

Literary World, 9:56, 1 Sep 1878

True, and Other Stories

Critic, NS 3:17, 10 Jan 1885

Independent, 37:75, 15 Jan 1885

Literary World, 16:308, 5 Sep 1885

Two Sides of a Story

Critic, NS 12:42, 27 Jul 1889

Independent, 41:1399, 24 Oct 1889

Literary World, 20:289, 31 Aug 1889

Would You Kill Him?

Chautauquan, 10:757, Mar 1890

Critic, NS 13:26, 18 Jan 1890

Harper's, 80:Literary Notes, 2, Jan 1890

Independent, 41:1577, 28 Nov 1889

Literary World, 20:458, 7 Dec 1889

Westminster Review, 134:216-8, Aug 1890

________, and Rose Hawthorne Lathrop

A Story of Courage

Critic, NS 23:378, 25 May 1895

Lathrop, Rose (Hawthorne)

A Transplanted Rose

Literary World, 13:401, 18 Nov 1881

See also Lathrop, George Parsons, and Rose Hawthorne Lathrop.

[Latimer, Elizabeth (Wormeley)]

My Wife and My Wife's Sister

Critic, 2:7, 14 Jan 1882

Dial, 2:220, Jan 1882

Literary World, 12:453, 3 Dec 1881

The Prince Incognito

Catholic World, 75:690-1, Aug 1902

Critic, 43:91, Jul 1903

Dial, 32:391, 1 Jun 1902

Princess Amélie

Critic, 2:253, 23 Sep 1882

Dial, 4:93, Aug 1883

Independent, 35:11, 23 Aug 1883

Literary World, 14:211, 30 Jun 1883

Salvage

Dial, 1:92-3, Sep 1880

Literary World, 11:280, 14 Aug 1880

Laughlin, Clara Elizabeth

Felicity

Dial, 42:315, 16 May 1907

Independent, 62:1267-8, 30 May 1907

Miladi

Critic, 44:381, Apr 1904

[Lawrence, Elizabeth]
A Heroic Sinner and the Pilgrim Spinster
By Gorham Silva [pseud.].
Independent, 45:1018, 27 Jul 1893
The Worm That Ceased To Turn
By Gorham Silva [pseud.].
Independent, 47:1579, 21 Nov 1895

Lawrence, Margaret Oliver (Woods)
Marion Graham
Literary World, 21:207, 21 Jun 1890

Lawson, Thomas William
Friday the Thirteenth
Independent, 62:798-9, 4 Apr 1907

Leahy, William Augustine
The Incendiary
Literary World, 28:228, 10 Jul 1897

[Leavitt, John McDowell]
Alicia
Literary World, 30:39, 4 Feb 1899
The American Cardinal
Literary World, 2:18-9, 1 Jul 1871

Le Cato, Nathaniel James Walter
Tom Burton
Critic, NS 10:102, 1 Sep 1888

Lecky, Walter [pseud.]
See McDermott, William A.

Le Conte, Caroline Eaton
The Statue in the Air
Critic, NS 29:76, 29 Jan 1898
Literary World, 28:377, 30 Oct 1897

Lee, Albert (1858-?)
The Gentleman Pensioner
Dial, 28:400-1, 16 May 1900
Literary World, 31:119, 1 Jun 1900
The Key of the Holy House
Dial, 26:245, 1 Apr 1899
Literary World, 30:93, 18 Mar 1899

Lee, Albert (1868-1946)
Four for a Fortune
Dial, 25:306, 1 Nov 1898
Harper's, 97:Literary Notes, 2, Jun 1898
Independent, 50:764, 9 Jun 1898
Literary World, 29:219, 9 Jul 1898
He, She, & They
Harper's, 99:Literary Notes, 4, Nov 1899
Independent, 51:3298, 7 Dec 1899
Literary World, 30:409, 25 Nov 1899
King Stork of the Netherlands
Dial, 30:111, 16 Feb 1901

Lee, Franklyn Warner
Senator Lars Erikson
Independent, 43:1844, 10 Dec 1891

Lee, Jennette Barbour (Perry)
Kate Wetherill
Critic, 37:85, Jul 1900
Independent, 52:1204, 17 May 1900
A Pillar of Salt
Critic, 38:377, Apr 1901
Literary World, 32:59, 1 Apr 1901
The Son of a Fiddler
Critic, 40:556, Jun 1902
Independent, 54:1843, 31 Jul 1902
Literary World, 33:76, 1 May 1902
Uncle William
Independent, 61:582-3,

6 Sep 1906

Lee, Margaret
A Brighton Night and A Brooklyn Bachelor
Critic, NS 23:203, 16 Mar 1895; NS 16:17, 11 Jul 1891
Divorce
Catholic World, 49:692-5, Aug 1889
Critic, 3:195, 28 Apr 1883
Independent, 35:43-4, 11 Jan 1883; 41:929, 18 Jul 1889
Literary World, 14:39, 10 Feb 1883; 20:163, 11 May 1889
Westminster Review, 134:93-4, Jul 1890
Lorimer and Wife
Critic, 1:203, 16 Jul 1881
Literary World, 12:280, 13 Aug 1881

Lee, Mary Catherine (Jenkins)
In the Cheering-Up Business
Critic, NS 15:310, 13 Jan 1891
Independent, 43:608, 23 Apr 1891
Lois Mallet's Dangerous Gift
Literary World, 34:35, Feb 1903
A Quaker Girl of Nantucket
Chautauquan, 9:625, Jul 1889
Critic, NS 11:155, 30 Mar 1889
Literary World, 20:113, 30 Mar 1889
A Soulless Singer
Critic, NS 23:460, 22 Jun 1895
Independent, 47:1170, 29 Aug 1895
Literary World, 26:170, 1 Jun 1895

Lee, Minnie Mary [pseud.]
See Wood, Julia Amanda (Sargent).

Lefevre, Edwin
The Golden Flood
Critic, 47:285, Sep 1905
Independent, 59:450-1, 24 Aug 1905
Sampson Rock of Wall Street
Dial, 42:378-9, 16 Jun 1907
Independent, 62:799, 4 Apr 1907
Wall Street Stories
Critic, 40:179, Feb 1902
Independent, 54:579, 6 Mar 1902

Leffingwell, Alsop
The Mystery of Bar Harbor
Critic, NS 8:128, 10 Sep 1887

Leggett, Mortimer Dormer
A Dream of a Modest Prophet
Critic, NS 15:167, 28 Mar 1891
Independent, 43:165, 29 Jan 1891; 43:456, 26 Mar 1891

Leland, Charles Godfrey
The Algonquin Legends of New England
Critic, NS 2:290, 20 Dec 1884
Literary World, 15:371, 1 Nov 1884

[Lennan, Katie]
Elmwood
Catholic World, 23:143-4, Apr 1876

Leonard, Mary Hall
A Code of Honor
Independent, 49:980, 29 Jul 1897

[Lesley, J. Peter]
Paul Dreifuss, His Holiday Abroad

[Lesley, J. Peter] (cont.)
By John W. Allen [pseud.].
Dial, 3:97-8, Sep 1882

Lewis, Alfred Henry
The Black Lion Inn
Critic, 43:380, Oct 1903
Literary World, 34:180, Jul 1903
The Boss
Dial, 36:22, 1 Jan 1904
Literary World, 34:349-50, Dec 1903
Peggy O'Neal
Critic, 43:285, Sep 1903
Dial, 35:156-7[220-1], 1 Oct 1903
Literary World, 34:179, Jul 1903
The President
Critic, 46:381, Apr 1905
Dial, 37:311-2, 16 Nov 1904
Independent, 57:923, 20 Oct 1904
Literary World, 35:281-2, Oct 1904
The Sunset Trail
Critic, 47:477, Nov 1905
Dial, 38:392, 1 Jun 1905
Independent, 59:1540-1, 28 Dec 1905
The Throwback
Critic, 49:191, Aug 1906
Wolfville
Critic, NS 28:320, 27 Nov 1897
Wolfville Days
Critic, 41:375, Oct 1902
Wolfville Folks
Independent, 65:550, 3 Sep 1908
Wolfville Nights
Critic, 42:184, Feb 1903
Dial, 33:334, 16 Nov 1902

Lewis, Julius A.
A Prince of the Blood
Literary World, 29:155, 14 May 1898

[Lewis, William H.]
Thomas Hard, Priest
By Lee Barton [pseud.].
Chautauquan, 10:251, Nov 1889

Libbey, Laura Jean
Florabel's Lover
Critic, NS 17:314, 4 Jun 1892
That Pretty Young Girl
Catholic World, 50:128-30, Oct 1889

Lichtenstein, Joy
For the Blue and Gold
Literary World, 32:92, 1 Jun 1901

Life and Alone
Catholic World, 12:431, Dec 1870

The Life Within
Critic, 43:91, Jul 1903

Lightner, Adna H. (Cornell)
Shadow and Sunshine
Independent, 37:1199, 17 Sep 1885

Lighton, William Rheem
Sons of Strength
Independent, 52:726, 22 Mar 1900
Uncle Mac's Nebrasky
Critic, 45:190, Aug 1904
Dial, 36:370, 1 Jun 1904

Liljencrantz, Ottilie Adaline
Randvar the Songsmith
Dial, 40:366, 1 Jun 1906
The Thrall of Leif the Lucky
Critic, 41:89-90, Jul 1902
Dial, 32:246, 1 Apr 1902
Literary World, 33:195, 1 Dec 1902
A Ward of King Canute
Critic, 43:188, Aug 1903
Dial, 34:372-3, 1 Jun 1903
Independent, 55:1690, 16 Jul 1903; 55:2741, 19

Nov 1903
Literary World, 34:140, Jun 1903

Lillibridge, William Otis
Ben Blair
Independent, 60:518, 1 Mar 1906
The Quest Eternal
Independent, 66:639, 25 Mar 1909

Lillie, Lucy Cecil (White)
Alison's Adventures
Critic, NS 23:460, 22 Jun 1895
The Colonel's Money
Critic, NS 9:17, 14 Jan 1888
Harper's, 76:Literary Notes, 3-4, Jan 1888
Esther's Fortune
Critic, NS 12:214, 2 Nov 1889
A Family Dilemma
Literary World, 25:470, 29 Dec 1894
A Girl's Ordeal
Literary World, 29:102, 2 Apr 1898
The Household of Glen Holly
Independent, 41:865, 4 Jul 1889
Jo's Opportunity
Critic, NS 6:101, 28 Aug 1886
Harper's, 73:Literary Notes, 3-4, Sep 1886
My Mother's Enemy
Critic, NS 10:102, 1 Sep 1888
Phil and the Baby, and False Witness
Harper's, 82:Literary Notes, 2, May 1891
Prudence
Critic, 2:174-5, 1 Jul 1882
Independent, 34:11, 25 May 1882
Rolf House
Harper's, 73:Literary Notes, 4, Aug 1886

Lin, Frank [pseud.]
See Atherton, Gertrude Franklin (Horn).

Lincoln, Jeanie Thomas (Gould)
A Genuine Girl
Critic, NS 27:253, 10 Apr 1897
Her Washington Season
Critic, NS 1:148, 29 Mar 1884
Independent, 36:650-1, 22 May 1884
A Javelin of Fate
Dial, 40:18-9, 1 Jan 1906
A Pretty Tory
Critic, 36:182, Feb 1900
Independent, 52:2522, 18 Oct 1900
An Unwilling Maid
Independent, 49:1544, 25 Nov 1897

Lincoln, Joseph Crosby
Cap'n Eri
Dial, 36:369, 1 Jun 1904
Independent, 56:859, 14 Apr 1904
Literary World, 35:111, Apr 1904
Mr. Pratt
Critic, 49:286, Sep 1906
Independent, 61:582-3, 6 Sep 1906
The "Old Home House"
Independent, 64:313, 6 Feb 1908
Our Village
Independent, 66:1344, 17 Jun 1909
Partners of the Tide
Critic, 47:285, Sep 1905
Dial, 38:394, 1 Jun 1905

Lindsay, Batterman
Derelicts of Destiny
Critic, 38:470, May 1901

Lindsey, William
Cinder-Path Tales
Critic, NS 27:219, 27

Lindsey, William (cont.)
Mar 1897
Independent, 48:1462, 29 Oct 1896

Linn, James Weber
The Chameleon
Literary World, 34:84, Apr 1903
The Second Generation
Dial, 32:388, 1 Jun 1902
Independent, 54:1192, 15 May 1902

[Lippincott, Sara Jane (Clarke)]
Stories and Sketches By Grace Greenwood [pseud.].
Independent, 45:577, 27 Apr 1893

Litchfield, Grace Denio
Criss-Cross
Critic, NS 4:185, 17 Oct 1885
Independent, 37:1488, 19 Nov 1885
Literary World, 16:385-6, 31 Oct 1885
A Hard-Won Victory
Critic, NS 10:178, 13 Oct 1888
Independent, 40:1073, 23 Aug 1888; 40:1275, 4 Oct 1888
Literary World, 19:250-1, 4 Aug 1888
In the Crucible
Critic, NS 27:354, 22 May 1897
Dial, 22:312, 16 May 1897
Independent, 49:948, 22 Jul 1897
Literary World, 28:145, 1 May 1897
The Knight of the Black Forest
Critic, NS 3:197, 25 Apr 1885
Independent, 37:815, 25 Jun 1885
Literary World, 16:267-8, 8 Aug 1885
Little Venice, and Other Stories
Chautauquan, 12:825, Mar 1891
Independent, 42:1842, 25 Dec 1890
The Moving Finger Writes
Critic, 38:377, Apr 1901; 38:567, Jun 1901
Independent, 53:568, 7 Mar 1901
Literary World, 32:11-2, 1 Jan 1901
Only an Incident
Critic, NS 1:184, 19 Apr 1884
Independent, 36:651, 22 May 1884
Westminster Review, 122:308, Jul 1884
The Supreme Gift
Independent, 64:1147, 21 May 1908

Litsey, Edwin Carlile
The Love Story of Abner Stone
Chautauquan, 36:336, Dec 1902
Independent, 54:2256, 18 Sep 1902
Literary World, 33:139, 1 Sep 1902

Little, Frances [pseud.]
See Macaulay, Fannie (Caldwell).

Livingston, Margaret Vere (Farrington)
Fra Lippo Lippi
Critic, NS 15:13-4, 10 Jan 1891
Independent, 42:1761, 11 Dec 1890
Westminster Review, 135:220, Feb 1891

Lloyd, John Uri
Etidorpha
Critic, NS 25:291, 25 Apr 1896; 39:183, Aug 1901

Literary World, 27:91, 21 Mar 1896
Red Head
Critic, 44:381, Apr 1904
Independent, 55:3070, 24 Dec 1903
The Right Side of the Car
Literary World, 29:205, 25 Jun 1898
Stringtown on the Pike
Catholic World, 72:406-7, Dec 1900
Chautauquan, 34:328, Dec 1901
Critic, 38:182, Feb 1901
Dial, 29:498-9, 16 Dec 1900
Independent, 52:3051, 20 Dec 1900; 53:2778, 21 Nov 1901
Literary World, 32:12, 1 Jan 1901
Warwick of the Knobs
Catholic World, 74:813-4, Mar 1902
Critic, 40:374, Apr 1902
Dial, 31:369-70, 16 Nov 1901
Independent, 53:2716-7, 14 Nov 1901
Literary World, 32:218, 1 Dec 1901

Lloyd, Nelson McAllister
The Chronic Loafer
Independent, 52:1391, 7 Jun 1900
A Drone and a Dreamer
Critic, 39:374, Oct 1901
Independent, 53:2656, 7 Nov 1901
Literary World, 32:143, 1 Sep 1901
Mrs. Radigan
Critic, 47:477, Nov 1905
Six Stars
Critic, 48:572-3, Jun 1906
Independent, 61:222, 26 Jul 1906
The Soldier of the Valley
Critic, 45:577, Dec 1904
Independent, 57:1454, 22 Dec 1904
Literary World, 35:331, Nov 1904

Locke, David Ross
The Demagogue
Critic, NS 15:193, 11 Apr 1891
Independent, 42:1720, 4 Dec 1890

Locke, James
The Stem of the Crimson Dahlia
Independent, 64:974, 30 Apr 1908

[Lockwood, Melancthon Clarence]
The New Minister
By Kenneth Paul [pseud.].
Literary World, 25:58, 24 Feb 1894

Lockwood, William Lewis
Trailers of the North
Catholic World, 83:686, Aug 1906

Lodge, Harriet (Newell)
A Bit of Finesse
Literary World, 26:251, 10 Aug 1895

Logan, Algernon Sydney
Amy Warren
Critic, 36:573, Jun 1900

Logan, Olive
See Sikes, Olive (Logan).

London, Jack
Before Adam
Independent, 62:620-1, 14 Mar 1907
Burning Daylight
Dial, 49:384, 16 Nov 1910
Independent, 69:1091-2, 17 Nov 1910
The Call of the Wild
Dial, 35:261, 16 Oct 1903
Independent, 55:1933, 13

London, Jack (cont.)
Aug 1903; 55:2742, 19 Nov 1903
Literary World, 34:229, Sep 1903
Children of the Frost
Critic, 41:583, Dec 1902
Dial, 33:330, 16 Nov 1902
A Daughter of the Snows
Chautauquan, 37:110, Apr 1903
Critic, 41:582-3, Dec 1902
The Faith of Men, and Other Stories
Catholic World, 79:691-2, Aug 1904
Critic, 45:190, Aug 1904
Independent, 56:1203, 26 May 1904
The Game
Critic, 47:285, Sep 1905
Independent, 58:1480, 29 Jun 1905
The God of His Fathers
Critic, 39:157-8, Aug 1901
Independent, 53:1868, 8 Aug 1901
Literary World, 32:125, 1 Aug 1901
The Iron Heel
Dial, 44:247, 16 Apr 1908
Independent, 64:865, 16 Apr 1908
The Kempton-Wace Letters
Critic, 43:380, Oct 1903
Dial, 35:69, 1 Aug 1903
Independent, 55:1930-2, 13 Aug 1903
Lost Face
Independent, 68:986, 5 May 1910
Love of Life
Independent, 64:104-5, 9 Jan 1908
Martin Eden
Dial, 47:386, 16 Nov 1909
Independent, 67:980-2, 20 Oct 1909
Moon-Face
Catholic World, 84:833-4, Mar 1907
Independent, 61:698, 20 Sep 1906
The Road
Independent, 64:421, 20 Feb 1908
The Sea Wolf
Dial, 38:16, 1 Jan 1905
Independent, 57:1138, 17 Nov 1904; 58:39-40, 5 Jan 1905
The Son of the Wolf
Literary World, 32:55, 1 Apr 1901
White Fang
Independent, 61:1055-6, 1 Nov 1906

Long, John Luther
The Fox-Woman
Critic, 36:170-1, Feb 1900
Literary World, 31:22, 20 Jan 1900
Heimweh
Critic, 47:578, Dec 1905
Madame Butterfly [and others]
Chautauquan, 38:416, Dec 1903
Critic, NS 30:526-7, Dec 1898
Literary World, 29:400, 26 Nov 1898
Miss Cherry-Blossom of Tokyo
Critic, NS 23:362, 18 May 1895
Dial, 18:272-3, 1 May 1895
Independent, 47:1075, 8 Aug 1895
Literary World, 26:105, 6 Apr 1895
Naughty Nan
Critic, 41:374, Oct 1902
Independent, 54:1134, 8 May 1902
Literary World, 33:55, 1 Apr 1902
The Prince of Illusion
Independent, 53:1684, 18

Jul 1901
Seffy
Critic, 48:573, Jun 1906
Sixty Jane
Critic, 43:579, Dec 1903
The Way of the Gods
Critic, 49:191, Aug 1906

Long, Lily Augusta
Apprentices to Destiny
Chautauquan, 19:126, Apr 1894
Critic, NS 21:237, 7 Apr 1894
Dial, 16:146, 1 Mar 1894
Literary World, 25:25, 27 Jan 1894
The Hemlock Avenue Mystery
By Roman Doubleday [pseud.].
Independent, 64:1036-7, 7 May 1908

Long, William Joseph
Wayeeses, the White Wolf
Independent, 63:1002, 24 Oct 1907

Longstreet, Rachel Abigail (Buchanan)
A Debutante in New York Society
Catholic World, 47:851, Sep 1888
Critic, NS 10:91, 25 Aug 1888
Independent, 40:817, 28 Jun 1888
Literary World, 19:187-8, 9 Jun 1888

Loomis, Charles Battell
Cheerful Americans
Critic, 43:579, Dec 1903
Literary World, 34:234, Sep 1903
The Four-Masted Cat-Boat, and Other Truthful Tales
Critic, 36:374, Apr 1900
Independent, 52:2522, 18 Oct 1900
A Holiday Touch
Independent, 66:639-40, 25 Mar 1909
Minerva's Manoeuvres
Critic, 42:478, Nov 1905
Independent, 59:696, 21 Sep 1905
More Cheerful Americans
Critic, 46:189, Feb 1905
Dial, 37:314, 16 Nov 1904

Lorimer, George Horace
The False Gods
Critic, 49:191, Aug 1906
Letters from a Self-Made Merchant to His Son
Chautauquan, 38:93, Sep 1903
Literary World, 33:195-6, 1 Dec 1902
Old Gorgon Graham
Critic, 45:476, Nov 1904
Literary World, 35:284, Oct 1904

Loring, Frederic W.
See also Six of One, by Half a Dozen of the Other.

The Lost Dispatch
Critic, NS 14:192, 18 Oct 1890

Loth, Moritz
"The Forgiving Kiss"
Literary World, 5:43, 1 Aug 1874

[Lothrop, Harriet Mulford (Stone)]
Grandmother Normandy
By Margaret Sidney [pseud.].
Independent, 35:44, 11 Jan 1883
Hester, and Other New England Stories
By Margaret Sidney [pseud.].
Independent, 39:1101, 1 Sep 1887
Literary World, 17:388,

[Lothrop, Harriet Mulford (Stone)] (cont.)
13 Nov 1886
A Little Maid of Concord Town
By Margaret Sidney [pseud.].
Chautauquan, 29:509, Aug 1899
Our Town
By Margaret Sidney [pseud.].
Independent, 41:1399, 24 Oct 1889
The Pettibone Name
By Margaret Sidney [pseud.].
Chautauquan, 7:254, Jan 1887
Critic, NS 5:56, 30 Jan 1886
Independent, 34:13, 6 Jul 1882
Rob
By Margaret Sidney [pseud.].
Chautauquan, 13:685-6, Aug 1891
Sally, Mrs. Tubbs
By Margaret Sidney [pseud.].
Literary World, 35:18, Jan 1904
The Stories Polly Pepper Told
By Margaret Sidney [pseud.].
Chautauquan, 29:509, Aug 1899

Loughead, Flora (Haines) Apponyi
The Abandoned Claim
Critic, NS 17:181, 26 Mar 1892
Independent, 43:1921, 24 Dec 1891
The Black Curtain
Literary World, 29:404, 26 Nov 1898
A Crown of Thorns
Critic, NS 17:167, 19 Mar 1892
The Man Who Was Guilty
Catholic World, 43:712-3, Aug 1886
Literary World, 17:253, 24 Jul 1886

Low, A. Maurice
The Supreme Surrender
Independent, 53:2363, 3 Oct 1901

Lowell, Robert Traill Spence
The New Priest in Conception Bay
Critic, NS 13:26, 18 Jan 1890
Literary World, 20:482, 21 Dec 1889
A Story or Two from an Old Dutch Town
Literary World, 10:28, 18 Jan 1879

Lubin, David
Let There Be Light
Catholic World, 72:270-2, Nov 1900

Ludlow, James Meeker
The Baritone's Parish
Independent, 48:628, 7 May 1896
The Captain of the Janizaries
Catholic World, 43:414, Jun 1886
Chautauquan, 6:547, Jun 1886
Critic, NS 5:194, 17 Apr 1886
Dial, 7:16, May 1886; 11:94, Aug 1890
Harper's, 81:Literary Notes, 1-2, Jun 1890; 88:Literary Notes, 2, Mar 1894
Independent, 38:756, 17 Jun 1886; 39:11, 21 Jul 1887
Literary World, 17:234, 10 Jul 1886
Deborah
Chautauquan, 34:323, Dec

1901
Critic, 39:375, Oct 1901
Dial, 32:88, 1 Feb 1902
Literary World, 32:139, 1 Sep 1901

A King of Tyre
Chautauquan, 15:775, Sep 1892
Critic, NS 16:165, 3 Oct 1891
Harper's, 83:Literary Notes, 4, Sep 1891
Independent, 43:1605, 29 Oct 1891

Sir Raoul
Dial, 40:16, 1 Jan 1906
Independent, 59:1049, 2 Nov 1905

That Angelic Woman
Harper's, 85:Literary Notes, 2-3, Jul 1892
Independent, 44:881, 23 Jun 1892
Literary World, 23:127, 9 Apr 1892

Ludlum, Jean Kate

At Brown's
Chautauquan, 13:686, Aug 1891
Independent, 43:608, 23 Apr 1891

Lummis, Charles Fletcher

The Enchanted Burro
Independent, 50:224, 17 Feb 1898

The Gold Fish of Gran Chimú
Critic, NS 25:443, 20 Jun 1896
Independent, 48:628-9, 7 May 1896

The King of the Broncos, and Other Stories of New Mexico
Critic, NS 29:414, 25 Jun 1898
Independent, 49:1544, 25 Nov 1897
Literary World, 29:10, 8 Jan 1898

The Land of Poco Tiempo
Literary World, 25:51, 24 Feb 1894

The Man Who Married the Moon
Chautauquan, 20:382, Dec 1894

A New Mexico David, and Other Sketches and Stories of the Southwest
Chautauquan, 14:762, Mar 1892

Lush, Charles Keeler

The Autocrats
Critic, 39:183, Aug 1901
Dial, 31:136-7, 1 Sep 1901
Independent, 53:1746, 25 Jul 1901

The Federal Judge
Dial, 24:80, 1 Feb 1898
Independent, 49:1695, 23 Dec 1897

Luska, Sidney [pseud.]
See Harland, Henry.

Lust, Adelina (Cohnfeldt)

A Tent of Grace
Chautauquan, 29:388, Jul 1899
Literary World, 30:141, 29 Apr 1899

Luther, Mark Lee

The Crucible
Dial, 44:45, 16 Jan 1908

The Favor of Princes
Chautauquan, 33:544, Aug 1901
Dial, 28:86, 1 Feb 1900

The Henchman
Catholic World, 77:115, Apr 1903
Critic, 42:69, Jan 1903
Dial, 34:88-9, 1 Feb 1903
Independent, 54:3099, 25 Dec 1902
Literary World, 34:60, Mar 1903

The Mastery
Dial, 37:312, 16 Nov 1904

Lutz, Ellen A.
One Woman's Story
Chautauquan, 21:775, Sep 1895

Lynch, Lawrence E. [pseud.]
See Van Deventer, Emma Murdock.

Lynde, Francis
Empire Builders
Independent, 63:1006, 24 Oct 1907
The Grafters
Dial, 36:367-8, 1 Jun 1904
Independent, 57:216, 28 Jul 1904
Literary World, 35:168, Jun 1904
The Helpers
Critic, 36:91, Jan 1900
Independent, 53:335, 7 Feb 1901
The King of Arcadia
Dial, 46:264-5, 16 Apr 1909
Independent, 66:764, 8 Apr 1909
The Master of Appleby
Critic, 42:85, Jan 1903; 42:563, Jun 1903
Dial, 34:89, 1 Feb 1903
Independent, 55:507, 26 Feb 1903
A Private Chivalry
Literary World, 32:87, 1 Jun 1901
The Quickening
Critic, 48:573, Jun 1906
Dial, 40:262, 16 Apr 1906
Independent, 60:1488, 21 Jun 1906
A Romance in Transit
Critic, NS 28:341, 4 Dec 1897
Independent, 49:1583, 2 Dec 1897
Literary World, 29:91, 19 Mar 1898
The Taming of Red Butte Western
Dial, 49:40, 16 Jul 1910
Independent, 69:423, 25 Aug 1910

Lyndon [pseud.]
See Hughes, Mrs. Reginald.

Lyon, Anne Bozeman
"No Saint"
Critic, NS 15:54, 31 Jan 1891

Lyon, Sidney [pseud.]
The Foolishness of Fools Is Folly
Critic, NS 14:165, 4 Oct 1890
For a Mess of Pottage
Independent, 42:967, 10 Jul 1890
Literary World, 21:303, 13 Sep 1890

Mabie, Hamilton Wright
A Child of Nature
Chautauquan, 34:319, Dec 1901

McAulay, Allan
See also The Affair at the Inn.

[Macaulay, Fannie (Caldwell)]
The Lady of the Decoration By Frances Little [pseud.].
Independent, 62:329, 7 Feb 1907

M'Caleb, Thomas
Anthony Melgrave
Critic, NS 18:106, 27 Aug 1892
Independent, 44:1329, 22 Sep 1892

McChesney, Dora Greenwell
Beatrix Infelix
Literature, 3:136, 13 Aug 1898
Coronet Strong of Ireton's Horse
Literary World, 34:124, May 1903

Miriam Cromwell, Royalist
Independent, 49:250, 25 Feb 1897
Rupert, by the Grace of God
Dial, 28:87, 1 Feb 1900
Independent, 51:1955-6, 20 Jul 1899

[Macchetta, Blanche Roosevelt (Tucker)]
Stage-Struck
By Blanche Roosevelt [pseud.].
Critic, NS 2:15, 12 Jul 1884
Dial, 5:66-7, Jul 1884
Independent, 36:907, 17 Jul 1884
Literary World, 15:242, 26 Jul 1884

McClellan, Mrs. George
See McClellan, Harriet (Hare).

McClellan, Harriet (Hare)
Broken Chords Crossed by the Echo of a False Note
Critic, NS 19:161, 18 Mar 1893
Independent, 45:53, 12 Jan 1893
Literary World, 24:42, 11 Feb 1893
A Carpet Knight
By Harford Flemming [pseud.].
Critic, NS 3:197, 25 Apr 1885
Dial, 5:329, Apr 1885
Independent, 37:751, 11 Jun 1885
Literary World, 16:113, 4 Apr 1885
Cupid and the Sphynx
By Harford Flemming [pseud.].
Literary World, 10:87, 15 Mar 1879

McClelland, Mary Greenway
Broadoaks
Dial, 15:93, 16 Aug 1893
Burkett's Lock
Critic, NS 11:209, 27 Apr 1889
Jean Monteith
Critic, NS 8:257, 19 Nov 1887
Literary World, 18:461, 10 Dec 1887
Madame Silva
Critic, NS 10:204, 27 Oct 1888
Manitou Island
Critic, NS 18:91, 20 Aug 1892
Independent, 44:1329, 22 Sep 1892
Literary World, 23:310, 10 Sep 1892
A Nameless Novel
Independent, 43:1069, 16 Jul 1891
Oblivion
Critic, NS 4:244-5, 21 Nov 1885
Literary World, 17:5, 9 Jan 1886
The Old Post-Road
Critic, NS 22:237, 13 Oct 1894
Literary World, 25:282, 8 Sep 1894
Princess
Critic, NS 6:137, 18 Sep 1886
Literary World, 17:368, 30 Oct 1886
St. John's Wooing
Harper's, 90:Literary Notes, 2, Jan 1895
Independent, 47:737, 30 May 1895
Literary World, 26:42, 9 Feb 1895

McConnell, Annie Bliss
Half Married
Critic, NS 7:17, 8 Jan 1887
Literary World, 18:140, 30 Apr 1887

McCook, Henry Christopher
The Latimers

McCook, Henry Christopher (cont.)
Independent, 50:322, 10 Mar 1898
Literary World, 29:28, 22 Jan 1898

McCray, Florine Thayer
Environment
Critic, NS 8:54, 30 Jul 1887
Literary World, 18:203, 25 Jun 1887
Wheels and Whims
Literary World, 15:265-6, 9 Aug 1884

[McCutcheon, Ben Frederick]
The Seventh Person
By Benjamin Brace [pseud.].
Independent, 62:385, 14 Feb 1907

McCutcheon, George Barr
The Alternative
Independent, 67:40, 1 Jul 1909
Beverly of Graustark
Critic, 45:577, Dec 1904
Dial, 37:312, 16 Nov 1904
Independent, 59:153-4, 20 Jul 1905
Literary World, 35:331, Nov 1904
Brewster's Millions
By Richard Greaves [pseud.].
Critic, 43:188, Aug 1903
Independent, 55:1521, 25 Jun 1903
Literary World, 34:150, Jun 1903
The Butterfly Man
Independent, 69:362, 18 Aug 1910
Castle Craneycrow
Critic, 41:479, Nov 1902
Dial, 32:242-3, 16 Oct 1902
Cowardice Court
Critic, 48:573, Jun 1906
Independent, 60:876, 12 Apr 1906
The Daughter of Anderson Crow
Independent, 64:313, 6 Feb 1908
The Day of the Dog
Critic, 44:562, Jun 1904
Graustark
Critic, 38:470, May 1901
Dial, 31:137, 1 Sep 1901
The Husbands of Edith
Independent, 65:211, 23 Jul 1908
Jane Cable
Independent, 61:941, 18 Oct 1906
The Man from Brodney's
Independent, 65:1247-8, 26 Nov 1908
Nedra
Independent, 59:1286, 30 Nov 1905
The Rose in the Ring
Independent, 69:1088-9, 17 Nov 1910
Westminster Review, 174:709-10, Dec 1910
The Sherrods
Dial, 35:157[221], 1 Oct 1903
Independent, 55:2523-4, 22 Oct 1903
Literary World, 34:261, Oct 1903
Truxton King
Westminster Review, 173:710-1, Jun 1910

[McDermott, William A.]
Mr. Billy Buttons
By Walter Lecky [pseud.].
Catholic World, 64:262-3, Nov 1896
Independent, 48:1653, 3 Dec 1896

McDonald, Robert
A Princess and a Woman
Dial, 23:93, 16 Aug 1897

McDougall, Walter Hugh
The Hidden City

Independent, 43:1762, 26 Nov 1891

[McDowell, Katherine Sherwood (Bonner)]
Dialect Tales
By Sherwood Bonner [pseud.].
Critic, 3:269, 9 Jun 1883
Dial, 4:70, Jul 1883
Independent, 35:11, 7 Jun 1883
Literary World, 14:364, 3 Nov 1883
Like unto Like
By Sherwood Bonner [pseud.].
Independent, 30:9, 10 Oct 1878
Suwanee River Tales
By Sherwood Bonner [pseud.].
Critic, NS 2:184, 18 Oct 1884
Dial, 5:212, Dec 1884
Independent, 36:1419, 6 Nov 1884
Literary World, 15:332-3, 4 Oct 1884

McElroy, John
The Red Acorn
Critic, 3:208, 5 May 1883
Dial, 3:280, Apr 1883
Literary World, 14:179, 2 Jun 1883

McElroy, Lucy (Cleaver)
Juletty
Critic, 39:86, Jul 1901
Dial, 31:31, 1 Jul 1901
Literary World, 32:91, 1 Jun 1901
The Silent Partner
Dial, 32:391, 1 Jun 1902
Literary World, 33:106, 1 Jul 1902

Macfarland, Margaret Russell
Odds Against Her
Critic, NS 10:177, 13 Oct 1888

McGlasson, Eva Wilder
See Brodhead, Eva Wilder (McGlasson).

McGowan, Alice
Judith of the Cumberlands
Independent, 65:1121-2, 12 Nov 1908
The Last Word
Literary World, 33:210, 1 Dec 1902
The Winning of Lance Cleverage
Independent, 68:367, 17 Feb 1910
See also Cooke, Grace McGowan, and Alice McGowan.

_______, and Grace McGowan Cooke
Return
Independent, 59:98, 13 Jul 1905; 59:1153-4, 16 Nov 1905

[McGowan, Archibald]
Christ the Socialist
Critic, NS 23:457-8, 22 Jun 1895

McGrath, Harold
Arms and the Woman
Independent, 52:262, 25 Jan 1900
The Best Man
Independent, 64:209, 23 Jan 1908
The Goose Girl
Independent, 67:550, 2 Sep 1909
The Grey Cloak
Dial, 35:66, 1 Aug 1903
Independent, 55:1692, 16 Jul 1903
Literary World, 34:210, Aug 1903
The Man on the Box
Critic, 46:478, May 1905
Independent, 58:270, 2 Feb 1905
The Princess Elopes
Dial, 38:394, 1 Jun 1905

McGrath, Harold (cont.)
A Splendid Hazard
Independent, 69:824, 13 Oct 1910

Mackaye, Harold Steele
The Panchronicon
Independent, 56:1336, 9 Jun 1904

McKean, Thomas
The Master Influence
Independent, 65:550, 3 Sep 1908

McKeever, Harriet Burn
Twice Crowned
Literary World, 3:172, 1 Apr 1873

Mackie, Pauline Bradford
See Hopkins, Pauline Bradford (Mackie).

McKnight, Charles
Old Fort Duquesne
Independent, 25:1257, 9 Oct 1873

Mackubin, Ellen
The King of the Town
Independent, 50:629, 12 May 1898
Literary World, 29:203, 25 Jun 1898

McLandburgh, Florence
The Automaton Ear, and Other Sketches
Galaxy, 22:138-9, Jul 1876

McLaws, Emily Lafayette
Jezabel
Catholic World, 76:127, Oct 1902
Critic, 41:280, Sep 1902
Independent, 54:2480, 16 Oct 1902
Literary World, 33:195, 1 Dec 1902
Maid of Athens
Independent, 60:1488-9, 21 Jun 1906
The Wedding
Catholic World, 86:695-6, Feb 1908
Independent, 64:531, 5 Mar 1908
When the Land Was Young
Chautauquan, 34:321-2, Dec 1901
Critic, 39:474, Nov 1901
Independent, 53:2656, 7 Nov 1901
Literary World, 32:139, 1 Sep 1901

McLaws, Lafayette
See McLaws, Emily Lafayette.

Maclay, Arthur Collins
Mito Yashiki
Dial, 10:216, Dec 1889

McLean, Sally Pratt
See Greene, Sarah Pratt (McLean).

McLeod, Clara Nevada
Then, and Not 'til Then
Literary World, 28:479, 25 Dec 1897

McMahon, Patrick Justin
Philip
Catholic World, 54:612, Jan 1892

McMinn, Edwin
Nemorama the Nautchnee
Chautauquan, 12:286, Nov 1890

McNeill, Orange
A Jesuit of To-Day
Catholic World, 62:850, Mar 1896
Literary World, 27:76, 7 Mar 1896

[Macnie, John]
The Diothas
By Ismar Thiusen [pseud.].
Independent, 35:9-10, 27

Dec 1883
Literary World, 15:27, 26 Jan 1884; 21:41, 1 Feb 1890

Macon, John Alfred
Uncle Gabe Tucker
Literary World, 14:364, 3 Nov 1883

McVickar, Henry Goelet
The Purple Light of Love
Critic, NS 23:158, 2 Mar 1895
Literary World, 25:231, 28 Jul 1894

_______, and Percy Collins
A Parish of Two
Independent, 55:2122-3, 3 Sep 1903
Literary World, 34:234, Sep 1903

Madison, Lucy (Foster)
A Colonial Maid
Literary World, 34:35, Feb 1903

Mag: A Story of To-Day
Independent, 30:12, 12 Sep 1878
Literary World, 9:47, 1 Aug 1878

[Magruder, Julia]
Across the Chasm
Independent, 37:1231, 24 Sep 1885
Literary World, 16:209, 13 Jun 1885
Dead Selves
Critic, NS 27:214, 27 Mar 1897
A Magnificent Plebian
Critic, NS 9:5, 7 Jan 1888
Harper's, 76:Literary Notes, 3-4, Feb 1888
Independent, 40:241, 23 Feb 1888
Literary World, 19:60, 18 Feb 1888
A Manifest Destiny
Independent, 52:2397, 4 Oct 1900
Literary World, 31:119, 1 Jun 1900
Miss Ayr of Virginia, & Other Stories
Critic, NS 27:214, 27 Mar 1897
Independent, 49:250, 25 Feb 1897
The Princess Sonia
Critic, NS 25:234, 4 Apr 1896
Struan
Literary World, 29:437, 10 Dec 1898
A Sunny Southerner
Independent, 53:2183, 12 Sep 1901
Literary World, 32:126, 1 Aug 1901
The Violet
Critic, NS 26:257, 31 Oct 1896
Independent, 49:219, 18 Feb 1897

Major, Charles
The Bears of Blue River
Literary World, 34:11-2, 1 Jan 1903
Dorothy Vernon of Haddon Hall
Catholic World, 75:688, Aug 1902
Dial, 33:67, 1 Aug 1902
Independent, 54:1309-10, 29 May 1902; 54:2771-2, 20 Nov 1902
A Forest Hearth
Critic, 44:93, Jan 1904
Dial, 36:23, 1 Jan 1904
Independent, 56:327, 11 Feb 1904
When Knighthood Was in Flower
By Edwin Caskoden [pseud.].
Dial, 25:172, 16 Sep 1898
Literary World, 29:370, 12 Nov 1898
Yolanda, Maid of Burgundy

Major, Charles (cont.)
Catholic World, 83:406, Jun 1906
Dial, 40:19, 1 Jan 1906

Malcolm, David
Fifty Thousand Dollars Ransom
Literary World, 27:204, 27 Jun 1896

Malone, Walter
The Coming of the King
Independent, 49:980, 29 Jul 1897; 50:727, 2 Jun 1898

Manley, R. M.
The Queen of Ecuador
Critic, NS 22:370, 1 Dec 1894

Mann, Mary Tyler (Peabody)
Juanita
Chautauquan, 7:574, Jun 1887
Literary World, 18:155, 14 May 1887

Mann, Rufus [pseud.]
See Shaler, Sophia Penn (Page).

Manning, Marie
See Gasch, Marie (Manning).

A Man's a Man for a' That
Literary World, 10:294, 13 Sep 1879

Marbourg, Dolores [pseud.]
See Bacon, Mary Schell (Hoke).

March, Anne [pseud.]
See Woolson, Constance Fenimore.

Marsh, Charles Leonard
Not on the Chart
Dial, 33:67, 1 Aug 1902
Opening the Oyster
Critic, NS 13:63, 8 Feb 1890
Dial, 10:216-7, Dec 1889

Marshall, Edward
The Middle Wall
Critic, 45:381, Oct 1904

Marshall, Luther
Thomas Boobig
Literary World, 26:202, 29 Jun 1895

Marston, Mrs. Mildred [pseud.]
See Scott, Anna (Kay).

Martin, Amarala (Arter)
Our Uncle and Aunt
Critic, NS 11:180, 13 Apr 1889

Martin, Caroline
The Blue Ridge Mystery
Literary World, 29:76, 5 Mar 1898

Martin, Elizabeth Gilbert (Davis)
Whom God Hath Joined
Catholic World, 43:560, Jul 1886; 44:127-8, Oct 1886; 44:141-2, Oct 1886
Critic, NS 6:135-6, 18 Sep 1886
Dial, 7:66, Jul 1886
Literary World, 17:213-4, 26 Jun 1886

Martin, Ellen
The Feet of Clay
Independent, 34:11, 2 Feb 1882
Literary World, 13:81, 11 Mar 1882

Martin, George Madden
Emmy Lou
Critic, 41:583, Dec 1902
Independent, 54:2718, 13 Nov 1902
The House of Fulfillment

Critic, 45:543, Dec 1904
Letitia: Nursery Corps, U. S. A.
Independent, 64:313, 6 Feb 1908

Martin, Helen (Reimensnyder)
The Betrothal of Elypholate
Independent, 64:312, 6 Feb 1908
The Crossways
Independent, 69:824, 13 Oct 1910
His Courtship
Dial, 43:65, 1 Aug 1907
Independent, 64:312, 6 Feb 1908
The Revolt of Anne Royle
Independent, 65:1249, 26 Nov 1908
A Story of the Amish
Critic, 48:475, May 1906
Tillie: A Mennonite Maid
Chautauquan, 41:286, May 1905
Critic, 45:190-1, Aug 1904
Dial, 36:373, 1 Jun 1904
Literary World, 35:113, Apr 1904
Warren Hyde
Literary World, 29:90, 19 Mar 1898

Mason, Caroline (Atwater)
The Binding of the Strong
Independent, 66:703, 1 Apr 1909
A Lily of France
Critic, 41:184, Aug 1902
Literary World, 32:187, 1 Nov 1901
The Minister of Carthage
Chautauquan, 29:206, May 1899
Literary World, 30:155, 13 May 1899
A Minister of the World
Independent, 47:1107, 15 Aug 1895
Literary World, 26:251, 10 Aug 1895
A Wind Flower
Literary World, 30:140, 29 Apr 1899
A Woman of Yesterday
Catholic World, 72:413-4, Dec 1900
Critic, 37:571, Dec 1900
Literary World, 31:268, 1 Dec 1900

Mason, Mrs. Eveleen Laura
Hiero-Salem
Catholic World, 50:832-3, Mar 1890
Independent, 42:221, 13 Feb 1890
Literary World, 21:35, 1 Feb 1890

[Mason, Fanny Witherspoon]
Daddy Dave
By Mary Frances [pseud.].
Critic, NS 6:197, 23 Oct 1886
Independent, 39:240, 24 Feb 1887

Mason, Mary Murdock
Mae Madden
Literary World, 6:117, 1 Jan 1876

Masterson, Kate
The Dobleys
Critic, 38:182, Feb 1901

Mathews, Frances Aymar
Billy Duane
Critic, 46:478, May 1905
His Will and Her Way
By A. X. [pseud.].
Catholic World, 47:851, Sep 1888
Critic, NS 9:306, 23 Jun 1888
A Little Tragedy at Tien-Tsin
Critic, 45:95, Jul 1904
Dial, 36:372, 1 Jun 1904
Independent, 56:1145-6, 19 May 1904
Literary World, 35:167, Jun 1904
The Marquise's Millions

Mathews, Frances Aymar (cont.)
Critic, 47:94, Jul 1905
A Married Man
Literary World, 30:449, 23 Dec 1899
The New Yorkers, and Other People
Critic, 37:468, Nov 1900
Pamela Congreve
Critic, 45:191, Aug 1904
The Undefiled
Dial, 43:65, 1 Aug 1907

Matthews, Brander
See Matthews, James Brander.

Matthews, James Brander
The Action and the Word
Dial, 29:125, 1 Sep 1900
Literary World, 31:267-8, 1 Dec 1900
A Confident To-Morrow
Critic, 36:91, Jan 1900
Dial, 27:491, 16 Dec 1899
Harper's, 100:Literary Notes, 2, Dec 1899
Independent, 52:128-9, 11 Jan 1900
Literary World, 31:78, 3 Mar 1900
A Family Tree, and Other Stories
Critic, NS 13:28, 18 Jan 1890; 21:271, 21 Apr 1894
Dial, 10:218, Dec 1889
Independent, 41:1576, 28 Nov 1889
Literary World, 21:4, 4 Jan 1890
His Father's Son
Critic, NS 25:2-3, 4 Jan 1896
Dial, 19:384, 16 Dec 1895
Harper's, 92:Literary Notes, 2, Dec 1895
Independent, 47:1579, 21 Nov 1895
Literary World, 26:476, 28 Dec 1895
In the Vestibule Limited
Critic, NS 17:340, 18 Jun 1892
Harper's, 85:Literary Notes, 1, Jun 1892
The Last Meeting
Dial, 6:181, Nov 1885
Independent, 37:1488, 19 Nov 1885
Literary World, 17:24, 23 Jan 1886
Outlines in Local Color
Critic, NS 28:359, 11 Dec 1897
Dial, 24:81, 1 Feb 1898
Independent, 50:521, 21 Apr 1898
Literary World, 29:44, 5 Feb 1898
The Royal Marine
Harper's, 90:Literary Notes, 1-2, Jan 1895
Literary World, 26:59, 23 Feb 1895
A Secret of the Sea, &c.
Critic, NS 6:172, 9 Oct 1886
Literary World, 18:27, 22 Jan 1887
The Story of a Story, and Other Stories
Critic, NS 20:87, 5 Aug 1893
Dial, 15:94, 16 Aug 1893
Harper's, 87:Literary Notes, 4, Jun 1893
Independent, 45:1019, 27 Jul 1893
Literary World, 24:194, 17 Jun 1893
Tales of Fantasy and Fact
Critic, NS 26:53, 25 Jul 1896
Dial, 21:289, 16 Nov 1896
Harper's, 93:Literary Notes, 1 Sep 1896
Independent, 48:1037, 30 Jul 1896
Literary World, 27:235, 25 Jul 1896
Tom Paulding
Critic, NS 18:296, 26

Nov 1892
Vignettes of Manhattan
Harper's, 89:Literary Notes, 3, Oct 1894
Literary World, 25:351, 20 Oct 1894
With My Friends
With H. C. Bunner, Walter Herries Pollock, George H. Jessop, and F. Anstey.
Critic, NS 17:7, 2 Jan 1892
Independent, 43:1882, 17 Dec 1891

_______, and H. C. Bunner
In Partnership
Critic, NS 2:161, 4 Oct 1884
Dial, 5:207, Dec 1884
Independent, 36:1324, 16 Oct 1884
Literary World, 15:386, 15 Nov 1884

_______, and George H. Jessop
A Tale of Twenty-Five Hours
Chautauquan, 15:774, Sep 1892
Critic, NS 18:177, 1 Oct 1892
Independent, 44:1229, 1 Sep 1892
Literary World, 23:294, 27 Aug 1892

Matthews, Washington, ed.
Navajo Legends
Independent, 49:1310, 7 Oct 1897

Maurice, Arthur Bartlett
New York in Fiction
Chautauquan, 33:104, Apr 1901

Mavericks
Critic, NS 18:31, 16 Jul 1892

Maxwell, Ellen (Blackmar)
The Bishop's Conversion
Chautauquan, 17:126, Apr 1893
Three Old Maids in Hawaii
Chautauquan, 25:222, May 1897
Independent, 49:219, 18 Feb 1897

May, Sophie [pseud.]
See Clarke, Rebecca Sophia.

May, Thomas P.
A Prince of Breffny
Critic, 1:337, 3 Dec 1881
Literary World, 12:398, 5 Nov 1881

Maynard, Cora
The Letter and the Spirit
Literary World, 29:434, 10 Dec 1898
Some Modern Heretics
Chautauquan, 25:575, Aug 1897
Independent, 49:57, 14 Jan 1897
Literary World, 27:478, 26 Dec 1896

Mayo, William Starbuck
Never Again
Independent, 25:12, 9 Jan 1873
Literary World, 3:121-2, 1 Jan 1873
Westminster Review, 99:295, Apr 1873

Mead, Leon
See Mead, William Leon.

Mead, Lucia True (Ames)
Memoirs of a Millionaire
Catholic World, 50:403-5, Dec 1889
Critic, NS 13:180, 12 Apr 1890
Dial, 10:215, Dec 1889
Independent, 41:1576, 28 Nov 1889

Mead, Lucia True (Ames) (cont.)
Literary World, 20:367, 26 Oct 1889

Mead, William Leon
The Bow-Legged Ghost, and Other Stories
Chautauquan, 30:327, Dec 1899
Independent, 52:195, 18 Jan 1900
Literary World, 31:12, 6 Jan 1900
In Thraldom
Critic, NS 9:5, 7 Jan 1888
Literary World, 19:11, 7 Jan 1888

Mears, Mary Martha
The Bird in the Box
Independent, 69:1092-3, 17 Nov 1910
The Breath of the Runners
Independent, 62:621, 14 Mar 1907
Emma Lou--Her Book
Independent, 48:628, 7 May 1896; 48:769, 4 Jun 1896

[Meeker, Mrs. Nellie J.]
Time's Scythe
By Jane Valentine [pseud.].
Critic, NS 11:283, 8 Jun 1889

Meekins, Lynn Roby
Adam Rush
Chautauquan, 38:95, Sep 1903
The Robb's Island Wreck, and Other Stories
Critic, NS 22:37, 21 Jul 1894
Some of Our People
Literary World, 29:370, 12 Nov 1898

Meline, Mary Miller
Charteris
Catholic World, 20:288, Nov 1874
In Six Months
Catholic World, 19:281, May 1874
The Mowbrays and Harringtons
Catholic World, 40:574, Jan 1885

Meredith, Katherine Mary Cheever
Drumsticks
Critic, NS 24:281, 2 Nov 1895
Green Gates
Chautauquan, 24:380, Dec 1896

Meredith, William Tuckey
Not of Her Father's Race
Catholic World, 52:290-1, Nov 1890
Critic, NS 14:321, 20 Dec 1890
Independent, 42:1842, 25 Dec 1890

Meriwether, Elizabeth (Avery)
The Master of Red Leaf
Literary World, 11:137-8, 24 Apr 1880

Merriman, Effie (Woodword)
Molly Miller
Chautauquan, 20:762, Mar 1895

Merron, Eleanor
As the Wind Blows
Independent, 49:252, 25 Feb 1897
Literary World, 27:251, 8 Aug 1896

Merwin, Samuel
His Little World
Dial, 35:265, 16 Oct 1903
The Merry Anne
Dial, 37:211, 1 Oct 1904
The Road-Builders
Independent, 60:224, 25 Jan 1906
The Road to Frontenac

Chautauquan, 34:346, Dec 1901
Dial, 32:89, 1 Feb 1902

_______, and Henry Kitchell Webster
Calumet 'K'
By Merwin-Webster.
Dial, 31:369, 16 Nov 1901
Comrade John
By Merwin-Webster.
Dial, 44:45, 16 Jan 1908
Independent, 64:259-60, 30 Jan 1908
The Short Line War
By Merwin-Webster.
Independent, 51:2163, 10 Aug 1899
Literary World, 30:183, 10 Jun 1899

Merwin-Webster
See Merwin, Samuel W., and Henry Kitchell Webster.

Metcalf, W. H.
A Summer in Oldport Harbor
Critic, NS 8:128, 10 Sep 1887
Literary World, 18:252, 6 Aug 1887

[Meyer, Annie (Nathan)]
Helen Brent, M. D.
Critic, NS 18:30-1, 16 Jul 1892
Literary World, 23:188-9, 4 Jun 1892
Robert Annys, Poor Priest
Critic, 39:86, Jul 1901
Independent, 53:1684, 18 Jul 1901
Literary World, 32:86, 1 Jun 1901

Meyers, Robert Cornelius V.
Miss Margery's Roses
Literary World, 10:214, 5 Jul 1879

Michaelis, Richard C.
Looking Forward
Critic, NS 14:106-7, 30 Aug 1890
Literary World, 21:283, 30 Aug 1890

Michelson, Miriam
The Awakening of Zojas
Independent, 68:987, 5 May 1900
In the Bishop's Carriage
Critic, 45:184, Aug 1904
Dial, 40:20, 1 Jan 1906
Literary World, 35:148, May 1904
The Madigans
Chautauquan, 41:285, May 1905
Critic, 46:93-4, Jan 1905
A Yellow Journalist
Critic, 48:573, Jun 1906

Mighels, Philip Verrill
Bruver Jim's Baby
Critic, 45:477, Nov 1904
Chatwit, the Man-Talk Bird
Critic, 48:573, Jun 1906
The Inevitable
Literary World, 34:12, 1 Jan 1903
Nella, the Heart of the Army
Literary World, 32:71, 1 May 1901
The Ultimate Passion
Critic, 47:285-6, Sep 1905
Dial, 39:115, 1 Sep 1905
Independent, 59:452, 24 Aug 1905

Miles, George Henry
Loretto; or the Choice
Catholic World, 11:720, Aug 1870

Miller, Alice (Duer)
Calderon's Prisoner
Critic, 44:93, Jan 1904
Independent, 55:2810, 26 Nov 1903
The Modern Obstacle
Critic, 43:77, Jul 1903

Miller, Alice (Duer) (cont.)
Dial, 34:375, 1 Jun 1903
Independent, 55:1692, 16 Jul 1903
Literary World, 34:179, Jul 1903

Miller, Annie (Jenness)
Barbara Thayer, Her Glorious Career
Catholic World, 39:856-7, Sep 1884
Literary World, 15:194, 14 Jun 1884
The Philosopher of Driftwood
Independent, 49:1546, 25 Nov 1897
Literary World, 28:297, 4 Sep 1897

[Miller, Cincinnatus Heine]
The Building of the City Beautiful
By Joaquin Miller [pseud.].
Dial, 16:188, 16 Mar 1894
The Destruction of Gotham
By Joaquin Miller [pseud.].
Critic, NS 6:64, 7 Aug 1886
Literary World, 17:317, 18 Sep 1886
First Fam'lies of the Sierras
By Joaquin Miller [pseud.].
Galaxy, 22:430-1, Sep 1876
Independent, 28:9, 6 Apr 1876
Literary World, 6:175, 1 May 1876
'49
By Joaquin Miller [pseud.].
Independent, 36:1419, 6 Nov 1884
Literary World, 16:307-8, 5 Sep 1885
The One Fair Woman
By Joaquin Miller [pseud.].
Independent, 28:9, 11 May 1876
Westminster Review, 106:280, Oct 1876
Shadows of Shasta
By Joaquin Miller [pseud.].
Critic, 1:122, 7 May 1881
Dial, 2:12, May 1881
True Bear Stories
By Joaquin Miller [pseud.].
Critic, 38:470, May 1901

Miller, Emily Clark (Huntington)
The King's Messengers
Chautauquan, 14:761, Mar 1892
Critic, NS 16:247, 7 Nov 1891
Thorn-Apples
Critic, NS 8:245, 12 Nov 1887
Independent, 40:560, 3 May 1888

Miller, Joaquin [pseud.]
See Miller, Cincinnatus Heine.

Millet, Francis Davis
A Capillary Crime, and Other Stories
Dial, 13:103, Aug 1892
Harper's, 84:Literary Notes, 3, May 1892
Independent, 44:664, 12 May 1892
Literary World, 23:165-6, 7 May 1892

Mills, Weymer Jay
Caroline of Courtlandt Street
Critic, 48:92, Jan 1906
The Girl I Left Behind Me
Independent, 69:1248-9, 8 Dec 1910

Mills, Willis
Scarlet or White?
Literary World, 28:195, 12 Jun 1897

Mitchell, Donald Grant
Dream Life
Critic, NS 12:294, 14 Dec 1889
Reveries of a Bachelor
Critic, NS 12:294, 14

Dec 1889
Seven Stories, with Basement and Attic
Independent, 36:172, 7 Feb 1884

Mitchell, Frederic Augustus
Chattanooga
Critic, NS 16:153, 26 Sep 1891
Independent, 43:1386, 17 Sep 1891
Sweet Revenge
Harper's, 95:Literary Notes, 2-3, Jul 1897
Independent, 49:882, 8 Jul 1897

Mitchell, John Ames
Amos Judd
Critic, NS 25:41, 18 Jan 1896
Harper's, 92:Literary Notes, 4, Feb 1896
Independent, 47:1727, 19 Dec 1895
Literary World, 27:76, 7 Mar 1896; 33:44, 1 Mar 1902
Gloria Victis
Independent, 50:224, 17 Feb 1898
Literary World, 29:74, 5 Mar 1898
The Pines of Lory
Literary World, 33:61, 1 Apr 1902
Romance of the Moon
Independent, 38:1414, 4 Nov 1886
That First Affair, and Other Sketches
Critic, NS 28:34, 17 Jul 1897
Literary World, 28:58, 20 Feb 1897
The Villa Claudia
Critic, 45:184-5, Aug 1904
Literary World, 35:169, Jun 1904

Mitchell, Langdon Elwyn
Love in the Backwoods
Critic, NS 27:219, 27 Mar 1897
Harper's, 94:Literary Notes, 2, Apr 1897
Independent, 48:1693, 10 Dec 1896
Literary World, 28:74, 6 Mar 1897

Mitchell, Silas Weir
The Adventures of François
Chautauquan, 28:315, Dec 1898
Critic, NS 30:516-7, Dec 1898
Dial, 25:458, 16 Dec 1898
Harper's, 98:Literary Notes, 4, Dec 1898
Independent, 50:1424, 17 Nov 1898
Literary World, 29:400, 26 Nov 1898
Literature, 3:499, 26 Nov 1898
The Autobiography of a Quack, and The Case of George Dedlow
Chautauquan, 32:452, Jan 1901
Bryan Maurice
Independent, 41:177, 7 Feb 1889
Literary World, 20:13, 5 Jan 1889
Characteristics
Chautauquan, 17:382, Jun 1893
Independent, 44:1599, 10 Nov 1892
Literary World, 23:383, 5 Nov 1892
Circumstance
Chautauquan, 34:328, Dec 1901
Critic, 40:65, Jan 1902
Dial, 32:87-8, 1 Feb 1902
Literary World, 32:219, 1 Dec 1901
A Comedy of Conscience

Mitchell, Silas Weir (cont.)
Critic, 43:188, Aug 1903
Literary World, 34:122, May 1903
Westminster Review, 161:475, Apr 1904
Constance Trescot
Critic, 47:185, Aug 1905
Dial, 39:42-3, 16 Jul 1905
Independent, 58:1011-2, 4 May 1905
A Diplomatic Adventure
Critic, 49:191, Aug 1906
Dr. North and His Friends
Critic, 38:85-6, Jan 1901
Dial, 30:196, 16 Mar 1901
Independent, 52:2933, 6 Dec 1902
Literary World, 32:5-6, 1 Jan 1901
Far in the Forest
Critic, NS 11:283, 8 Jun 1889
Literary World, 20:203, 22 Jun 1889
The Guillotine Club and Other Stories
Independent, 69:1090, 17 Nov 1910
Hephzibah Guinness [and others]
Literary World, 11:215, 19 Jun 1880
Hugh Wynne, Free Quaker
Chautauquan, 26:344-5, Dec 1897
Critic, NS 28:214-5, 16 Oct 1897
Dial, 23:285-6, 16 Nov 1897
Independent, 49:1308, 7 Oct 1897; 49:1505, 18 Nov 1897
Literary World, 28:369-70, 30 Oct 1897
Literature, 1:21-2, 23 Oct 1897
Westminster Review, 149:714, Jun 1898
In War Time
Critic, NS 2:293, 20 Dec 1884
Dial, 5:329, Apr 1885
Independent, 37:74, 15 Jan 1885
Literary World, 16:83-4, 7 Mar 1885
Little Stories
Critic, 43:579, Dec 1903
Philip Vernon
Critic, NS 24:407, 14 Dec 1895
Independent, 47:1075, 8 Aug 1895
The Red City
Dial, 45:456-7, 16 Dec 1908
Independent, 65:1182-3, 12 Nov 1908
Roland Blake
Catholic World, 44:417-8, Jun 1887
Critic, NS 6:317, 25 Dec 1886
Independent, 38:1701, 30 Dec 1886
Literary World, 17:465, 11 Dec 1886
Westminster Review, 128:134, Apr 1887
Two Strings to His Bow
Critic, NS 22:136, 1 Sep 1894
Literary World, 25:218, 14 Jul 1894
When All the Woods Are Green
Dial, 18:52, 16 Jan 1895
Literary World, 25:392, 17 Nov 1894

Moffat, William David
Not Without Honor
Literary World, 27:456-7, 12 Dec 1896

Monroe, Forest [pseud.]
See Wiechmann, Ferdinand Gerhard.

Montague, Charles Howard
The Countess Muta
Independent, 42:788, 5 Jun 1890

______, and C. W. Dyar
Written in Red
Critic, NS 14:95, 23 Aug 1890

[Monti, Luigi]
Leone
Critic, 2:253, 23 Sep 1882
Independent, 34:12, 31 Aug 1882
Literary World, 13:253, 29 Jul 1882

Moodey, Martha Livingston
Alan Thorne
Critic, NS 11:233, 11 May 1889
The Tragedy of Brinkwater
Critic, NS 7:217, 30 Apr 1887
Literary World, 18:169, 28 May 1887

Moore, B. P.
Endura
Critic, NS 5:128, 13 Mar 1886
Literary World, 17:166, 15 May 1886

Moore, Susan Teackle
Ryle's Open Gate
Chautauquan, 13:552, Jul 1891
Critic, NS 17:63, 8 Aug 1891

Moos, Herman M.
Hannah
Galaxy, 13:134-6, Jan 1872
Literary World, 1:156, 1 Mar 1871

More, Paul Elmer
The Great Refusal
Critic, NS 23:258, 6 Apr 1895
Literary World, 26:58, 23 Feb 1895

[Morgan, Carrie A.]
Mistaken Paths
By Herbert G. Dick [pseud.].
Literary World, 18:252-3, 6 Aug 1887
Sounding Brass
By Herbert G. Dick [pseud.].
Critic, NS 12:135, 21 Sep 1889

Morgan, Emily Malbone
The Flight of the "Swallow"
Chautauquan, 19:486, Jul 1894
Literary World, 25:218, 14 Jul 1894
A Poppy Garden
Chautauquan, 17:636, Aug 1893

Morgan, George
The Issue
Critic, 45:477, Nov 1904
Dial, 36:370, 1 Jun 1904
Independent, 57:154, 21 Jul 1904; 57:1137, 17 Nov 1904
Literary World, 35:144-5, May 1904
John Littlejohn of J
Critic, NS 27:440, 26 Jun 1897
Dial, 22:156, 1 Mar 1897
Independent, 49:26, 7 Jan 1897
Literary World, 28:73-4, 6 Mar 1897

Morris, Clara
Left in Charge
Dial, 36:372, 1 Jun 1904
A Pasteboard Crown
Dial, 33:65, 1 Aug 1902
Independent, 54:1783, 24 Jul 1902
Literary World, 33:119, 1 Aug 1902

[Morris, Eugenia Laura (Tuttle)]
A Hilltop Summer

[Morris, Eugenia Laura (Tuttle)] (cont.)
By Alyn Yates Keith [pseud.].
Chautauquan, 21:126, Apr 1895
Literary World, 25:455, 15 Dec 1894

A Lost Illusion
By Alyn Yates Keith [pseud.].
Critic, NS 16:29, 18 Jul 1891

A Spinster's Leaflets
By Alyn Yates Keith [pseud.].
Critic, NS 21:167, 10 Mar 1894
Literary World, 25:37, 10 Feb 1894

Morris, Gouverneur

Aladdin O'Brien
Critic, 42:67, Jan 1903
Independent, 55:451, 19 Feb 1903
Literary World, 33:194, 1 Dec 1902

Ellen and Mr. Man
Critic, 46:285, Mar 1905

The Footprint
Independent, 64:974, 30 Apr 1908

The Pagan's Progress
Critic, 45:542, Dec 1904
Independent, 62:621, 14 Mar 1907
Literary World, 35:329, Nov 1905

Tom Beauling
Critic, 39:466, Nov 1901
Literary World, 33:73, 1 May 1902

The Voice in the Rice
Independent, 68:763-4, 7 Apr 1910

Morris, Henry O.

Waiting for the Signal
Literary World, 29:370, 12 Nov 1898

Morrison, Mary Gray

The Sea-Farers
Chautauquan, 31:532, Aug 1900
Critic, 37:278, Sep 1900

Morrow, William Chambers

The Ape, The Idiot, & Other People
Critic, NS 27:254, 10 Apr 1897
Independent, 49:650, 20 May 1897; 49:719, 3 Jun 1897

A Man, His Mark
Literary World, 31:74, 3 Mar 1900

Morse, Clara Frances

Blush Roses
Independent, 30:12, 26 Sep 1878

Morse, Lucy (Gibbons)

The Chezzles
Chautauquan, 9:625, Jul 1889

Rachel Stanwood
Critic, NS 21:109-10, 17 Feb 1894
Literary World, 24:369, 4 Nov 1893

Morton, A. J.

Beyond the Palaeocrystic Sea
Dial, 21:19, 1 Jul 1896

Moss, Mary

The Poet and the Parish
Dial, 42:16-7, 1 Jan 1907

A Sequence in Hearts
Dial, 35:264, 16 Oct 1903; 36:22, 1 Jan 1904
Independent, 55:2697, 12 Nov 1903
Literary World, 35:19, Jan 1905

Mott, Edward Harold

The Black Homer of Jimtown

Chautauquan, 31:533, Aug 1900
The Old Settler and His Tales of Sugar Swamp
Literary World, 20:305, 14 Sep 1889
The Old Settler, the Squire, and Little Peleg
Literary World, 26:331, 5 Oct 1895

Moulton, Ellen Louise (Chandler)
Miss Eyre from Boston, and Others
Critic, NS 12:98, 31 Aug 1889
Literary World, 20:242, 20 Jul 1889
Some Women's Hearts
Independent, 26:11, 2 Jul 1874
Literary World, 5:11-2, 1 Jun 1874
Stories Told at Twilight
Chautauquan, 12:285, Nov 1890
Critic, NS 15:28, 17 Jan 1891

Moulton, Louise
See Moulton, Ellen Louise (Chandler).

Mowbray, J. P. [pseud.]
See Wheeler, Andrew Carpenter.

[Munday, John William]
The Lost Canyon of the Toltecs
By Charles Sumner Seeley [pseud.].
Literary World, 25:41, 10 Feb 1894
The Spanish Galleon
By Charles Sumner Seeley [pseud.].
Dial, 21:277-8, Dec 1891

Munkittrick, Richard Kendall
The Moon Prince, and Other Nabobs
Harper's, 86:Literary Notes, 3, Feb 1893
The Slambangaree, and Other Stories
Independent, 50:224, 17 Feb 1898

Munn, Charles Clark
The Castle Builders
Independent, 69:1092, 17 Nov 1910
The Girl from Tim's Place
Independent, 60:1376-7, 7 Jun 1906
The Hermit
Dial, 35:264, 16 Oct 1903
Literary World, 34:308-9, Nov 1903
Rockhaven
Dial, 32:392, 1 Jun 1902
Literary World, 33:91, 1 Jun 1902
Uncle Terry
Literary World, 32:86, 1 Jun 1901

Munroe, Charles Kirk
Campmates
Harper's, 82:Literary Notes, 3, May 1891
Canoemates
Harper's, 86:Literary Notes, 3, Feb 1893
Chrystal, Jack & Co. and Delta Bixby
Harper's, 78:Literary Notes, 4, Jun 1899
The Copper Princess
Harper's, 98:Literary Notes, 1-2, Mar 1899
Dorymates
Harper's, 80:Literary Notes, 3, Dec 1889
The Flamingo Feather
Harper's, 75:Literary Notes, 2, Aug 1887
"Forward March"
Harper's, 99:Literary Notes, 3, Oct 1899
The Fur Seal's Tooth
Harper's, 90:Literary Notes, 1-2, Dec 1894

Munroe, Charles Kirk (cont.)
The Painted Desert
Harper's, 95:Literary Notes, 3-4, Nov 1897
Raftmates
Harper's, 87:Literary Notes, 3, Jul 1893
The Ready Rangers
Chautauquan, 26:127, Oct 1897
Rick Dale
Harper's, 93:Literary Notes, 1, Nov 1896
Snow-Shoes and Sledges
Harper's, 92:Literary Notes, 4, Dec 1895
Through Swamp and Glade
Chautauquan, 25:112, Apr 1897
Wakulla
Critic, NS 5:117, 6 Mar 1886
Independent, 37:1676, 24 Dec 1885
With Crockett and Bowie
Chautauquan, 26:460, Jan 1898

Munroe, Kirk
See Munroe, Charles Kirk.

Munsey, Frank Andrew
Afloat in a Great City
Critic, NS 8:258, 19 Nov 1887
The Boy Broker
Independent, 40:1473, 15 Nov 1888
Derringforth
Critic, NS 22:370, 1 Dec 1894
A Tragedy of Errors
Critic, NS 12:214, 2 Nov 1889

Murfree, Fanny Noailles Dickinson
Felicia
Catholic World, 53:920-1, Sep 1891
Chautauquan, 13:805, Sep 1891
Critic, NS 16:51, 1 Aug 1891
Independent, 43:1068, 16 Jul 1891

[Murfree, Mary Noailles]
The Amulet
By Charles Egbert Craddock [pseud.].
Dial, 42:227, 1 Apr 1907
Independent, 62:501, 28 Feb 1907
The Bushwackers, & Other Stories
By Charles Egbert Craddock [pseud.].
Independent, 51:2628, 28 Sep 1899
Literary World, 30:251, 5 Aug 1899
The Despot of Broomsedge Cove
By Charles Egbert Craddock [pseud.].
Catholic World, 48:842-3, Mar 1889
Chautauquan, 9:434, Apr 1889
Critic, NS 11:115, 9 Mar 1889
Dial, 9:292, Mar 1889
Independent, 41:402, 28 Mar 1889
Literary World, 20:51, 16 Feb 1889
Down the Ravine
By Charles Egbert Craddock [pseud.].
Critic, NS 3:293, 20 Jun 1885
Dial, 6:123, Sep 1885
Independent, 37:1103-4, 27 Aug 1885
Literary World, 16:203, 13 Jun 1885
The Fair Mississippian
By Charles Egbert Craddock [pseud.].
Dial, 46:86, 1 Feb 1909
The Frontiersman
By Charles Egbert Craddock [pseud.].
Critic, 45:94, Jul 1904
Literary World, 35:223,

Aug 1904

His Vanished Star

By Charles Egbert Craddock [pseud.].

Dial, 17:123, 1 Sep 1894

Literary World, 25:212-3, 14 Jul 1894

In the Clouds

By Charles Egbert Craddock [pseud.].

Catholic World, 44:705-8, Feb 1887

Chautauquan, 7:384, Mar 1887

Critic, NS 7:27, 15 Jan 1887

Dial, 7:269-71, Mar 1887

Independent, 38:1665, 23 Dec 1886

Literary World, 18:27, 22 Jan 1887

In the "Stranger People's" Country

By Charles Egbert Craddock [pseud.].

Critic, NS 17:67, 30 Jan 1892

Dial, 12:425, Apr 1892

Harper's, 83:Literary Notes, 1-2, Nov 1891

Independent, 43:1882, 17 Dec 1891

Westminster Review, 137:223, Jan 1892

In the Tennessee Mountains

By Charles Egbert Craddock [pseud.].

Chautauquan, 5:556, Jun 1885

Critic, NS 2:75, 16 Aug 1884

Dial, 5:43, Jun 1884

Independent, 36:747, 12 Jun 1884

Literary World, 15:179, 31 May 1884

The Juggler

By Charles Egbert Craddock [pseud.].

Critic, NS 29:215, 26 Mar 1898

Dial, 24:79, 1 Feb 1898

Independent, 49:1623, 9 Dec 1897

Literary World, 28:478, 25 Dec 1897

Literature, 3:18, 9 Jul 1898

The Mystery of Witch-Face Mountain, and Other Stories

By Charles Egbert Craddock [pseud.].

Critic, NS 25:161-2, 7 Mar 1896

Dial, 20:174, 16 Mar 1896

Independent, 47:1727, 19 Dec 1895

Literary World, 27:121, 18 Apr 1896

The Phantoms of the Foot-Bridge, and Other Stories

By Charles Egbert Craddock [pseud.].

Critic, NS 23:440, 15 Jun 1895

Dial, 19:95, 16 Aug 1895

Harper's, 88:Literary Notes, 1, May 1894

Independent, 47:737, 30 May 1895

Literary World, 26:90, 23 Mar 1895

The Prophet of the Great Smoky Mountains

By Charles Egbert Craddock [pseud.].

Catholic World, 42:427-8, Dec 1885

Critic, NS 4:195, 24 Oct 1885

Dial, 6:179-80, Nov 1885

Independent, 37:1488, 19 Nov 1885

Literary World, 16:383-4, 31 Oct 1885

A Spectre of Power

By Charles Egbert Craddock [pseud.].

Critic, 43:284-5, Sep 1903

Dial, 35:65, 1 Aug 1903

Literary World, 34:209, Aug 1903

The Storm Centre

[Murfree, Mary Noailles] (cont.)
By Charles Egbert Craddock [pseud.].
Critic, 47:284, Sep 1905
Dial, 39:115, 1 Sep 1905
Independent, 59:210, 27 Jul 1905
The Story of Keedon Bluffs
By Charles Egbert Craddock [pseud.].
Chautauquan, 8:327, Feb 1888
Critic, NS 8:336, 31 Dec 1887
The Story of Old Fort Loudon
By Charles Egbert Craddock [pseud.].
Chautauquan, 29:311, Jun 1899
Critic, NS 31:472, May 1899
Independent, 51:1033, 13 Apr 1899
Literary World, 30:53-4, 18 Feb 1899
Where the Battle Was Fought
By Charles Egbert Craddock [pseud.].
Dial, 5:204-5, Dec 1884
Independent, 36:1292, 9 Oct 1884
Literary World, 15:306-7, 20 Sep 1884
The Windfall
By Charles Egbert Craddock [pseud.].
Dial, 42:315-6, 16 May 1907
Independent, 63:100, 11 Jul 1907
The Young Mountaineers
By Charles Egbert Craddock [pseud.].
Independent, 49:1695, 23 Dec 1897
Literary World, 28:359, 16 Oct 1897

Murray, Charles Theodore
Mlle. Fouchette
Dial, 33:63, 1 Aug 1902

Murray, William Henry Harrison
Adirondack Tales
Literary World, 20:258-9, 3 Aug 1889
The Doom of Mamelons
Independent, 40:497, 19 Apr 1888
How Deacon Turman and Parson Whitney Kept New Year's, and Other Stories
Critic, NS 8:258, 19 Nov 1887
Literary World, 19:26, 21 Jan 1888
The Story That the Keg Told Me, and The Story of the Man Who Didn't Know Much
Critic, NS 12:17, 13 Jul 1889

Musick, John Roy
Braddock
Chautauquan, 18:254, Nov 1893
Brother Against Brother
Literary World, 19:60, 18 Feb 1888
Calamity Row
Critic, NS 9:5, 7 Jan 1888
A Century Too Soon
Chautauquan, 17:637, Aug 1893
Independent, 45:1018, 27 Jul 1893
Columbia
Critic, NS 16:152-3, 26 Sep 1891
Independent, 43:1068, 16 Jul 1891
Estevan
Chautauquan, 16:127, Oct 1892
Independent, 44:1229, 1 Sep 1892
Humbled Pride
Chautauquan, 19:126, Apr 1894
Independence
Chautauquan, 18:254, Nov 1893
The Pilgrims

Chautauquan, 17:126, Apr 1893
Pocahontas
Chautauquan, 17:126, Apr 1893
Saint Augustine
Independent, 44:1834, 22 Dec 1892
Sustained Honor
Chautauquan, 19:126, Apr 1894
Union
Chautauquan, 19:381, Jan 1894
The Witch of Salem
Chautauquan, 17:637, Aug 1893
Independent, 45:1282, 21 Sep 1893

My Intimate Enemy
Literary World, 8:216-7, 1 May 1878

My Mother-in-Law
Literary World, 8:76, 1 Oct 1877

Myrick, Herbert
Cache la Poudre
Independent, 60:457, 22 Feb 1906

Nason, Frank Lewis
The Blue Goose
Literary World, 34:123, May 1903
To the End of the Trail
Dial, 33:242, 16 Oct 1902
Literary World, 33:106, 1 Jul 1902
The Vision of Elijah Berl
Dial, 38:392, 1 Jun 1905
Independent, 59:209-10, 27 Jul 1905

Naylor, James Ball
In the Days of St. Clair
Critic, 42:85, Jan 1903
Dial, 32:243, 16 Oct 1902
Independent, 54:2719, 13 Nov 1902
Literary World, 33:195, 1 Dec 1902
The Kentuckian
Dial, 40:365, 1 Jun 1906
Independent, 60:1220, 24 May 1906
Ralph Marlowe
Chautauquan, 34:340, Dec 1901
Critic, 39:86, Jul 1901
Independent, 53:2124, 5 Sep 1901
Literary World, 32:87, 1 Jun 1901
The Sign of the Prophet
Dial, 31:372, 16 Nov 1901
Independent, 53:2903, 5 Dec 1901
Literary World, 32:187, 1 Nov 1901
Under Mad Anthony's Banner
Critic, 43:476, Nov 1903
Dial, 35:158-9[222-3], 1 Oct 1903

Neale, Walter, and Elizabeth H. Hancock
The Betrayal
Westminster Review, 174:109, Jul 1910

Needham, Elizabeth Annable
Mrs. Whilling's Faith Cure
Independent, 43:1142, 30 Jul 1891

Needham, Mrs. George C.
See Needham, Elizabeth Annable.

Needham, George Carter
Conflict and Conquest
Independent, 48:1462, 29 Oct 1896
Father Flynn
Independent, 43:1142, 30 Jul 1891

Neff, Elizabeth (Hyer)
Altars to Mammon
Dial, 44:245-6, 16 Apr

Neff, Elizabeth (Hyer) (cont.)
1908
Independent, 64:810, 9 Apr 1908

Nelson, Alice Ruth (Moore) Dunbar
The Goodness of St. Rocque, and Other Stories
Critic, 36:183, Feb 1900

Newberry, Fanny E.
Bryan's House
Independent, 44:1260, 8 Sep 1892
The Impress of a Gentlewoman
Independent, 43:1605, 29 Oct 1891
Joyce's Investment
Literary World, 30:377, 11 Nov 1899
Not for Profit
Literary World, 25:302, 22 Sep 1894
Sara, A Princess
Independent, 44:1229, 1 Sep 1892
Transplanted
Independent, 42:1415, 9 Oct 1890
Literary World, 21:155, 10 May 1890

Newcomb, Simon
His Wisdom the Defender
Critic, 38:182, Feb 1901
Dial, 29:499, 16 Dec 1900
Literary World, 31:221, 1 Nov 1900

Newell, Charles Martin
Kalani of Oahu
Critic, 1:241-3, 10 Sep 1881
Independent, 34:12, 30 Mar 1882
Literary World, 12:320, 24 Sep 1881
Kaméhaméha, the Conquering King
Dial, 6:122-3, Sep 1885
Independent, 37:1231, 24 Sep 1885

[Newell, Robert Henry]
There Was Once a Man By Orpheus C. Kerr [pseud.].
Independent, 36:907, 17 Jul 1884
Literary World, 15:242-3, 26 Jul 1884

Newton, William Wilberforce
The Priest and the Man
Critic, 3:265, 9 Jun 1883
Dial, 4:69, Jul 1883
Independent, 35:11, 13 Sep 1883
Literary World, 14:158-9, 19 May 1883

Nicholas, Anna
An Idyl of the Wabash, and Other Stories
Independent, 51:210, 19 Jan 1899

Nicholson, Meredith
The House of a Thousand Candles
Dial, 40:155, 1 Mar 1906
Independent, 60:48, 4 Jan 1906
The Little Brown Jug at Kildare
Dial, 45:214, 1 Oct 1908
Independent, 65:1070, 5 Nov 1908
The Lords of High Decision
Dial, 48:245, 1 Apr 1910
The Main Chance
Dial, 35:155[219], 1 Oct 1903
Independent, 55:2238, 17 Sep 1903; 55:2740-1, 19 Nov 1903
Literary World, 34:151, Jun 1903
The Port of Missing Men
Dial, 42:227-8, 1 Apr 1907
Rosalind at Red Gate

Independent, 64:208, 23 Jan 1908
The Siege of the Seven Suitors
Independent, 69:1089, 17 Nov 1910
Zelda Dameron
Literary World, 35:378, Dec 1904

Nicolls, William Jasper
Graystone
Critic, 41:375, Oct 1902
Dial, 32:392, 1 Jun 1902

[Nitsch, Helen Alice (Matthews)]
Gentle Breadwinners
By Catherine Owen [pseud.].
Chautauquan, 8:445, Apr 1888
Independent, 40:689, 31 May 1888
Literary World, 19:67, 3 Mar 1888
Molly Bishop's Family
By Catherine Owen [pseud.].
Chautauquan, 9:125, Nov 1888
Critic, NS 10:273, 1 Dec 1888
Independent, 40:1345, 18 Oct 1888
Literary World, 19:365, 27 Oct 1888

Nixon, Mary F.
See Roulet, Mary F. (Nixon).

Noble, Annette Lucille
A Crazy Angel
Critic, 39:576, Dec 1901
Literary World, 33:8, 1 Jan 1902
Eunice Lathrop, Spinster
Independent, 34:11, 2 Feb 1882
Literary World, 13:42, 11 Feb 1882
In a Country Town
Independent, 42:788, 5 Jun 1890
Love and Shawl-Straps
Chautauquan, 20:253, Nov 1894
Critic, NS 22:370, 1 Dec 1894
Miss Janet's Old House
Critic, NS 2:220, 8 Nov 1884
The Professor's Dilemma
Independent, 49:1546, 25 Nov 1897
Literary World, 28:343, 2 Oct 1897
Literature, 1:148, 20 Nov 1897
The Ryhoves of Antwerp
Literary World, 21:439, 22 Nov 1890
Uncle Jack's Executors
Independent, 32:12, 26 Aug 1880
Literary World, 11:263, 31 Jul 1880

[Noble, Lucretia Gray]
A Reverend Idol
Dial, 3:37-8, Jun 1882
Literary World, 13:176, 3 Jun 1882

Norris, Frank
Blix
Chautauquan, 30:329, Dec 1899
Independent, 51:2830, 19 Oct 1899
A Deal in Wheat
Critic, 44:382, Apr 1904
McTeague
Independent, 51:968, 6 Apr 1899
Literary World, 30:88-9, 18 Mar 1899; 30:99, 1 Apr 1899
A Man's Woman
Critic, 36:352-3, Apr 1900
Independent, 52:611, 8 Mar 1900
Literary World, 31:140, 1 Jul 1900
Moran of the Lady Letty
Independent, 50:1129, 20 Oct 1898

Norris, Frank (cont.)
Literary World, 29:404, 26 Nov 1898
Literature, 3:578, 17 Dec 1898
The Octopus
Chautauquan, 33:539, Aug 1901
Dial, 31:136, 1 Sep 1901; 32:242, 1 Apr 1903
Independent, 53:1139-40, 16 May 1901; 53:2778, 21 Nov 1901
The Pit
Chautauquan, 37:100, Apr 1903
Independent, 55:2741, 19 Nov 1903; 55:331-2, 5 Feb 1903
Literary World, 34:54, Mar 1903

Norris, Mary Harriott
Dorothy Delafield
Critic, NS 7:216, 30 Apr 1887
Independent, 39:1101, 1 Sep 1887
The Grapes of Wrath
Critic, 39:279, Sep 1901
Dial, 31:32, 1 Jul 1901
Independent, 53:2122-3, 5 Sep 1901
Literary World, 32:143, 1 Sep 1901
The Gray House of the Quarries
Literary World, 29:203, 25 Jun 1898
Westminster Review, 154:594, Nov 1900
Lakewood
Chautauquan, 22:639, Feb 1896
Literary World, 27:236, 25 Jul 1896
Phebe
Chautauquan, 12:825, Mar 1891
Critic, NS 15:28, 17 Jan 1891

North, Barclay [pseud.]
See Hudson, William Cadwalader.

North, Leigh [pseud.]
See Phelps, Elizabeth Steward (Natt).

Norton, Charles Ledyard
A Soldier of the Legion
Independent, 50:1346, 10 Nov 1898

Norton, Frank Henry
The Malachite Cross
Literary World, 28:324, 18 Sep 1897

Oakley, Hester Caldwell
As Having Nothing
Independent, 50:492, 18 Aug 1898
Literary World, 29:268, 20 Aug 1898

Oakum, John [pseud.]
See Phillips, Walter Polk.

[Obenchain, Eliza Caroline (Calvert)]
Aunt Jane of Kentucky
By Eliza Calvert Hall [pseud.].
Catholic World, 85:688-9, Aug 1907
Independent, 62:1212, 23 May 1907

Oberholtzer, Sara Louise (Vickers)
Hope's Heart Bells
Independent, 36:172, 7 Feb 1884

O'Brien, Dillon
Frank Blake
Catholic World, 24:860, Mar 1877

O'Brien, Fitz-James
The Diamond Lens, with Other Stories
Literary World, 16:202, 13 Jun 1885

O'Connor, William Douglas
Three Tales
Critic, NS 17:99-199, 13 Feb 1892
Dial, 12:279, Dec 1891
Independent, 43:1844, 10 Dec 1891

Odell, Samuel W.
Adam Lore's Choice
Chautauquan, 10:379, Dec 1889

O'Donnell, Jessie Fremont
A Soul from Pudge's Corners
Chautauquan, 17:126, Apr 1893

O'Higgins, Harvey Jerrold
The Smoke-Eaters
Critic, 46:478, May 1905
Dial, 38:393, 1 Jun 1905

Oldboy, Oliver [pseud.]
George Bailey
Dial, 1:93, Sep 1880
Independent, 32:12, 19 Aug 1880

Older, Cora Miranda (Baggerly)
The Giants
Dial, 39:308, 16 Nov 1905
The Socialist and the Prince
Critic, 43:188-9, Aug 1903
Dial, 34:242, 1 Apr 1903

Oldham, Henry
The Man from Texas
Westminster Review, 123 (NS 67):291, Jan 1885

Oliphant, Margaret (Wilson), and Thomas Bailey Aldrich, Jr.
The Second Son
Independent, 40:689, 31 May 1888
Literary World, 19:90, 17 Mar 1888

Olney, Ellen W.
See Kirk, Ellen Warner (Olney).

O'Neill, Rose Cecil
The Lady in the White Veil
Independent, 67:423-4, 19 Aug 1909
The Loves of Edwy
Independent, 57:621, 15 Sep 1904
Literary World, 35:282, Oct 1904

The Opal
Dial, 38:392, 1 Jun 1905
Independent, 58:1009, 4 May 1905

Oppenheim, James
Doctor Rast
Independent, 68:581, 17 Mar 1910

Optic, Oliver [pseud.]
See Adams, William Taylor.

Orcutt, William Dana
The Flower of Destiny
Dial, 38:393, 1 Jun 1905
Robert Cavelier
Critic, 45:381, Oct 1904
Dial, 36:367, 1 Jun 1904
Literary World, 35:206, Jul 1904
The Spell
Dial, 46:265, 16 Apr 1909

O'Reilly, Bernard
The Two Brides
Catholic World, 29:719, Aug 1879

O'Reilly, John Boyle
Moondyne
Catholic World, 29:718-9, Aug 1879
Independent, 31:11, 7 Aug 1879
Literary World, 10:214, 5 Jul 1879; 10:326,

O'Reilly, John Boyle (cont.)
11 Oct 1879
See also The King's Men.

Orleanian [pseud.]
See Wharton, Edward Clifton.

Osborne, Duffield
See Osborne, Samuel Duffield.

Osborne, Samuel Duffield
The Lion's Brood
Critic, 39:183, Aug 1901
Independent, 53:1564, 4 Jul 1901
The Robe of Nessus
Critic, NS 14:30, 19 Jul 1890
Literary World, 21:267, 16 Aug 1890
The Spell of Ashtaroth
Catholic World, 47:557-9, Jul 1888
Chautauquan, 9:63, Oct 1888
Critic, NS 9:315-6, 30 Jun 1888
Literary World, 19:170, 26 May 1888

Osbourne, Lloyd
The Adventurer
Independent, 64:209, 23 Jan 1908
Baby Bullet
Critic, 47:579, Dec 1905
Infatuation
Independent, 66:761-2, 8 Apr 1909
Love, the Fiddler
Critic, 43:579, Dec 1903
The Queen versus Billy, and Other Stories
Critic, 37:569, Dec 1900
Independent, 53:735, 28 Mar 1901
Wild Justice
Critic, 48:476, May 1906

________, and Robert Louis Stevenson
The Ebb-Tide
Critic, NS 22:88-9, 11 Aug 1894
Dial, 17:122-3, 1 Sep 1894
Harper's, 89:Literary Notes, 2-3, Nov 1894
The Wrecker
Catholic World, 55:918-9, Sep 1892
The Wrong Box
Catholic World, 50:131, Oct 1889
Chautauquan, 10:251, Nov 1889
Dial, 10:57, Jul 1889
Literary World, 20:236-7, 20 Jul 1889

Osgood, Irene (De Bellot)
The Shadow of Desire
Catholic World, 57:582-3, Jul 1893

Ottolengui, Rodrigues
An Artist in Crime
Independent, 45:53, 12 Jan 1893
Literary World, 24:26, 28 Jan 1893
A Conflict of Evidence
Chautauquan, 17:761, Sep 1893
Critic, NS 20:136, 26 Aug 1893
Literary World, 24:227, 15 Jul 1893
The Crime of the Century
Independent, 48:494, 26 Mar 1896
Literary World, 27:172, 30 May 1896
Final Proof
Literary World, 29:435, 10 Dec 1898
A Modern Wizard
Critic, NS 21:357, 26 May 1894
Literary World, 25:219, 14 Jul 1894

Overton, Gwendolen
Anne Carmel
Critic, 43:286, Sep 1903

Captains of the World
Critic, 46:94, Jan 1905
The Golden Chain
Independent, 56:1504-5, 30 Jun 1904
The Heritage of Unrest
Critic, 38:559, Jun 1901
Dial, 31:28, 1 Jul 1901
Independent, 53:564, 4 Jul 1901

Owen, Catherine [pseud.]
See Nitsch, Helen Alice (Matthews).

Owen, Mary Alicia
Voodoo Tales
Chautauquan, 17:761, Sep 1893
Critic, NS 19:398, 17 Jun 1893
Dial, 14:338-9, 1 Jun 1893
Independent, 45:1282, 21 Sep 1893
Literary World, 24:179, 3 Jun 1893

P., G. H.
See Putnam, George Haven.

Pacheco, Mary
The New Don Quixote
Literary World, 32:87, 1 Jun 1901

Paddock, Mrs. A. G.
See Paddock, Mrs. Cornelia.

Paddock, Mrs. Cornelia
The Fate of Madame La Tour
Chautauquan, 31:106, Apr 1900
Literary World, 12:239, 16 Jul 1881
In the Toils
Independent, 31:12, 21 Aug 1879
Literary World, 10:310, 27 Sep 1879; 21:71, 1 Mar 1890

Page, Stanton [pseud.]
See Fuller, Henry Blake.

Page, Thomas Nelson
Among the Camps
Catholic World, 54:609, Jan 1902
Chautauquan, 14:510, Jan 1892
Critic, NS 17:8, 2 Jan 1892
Bred in the Bone
Critic, 46:189, Feb 1905
Independent, 57:100-1, 14 Jul 1904
Literary World, 35:205, Jul 1904
The Burial of the Guns
Dial, 17:333, 1 Dec 1894
Independent, 47:53, 10 Jan 1895
Literary World, 25:455, 15 Dec 1894
Elsket, and Other Stories
Catholic World, 54:609, Jan 1902
Chautauquan, 14:510, Jan 1892
Dial, 12:278-9, Dec 1891
Independent, 43:1882, 17 Dec 1891
Gordon Keith
Critic, 43:380, Oct 1903
Dial, 35:66-7, 1 Aug 1903
Independent, 55:1993-4, 20 Aug 1903
Literary World, 34:168-9, Jul 1903
In Ole Virginia
Chautauquan, 24:376, Dec 1896
Critic, NS 8:14-5, 2 Jul 1887
Independent, 39:1102, 1 Sep 1887
Literary World, 18:203, 25 Jun 1887; 28:74, 6 Mar 1897
John Marvel, Assistant
Dial, 47:386, 16 Nov 1909
Marse Chan
Independent, 44:1835, 22

Page, Thomas Nelson (cont.)
Dec 1892
Meh Lady
Independent, 38:726, 10 Jun 1886
The Old Gentleman of the Black Stock
Critic, NS 28:321, 27 Nov 1897; 38:279, Mar 1901
Independent, 49:1085, 19 Aug 1897
Literary World, 28:324, 18 Sep 1897; 32:71, 1 May 1901
On Newfound River
Catholic World, 54:138-9, Oct 1891
Critic, NS 16:51-2, 1 Aug 1891
Dial, 12:278, Dec 1891
Independent, 43:1068, 16 Jul 1891; 62:677, 21 Mar 1907
Pastime Stories
Critic, NS 22:54, 28 Jul 1894
Harper's, 89:Literary Notes, 3, Jun 1894
Independent, 50:797, 16 Jun 1898
Literary World, 25:219, 14 Jul 1894; 29:237, 23 Jul 1898
Polly
Critic, NS 22:347, 24 Nov 1894
Red Rock
Chautauquan, 28:420-1, Jan 1899
Critic, NS 31:83-4, Jan 1899
Dial, 25:458-9, 16 Dec 1898
Independent, 51:769-70, 16 Mar 1899; 51:1565, 8 Jun 1899; 51:3171, 23 Nov 1899
Literary World, 29:438, 10 Dec 1898
Santa Claus's Partner
Critic, 36:91, Jan 1900
Literary World, 31:26, 20 Jan 1900
Two Little Confederates
Chautauquan, 9:189, Dec 1888
Critic, NS 10:231, 10 Nov 1888
Independent, 40:1377, 25 Oct 1888
Literary World, 19:417, 24 Nov 1888
Two Prisoners
Critic, NS 30:105, Jul-Aug 1898; 43:579, Dec 1903
Independent, 50:797, 16 Jun 1898
Unc' Edinburg
Chautauquan, 22:379, Dec 1895
Literary World, 26:476, 28 Dec 1895
Works
Critic, NS 20:390-1, 16 Dec 1893
Independent, 61:1351-2, 6 Dec 1906

Paine, Albert Bigelow
The Bread Line
Critic, 38:182, Feb 1901
Independent, 53:792, 4 Apr 1901
The Commuters
Critic, 44:562, Jun 1904
Independent, 56:1145, 19 May 1904
From Van Dweller to Commuter
Independent, 64:312, 6 Feb 1908
The Great White Way
Critic, 41:184, Aug 1902
Dial, 32:20, 1 Jan 1902
Independent, 54:519, 27 Feb 1902
Literary World, 33:28, 1 Feb 1902
The Lucky Piece
Critic, 49:191-2, Aug 1906
The Van Dwellers
Critic, 40:281, Mar 1902
Dial, 31:373, 16 Nov

1901
Literary World, 33:9, 1 Jan 1902

Paine, Ralph Delahaye
The Praying Skipper, and Other Stories
Independent, 60:1375-6, 7 Jun 1906

A Palace-Prison
Independent, 36:1163, 11 Sep 1884
Literary World, 15:264-5, 9 Aug 1884

Palmer, Fanny (Purdy)
A Dead Level, and Other Episodes
Literary World, 24:42, 11 Feb 1893

Palmer, Frederick
The Big Fellow
Dial, 45:455-6, 16 Dec 1908
Westminster Review, 173:354, Mar 1910
Lucy of the Stars
Critic, 49:192, Aug 1906
Dial, 40:366, 1 Jun 1906
Independent, 61:759, 27 Sep 1906
The Vagabond
Critic, 43:476, Nov 1903
Dial, 35:262, 16 Oct 1903
Independent, 55:2876, 3 Dec 1903

[Palmer, John Williamson]
After His Kind
By John Coventry [pseud.].
Critic, NS 5:43, 23 Jan 1886
Literary World, 17:102, 20 Mar 1886

Palmer, Lynde [pseud.]
See Peebles, Mary Louise (Parmalee).

Palmer, Mary Towle
The Doctor of Deane
Critic, NS 9:258, 26 May 1888
Independent, 40:625, 17 May 1888
Literary World, 19:105, 31 Mar 1888

Pangborn, Georgia (Wood)
Roman Biznet
Independent, 54:2368, 2 Oct 1902
Literary World, 33:94, 1 Jun 1902

Pansy [pseud.]
See Alden, Isabella (Macdonald).

Parker, Clara
An Eventful Night
Critic, 37:279, Sep 1900
Independent, 52:2459, 11 Oct 1900

Parker, Helen Eliza (Fitch)
Constance of Alymer
Independent, 42:258, 20 Feb 1890

Parker, Jane (Marsh)
The Midnight Cry
Critic, NS 5:244, 15 May 1886
Literary World, 17:367, 30 Oct 1886

Parker, Lottie Blair
Homespun
Dial, 47:183, 16 Sep 1909

Parrish, Randall
Beth Norvell
Dial, 43:318, 16 Nov 1907
Bob Hampton of Placer
Dial, 42:16, 1 Jan 1907
Don MacGrath
Independent, 69:1089, 17 Nov 1910
Keith of the Border
Catholic World, 92:260, Nov 1910

Parrish, Randall (cont.)
The Last Voyage of the Donna Isabel
Dial, 45:295-6, 1 Nov 1908
My Lady of the North
Critic, 46:94, Jan 1905
Dial, 37:312, 16 Nov 1904
Independent, 58:1132, 18 May 1905
Literary World, 35:330, Nov 1904
My Lady of the South
Dial, 48:19, 1 Jan 1910
Prisoners of Chance
Dial, 44:351, 1 Jun 1908
A Sword of the Old Frontier
Dial, 40:16, 1 Jan 1906
When Wilderness Was King
Dial, 36:367, 1 Jun 1904

Parsons, Caroline
Esther Hills, Housemaid
Catholic World, 75:261, May 1902

[Parsons, Julia (Worth)]
The Full Stature of a Man
By Julian Worth [pseud.].
Chautauquan, 7:254, Jan 1887

Partridge, William Ordway
The Angel of Clay
Critic, 37:87, Jul 1900
Dial, 29:22, 1 Jul 1900
Literary World, 31:267, 1 Dec 1900

Patch, Kate Whiting
Middleway
Independent, 49:1662, 16 Dec 1897
Literary World, 29:155, 14 May 1898

Pattee, Fred Lewis
Mary Garvin
Dial, 32:390-1, 1 Jun 1902
Literary World, 33:102, 1 Jul 1902

Paul, Kenneth [pseud.]
See Lockwood, Melancthon Clarence.

Paul, Mrs. Marjorie
The Passing of Alix
Independent, 47:1690, 12 Dec 1895

Paull, Minnie E. (Kenney)
Gypsie
Independent, 34:11, 3 Aug 1882

Payne, Will
See Payne, William Hudson.

Payne, William Hudson
Jerry, the Dreamer
Dial, 21:95, 16 Aug 1896
Harper's, 93:Literary Notes, 3, Aug 1896
Literary World, 27:330, 3 Oct 1896
Mr. Salt
Dial, 36:121, 16 Feb 1904
The Money Captain
Dial, 25:306, 1 Nov 1898
Independent, 50:1942, 29 Dec 1898
Literary World, 29:456, 24 Dec 1898
Literature, 3:578, 17 Dec 1898
On Fortune's Road
Critic, 42:86, Jan 1903
Dial, 33:329, 16 Nov 1902
The Story of Eva
Dial, 31:137-8, 1 Sep 1901
Independent, 53:1383, 13 Jun 1901
When Love Speaks
Dial, 42:228, 1 Apr 1907

Paynter, Mary Moncure
Caleb, the Irrepressible
Independent, 35:11, 23

Aug 1883
Literary World, 14:195, 16 Jun 1883

Payson, William Farquhar
Barry Gordon
Dial, 46:86-7, 1 Feb 1909
The Copy-Maker
Literary World, 29:76, 5 Mar 1898
Debonnaire
Critic, 47:189-90, Aug 1905
John Vytal
Critic, 39:86, Jul 1901
Dial, 31:26, 1 Jul 1901
Independent, 53:2054, 29 Aug 1901
Periwinkle
Independent, 69:1093, 17 Nov 1910
The Title-Mongers
Literary World, 29:435, 10 Dec 1898
The Triumph of Life
Critic, 43:376, Oct 1903
Dial, 35:155-6 [219-20], 1 Oct 1903
Independent, 55:1405-6, 4 Jun 1903
Literary World, 34:153, Jun 1903

Peake, Elmore Elliott
The Darlingtons
Critic, 38:85-6, Jan 1901
The House of Hawley
Independent, 59:392, 17 Aug 1905
The Pride of Tellfair
Critic, 42:378, Apr 1903
Dial, 34:243, 1 Apr 1903
Independent, 55:569-70, 5 Mar 1903
Literary World, 34:76-7, Apr 1903
See also The Railroad.

Peale, Margaret
In the Time of the Cherry Viewing
Critic, NS 12:256, 23 Nov 1889

Pearson, Frederick W.
Her Sacrifice
Critic, NS 12:161, 5 Oct 1889
Miñon
Critic, NS 9:152, 31 Mar 1888
Independent, 40:241, 23 Feb 1888

Peattie, Elia (Wilkinson)
The Beleaguered Forest
Critic, 39:263, Sep 1901
Dial, 32:18-9, 1 Jan 1902
Independent, 53:2778, 21 Nov 1901
The Edge of Things
Critic, 43:579, Dec 1903
Dial, 35:264, 16 Oct 1903
Independent, 55:2633-4, 5 Nov 1903
The Judge
Literary World, 29:140, 30 Apr 1898
A Mountain Woman
Critic, NS 26:88, 8 Aug 1896
Dial, 22:23-4, 1 Jan 1897
Pippins and Cheese
Independent, 49:1660, 16 Dec 1897
The Shape of Fear, and Other Ghostly Tales
Critic, 45:477, Nov 1904
Dial, 37:41-2, 16 Jul 1904
Literary World, 29:370, 12 Nov 1898

Peck, Samuel Minturn
Alabama Sketches
Critic, 40:471, May 1902
Dial, 32:390, 1 Jun 1902

[Peebles, Mary Louise (Parmalee)]
A Question of Honor
By Lynde Palmer [pseud.].

[Peebles, Mary Louise (Parmalee)] (cont.)
Literary World, 24:369, 4 Nov 1893; 26:25, 26 Jan 1895

Peeke, Margaret Bloodgood (Peck)
Born of Flame
Independent, 44:1260, 8 Sep 1892

Pelletreau, Charles
Sylvester Romaine
Independent, 45:53, 12 Jan 1893

Pemberton, Caroline H.
Stephen the Black
Literary World, 31:76, 3 Mar 1900

Pemberton, Jeannette
Buffeting
Critic, NS 19:216, 8 Apr 1893
Independent, 45:53, 12 Jan 1893
Literary World, 24:42, 11 Feb 1896

Pendleton, Edmund
A Conventional Bohemian
Independent, 38:398, 1 Apr 1886
Literary World, 17:146, 1 May 1886
One Woman's Way
Critic, NS 16:164, 3 Oct 1891
A Virginia Inheritance
Critic, NS 10:113, 8 Sep 1888
Independent, 40:1644, 20 Dec 1888
Literary World, 19:343, 13 Oct 1888

Pendleton, Louis Beauregard
Bewitched
Critic, NS 10:177-8, 13 Oct 1888
Literary World, 19:315, 29 Sep 1888
Carita
Independent, 50:659, 19 May 1898
Literary World, 29:106, 2 Apr 1898
Corona of the Nantahalas
Critic, NS 24:407-8, 14 Dec 1895
Independent, 47:875, 27 Jun 1895
Literary World, 26:202, 29 Jun 1895
A Forest Drama
Independent, 57:807, 6 Oct 1904
Literary World, 35:257, Sep 1904
In Assyrian Tents
Literary World, 35:204, Jul 1904
In the Okefenokee
Chautauquan, 22:511, Jan 1896
In the Wire-Grass
Literary World, 20:274, 17 Aug 1889
Lost Prince Almon
Independent, 51:634, 2 Mar 1899
The Sons of Ham
Independent, 47:737, 30 May 1895
Literary World, 26:85-6, 23 Mar 1895
The Wedding Garment
Catholic World, 60:135, Oct 1894
Literary World, 25:218, 14 Jul 1894

Penn, Rachel [pseud.]
See Willard, Caroline McCoy (White).

Pennell, William Wesley
The Buckeye Doctor
Critic, 44:93, Jan 1904

Pennington, Jeanne Gillespie
Some Marked Passages, and Other Stories
Independent, 51:634, 2

Mar 1899
Literary World, 30:92, 18 Mar 1899

Pennot, Peter [pseud.]
See Round, William Marshall Fitts.

Peple, Edward Henry
The Prince Chap
Critic, 45:577, Dec 1904
Semiramis
Independent, 63:946, 17 Oct 1907
The Spitfire
Independent, 65:786, 1 Oct 1908

Perch, Philemon [pseud.]
See Johnston, Richard Malcolm.

Perkins, Frederic Beecher
Scrope
Independent, 26:12, 13 Aug 1874
Literary World, 5:35-6, 1 Aug 1874
See also Six of One, by Half a Dozen of the Other.

[Perley, Mrs. T. E.]
From Timber to Town
Independent, 43:1283, 27 Aug 1891

Perry, Alice
Esther Pennefather
Literary World, 9:13, 1 Jun 1878
The Schoolmaster's Trial
Critic, 1:52, 26 Feb 1881
Dial, 1:264, Apr 1881
Literary World, 12:115, 26 Mar 1881

Perry, Bliss
The Broughton House
Catholic World, 51:825-6, Sep 1890
Chautauquan, 11:383, Jun 1890
Critic, NS 14:192, 18 Oct 1890
Dial, 11:93, Aug 1890
Independent, 42:967, 10 Jul 1890
Literary World, 21:200, 21 Jun 1890
The Plated City
Dial, 19:94, 16 Aug 1895
Independent, 47:1075, 8 Aug 1895
The Powers at Play
Dial, 28:88, 1 Feb 1900
Independent, 51:2829, 19 Oct 1899
Salem Kittredge, and Other Stories
Critic, NS 22:136, 1 Sep 1894
Literary World, 25:218, 14 Jul 1894

Perry, Nora
A Book of Love Stories
Critic, 1:191, 16 Jul 1881
Dial, 2:87-8, Aug 1881
For a Woman
Critic, NS 4:185, 17 Oct 1885
Dial, 6:180, Nov 1885
Independent, 37:1488, 19 Nov 1885
Literary World, 16:374, 17 Oct 1885
The Tragedy of the Unexpected, and Other Stories
Dial, 1:75, Aug 1880
Literary World, 11:347, 9 Oct 1880

Peterson, Henry
Pemberton
Literary World, 29:455, 24 Dec 1898

Phelps, Charles Edward Davis, and Leigh North [pseud.]
The Bailiff of Tewkesbury
Dial, 16:20, 1 Jan 1894

Phelps, Elizabeth Stewart (Natt)
See Phelps, Charles Edward Davis, and Leigh North [pseud.].

Phelps, Elizabeth Stuart
See Ward, Elizabeth Stuart (Phelps).

Philips, Melville
The Devil's Hat
Literary World, 18:185, 11 Jun 1887

Phillips, Barnet
Burning Their Ships
Literary World, 10:341, 25 Oct 1879

Phillips, David Graham
The Cost
Critic, 45:191, Aug 1904
Dial, 36:369-70, 1 Jun 1904
Literary World, 35:204, Jul 1904
The Fashionable Adventures of Joshua Craig
Dial, 46:264, 16 Apr 1909
The Fortune Hunter
Critic, 49:286, Sep 1906
Independent, 61:213, 26 Jul 1906
Her Serene Highness
Independent, 54:1668-9, 10 Jul 1902
Literary World, 33:123, 1 Aug 1902
The Hungry Heart
Dial, 47:386-7, 16 Nov 1909
Independent, 67:758-60, 30 Sep 1909; 67:1153, 18 Nov 1909
The Husband's Story
Dial, 49:289, 16 Oct 1910
Light-Fingered Gentry
Dial, 43:253, 16 Oct 1907
The Master Rogue
Critic, 44:382, Apr 1904
Old Wives for New
Dial, 44:350, 1 Jun 1908
Independent, 64:808-9, 9 Apr 1908
The Plum Tree
Critic, 46:564, Jun 1905
Independent, 59:450-2, 24 Aug 1905
The Second Generation
Dial, 42:314, 16 May 1907
Independent, 62:1415, 13 Jun 1907; 63:1226-8, 21 Nov 1907
The Social Secretary
Critic, 48:92-3, Jan 1906
Independent, 59:1482, 21 Dec 1905

Phillips, Henry Wallace
Fables for Our Time
Literary World, 27:416, 28 Nov 1896
Red Saunders
Critic, 41:375, Oct 1902

Phillips, Samuel Louis
Prince Como II
Literary World, 24:148, 6 May 1893

Phillips, Waldorf Henry
Who Is Your Wife?
Literary World, 11:394-5, 6 Nov 1880

[Phillips, Walter Polk]
Oakum Pickings
By John Oakum [pseud.].
Galaxy, 22:716, Nov 1876

Phineas [pseud.]
See Hanifin, John M.

Piatt, Donn
The Lone Grave of the Shenandoah, and Other Tales
Critic, NS 10:91, 25 Aug 1888

Picard, Florence (Willingham)
The Ides of March
Literary World, 30:251, 5 Aug 1899

Picard, George Henry
A Matter of Taste
Independent, 36:1646, 25 Dec 1884
Literary World, 16:31, 24 Jan 1885
A Mission Flower
Catholic World, 43:131-2, Apr 1886
Critic, NS 4:209, 31 Oct 1885
Dial, 6:180-1, Nov 1885
Independent, 37:1565, 3 Dec 1885
Literary World, 16:399-400, 14 Nov 1885
Old Boniface
Catholic World, 44:412, Dec 1886
Critic, NS 6:249, 20 Nov 1886
Independent, 38:1665, 23 Dec 1886
Literary World, 17:392, 13 Nov 1886

Pidgin, Charles Felton
Blennerhassett
Chautauquan, 34:322-3, Dec 1901
Dial, 31:366, 16 Nov 1901
Independent, 53:2479, 17 Oct 1901
The Climax
Chautauquan, 38:518, Jan 1904
Dial, 33:333, 16 Nov 1902
Quincy Adams Sawyer and Mason's Corner Folks
Critic, 38:279, Mar 1901

Pier, Arthur Stanwood
The Ancient Grudge
Dial, 39:309, 16 Nov 1905
The Pedagogues
Chautauquan, 29:605, Sep 1899
Dial, 27:75, 1 Aug 1899
Independent, 51:2162, 10 Aug 1899
Literary World, 30:233, 22 Jul 1899
The Sentimentalists
Critic, 38:377, Apr 1901
Dial, 30:268, 16 Apr 1901
Independent, 53:1561-2, 4 Jul 1901

Pierce, Gilbert Ashville
Zachariah, the Congressman
Dial, 1:12, May 1880
Literary World, 11:112, 27 Mar 1880

Pierce, Squier Littell
Di
Critic, NS 16:53, 1 Aug 1891
Independent, 43:1142, 30 Jul 1891
Stolen Steps
Critic, NS 18:31-2, 16 Jul 1892

Pike, Louise
Southern Echoes
Critic, 38:182, Feb 1901

Pinkerton, Allan
Claude Melnotte as a Detective, and Other Stories
Literary World, 6:18, 1 Jul 1875
The Expressman and the Detective
Literary World, 5:108, 1 Dec 1874

Pinkham, Edwin George
Fate's a Fiddler
Catholic World, 88:407-8, Dec 1908
Independent, 65:550, 3 Sep 1908

Pitkin, Helen
An Angel by Brevet

Pitkin, Helen (cont.)
Independent, 58:844, 13 Apr 1905

Pixley, Frank
See Read, Opie, and Frank Pixley.

Plant, Charles P.
John Rigdon
Westminster Review, 162:714-5, Dec 1904

Plantz, Myra (Goodwin)
A Great Appointment
Literary World, 27:236, 25 Jul 1896

Plympton, Almira George
A Bud of Promise
Literary World, 26:428, 30 Nov 1895
A Willing Transgressor, and Other Stories
Critic, NS 28:361, 11 Dec 1897
Independent, 49:948, 22 Jul 1897

Pollard, Percival
Cape of Storms
Literary World, 30:408, 25 Nov 1899
Dreams of To-Day
Independent, 49:1546, 25 Nov 1897

Pollock, Walter Herries
See The Broken Shaft; also Matthews, Brander, With My Friends.

Pool, Maria Louise
Against Human Nature
Critic, NS 26:56, 25 Jul 1896
Independent, 47:1579, 21 Nov 1895; 47:1689, 12 Dec 1895
Literary World, 26:458, 14 Dec 1895
Boss and Other Dogs
Critic, NS 27:426, 19 Jun 1897
Independent, 49:250, 25 Feb 1897
Literary World, 28:90-1, 20 Mar 1897
Dally
Critic, NS 16:140, 19 Sep 1891
Harper's, 83:Literary Notes, 2, Oct 1891
Friendship and Folly
Independent, 50:1941, 29 Dec 1898
Literary World, 29:371, 12 Nov 1898
Westminster Review, 155:231, Feb 1901
A Golden Sorrow
Independent, 51:563, 23 Feb 1899
Literary World, 30:6, 7 Jan 1899
In a Dike Shanty
Independent, 48:976, 16 Jul 1896
Literary World, 27:234, 25 Jul 1896
In Buncombe County
Critic, NS 27:253, 10 Apr 1897
Literary World, 27:477, 26 Dec 1896
In the First Person
Critic, NS 27:439, 26 Jun 1897
Harper's, 93:Literary Notes, 4, Nov 1896
Independent, 48:1693, 10 Dec 1896
Literary World, 28:139-40, 1 May 1897
Katharine North
Critic, NS 20:51, 22 Jul 1893
Harper's, 86:Literary Notes, 3, Mar 1893
Independent, 45:1154, 24 Aug 1893
Literary World, 24:146-7, 6 May 1893
The Meloon Farm
Literary World, 31:163-4, 1 Sep 1900

Mrs. Gerald
Critic, NS 27:58, 23 Jan 1897
Harper's, 93:Literary Notes, 4, Sep 1896
Independent, 49:91, 21 Jan 1897
Literary World, 27:267, 22 Aug 1896

Mrs. Keats Bradford
Critic, NS 18:176-7, 1 Oct 1892
Harper's, 85:Literary Notes, 2-3, Oct 1892
Independent, 44:1330, 22 Sep 1892
Literary World, 23:261, 30 Jul 1892

Out of Step
Critic, NS 22:428, 22 Dec 1894
Harper's, 89:Literary Notes, 2-3, Oct 1894
Literary World, 25:267, 25 Aug 1894

The Red-Bridge Neighborhood
Critic, NS 29:356, 28 May 1898
Harper's, 96:Literary Notes, 1, Apr 1898
Literary World, 29:124, 16 Apr 1898

Roweny in Boston
Catholic World, 55:130, Apr 1892
Critic, NS 17:314, 4 Jun 1892
Harper's, 84:Literary Notes, 2, May 1892
Independent, 44:881, 23 Jun 1892
Literary World, 23:110, 26 Mar 1892

Sand 'n' Bushes
Independent, 51:1439-40, 25 May 1899; 51:1565, 8 Jun 1899
Literary World, 30:183, 10 Jun 1899

Tenting at Stony Beach
Critic, NS 15:310, 13 Jun 1891
Literary World, 19:234, 21 Jul 1888

The Two Salomes
Critic, NS 20:255, 21 Oct 1893
Harper's, 87:Literary Notes, 4, Oct 1893
Literary World, 24:367, 4 Nov 1893

Vacation in a Buggy
Literary World, 18:349-50, 15 Oct 1887

A Widower & Some Spinsters
Independent, 51:3297, 7 Dec 1899
Literary World, 31:71, 3 Mar 1900; 31:269, 1 Dec 1900

Poor, Agnes Blake

Boston Neighbours in Town and Out
Independent, 50:659, 12 May 1898
Literary World, 29:141, 30 Apr 1898

Brothers and Strangers
Critic, NS 20:255, 21 Oct 1893
Literary World, 24:333, 7 Oct 1893

Porter, Mrs. A. E.
See Porter, Lydia Ann (Emerson).

Porter, David Dixon

Adventures of Harry Marline
Independent, 37:1454, 12 Nov 1885

Allan Dare and Robert le Diable
Dial, 5:330-1, Apr 1885
Independent, 37:459, 9 Apr 1885
Literary World, 15:349, 18 Oct 1884; 16:112-3, 4 Apr 1885

Arthur Merton
Literary World, 20:387, 9 Nov 1889

The Lady of the Spur
Dial, 49:384, 16 Nov 1910

Porter, Gene Stratton
Freckles
Independent, 59:153, 20 Jul 1905
The Song of the Cardinal
Independent, 55:1578, 2 Jul 1903

[Porter, Linn Boyd]
His Private Character
By Albert Ross [pseud.].
Critic, NS 12:162, 5 Oct 1889
Out of Wedlock
By Albert Ross [pseud.].
Critic, NS 23:203, 16 Mar 1895

Porter, Lydia Ann (Emerson)
Cousin Polly's Gold Mine
Independent, 30:10, 31 Oct 1878
Married for Both Worlds
Literary World, 2:4-5, 1 Jun 1871

Porter, Rose
A Daughter of Israel
Independent, 51:838, 23 Mar 1899
Driftings from Mid-Ocean
Critic, NS 13:16, 11 Jan 1890
In the Mist
Literary World, 10:140, 26 Apr 1879
A Modern Saint Christopher
Independent, 40:50, 12 Jan 1888
Uplands and Lowlands
Literary World, 3:75, 1 Oct 1872

[Porter, William Sydney]
Cabbages and Kings
By O. Henry [pseud.].
Critic, 46:189, Feb 1905
Independent, 58:328, 9 Feb 1905
The Four Million
By O. Henry [pseud.].
Critic, 49:93, Jul 1906
Independent, 61:161, 19 Jul 1906
Options
By O. Henry [pseud.].
Independent, 68:321, 10 Feb 1910
Strictly Business
By O. Henry [pseud.].
Catholic World, 91:393, Jun 1910
Independent, 68:989, 5 May 1910
The Trimmed Lamp, and Other Stories of the Four Million
By O. Henry [pseud.].
Independent, 63:880, 10 Oct 1907
The Voice of the City
By O. Henry [pseud.].
Independent, 65:552, 3 Sep 1908
Whirligigs
By O. Henry [pseud.].
Independent, 69:987-8, 3 Nov 1910

Post, Melville Davisson
Dwellers in the Hills
Critic, 39:375, Oct 1901
The Man of Last Resort
Independent, 50:123, 27 Jan 1898
The Strange Schemes of Randolph Mason
Critic, NS 27:218, 27 Mar 1897
Literary World, 27:329, 3 Oct 1896

Post, Waldron Kintzing
Harvard Stories
Independent, 45:921, 6 Jul 1893
Literary World, 24:239, 29 Jul 1893
Smith Brunt
Independent, 52:2522, 18 Oct 1900

Potter, Margaret Horton
See Black, Margaret Horton (Potter).

Potter, Mary Knight
Counsels of Croesus

Literary World, 34:12, 1 Jan 1903

Powell, Richard Stillman [pseud.]
See Barbour, Ralph Henry; also Bickford, Luther H., and Richard Stillman Powell.

Pratt, Cornelia Atwood
See Comer, Cornelia Atwood (Pratt).

Prentiss, Elizabeth (Payson)
Avis Benson
Literary World, 11:28, 17 Jan 1880
The Home at Graylock
Independent, 28:8, 16 Nov 1876
Pemaquid
Literary World, 8:164, 1 Feb 1878

Preston, Harriet Waters
Aspendale
Literary World, 1:115-6, 1 Jan 1871
Is That All?
Literary World, 7:114-5, 1 Jan 1877
Love in the Nineteenth Century
Independent, 25:984-5, 7 Aug 1873
A Year in Eden
Dial, 7:291, Apr 1887
Independent, 39:398, 31 Mar 1887
Literary World, 18:19, 22 Jan 1887

_______, and Louise Preston Dodge
The Guardians
Critic, NS 10:244, 17 Nov 1888
Dial, 9:161, Nov 1888

Preston, Margaret (Junkin)
Aunt Dorothy
Catholic World, 52:763-4, Feb 1891

Price, Ella Brown
The Major's Love
Critic, NS 9:258, 26 May 1888

Prince, Helen Choate (Pratt)
At the Sign of the Silver Crescent
Critic, NS 29:298, 30 Apr 1898
Dial, 25:22, 1 Jul 1898
Independent, 50:592, 5 May 1898
The Story of Christine Rochefort
Critic, NS 23:434-5, 15 Jun 1895
Dial, 19:19, 1 Jul 1895
Independent, 47:875, 27 Jun 1895; 47:1579, 21 Nov 1895
The Strongest Master
Dial, 33:330, 16 Nov 1902
Literary World, 33:194, 1 Dec 1902
A Transatlantic Chatelaine
Critic, NS 27:270, 17 Apr 1897
Dial, 22:312, 16 May 1897
Independent, 49:980, 29 Jul 1897
Literary World, 28:164, 15 May 1897

Pullen, Elisabeth (Jones) Cavazza
Don Finimondone
Dial, 13:103-4, Aug 1892
Independent, 44:1130, 11 Aug 1892
Mr. Whitman
Dial, 33:63-4, 1 Aug 1902

A Pure Souled Liar
Critic, NS 10:54, 4 Aug 1888

Putnam, Eleanor [pseud.]
See Bates, Harriet Leonora (Vose).

[Putnam, George Haven]
The Artificial Mother
By G. H. P. [pseud.].
Chautauquan, 20:253, Nov 1894

Putnam, George Israel
In Blue Uniform
Catholic World, 57:580, Jul 1893
Critic, NS 20:237, 14 Oct 1893
Independent, 45:1453, 26 Oct 1893
Literary World, 24:226, 15 Jul 1893
On the Offensive
Critic, NS 21:374, 2 Jun 1894
Literary World, 25:139, 5 May 1894

Pyle, Howard
Rejected of Men
Independent, 55:1934, 13 Aug 1903
The Rose of Paradise
Harper's, 75:Literary Notes, 3, Sep 1887
Within the Capes
Dial, 6:123-4, Sep 1885
The Wonder Clock
Harper's, 75:Literary Notes, 4, Nov 1887

Quick, Herbert
See Quick, John Herbert.

Quick, John Herbert
Aladdin & Co.
Critic, 45:381, Oct 1904
Dial, 36:372, 1 Jun 1904
The Broken Lance
Dial, 44:45-6, 16 Jan 1908
Independent, 64:156-7, 16 Jan 1908
Double Trouble
Dial, 40:263, 16 Apr 1906

Quigg, Lemuel Ely
Tin-Types Taken in the Streets of New York
Critic, NS 14:166, 4 Oct 1890; NS 15:194, 11 Apr 1891
Independent, 42:788, 5 Jun 1890
Literary World, 21:126, 12 Apr 1890

Quincy, Josiah Phillips
The Peckster Professorship
Critic, NS 11:130, 16 Mar 1889
Dial, 9:293-4, Mar 1889
Literary World, 19:388, 10 Nov 1888

[Quincy, Samuel Miller]
The Man Who Was Not a Colonel
By a High Private.
Galaxy, 23:712, May 1877

Raffensperger, Mrs. Anna Frances
Led in Unknown Paths
Chautauquan, 14:383, Dec 1891
Critic, NS 16:248, 7 Nov 1891
Those Raeburn Girls
Chautauquan, 11:126, Apr 1890
Independent, 42:560-1, 24 Apr 1890

Ragan, Emily Lee (Sherwood)
Willis Peyton's Inheritance
Independent, 42:258, 20 Feb 1890

The Railroad
By Frank Hamilton Spearman, Elmore Elliott Peake, F. B. Tracy, William McLeod Raine, James A. Hill.
Critic, 38:471, May 1901

Raimond, C. E. [pseud.]
See Robins, Elizabeth.

Raine, William McLeod
See The Railroad.

Ralph, Julian
Alone in China, and Other Stories
Harper's, 94:Literary Notes, 1, Dec 1896
Literary World, 28:4, 9 Jan 1897
An Angel in a Web
Critic, NS 31:260-1, Mar 1899
Harper's, 98:Literary Notes, 3, Mar 1899
Literary World, 30:22, 21 Jan 1899
Dixie
Harper's, 92:Literary Notes, 1-2, Jan 1896
The Millionairess
Dial, 33:332-3, 16 Nov 1902
Literary World, 33:172, 1 Nov 1902
People We Pass
Dial, 20:174, 16 Mar 1896
Harper's, 92:Literary Notes, 1, Jan 1896
Independent, 47:1690, 12 Dec 1895
The Prince of Georgia, and Other Tales
Critic, 36:90, Jan 1900
Harper's, 99:Literary Notes, 4, Oct 1899
Independent, 51:2630, 28 Sep 1899; 51:3172, 23 Nov 1899
Literary World, 30:295, 16 Sep 1899

Rand, Edward Augustus
After the Freshet
Independent, 34:11, 3 Aug 1882
Behind Manhattan Gables
Literary World, 27:479, 26 Dec 1896
The Drummer-Boy of the Rappahannock
Chautauquan, 10:505, Jan 1890

Rathborne, St. George Henry
A Bar Sinister
Literary World, 28:255, 7 Aug 1897
A Goddess of Africa
Literary World, 28:244, 24 Jul 1897
Her Rescue from the Turks
Literary World, 28:27, 23 Jan 1897
Masked in Mystery
Literary World, 28:195, 12 Jun 1897
A Sailor's Sweetheart
Dial, 1:137-8, Nov 1880

Ravenswood [pseud.]
See Beebe, Charles Washington.

Ray, Anna Chapin
The Bridge Builders
Catholic World, 89:822, Sep 1909
Dial, 47:183, 16 Sep 1909
By the Good Sainte Anne
Literary World, 35:148, May 1904
Dick
Chautauquan, 25:112, Apr 1897
The Dominant Strain
Critic, 44:477, May 1904
Each Life Unfulfilled
Chautauquan, 29:311, Jun 1899
Literary World, 30:155, 13 May 1899
Half a Dozen Girls
Chautauquan, 25:112, Apr 1897
Hearts and Creeds
Critic, 48:574, Jun 1906
Independent, 61:698-9, 20 Sep 1906
In Blue Creek Cañon
Independent, 44:1835, 22 Dec 1892
Over the Quicksands
Independent, 69:138, 21

Ray, Anna Chapin (cont.)
Jul 1910
Quickened
Independent, 65:550-1, 3 Sep 1908
Sheba
Critic, 44:284, Mar 1904
Ursula's Freshman
Critic, 44:93-4, Jan 1904

Raymond, Evelyn (Hunt)
The Little Lady of the Horse
Chautauquan, 20:762, Mar 1895
The Little Red Schoolhouse
Literary World, 28:464, 11 Dec 1897
Mixed Pickles
Chautauquan, 17:486, Jul 1893
Monica, the Mesa Maiden
Catholic World, 56:432, Dec 1892
Independent, 44:1834, 22 Dec 1892

[Raymond, George Lansing]
Modern Fishers of Men . . .
Independent, 31:12, 6 Mar 1879; 38:1665, 23 Dec 1886
Literary World, 10:87, 15 Mar 1879

Raymond, Ross
No Laggards We
Critic, 1:152, 4 Jun 1881
Literary World, 12:246, 16 Jul 1881

[Raymond, Rossiter Worthington]
Brave Hearts
By Robertson Gray [pseud.].
Galaxy, 17:140-1, Jan 1874
Literary World, 4:82-3, Nov 1873
Camp and Cabin
Literary World, 11:198, 5 Jun 1880

Raymond, Walter
Two Men o' Mendip
Literary World, 30:106, 1 Apr 1899

Rayner, Emma
Doris Kingsley
Literary World, 33:44, 1 Mar 1902
Free To Serve
Critic, NS 29:265, 16 Apr 1898
Dial, 24:296, 1 May 1898
Independent, 49:1544, 25 Nov 1897
Literary World, 29:75, 5 Mar 1898
Handicapped Among the Free
Literary World, 34:139, Jun 1903
Visiting the Sin
Catholic World, 73:112-3, Apr 1901

Read, Emily
See Reeves, Marian Calhoun Legaré, and Emily Read.

Read, Opie Percival
An Arkansas Planter
Literary World, 28:90, 20 Mar 1897
Bolanyo
Dial, 23:286, 16 Nov 1897
Independent, 49:1310, 21 Oct 1897
The Colossus
Critic, NS 19:400, 404, 17 Jun 1893
Independent, 45:1154, 24 Aug 1893
Emmett Bonlore
Independent, 43:1922, 24 Dec 1891
In the Alamo
Critic, 39:86, Jul 1901
Judge Elbridge
Literary World, 31:93, 1 Apr 1900
A Kentucky Colonel
Critic, NS 14:321, 20 Dec 1890

Independent, 42:1604, 13 Nov 1890
Len Gansett
Literary World, 19:154, 12 May 1888
Miss Madam, and Other Sketches
Catholic World, 56:727, Feb 1893
"Old Folks"
Independent, 49:1149, 2 Sep 1897
Old Lim Jucklin
Independent, 59:1543, 28 Dec 1905
The Starbucks
Dial, 33:334, 16 Nov 1902
A Tennessee Judge
Literary World, 25:42, 10 Feb 1894
"Turk"
Dial, 37:314, 16 Nov 1904
Up Terrapin River
Critic, NS 12:135-6, 21 Sep 1889
Literary World, 20:324, 28 Sep 1889
The Waters of Caney Fork
Literary World, 29:181-2, 11 Jun 1898
A Yankee from the West
Literary World, 30:22, 21 Jan 1899

_______, and Frank Pixley
The Carpetbagger
Chautauquan, 30:329, Dec 1899

Reed, Anna Stevens
A Single Strand
Literary World, 19:188, 9 Jun 1888

Reed, Helen Leah
Brenda's Cousin at Radcliffe
Critic, 42:285, Mar 1903
Miss Theodora
Independent, 50:191, 21 Jul 1898
Literary World, 29:371, 12 Nov 1898

Reed, Isaac George
Erring Yet Noble
Independent, 36:299, 6 Mar 1884

Reed, Myrtle
At the Sign of the Jack o' Lantern
Dial, 39:308-9, 16 Nov 1905
Independent, 59:576, 7 Sep 1905
The Book of Clever Beasts
Chautauquan, 41:285, May 1905
Critic, 45:577, Dec 1904
Flower of the Dusk
Catholic World, 88:550-1, Jan 1909
Lavender and Old Lace
Critic, 41:584, Dec 1902
The Master's Violin
Critic, 46:189, Feb 1905
Independent, 57:977, 27 Oct 1904
The Shadow of Victory
Dial, 35:263, 16 Oct 1903
Independent, 55:2696, 12 Nov 1903
Literary World, 34:307-8, Nov 1903
A Spinner in the Sun
Independent, 62:215-6, 24 Jan 1907

Reed, Verner Zevola
Lo-To-Kah
Critic, NS 27:252, 10 Apr 1897
Independent, 49:980, 29 Jul 1897
Literary World, 28:107, 3 Apr 1897
Tales of the Sun-Land
Independent, 49:1149, 2 Sep 1897
Literary World, 28:297, 4 Sep 1897; 30:123, 15 Apr 1899

Reeder, A. P.
Around the Golden Deep
Critic, NS 11:40, 26 Jan 1889
Literary World, 20:259, 3 Aug 1889

Reese, Cara
"And She Got All That"
Chautauquan, 26:688, Mar 1898
Literary World, 29:205, 25 Jun 1898

Reeves, Marian Calhoun Legaré
A Little Maid of Arcadie
Critic, NS 10:66, 11 Aug 1888
Literary World, 19:365, 27 Oct 1888
Wearithorne
By "Fadette" [pseud.].
Literary World, 3:11, 1 Jun 1872

______, and Emily Read
Pilot Fortune
Critic, NS 3:172, 11 Apr 1885
Literary World, 16:113, 4 Apr 1885

Reid, Christian [pseud.]
See Tiernan, Frances Christine (Fisher).

Reid, Mayne
The Castaways
Galaxy, 11:145-6, Jan 1871

Remington, Frederic
Crooked Trails
Harper's, 97:Literary Notes, 3, Oct 1898
Independent, 50:1704, 8 Dec 1898
Literary World, 29:403, 26 Nov 1898
John Ermine of the Yellowstone
Independent, 55:506, 26 Feb 1903
Literary World, 34:53-4, Mar 1903
Men with the Bark On
Chautauquan, 31:533, Aug 1900
Independent, 52:2397, 4 Oct 1900
Pony Tracks
Critic, NS 24:261-2, 26 Oct 1895
Dial, 19:148, 16 Sep 1895
Harper's, 91:Literary Notes, 4, Oct 1895
Independent, 47:1140, 22 Aug 1895
Sundown Leflare
Harper's, 98:Literary Notes, 2, Feb 1898
Literary World, 30:92, 18 Mar 1899

Reynolds, Beatrice
The Match-Maker
Literary World, 9:56, 1 Sep 1878

[Rhoades, Cornelia Harsen]
Silver Linings
By Nina Rhoades [pseud.]
Critic, 44:188, Feb 1904

Rhoades, Nina [pseud.]
See Rhoades, Cornelia Harsen.

Rhodes, Harrison Garfield
The Lady and the Ladder
Critic, 49:192, Aug 1906

Rhone, Mrs. D. L.
See Rhone, Rosamond (Dodson).

Rhone, Rosamond (Dodson)
Among the Dunes
Independent, 50:489, 14 Apr 1898
The Days of the Son of Man
Critic, 42:86, Jan 1903
Literary World, 33:105, 1 Jul 1902

Rice, Alice Caldwell (Hegan)
Lovey Mary
Chautauquan, 37:100-1, Apr 1903
Critic, 42:477-8, Apr 1907
Independent, 55:686, 19 Mar 1903
Mr. Opp
Chautauquan, 55:288, Jul 1909
Mrs. Wiggs of the Cabbage Patch
Critic, 40:374, Apr 1902
Independent, 53:3090, 26 Dec 1901
Literary World, 33:8, 1 Jan 1902
Sandy
Independent, 59:209, 27 Jul 1905

Richards, Laura Elizabeth (Howe)
Bethesda Pool
Critic, NS 24:178, 21 Sep 1895
Geoffrey Strong
Critic, 41:184, Aug 1902
Independent, 53:2658, 7 Nov 1901
Literary World, 32:138, 1 Sep 1901
The Golden Windows
Chautauquan, 41:96, Mar 1905
In Verona
Critic, NS 22:330, 17 Nov 1894
Mrs. Tree's Will
Critic, 47:579, Dec 1905
Narcissa
Critic, NS 22:330, 17 Nov 1894
Nautilus
Critic, NS 24:408, 14 Dec 1895
Rosin the Beau
Literary World, 29:205, 25 Jun 1898
"Some Say"
Literary World, 27:457, 12 Dec 1896
Three Margarets
Literary World, 28:478, 25 Dec 1897

[Richardson, Charles Francis]
The End of the Beginning
Chautauquan, 25:431, Jul 1897
Critic, NS 26:383, 5 Dec 1896
Independent, 48:1693, 10 Dec 1896

Richardson, Leander Pease
Lord Dunmersey
Critic, NS 12:162, 5 Oct 1889

Richardson, Norval
The Lead of Honor
Catholic World, 92:393, Dec 1910

Rickert, Martha Edith
Folly
Dial, 41:114, 1 Sep 1906
Independent, 60:1040-2, 3 May 1906
The Golden Hawk
Independent, 63:42, 4 Jul 1907
The Reaper
Critic, 46:94, Jan 1905

Riddle, Albert Gallatin
Alice Brand
Literary World, 5:149, 1 Mar 1875
Ansel's Cave
Critic, NS 20:136, 26 Aug 1893
Bart Ridgeley
Literary World, 3:134, 1 Feb 1873
Castle Gregory
Critic, NS 2:256, 29 Nov 1884
The House of Ross, and Other Tales
Literary World, 12:146, 23 Apr 1881
The Portrait
Literary World, 4:89,

Riddle, Albert Gallatin (cont.)
Nov 1873
The Tory's Daughter
Critic, NS 11:117, 9 Mar 1889
Dial, 9:293, Mar 1889
Literary World, 20:131, 13 Apr 1889

Rideout, Henry Milner
Beached Keels
Independent, 62:915, 18 Apr 1907
Dragon's Blood
Independent, 67:424, 19 Aug 1909

Ridgeway, Algernon [pseud.]
See Wood, Anna Cogswell.

Riis, Jacob August
Children of the Tenements
Independent, 56:860, 14 Apr 1904
Nibsy's Christmas
Critic, NS 20:412-3, 23 Dec 1893
Out of Mulberry Street
Chautauquan, 29:311, Jun 1899

Riley, James Whitcomb
The Boss Girl, and Other Sketches
Literary World, 17:351, 16 Oct 1886

Risley, Richard Voorhees
The Life of a Woman
Chautauquan, 36:336, Dec 1902
Dial, 33:327, 16 Nov 1902
Literary World, 34:33, Feb 1903
Men's Tragedies
Critic, NS 32:647, Jul 1899
Dial, 27:76, 1 Aug 1899
Independent, 51:2025, 27 Jul 1899
Literary World, 30:250, 5 Aug 1899
The Sentimental Vikings
Literary World, 28:127, 17 Apr 1897

Rivers, George Robert Russell
Captain Shays
Dial, 23:286, 16 Nov 1897
Literary World, 28:342, 2 Oct 1897
The Count's Snuff-Box
Dial, 26:124, 16 Feb 1899
Independent, 51:281, 26 Jan 1899
Literary World, 29:456, 24 Dec 1898

Rives, Amélie
See Troubetzkoy, Amélie (Rives) Chanler.

Rives, Hallie Erminie
The Castaway
Independent, 57:157, 21 Jul 1904
Literary World, 35:197, Jul 1904
Hearts Courageous
Chautauquan, 38:93, Sep 1903
Critic, 41:375, Oct 1902
Dial, 33:65, 1 Aug 1902
Independent, 54:2369, 2 Oct 1902
The Kingdom of Slender Swords
Independent, 68:930-1, 28 Apr 1910

Roberts, Charles Humphrey
Down the O-hi-o
Critic, NS 15:287, 16 May 1891
Dial, 12:49, Jun 1891
Independent, 43:1283, 27 Aug 1891

Roberts, J. W.
Looking Within
Independent, 45:1251, 14 Sep 1893

Roberts, Ralph
Delivered from Afar
Critic, NS 3:280-1, 13 Jun 1885
Independent, 37:1167, 10 Sep 1885

Robertson, Harrison
"If I Were a Man"
Critic, NS 31:566, Jun 1899
Independent, 51:968, 6 Apr 1899
The Inlander
Critic, 38:568, Jun 1901
Independent, 53:1685, 18 Jul 1901
The Opponents
Independent, 54:1966, 14 Aug 1902
Literary World, 33:124, 1 Aug 1902
The Pink Typhoon
Critic, 49:192, Aug 1906
Red Blood and Blue
Critic, 37:278, Sep 1900

Robertson, Morgan Andrew
Down to the Sea
Critic, 47:382, Oct 1905
Independent, 58:1250, 1 Jun 1905
Futility
Literary World, 29:322, 1 Oct 1898
Land Ho!
Dial, 40:19, 1 Jan 1906
Independent, 60:455-6, 22 Feb 1906
Masters of Men
Dial, 31:33, 1 Jul 1901
Sinful Peck
Dial, 35:68, 1 Aug 1903
Independent, 55:2058, 27 Aug 1903
Literary World, 34:169, Jul 1903
Spun-Yarn
Independent, 50:730, 2 Jun 1898
"Where Angels Fear To Tread," and Other Tales of the Sea
Critic, 36:91-2, Jan 1900
Independent, 52:195, 18 Jan 1900

Robins, Edward
Romances of Early America
Chautauquan, 38:200, Oct 1903

[Robins, Elizabeth]
Come and Find Me
By C. E. Raimond [pseud.].
Dial, 44:245, 16 Apr 1908
Independent, 64:867, 16 Apr 1908
The Convert
Dial, 44:44, 16 Jan 1908
A Dark Lantern
Dial, 39:115, 1 Sep 1905
Independent, 59:210, 27 Jul 1905; 59:1051, 16 Nov 1905
The Fatal Gift of Beauty, and Other Stories
By C. E. Raimond [pseud.].
Independent, 49:57, 14 Jan 1897
Literary World, 28:180, 29 May 1897
The Florentine Frame
Dial, 48:244, 1 Apr 1910
Independent, 68:368, 17 Feb 1910
George Mandeville's Husband
By C. E. Raimond [pseud.].
Critic, NS 22:370, 1 Dec 1894
The Magnetic North
Dial, 37:39, 16 Jul 1904
The Mills of the Gods
Independent, 65:1064-5, 5 Nov 1908
The New Moon
By C. E. Raimond [pseud.].
Independent, 47:875, 27 Jun 1895
Literary World, 26:171, 1 Jun 1895
The Open Question
By C. E. Raimond [pseud.].
Critic, NS 31:157-60,

[Robins, Elizabeth] (cont.)
Feb 1899
Dial, 26:244-5, 1 Apr 1899
Independent, 51:562, 23 Feb 1899
Literary World, 30:51-2, 18 Feb 1899
Literature, 3:498-9, 26 Nov 1898
Under the Southern Cross
Independent, 64:421, 20 Feb 1908

Robinson, Edith
A Forced Acquaintance
Critic, NS 7:241, 14 May 1887
A Little Puritan Rebel
Independent, 50:1787, 15 Dec 1898
A Loyal Little Maid
Critic, NS 28:34, 17 Jul 1897
Penhallow Tales
Critic, NS 27:75-6, 30 Jan 1897
Independent, 49:57, 14 Jan 1897

Robinson, Edward A., and George A. Wall
The Disk
By Robinson and Wall.
Literary World, 15:194, 14 Jun 1884
Westminster Review, 123 (NS 67):291-2, Jan 1885
The Gun-Bearer
Chautauquan, 19:486, Jul 1894

Robinson, Harry Perry
Men Born Equal
Dial, 18:271, 1 May 1895
Harper's, 91:Literary Notes, 3, Jun 1895
Independent, 47:737, 30 May 1895
Literary World, 26:105, 6 Apr 1895

Robinson, Nina Hill
Aunt Dice, the Story of a Faithful Slave
Independent, 49:1624, 9 Dec 1897

Robinson, Rowland Evans
Danvis Folks
Literary World, 25:365, 3 Nov 1894
A Danvis Pioneer
Critic, 37:86, Jul 1900
Independent, 52:954, 19 Apr 1900
Literary World, 31:90, 1 Apr 1900
A Hero of Ticonderoga
Literary World, 29:322, 1 Oct 1898
Sam Lovel's Boy
Literary World, 32:41, 1 Mar 1901
Sam Lovel's Camps
Independent, 41:769, 13 Jun 1889
Uncle Lisha's Outing
Independent, 49:1695, 23 Dec 1897
Literary World, 29:44, 5 Feb 1898
Uncle Lisha's Shop
Chautauquan, 8:444, Apr 1888
Critic, NS 8:258, 19 Nov 1887
Literary World, 19:26, 21 Jan 1888

[Robinson, Stephen T.]
The Shadow of the War
Critic, NS 2:29, 19 Jul 1884
Independent, 36:1163, 11 Sep 1884
Literary World, 15:217, 28 Jun 1884

Robinson, Suzanne (Antrobus)
The King's Messenger
Independent, 53:2656, 7 Nov 1901

Robinson, W. A.
His Way and Hers

Chautauquan, 21:492, Jul 1895

Rockwood, Caroline Washburn
In Biscayne Bay
Critic, NS 17:324, 11 Jun 1892
Independent, 44:413, 24 Mar 1892

Rodney, George Brydges
In Buff and Blue
Critic, NS 28:267, 6 Nov 1897
Dial, 23:285, 16 Nov 1897
Independent, 49:980, 29 Jul 1897
Literary World, 28:342, 2 Oct 1897

Roe, Azel Stevens
Resolution
Literary World, 2:108, 1 Dec 1871

Roe, Edward Payson
Barriers Burned Away
Independent, 25:236, 20 Feb 1873
A Day of Fate
Dial, 1:131-3, Nov 1880
Independent, 32:12, 4 Nov 1880
Literary World, 11:394, 6 Nov 1880
The Earth Trembled
Chautauquan, 8:199, Dec 1887
Critic, NS 8:257, 19 Nov 1887
Independent, 39:1693, 29 Dec 1887
A Face Illumined
Literary World, 10:28, 18 Jan 1879
Found, yet Lost
Critic, NS 10:6, 7 Jul 1888
He Fell in Love with His Wife
Critic, NS 6:196, 23 Oct 1886
Independent, 38:1337, 21 Oct 1886
His Sombre Rivals
Independent, 36:75, 17 Jan 1884
Literary World, 14:343, 20 Oct 1883
The Hornet's Nest
Literary World, 18:187, 11 Jun 1887
"Miss Lou"
Critic, NS 11:40, 26 Jan 1889
Literary World, 19:388, 10 Nov 1888
Near to Nature's Heart
Galaxy, 23:285-6, Feb 1877
Independent, 28:8, 2 Nov 1876
Literary World, 7:89, 1 Nov 1876
Westminster Review, 107:140, Jan 1877
An Original Belle
Catholic World, 47:417, Jun 1888
Critic, NS 4:195-6, 24 Oct 1885; NS 10:177, 13 Oct 1888
Independent, 37:1454, 12 Nov 1885
Literary World, 16:386, 31 Oct 1885
Taken Alive, and Other Stories
Catholic World, 50:693-4, Feb 1890
Critic, NS 14:165, 4 Oct 1890
An Unexpected Result, and Other Stories
Critic, 3:232, 19 May 1883
Independent, 35:11, 7 Jun 1883
Without a Home
Critic, 1:322, 19 Nov 1881; NS 3:292, 20 Jun 1885
Literary World, 12:387-8, 5 Nov 1881
A Young Girl's Wooing

Roe, Edward Payson (cont.)
Critic, NS 2:233, 15 Nov 1884
Independent, 36:1646, 25 Dec 1884
Literary World, 15:369-70, 1 Nov 1884

Roe, Edward Reynolds
Brought to Bay
Independent, 34:11, 3 Aug 1882
Literary World, 13:201, 17 Jun 1882
May and June
Critic, NS 10:90, 25 Aug 1888
The World Against Her
Critic, NS 16:248, 7 Nov 1891

[Roe, Mary Abigail]
Free, yet Forging Their Own Chains
By C. M. Cornwall [pseud.].
Galaxy, 21:860, Jun 1876
Independent, 28:9, 11 May 1876
Left in the Wilderness
Critic, NS 6:222, 6 Nov 1886
A Long Search
Critic, NS 5:105, 27 Feb 1886
Literary World, 17:278-9, 21 Aug 1886

[Roe, William James]
Bellona's Husband
By Hudor Genone [pseud.].
Critic, NS 8:54, 30 Jul 1887
Independent, 39:1166, 15 Sep 1887
Cut
By G. I. Cervus [pseud.].
Critic, NS 6:52, 31 Jul 1886
Literary World, 17:350, 16 Oct 1886
Inquirendo Island
By Hudor Genone [pseud.].
Critic, NS 5:181, 10 Apr 1886
Independent, 38:304, 11 Mar 1886
Literary World, 17:166, 15 May 1886
The Last Tenet Imposed upon the Khan of Tomathoz
By Hudor Genone [pseud.].
Independent, 44:1563, 3 Nov 1892
A Model Wife
By G. I. Cervus [pseud.].
Critic, NS 4:186, 17 Oct 1885
Independent, 37:1565, 3 Dec 1885
White Feathers
By G. I. Cervus [pseud.].
Critic, NS 3:17, 10 Jan 1885
Independent, 37:395, 26 Mar 1885
Literary World, 16:276, 8 Aug 1885

Rogers, Anna (Alexander)
Peace and the Vices
Critic, 44:562, Jun 1904
Literary World, 35:149, May 1904
Sweethearts and Wives
Independent, 51:2570, 21 Sep 1899

Rogers, Robert Cameron
Old Dorset
Critic, NS 27:253, 10 Apr 1897
Independent, 49:156, 4 Feb 1897

Rohlfs, Anna Katharine (Green)
Agatha Webb
Literary World, 30:236, 22 Jul 1899
Behind Closed Doors
Critic, NS 11:29, 19 Jan 1889
Independent, 41:466, 11 Apr 1889
Literary World, 19:388, 10 Nov 1888

The Circular Study
Critic, 38:182, Feb 1901
Literary World, 31:223, 1 Nov 1900
Cynthia Wakeham's Money
Catholic World, 56:137, Oct 1892
Critic, NS 18:118, 3 Sep 1892
Independent, 44:1330, 22 Sep 1892
Literary World, 23:278, 13 Aug 1892
The Doctor, His Wife, and the Clock
Chautauquan, 21:126, Apr 1895
Literary World, 26:106, 6 Apr 1895
Doctor Izard
Critic, NS 25:335, 9 May 1896
Independent, 47:1075, 8 Aug 1895
Literary World, 26:217, 13 Jul 1895
The Filigree Ball
Independent, 55:740-1, 26 Mar 1903
Literary World, 34:122, May 1903
The Forsaken Inn
Independent, 42:788, 5 Jun 1890
Hand and Ring
Independent, 35:11, 22 Nov 1883
Literary World, 15:27, 26 Jan 1884
The Leavenworth Case
Independent, 31:12, 9 Jan 1879
Literary World, 10:28, 18 Jan 1879
Lost Man's Lane
Critic, NS 29:413-4, 25 Jun 1898
Independent, 50:726, 2 Jun 1898
Literary World, 29:187, 11 Jun 1898
Marked "Personal"
Critic, NS 20:299, 11 Nov 1893
Independent, 45:889, 29 Jun 1893
Literary World, 24:210, 1 Jul 1893
A Matter of Millions
Critic, NS 14:335, 27 Dec 1890
The Mill Mystery
Critic, NS 5:216, 1 May 1886
Independent, 38:366, 25 Mar 1886
Literary World, 17:112, 3 Apr 1886
Miss Hurd, an Enigma
Literary World, 25:352, 20 Oct 1894
A Mysterious Disappearance
Literary World, 11:11, 3 Jan 1880
The Old Stone House, and Other Stories
Independent, 44:413, 24 Mar 1892
Literary World, 23:89, 12 Mar 1892
One of My Sons
Literary World, 33:61, 1 Apr 1902
7 to 12
Critic, NS 7:319, 25 Jun 1887
Literary World, 18:186, 4 Jun 1887
The Sword of Damocles
Critic, 1:152, 4 Jun 1881
Literary World, 12:167, 7 May 1881
That Affair Next Door
Independent, 49:252, 25 Feb 1897
Literary World, 28:127, 17 Apr 1897
The Woman in the Alcove
Critic, 49:93, Jul 1906
Independent, 61:338-9, 9 Aug 1906
X Y Z
Independent, 35:11, 2 Aug 1883
Literary World, 14:244, 28 Jul 1883

Rohlfs, Anna Katharine (Green) (cont.)
Westminster Review, 120:280, Oct 1883

Rollins, Alice Marland (Wellington)
The Story of a Ranch
Critic, NS 5:30, 16 Jan 1886
Literary World, 17:43, 6 Feb 1886
The Three Tetons
Critic, NS 8:138, 17 Sep 1887
Independent, 39:1231, 29 Sep 1887
Literary World, 18:261-2, 20 Aug 1887
Uncle Tom's Tenement
Critic, NS 10:138, 22 Sep 1888
Independent, 41:17, 3 Jan 1889
Literary World, 19:315, 29 Sep 1888

Rollins, Clara Harriot (Sherwood)
A Burne-Jones Head, and Other Sketches
Critic, NS 23:27, 12 Jan 1895
Literary World, 25:219, 14 Jul 1894
Threads of Life
Independent, 50:224, 17 Feb 1898
Literary World, 29:203, 25 Jun 1898

Rollins, Frank West
Break o' Day Tales
Literary World, 25:233, 28 Jul 1894
The Lady of the Violets
Independent, 50:222, 17 Feb 1898
Literary World, 29:23, 22 Jan 1898

Rood, Henry Edward
The Company Doctor
Chautauquan, 22:127, Oct 1895
Independent, 47:875, 27 Jun 1895
Literary World, 26:155, 18 May 1895
Hardwicke
Dial, 32:388, 1 Jun 1902
Independent, 54:1844, 31 Jul 1902

Roosevelt, Blanche [pseud.]
See Macchetta, Blanche Roosevelt (Tucker).

Roosevelt, Robert Barnwell
Love and Luck
Critic, NS 6:101, 28 Aug 1886
Harper's, 73:Literary Notes, 2, Sep 1886
Independent, 38:1336, 21 Oct 1886
Literary World, 17:316, 18 Sep 1886

Roseboró, Viola
The Joyous Heart
Literary World, 34:210, Aug 1903
Old Ways and New
Dial, 14:115, 16 Feb 1893
Independent, 44:1599, 10 Nov 1892
Literary World, 23:385, 5 Nov 1892

Ross, Albert [pseud.]
See Porter, Linn Boyd.

Ross, Clinton
The Adventures of Three Worthies
Critic, NS 16:140, 19 Sep 1891
Independent, 43:1386, 17 Sep 1891
Bobbie McDuff
Dial, 25:76, 1 Aug 1898
Chalmette
Dial, 24:296, 1 May 1898
Independent, 49:1623, 9

Dec 1897
Literary World, 28:464, 11 Dec 1897

A Gallery of a Random Collector
Literary World, 19:284, 1 Sep 1888

Improbable Tales
Critic, NS 17:290, 21 May 1892
Independent, 44:413, 24 Mar 1892
Literary World, 23:58, 13 Feb 1892

The Meddling Hussy
Literary World, 28:193, 12 Jun 1897

The Puppet
Critic, NS 27:58, 23 Jan 1897
Literary World, 28:28, 23 Jan 1897

The Scarlet Coat
Critic, NS 27:58, 23 Jan 1897
Dial, 22:156, 1 Mar 1897
Independent, 48:1697, 10 Dec 1896
Literary World, 28:43, 6 Feb 1897

The Silent Workman
Literary World, 18:186, 11 Jun 1887

The Speculator
Chautauquan, 13:685, Aug 1891
Critic, NS 15:263, 16 May 1891

A Trooper of the Empress
Dial, 25:76, 1 Aug 1898

Zuleka
Critic, NS 27:425, 19 Jun 1897
Independent, 49:882, 8 Jul 1897
Literary World, 28:194, 12 Jun 1897

Rossiter, William Sidney

An Accidental Romance, and Other Stories
Literary World, 27:365, 31 Oct 1896

Roulet, Mary F. (Nixon)

God, the King, My Brother
Dial, 29:307, 1 Nov 1900

[Round, William Marshall Fitts]

Achsah
By Peter Pennot [pseud.].
Catholic World, 23:719, Aug 1876
Galaxy, 22:859-60, Jun 1876
Independent, 28:9, 11 May 1876
Literary World, 6:179, 1 May 1876

Hal
Literary World, 11:112, 27 Mar 1880

Rosecroft
Literary World, 12:245, 16 Jul 1881

Rouse, Adelaide Louise

The Deane Girls
Independent, 47:1335, 3 Oct 1895

The Letters of Theodora
Critic, 47:286, Sep 1905

Under My Own Roof
Literary World, 33:105-6, 1 Jul 1902

Wendover House
Chautauquan, 16:509-10, Jan 1893

Rowe, Henrietta (Gould)

A Maid of Bar Harbor
Dial, 33:66, 1 Aug 1902

Queenshithe
Chautauquan, 22:639, Feb 1896

Re-Told Tales of the Hills and Shores of Maine
Chautauquan, 19:127, Apr 1894

Rowland, Henry Cottrell

The Countess Diane
Independent, 65:1463, 17 Dec 1908

In the Shadow
Dial, 41:116, 1 Sep 1906

Rowland, Henry Cottrell (cont.)
The Mountain of Fears
Independent, 60:744, 29 Mar 1906
Sea Scamps
Critic, 43:476, Nov 1903
To Windward
Critic, 45:477, Nov 1904
Independent, 56:1204, 26 May 1904
Literary World, 35:205, Jul 1904
The Wanderers
Critic, 46:564, Jun 1905
Independent, 58:1250-1, 1 Jun 1905

Royce, Josiah
The Feud of Oakfield Creek
Catholic World, 44:419, Jun 1887
Critic, NS 7:241, 14 May 1887
Dial, 8:67-8, Jul 1887
Independent, 39:592, 12 May 1887
Literary World, 18:155, 14 May 1887
Westminster Review, 128:385, Jun 1887

Ruben, Edward
The Path to Fame
Critic, NS 11:283, 8 Jun 1889
Independent, 41:769, 13 Jun 1889

Ruddy, Ella Augusta (Giles)
Bachelor Ben
Literary World, 6:36, 1 Aug 1875
Maiden Rachel
Independent, 31:11, 7 Aug 1879
Literary World, 10:214, 5 Jul 1879
Out from the Shadows
Independent, 28:9, 15 Jun 1876

Runkle, Bertha Brooks
The Helmet of Navarre
Chautauquan, 33:99, Apr 1901
Critic, 38:558-9, Jun 1901
Dial, 31:29, 1 Jul 1901
Independent, 53:1323, 6 Jun 1901; 53:2777, 21 Nov 1901
Literary World, 32:83, 1 Jun 1901
The Truth About Tolna
Dial, 40:367, 1 Jun 1906
Independent, 60:1046-7, 3 May 1906

Russell, Ernest E.
The Reason Why
Literary World, 27:285, 5 Sep 1896

Russell, Frances E.
A Quaint Spinster
Critic, NS 23:438, 15 Jun 1895

Ryan, Marah Ellis (Martin)
The Bondwoman
Literary World, 30:408, 25 Nov 1899
A Chance Child [and others]
Critic, NS 27:253, 10 Apr 1897
A Flower of France
Critic, NS 22:86-7, 11 Aug 1894
Dial, 16:366, 16 Jun 1894
Literary World, 25:303, 22 Sep 1894
The Flute of the Gods
Independent, 67:1264, 2 Dec 1909
For the Soul of Rafael
Dial, 41:39, 16 Jul 1906
Merze
Catholic World, 50:128, Oct 1889
A Pagan of the Alleghanies
Critic, NS 17:100, 13 Feb 1892
Independent, 43:1844, 10 Dec 1891

<u>Squaw Elouise</u>
Independent, 44:1834, 22 Dec 1892
Literary World, 24:58, 25 Feb 1893

S., D. T. [pseud.]
See Balch, Elizabeth.

S., E. A. B.
See Shackelford, Miss E. A. B.

Sage, William
<u>By Divine Right</u>
Dial, 43:64, 1 Aug 1907
Independent, 63:572, 5 Sep 1907
<u>The Claybornes</u>
Critic, 41:375, Oct 1902
Dial, 32:243, 16 Oct 1902
Literary World, 33:138, 1 Sep 1902
<u>The District Attorney</u>
Critic, 49:287, Sep 1906
Dial, 41:38, 16 Jul 1906
Independent, 61:214, 26 Jul 1906
<u>Frenchy, the Story of a Gentleman</u>
Dial, 37:42, 16 Jul 1904
<u>Robert Tournay</u>
Dial, 29:125-6, 1 Sep 1900
Independent, 53:333-4, 7 Feb 1901
Literary World, 31:140, 1 Jul 1900

Saltus, Edgar Everston
<u>Eden</u>
Catholic World, 48:128-9, Oct 1888
Critic, NS 10:63-4, 11 Aug 1888
<u>Enthralled</u>
Critic, NS 21:272, 21 Apr 1894
<u>Love and Lore</u>
Literary World, 21:430, 22 Nov 1890
<u>Mary Magdalen</u>
Critic, NS 16:28, 18 Jul 1891
Literary World, 27:91, 21 Mar 1896
<u>Mr. Incoul's Misadventure</u>
Critic, NS 8:54, 30 Jul 1887
Dial, 8:147, Nov 1887
Independent, 39:1269, 6 Oct 1887
Literary World, 18:347, 15 Oct 1887
<u>The Pace That Kills</u>
Catholic World, 50:130, Oct 1889
Literary World, 20:289, 31 Aug 1889
<u>The Perfume of Eros</u>
Critic, 49:574, Jun 1906
<u>The Truth About Tristrem Varick</u>
Catholic World, 47:555-7, Jul 1888
Critic, NS 9:191, 21 Apr 1888; NS 23:458, 22 Jun 1895

Samuels, Samuel
<u>From the Forecastle to the Cabin</u>
Harper's, 74:Literary Notes, 1, May 1887

Sanborn, Alvan Francis
<u>Meg McIntyre's Raffle, and Other Stories</u>
Critic, NS 27:76, 30 Jan 1897; NS 27:255, 10 Apr 1897
Independent, 49:57, 14 Jan 1897
Literary World, 28:107-8, 3 Apr 1897

Sanborn, Edwin Webster
<u>People at Pisgah</u>
Chautauquan, 16:508, Jan 1893
Critic, NS 18:177, 1 Oct 1892
Independent, 44:1563, 3 Nov 1892
Literary World, 23:310, 10 Sep 1892

Sanborn, Mary Farley (Sanborn)
It Came To Pass
Independent, 44:1261, 8 Sep 1892
Lynette and the Congressman
Dial, 40:16, 1 Jan 1906
Independent, 59:1229, 26 Nov 1905
Paula Ferris
Independent, 45:1453, 26 Oct 1893
Literary World, 24:258, 12 Aug 1893
Sweet and Twenty
Critic, NS 16:182, 10 Oct 1891

Sanderson, James Gardner
Cornell Stories
Independent, 50:264, 28 Jul 1898
Literary World, 29:236-7, 23 Jul 1898

Sanford, Frederick R.
The Bursting of a Boom
Critic, NS 13:154-5, 29 Mar 1890

Sangster, Margaret Elizabeth (Munson)
Eleanor Lee
Critic, 43:580, Dec 1903
Janet Ward
Critic, 41:584, Dec 1902
Literary World, 33:172-3, 1 Nov 1902

Sargent, J. L.
See Wilson, Elizabeth (Sargent), and J. L. Sargent.

Satterthwait, Mrs. Elisabeth Carpenter
A Son of the Carolinas
Independent, 51:635, 2 Mar 1899

Saunders, Margaret Marshall
Deficient Saints
Independent, 51:3501, 28 Dec 1899
Rose à Charlitte
Dial, 25:305, 1 Nov 1898
Independent, 50:1346, 10 Nov 1898

Saunders, Marshall
See Saunders, Margaret Marshall.

Saunders, Ripley Dunlap
John Kenadie
Critic, 42:381, Apr 1903
Dial, 32:392, 1 Jun 1902
Independent, 54:1967, 14 Aug 1902
Literary World, 33:123, 1 Aug 1902

Savage, Minot Judson
Bluffton
Literary World, 9:13, 1 Jun 1878

A Savage of Civilization
Literary World, 27:92, 21 Mar 1896

Savage, Richard Henry
Checked Through
Westminster Review, 146:471, Oct 1896
A Daughter of Judas
Critic, NS 23:203, 16 Mar 1895
For Her Life
Literary World, 28:377, 30 Oct 1897
Her Foreign Conquest
Westminster Review, 147:227, Feb 1897
The Little Lady of Lagunitas
Literary World, 28:228, 10 Jul 1897
Lost Countess Falka
Literary World, 28:73, 6 Mar 1897
A Modern Corsair
Literary World, 28:210, 26 Jun 1897
My Official Wife

Westminster Review, 136:348, Sep 1891
Prince Schamyl's Wooing
Literary World, 28:228, 10 Jul 1897

Savidge, Eugene Coleman
The American in Paris
Critic, NS 25:5, 4 Jan 1896
Dial, 19:384, 16 Dec 1895
Wallingford
Critic, NS 8:30, 16 Jul 1887
Literary World, 18:268, 20 Aug 1887

Sawyer, Edith Augusta
Mary Cameron
Critic, 36:472, May 1900
Literary World, 30:250, 5 Aug 1899

Sawyer, Walter Leon
A Local Habitation
Literary World, 31:26, 20 Jan 1900

Saxon, Van [pseud.]
See Simpson, Mrs. Evangeline M.

Sayre, Theodore Burt
The Son of Carleycroft
Critic, 37:569, Dec 1900

Schallenberger, V.
See Simmons, Vesta S.

Schayer, Julia (Thompson) von Stosch
Tiger Lily, and Other Stories
Critic, 3:296, 30 Jun 1883
Independent, 35:11, 28 Jun 1883
Literary World, 14:244-5, 28 Jul 1883

Schindler, Solomon
Young West
Critic, NS 23:202-3, 16 Mar 1895

Schwartz, Julia Augusta
Vassar Studies
Independent, 51:2024, 27 Jul 1899
Literary World, 30:237, 22 Jul 1899

Scofield, Charles Josiah
A Subtle Adversary
Chautauquan, 16:127, Oct 1892

Scollard, Clinton
The Cloistering of Ursula
Critic, 40:375, Apr 1902
Dial, 32:391, 1 Jun 1902
Independent, 54:1433-4, 12 Jun 1902
Count Falcon of the Eyrie
Critic, 44:477-8, May 1904
A Man-at-Arms
Dial, 25:22, 1 Jul 1898
Independent, 50:727, 2 Jun 1898
Literary World, 29:203-4, 25 Jun 1898
The Son of a Tory
Critic, 39:375, Oct 1901
Dial, 31:34, 1 Jul 1901

[Scott, Anna (Kay)]
Korno Siga, the Mountain Chief
By Mrs. Mildred Marston [pseud.].
Chautauquan, 11:127, Apr 1890

Scott, Leroy
To Him That Hath
Dial, 43:253, 16 Oct 1907
Independent, 63:817-8, 3 Oct 1907; 63:1226-8, 21 Nov 1907
The Walking Delegate
Catholic World, 81:400, Jun 1905
Independent, 59:450-2, 24 Aug 1905

Scribner, Frank Kimball
The Honor of a Princess
Independent, 49:980, 29 Jul 1897
The Love of the Princess Alice
Independent, 51:562, 23 Feb 1899
See also Bentley, Charles S., and Frank Kimball Scribner.

Scudder, Horace Elisha
The Dwellers in Five-Sisters Court
Independent, 28:9, 29 Jun 1876
Stories and Romances
Critic, NS 5:305, 19 Jun 1886
Dial, 1:136, Nov 1880
Literary World, 11:407-8, 20 Nov 1880

Scudder, Moses Lewis
Almost an Englishman
Independent, 30:11, 2 Jan 1879

Searing, Anne Eliza (Pidgeon)
A Social Experiment
Critic, NS 4:161, 3 Oct 1885
Literary World, 16:342, 3 Oct 1885

Sears, Hamblen
See Sears, Joseph Hamblen.

Sears, Joseph Hamblen
A Box of Matches
Literary World, 35:379-80, Dec 1904
Fur and Feather Tales
Harper's, 98:Literary Notes, 4, May 1899
Independent, 51:2230, 17 Aug 1899
Literary World, 30:141, 29 Apr 1899
None but the Brave
Dial, 32:386, 1 Jun 1902
Independent, 54:2024, 21 Aug 1902
Literary World, 33:138, 1 Sep 1902

Seawell, Molly Elliot
The Berkeley's and Their Neighbors
Independent, 44:1835, 22 Dec 1892
Literary World, 23:407, 19 Nov 1892
The Château of Montplaisir
Critic, 49:574, Jun 1906
Children of Destiny
Critic, NS 19:307, 13 May 1893
Literary World, 24:179, 3 Jun 1893
Decatur and Somers
Chautauquan, 20:762, Mar 1895
The Fortunes of Fifi
Critic, 43:580, Dec 1903
Dial, 35:265, 16 Oct 1903
Independent, 56:43-4, 7 Jan 1904
Francezka
Critic, 41:584, Dec 1902
Dial, 33:330-1, 16 Nov 1902
Independent, 55:330, 5 Feb 1903
The History of Lady Betty Stair
Independent, 49:1695, 23 Dec 1897
Literary World, 29:28, 22 Jan 1898
The House of Egremont
Catholic World, 72:404-6, Dec 1900
Critic, 38:86, Jan 1901
Independent, 52:2937, 6 Dec 1900
Literary World, 32:38, 1 Mar 1901
The Loves of the Lady Arabella
Independent, 50:1941, 29 Dec 1898
Literary World, 29:354, 29 Oct 1898
Maid Marian, and Other

Stories
Critic, NS 16:153, 26 Sep 1891
Papa Bouchard
Catholic World, 74:680, Feb 1902
Dial, 31:371, 16 Nov 1901
Literary World, 32:218, 1 Dec 1901
The Rock of the Lion
Harper's, 96:Literary Notes, 1, Mar 1898
Independent, 50:222, 17 Feb 1898
The Sprightly Romance of Marsac
Critic, NS 26:296, 14 Nov 1896
Independent, 48:1693, 10 Dec 1896
A Strange, Sad Comedy
Critic, NS 25:424, 13 Jun 1896
Independent, 48:1007, 23 Jul 1896
Literary World, 27:251-2, 8 Aug 1896
Throckmorton
Catholic World, 51:689-90, Aug 1890
Critic, NS 14:105, 30 Aug 1890
Independent, 42:1344, 25 Sep 1890
Literary World, 21:289, 30 Aug 1890
A Virginia Cavalier
Dial, 22:156, 1 Mar 1897
Harper's, 94:Literary Notes, 1, Jan 1897

Sedgwick, Anne Douglas
Amabel Channice
Independent, 65:1062-3, 5 Nov 1908
The Confounding of Camelia
Critic, NS 32:646-7, Jul 1899
Independent, 51:2570, 21 Sep 1899
Literary World, 30:139, 29 Apr 1899
The Dull Miss Archinard
Independent, 50:726, 2 Jun 1898
Literary World, 29:188, 11 Jun 1898
Literature, 3:135-6, 13 Aug 1898
Paths of Judgment
Critic, 46:94, Jan 1905
Literary World, 35:380-1, Dec 1904
The Rescue
Chautauquan, 35:621, Sep 1902
Critic, 41:58-60, Jul 1902
Dial, 33:63, 1 Aug 1902
Independent, 54:1843, 31 Jul 1902
Literary World, 33:105, 1 Jul 1902
The Shadow of Life
Independent, 60:1041-2, 3 May 1906; 61:1158-60, 15 Nov 1906

Seeley, Charles Sumner [pseud.]
See Munday, John William.

Seely, Edward Howard
A Border Leander
Chautauquan, 17:762, Sep 1893
Critic, NS 20:183, 16 Sep 1893
Literary World, 24:257, 12 Aug 1893
The Jonah of Lucky Valley, and Other Stories
Critic, NS 17:301, 28 May 1892
Harper's, 85:Literary Notes, 2, August 1892
Independent, 44:664, 12 May 1892
Literary World, 23:182, 21 May 1892
A Lone Star Bo-Peep
Critic, NS 5:43, 23 Jan 1886
Literary World, 16:317,

Seely, Edward Howard (cont.)
19 Sep 1885
A Nymph of the West
Critic, NS 10:138, 22 Sep 1888
Independent, 40:817, 28 Jun 1888
Literary World, 19:187, 9 Jun 1888
A Ranchman's Stories
Independent, 38:495, 22 Apr 1886
Literary World, 17:146, 1 May 1886

Seely, Howard
See Seely, Edward Howard.

Seemüller, Anne Moncure (Crane)
Reginald Archer
Galaxy, 12:896-8, Jun 1871
Literary World, 1:172, 1 Apr 1871

[Sellers, Elizabeth Jaudon]
From 18 to 20
Critic, NS 10:114, 8 Sep 1888

Seton, Ernest Thompson
The Biography of a Silver-Fox
Independent, 66:867-8, 22 Apr 1909

Seton, William
The Poor Millionaire
Catholic World, 39:715-6, Aug 1884
Rachel's Fate, and Other Tales
Catholic World, 36:431, Dec 1882
The Romance of the Charter Oak
Catholic World, 13:288, May 1871
The Shamrock Gone West, and Moida
Catholic World, 39:715-6, Aug 1884

Severance, Mark Sibley
Hammersmith
Literary World, 9:31, 1 Jul 1878

Severy, Melvin Linwood
Gillette's Social Redemption
Independent, 63:1177, 14 Nov 1907

[Shackelford, Miss E. A. B.]
Virginia Dare
By E. A. B. S.
Critic, NS 19:60-1, 4 Feb 1893
Literary World, 24:42-3, 11 Feb 1893

Shackleton, Robert
The Great Adventurer
Critic, 45:95, Jul 1904
Dial, 36:368, 1 Jun 1904
Independent, 56:1032-3, 5 May 1904
Literary World, 35:205, Jul 1904
Many Waters
Critic, 42:285, Mar 1903
Dial, 32:390, 1 Jun 1902
Literary World, 33:94, 1 Jun 1902
Toomey and Others
Critic, 37:278, Sep 1900

Shafer, Sara (Andrew)
Beyond Chance of Change
Critic, 47:94, Jul 1905
Dial, 38:394, 1 Jun 1905
Independent, 58:959, 27 Apr 1905
The Day Before Yesterday
Dial, 36:372, 1 Jun 1904

Shaler, Sophia Penn (Page)
The Prelude and the Play
By Rufus Mann [pseud.].
Dial, 29:124-5, 1 Sep 1900

Sharp, William
See Teuffel, Blanche Willis (Howard) von, and William Sharp.

Shaw, Adele Marie
The Coast of Freedom
Catholic World, 76:124-5, Oct 1902
Chautauquan, 37:101, Apr 1903
Dial, 32:386, 1 Jun 1902
Independent, 54:1550, 26 Jun 1902

Shaw, Edward Richard
Legends of Fire Island Beach and the South Side
Independent, 47:1303, 26 Sep 1895
The Pot of Gold
Critic, NS 10:219, 3 Nov 1888

Shaw, Marian
Queen Bess
Independent, 37:1040, 13 Aug 1885
Literary World, 16:277, 8 Aug 1885

Shedd, Harry Graves
Over Grass-Grown Trails
Chautauquan, 33:544, Aug 1901
Critic, 38:182, Feb 1901

Sheldon, Charles Monroe
Born to Serve
Independent, 53:788, 4 Apr 1901
The Crucifixion of Philip Strong
Critic, NS 23:457, 22 Jun 1895
Independent, 47:971, 18 Jul 1895
Literary World, 26:7, 12 Jan 1895
The Heart of the World
Independent, 59:582, 7 Sep 1905
His Brother's Keeper
Literary World, 27:381, 31 Oct 1896
In His Steps
Independent, 49:883, 8 Jul 1897
John King's Question Class
Literary World, 30:408, 25 Nov 1899
The Redemption of Freetown
Independent, 50:1059, 13 Oct 1898
The Reformer
Chautauquan, 38:312, Nov 1903
Robert Hardy's Seven Days
Independent, 45:1453, 26 Oct 1893
Literary World, 24:292, 9 Sep 1893
Who Killed Joe's Baby?
Independent, 53:788, 4 Apr 1901

Sheldon, Mrs. Georgie [pseud.]
See Downs, Sarah Elizabeth (Forbush).

Sheldon, Ruth Louise
Flexible Morals
Literary World, 30:123, 15 Apr 1899

Shelton, Frederick William
The Rector of St. Bardolph's
Independent, 34:11, 2 Mar 1882

Shelton, William Henry
The Last Three Soldiers
Chautauquan, 26:460, Jan 1898
Independent, 49:1695, 23 Dec 1897
Literary World, 28:464, 11 Dec 1897
A Man Without a Memory, and Other Stories
Critic, NS 23:458, 22 Jun 1895
Independent, 47:875, 27 Jun 1895
Literary World, 26:154, 18 May 1895

Sheppard, Francis Henry
Love Afloat
Galaxy, 20:137-9, Jul 1875

Sherlock, Charles Reginald
The Red Anvil
Critic, 42:86, Jan 1903

[Sherman, Charles Pomeroy]
A Bachelor's Wedding Trip
Critic, NS 11:64, 9 Feb 1899

Sherman, Frank Dempster
See Bangs, John Kendrick, and Frank Dempster Sherman.

Sherwood, Emily Lee
See Ragan, Emily Lee (Sherwood).

Sherwood, Mrs. John
See Sherwood, Mary Elizabeth (Wilson).

Sherwood, Margaret Pollock
The Coming of the Tide
Dial, 40:19, 1 Jan 1906
Daphne
Independent, 56:859-60, 14 Apr 1904
An Experiment in Altruism
By Elizabeth Hastings [pseud.].
Critic, NS 23:431, 15 Jun 1895
Literary World, 26:195, 29 Jun 1895
Henry Worthington, Idealist
Chautauquan, 30:442, Jan 1900
Dial, 27:492, 16 Dec 1899
Independent, 51:2829, 19 Oct 1899
Literary World, 31:76, 3 Mar 1900
A Puritan Bohemia
Critic, NS 27:93, 6 Feb 1897
Independent, 49:59, 14 Jan 1897
Literary World, 28:43, 6 Feb 1897
The Story of King Sylvain and Queen Aimée
Independent, 57:510, 1 Sep 1904

Sherwood, Mary Elizabeth (Wilson)
Sweet-Brier
Critic, NS 12:161, 5 Oct 1889
A Transplanted Rose
Catholic World, 55:765-6, Aug 1892
Critic, 2:310, 18 Nov 1882
Dial, 3:140, Nov 1882
Harper's, 86:Literary Notes, 3, Feb 1893
Independent, 34:11, 23 Nov 1882

Shevitch, S.
See Ventura, Luigi Donato, and S. Shevitch.

Shipman, Louis Evan
The Curious Courtship of Kate Poins
Independent, 53:2243, 19 Sep 1901
Literary World, 32:142, 1 Sep 1901
D'Arcy of the Guards
Critic, NS 32:647, Jul 1899
Literary World, 30:237, 22 Jul 1899
The Quality of Youth
Critic, 45:191, Aug 1904
Urban Dialogues
Independent, 49:250, 25 Feb 1897

Shuey, Lillian (Hinman)
Don Luis' Wife
Independent, 50:224, 17 Feb 1898
Literary World, 29:140, 30 Apr 1898

Sibley, Edwin Day
Stillman Gott
Independent, 54:2599, 30 Oct 1902

Sibley, Louise Florence Maria (Lyndon)
A Lighthouse Village
Literary World, 33:61, 1 Apr 1902

Sidney, Margaret [pseud.]
See Lothrop, Harriet Mulford (Stone).

Sikes, Olive (Logan)
Get Thee Behind Me, Satan
Literary World, 3:28, 1 Jul 1872
They Met By Chance
Independent, 25:984, 7 Aug 1873
Literary World, 4:37-8, 1 Aug 1873

Sikes, Mrs. William Wirt
See Sikes, Olive (Logan).

Silva, Gorham [pseud.]
See Lawrence, Elizabeth.

[Simmons, Vesta S.]
Green Tea
By V. Schallenberger.
Catholic World, 56:432, Dec 1892
Literary World, 24:58, 25 Feb 1893
Westminster Review, 137:466, Apr 1892

[Simpson, Mrs. Evangeline M.]
Marplot Cupid
By Van Saxon [pseud.].
Independent, 36:523, 24 Apr 1884

Sinclair, Ellery
Christie's Choice
Critic, NS 5:216, 1 May 1886
Victor
Critic, NS 9:152, 31 Mar 1888
Independent, 40:625, 17 May 1888

Sinclair, Upton
The Jungle
Critic, 48:476, May 1906
Dial, 40:262, 16 Apr 1906
Independent, 60:740-1, 29 Mar 1906; 61:1158-60, 15 Nov 1906
King Midas
Literary World, 33:58, 1 Apr 1902
Manassas
Chautauquan, 44:133, Sep 1906
Dial, 38:15-6, 1 Jan 1905
Independent, 57:1149-51, 17 Nov 1904
Literary World, 35:327, Nov 1904
The Metropolis
Dial, 44:246-7, 16 Apr 1908
Independent, 65:264, 30 Jul 1908
Prince Hagan
Critic, 43:380, Oct 1903
Independent, 55:2292, 24 Sep 1903
Literary World, 34:137-8, Jun 1903
Springtime and Harvest
Literary World, 32:83-4, 1 Jun 1901

Six of One, by Half a Dozen of the Other
By Harriet Beecher Stowe, Adeline D. T. Whitney, Lucretia P. Hale, Frederic W. Loring, Frederic B. Perkins, Edward E. Hale.
Literary World, 3:22, 1 Jul 1872

Skeel, Adelaide
See Kelley, Adelaide (Skeel).

Skinner, Charles Montgomery
With Feet to the Earth
Independent, 49:1547, 25 Nov 1897

Skinner, Henrietta Channing (Dana)
Espiritu Santo
Catholic World, 69:119-21, Apr 1899
Dial, 27:20, 1 Jul 1899
Literary World, 30:116, 15 Apr 1899
Heart and Soul
Independent, 53:2305, 26 Sep 1901
Literary World, 32:142, 1 Sep 1901

Slee, Richard, and Cornelia Atwood Pratt
Dr. Berkeley's Discovery
Critic, 36:374, Apr 1900
Literary World, 31:76, 3 Mar 1900

Sleight, Mary Breck
The Flag on the Mill
Critic, NS 9:4, 7 Jan 1888
Independent, 40:560, 3 May 1888
The House at Crague
Chautauquan, 6:425, Apr 1886
Critic, NS 5:92, 20 Feb 1886
Literary World, 17:350, 16 Oct 1886
An Island Heroine
Literary World, 30:23, 21 Jan 1899
The Osego Chronicles
Literary World, 11:28, 17 Jan 1880
Pulpit and Easel
Chautauquan, 6:60, Oct 1885
Critic, NS 3:257, 30 May 1885

Slosson, Annie (Trumbull)
Aunt Abby's Neighbors
Critic, 41:584, Dec 1902
Literary World, 33:196, 1 Dec 1902
Aunt Liefy
Chautauquan, 16:509, Jan 1893
Critic, NS 19:95, 18 Feb 1893
A Dissatisfied Soul
Independent, 65:556, 3 Sep 1908
Dumb Foxglove, and Other Stories
Harper's, 98:Literary Notes, 3, Dec 1898
Literary World, 30:167, 27 May 1899
Fishin' Jimmy
Chautauquan, 10:251-2, Nov 1889
Critic, NS 12:42, 27 Jul 1889
Independent, 41:1026, 8 Aug 1889
The Heresy of Mehetabel Clark
Critic, NS 17:314, 4 Jun 1892
Harper's, 85:Literary Notes, 4, Aug 1892
Literary World, 23:214, 18 Jun 1892
Seven Dreamers
Critic, NS 15:108, 28 Feb 1891
Harper's, 82:Literary Notes, 3, Feb 1891
White Christopher
Independent, 53:788, 4 Apr 1901

Smart, Charles
Driven from the Path
Literary World, 4:49-50, 1 Aug 1873

Smart, Helen Hamilton (Gardener)
Pray You, Sir, Whose Daughter?
Literary World, 23:278, 13 Aug 1892
Pushed by Unseen Hands
Independent, 44:1261, 8 Sep 1892
A Thoughtless Yes
Independent, 42:1344, 25 Sep 1890

Smith, Alice Prescott
The Legatee
Dial, 35:66, 1 Aug 1903
Westminster Review, 160:112, Jul 1903
Montlivet
Dial, 42:17, 1 Jan 1907
Off the Highway
Independent, 59:154, 20 Jul 1905

Smith, Ann Eliza (Brainerd)
Atla
By Mrs. J. Gregory Smith.
Critic, NS 5:216, 1 May 1886
Harper's, 72:Literary Notes, 1-2, May 1886; 74:Literary Notes, 3, Jan 1887
Literary World, 17:198, 12 Jun 1886
The Garden of the Hesperides
Independent, 39:1038, 18 Aug 1887

Smith, Arthur Cosslett
The Turquoise Cup
Chautauquan, 41:285, May 1905
Independent, 55:801, 2 Apr 1903

Smith, Francis Hopkinson
At Close Range
Critic, 47:94, Jul 1905
Independent, 58:958, 27 Apr 1905
Caleb West, Master Diver
Chautauquan, 28:215-6, Nov 1898
Critic, NS 29:280, 23 Apr 1898
Dial, 24:355-6, 1 Jun 1898
Independent, 50:627, 12 May 1898; 50:1424, 17 Nov 1898
Literary World, 29:187-8, 11 Jun 1898
Literature, 8:328, 8 Oct 1898
Colonel Carter of Cartersville
Catholic World, 53:604, Jul 1891
Critic, NS 16:28-9, 18 Jul 1891
Dial, 12:49, Jun 1891
Westminster Review, 136:231, Aug 1891
Colonel Carter's Christmas
Independent, 55:3068, 24 Dec 1903
A Day at Laguerre's, and Other Days
Critic, NS 17:309, 4 Jun 1892
Independent, 44:664, 12 May 1892
The Fortunes of Oliver Horn
Chautauquan, 37:100, Apr 1903
Critic, 41:584, Dec 1902
Dial, 33:326, 16 Nov 1902
Independent, 54:2367-8, 2 Oct 1902
Literary World, 33:171, 1 Nov 1902
A Gentleman Vagabond, and Some Others
Critic, NS 25:6, 4 Jan 1896
Dial, 20:173, 16 Mar 1896
Independent, 47:1690, 12 Dec 1895
Literary World, 27:188, 13 Jun 1896
The Other Fellow
Chautauquan, 30:327-8, Dec 1899
Dial, 28:88, 1 Feb 1900
Independent, 51:3300, 7 Dec 1899
Literary World, 31:29, 20 Jan 1900
Peter
Dial, 45:213-4, 1 Oct 1908
Independent, 65:718-9, 24 Sep 1908
The Romance of an Old-Fashioned Gentleman

Smith, Francis Hopkinson (cont.)
Independent, 63:1466, 19 Dec 1907
The Tides of Barnegat
Dial, 41:243, 16 Oct 1906
Independent, 61:882-3, 11 Oct 1906
Tom Grogan
Chautauquan, 23:783, Sep 1896
Critic, NS 25:290, 25 Apr 1896; NS 26:156, 12 Sep 1896
Dial, 20:336, 1 Jun 1896
Independent, 48:769, 4 Jun 1896; 48:943, 9 Jul 1896
Literary World, 27:172, 30 May 1896
Westminster Review, 146:232, Aug 1896
The Under Dog
Critic, 43:189, Aug 1903
Independent, 55:1692, 16 Jul 1903
Literary World, 34:179, Jul 1903
The Veiled Lady, and Other Men and Women
Independent, 63:102-3, 11 Jul 1907
A White Umbrella in Mexico
Critic, NS 11:256, 25 May 1889
Independent, 41:464, 11 Apr 1889
The Wood Fire in No. 3
Critic, 47:579, Dec 1905; 48:476-7, May 1906
Independent, 60:225, 25 Jan 1906

Smith, Gertrude
Dedora Heywood
Critic, NS 25:462, 27 Jun 1896
Independent, 48:628, 7 May 1896
Literary World, 27:172, 30 May 1896
The Rousing of Mrs. Potter, and Other Stories
Critic, NS 21:237, 7 Apr 1894
Literary World, 25:58, 24 Feb 1894

Smith, Mrs. J. Gregory
See Smith, Ann Eliza (Brainerd).

Smith, Jeanie Oliver (Davidson)
Donald Moncrieff
Critic, NS 21:408, 16 Jun 1894
The Mayor of Kanemeta
Critic, NS 21:408, 16 Jun 1894
Literary World, 24:242, 29 Jul 1893

Smith, John Talbot
The Art of Disappearing
Catholic World, 77:116-7, Apr 1903
His Honor, the Mayor, and Other Tales
Catholic World, 53:439-40, Jun 1891
Independent, 43:1218, 13 Aug 1891
Saranac
Catholic World, 57:723-4, Aug 1893
Solitary Island
Catholic World, 47:719-20, Aug 1888

Smith, Johnston [pseud.]
See Crane, Stephen.

Smith, Joseph Emerson
Oakridge
Literary World, 5:166, 1 Apr 1875

Smith, Mrs. Julia P.
His Young Wife
Independent, 28:8, 7 Dec 1876
The Married Belle
Literary World, 3:91, 1 Nov 1872
Ten Old Maids . . .

Literary World, 5:92, 1 Nov 1874

Smith, Logan Pearsoll
The Youth of Parnassus
Literary World, 27:188, 13 Jun 1896

[Smith, Mary E.]
Carroll O'Donoghue
By Christine Faber [pseud.].
Catholic World, 33:720, Aug 1881
A Chivalrous Deed and What Came of It
By Christine Faber [pseud.].
Catholic World, 53:924, Sep 1891
The Guardian's Mystery
By Christine Faber [pseud.].
Catholic World, 45:698, 700, Aug 1887
An Original Girl
By Christine Faber [pseud.].
Catholic World, 73:815, Sep 1901
An Ugly Heroine
By Christine Faber [pseud.].
Independent, 35:11, 7 Jun 1883
Literary World, 14:195, 16 Jun 1883

Smith, Minna Caroline
Mary Paget
Chautauquan, 31:314, Jun 1900
Dial, 29:23, 1 Jul 1900
Independent, 52:611, 8 Mar 1900

Smith, Ruel Perley
Prisoners of Fortune
Dial, 42:378, 16 Jun 1907
Independent, 62:674, 21 Mar 1907

Smith, William Hawley
The Evolution of "Dodd" . . .
Critic, NS 3:222, 9 May 1885

Sola [pseud.]
See Anderson, Olive Santa Louise.

Sommers, Lillian E.
Jerome Leaster of Roderick, Leaster & Co.
Independent, 43:457, 26 Mar 1891

Southwick, Albert Plympton
Bijou
Critic, NS 12:186, 19 Oct 1889
Independent, 41:1659, 12 Dec 1889

Southworth, Mrs. E. D. E. N.
See Southworth, Emma Dorothy Eliza (Nevitte).

Southworth, Emma Dorothy Eliza (Nevitte)
The Bridal Eve
Critic, 1:276, 8 Oct 1881
Independent, 35:11, 31 May 1883
Ishmael
Independent, 28:9, 11 May 1876
Self-Raised
Independent, 28:9, 15 Jun 1876
Tried for Her Life
Literary World, 2:12, 1 Jun 1871

Sparhawk, Frances Campbell
A Chronicle of Conquest
Chautauquan, 11:650, Aug 1890
Critic, NS 16:128, 12 Sep 1891
Literary World, 21:126, 12 Apr 1890
Honor Dalton
Independent, 56:212, 28 Jan 1904
A Lazy Man's Work
Critic, 1:109, 23 Apr 1881
Literary World, 12:162, 7 May 1881

Sparhawk, Frances Campbell (cont.)
Onoqua
Chautauquan, 16:127, Oct 1892; 17:126, Apr 1893
Critic, NS 18:32, 16 Jul 1892
Independent, 44:1130, 11 Aug 1892
Literary World, 23:261, 30 Jul 1892
Senator Intrigue and Inspector Noseby
Independent, 47:1107, 15 Aug 1895

Spear, John W.
Grace Winslow
Literary World, 15:264, 9 Aug 1884
Out of the Toils
Chautauquan, 7:506, May 1887
Rudolph of Rosenfeldt
Chautauquan, 12:286, Nov 1890

Spearman, Frank Hamilton
The Close of the Day
Independent, 56:1087-8, 12 May 1904
Literary World, 35:79, Mar 1904
The Daughter of a Magnate
Dial, 36:121, 16 Feb 1904
Independent, 56:1336, 9 Jun 1904
Doctor Bryson
Dial, 33:330, 16 Nov 1902
Independent, 55:391-2, 12 Feb 1903
Literary World, 34:12, 1 Jan 1903
Held for Orders
Literary World, 33:61-2, 1 Apr 1902
The Nerve of Foley, and Other Railroad Stories
Critic, 36:548, Jun 1900
Literary World, 31:90, 1 Apr 1900
See also The Railroad.

Spears, John Randolph
The Port of Missing Ships, and Other Stories of the Sea
Critic, NS 27:426, 19 Jun 1897
Independent, 49:650, 20 May 1897; 49:719, 3 Jun 1897
Literary World, 28:195, 12 Jun 1897

Spencer, Mrs. George E.
See Spencer, William Loring (Nuñez).

Spencer, Lilian
After All
Critic, NS 4:114, 5 Sep 1885
Literary World, 16:342, 3 Oct 1885

Spencer, William Loring (Nuñez)
Calamity Jane
By Mrs. George E. Spencer.
Critic, NS 8:128, 10 Sep 1887
Literary World, 18:284, 3 Sep 1887
Dennis Day, Carpet-Bagger
By Mrs. George E. Spencer.
Critic, NS 8:54, 30 Jul 1887
A Plucky One
By Mrs. George E. Spencer.
Literary World, 18:140, 30 Apr 1887
Salt Lake Fruit
By an American.
Critic, NS 2:5, 5 Jul 1884

Spenser, Mary Clare
The Benefit of the Doubt
Independent, 35:11, 19 Apr 1883

Literary World, 14:229, 14 Jul 1883
Brinka, an American Countess
Critic, NS 9:192, 21 Apr 1888
Independent, 40:753, 14 Jun 1888

Spofford, Harriet Elizabeth (Prescott)
Hester Stanley at St. Mark's
Critic, 2:326, 2 Dec 1882
Independent, 35:43, 11 Jan 1883
An Inheritance
Critic, NS 28:187, 2 Oct 1897
Dial, 22:312, 16 May 1897
Independent, 49:851, 1 Jul 1897
Literary World, 28:211, 26 Jun 1897
A Lost Jewel
Critic, NS 15:27, 17 Jan 1891
Independent, 43:201, 5 Feb 1891
The Maid He Married
Literary World, 30:249, 5 Aug 1899
The Marquis of Carabas
Critic, 2:227, 26 Aug 1882
Dial, 3:97, Sep 1882
Independent, 34:12, 5 Oct 1882
Literary World, 13:252-3, 29 Jul 1882
The Master Spirit
Independent, 48:629, 7 May 1896
Old Washington
Critic, 48:477, May 1906
Independent, 60:1219, 24 May 1906
Priscilla's Love-Story
Independent, 50:729, 2 Jun 1898
Literary World, 29:155, 14 May 1898
A Scarlet Poppy, and Other Stories
Critic, NS 22:328, 17 Nov 1894
Dial, 17:333-4, 1 Dec 1894
Harper's, 90:Literary Notes, 4, Feb 1895
Literary World, 25:301, 22 Sep 1894
That Betty
Critic, 44:94, Jan 1904
Dial, 36:23, 1 Jan 1904
The Thief in the Night
Galaxy, 13:712-3, May 1872
Literary World, 2:147-8, 1 Mar 1872

Sprague, William Cyrus
Felice Constant
Dial, 37:39, 16 Jul 1904

Springer, Mary Elizabeth
"Lady Hancock"
Critic, 38:279, Mar 1901

Springer, Rebecca (Ruter)
Beechwood
Independent, 25:236, 20 Feb 1873
Literary World, 3:138, 1 Feb 1873
Self
Literary World, 12:10, 1 Jan 1881

Staats [pseud.]
See Staats, William.

[Staats, William]
A Tight Squeeze
By Staats [pseud.].
Literary World, 10:307-8, 27 Sep 1879

Stafford, William A. H.
Broken Bonds
Literary World, 17:350, 16 Oct 1886

Stanley, Caroline Hart (Abbot)
A Modern Madonna
Dial, 42:379-80, 16 Jun

Stanley, Caroline Hart (Abbot) (cont.)
1907
Order No. 11
Critic, 45:477, Nov 1904

Stanley, Hiram Alonzo
The Backwoodsman
Dial, 32:89, 1 Feb 1902

Stapleton, Patience (Tucker)
The Major's Christmas, and Other Stories
Critic, NS 5:145, 20 Mar 1886

Steele, James William
Frontier Army Sketches
Dial, 3:140, Nov 1882
Independent, 35:12, 7 Jun 1883

Steell, Willis
Isidra
Critic, NS 9:258, 26 May 1888
Literary World, 29:102-3, 2 Apr 1898

Stephens, Robert Neilson
The Bright Face of Danger
Independent, 57:395, 18 Aug 1904
Literary World, 35:145-6, May 1904
Captain Ravenshaw
Dial, 31:366, 16 Nov 1901
Literary World, 33:44, 1 Mar 1902
The Continental Dragoon
Dial, 25:22, 1 Jul 1898
Independent, 50:727, 2 Jun 1898
Literary World, 29:268, 20 Aug 1898
An Enemy to the King
Dial, 24:295, 1 May 1898
Literary World, 28:515, 11 Dec 1897
The Flight of Georgiana
Independent, 60:111, 11 Jan 1906
A Gentleman Player
Dial, 27:175, 16 Sep 1899
Literary World, 30:219, 8 Jul 1899
The Mystery of Murray Davenport
Critic, 43:381, Oct 1903
Literary World, 34:117, May 1903
Philip Winwood
Dial, 29:307, 1 Nov 1900
Independent, 53:162, 17 Jan 1901
Literary World, 31:140, 1 Jul 1900
The Road to Paris
Dial, 26:124, 16 Feb 1899
Literary World, 30:23, 21 Jan 1899

Stephenson, Henry Thew
Patroon Van Volkenberg
Critic, 38:182, Feb 1901
Dial, 31:26, 1 Jul 1901

Stephenson, Nathaniel Wright
The Beautiful Mrs. Moulton
Literary World, 33:172, 1 Nov 1902
Eleanor Dayton
Dial, 35:157 [221], 1 Oct 1903
Independent, 55:3132-3, 31 Dec 1903
They That Took the Sword
Critic, 39:279, Sep 1901
Dial, 31:367, 16 Nov 1901

Sterne, Stuart [pseud.]
See Bloede, Gertrude.

Stetson, Charlotte Perkins
See Gilman, Charlotte (Perkins) Stetson.

Stetson, Grace Ellery (Channing)
The Sister of a Saint, and Other Stories
Critic, NS 25:289, 25 Apr 1896

Independent, 48:526, 16 Apr 1896

Stevens, Mary Fletcher
By Subtle Fragrance Held
Chautauquan, 16:508, Jan 1893
Critic, NS 19:127, 4 Mar 1893
Literary World, 24:148, 6 May 1893

Stevens, Sheppard
See Stevens, Susan Sheppard (Pierce).

Stevens, Susan Sheppard (Pierce)
I Am the King
Literary World, 30:7, 7 Jan 1899
In the Eagle's Talons
Catholic World, 75:834-5, Sep 1902
Dial, 33:67, 1 Aug 1902
Literary World, 33:140, 1 Sep 1902
The Sword of Justice
Critic, 36:90, Jan 1900
Independent, 52:2522, 18 Oct 1900
Literary World, 30:409, 25 Nov 1899

Stevenson, Burton Egbert
Affairs of State
Dial, 42:16, 1 Jan 1907
Independent, 62:386, 14 Feb 1907
At Odds with the Regent
Literary World, 32:187, 1 Nov 1901
Cadets of Gascony
Independent, 56:1202-3, 26 May 1904
Literary World, 35:169, Jun 1904
The Girl with the Blue Sailor
Critic, 49:287, Sep 1906
The Heritage
Chautauquan, 38:91, Sep 1903
Critic, 42:86, Jan 1903
Dial, 33:327, 16 Nov 1902
The Holladay Case
Critic, 44:478, May 1904
Literary World, 35:15, Jan 1904
The Marathon Mystery
Critic, 46:285, Mar 1905
Dial, 38:128, 16 Feb 1905
A Soldier of Virginia
Dial, 31:135, 1 Sep 1901
Independent, 53:2121, 5 Sep 1901

Stevenson, Edward Irenaeus Prime
Janus
Dial, 22:22-3, 1 Jan 1897
Independent, 41:370, 21 Mar 1889
Literary World, 20:242, 20 Jul 1889
Left to Themselves
Chautauquan, 13:686, Aug 1891

Stevenson, Robert Louis
See Osbourne, Lloyd, and Robert Louis Stevenson.

Stickney, Mary Etta (Smith)
Brown of Lost River
Literary World, 31:163, 1 Sep 1900

[Stillman, Annie Raymond]
How They Kept the Faith
By Grace Raymond [pseud.].
Literary World, 20:305, 14 Sep 1889

Stimpson, Herbert Baird
The Tory Maid
Independent, 51:3501, 28 Dec 1899

Stimson, Frederic Jesup
The Crime of Henry Vane
By J. S. of Dale [pseud.].
Critic, NS 2:17, 12 Jul 1884

Stimson, Frederic Jesup (cont.)
Dial, 5:67, Jul 1884
Independent, 36:971, 31 Jul 1884
Literary World, 15:226, 12 Jul 1884
First Harvests
Chautauquan, 9:434, Apr 1889
Critic, NS 11:39, 26 Jan 1889
Independent, 41:402, 28 Mar 1889
Literary World, 20:4-5, 5 Jan 1889
Guerndale
By J. S. of Dale [pseud.].
Critic, 2:161, 17 Jun 1882
Dial, 3:60, Jul 1882
Independent, 34:12, 7 Sep 1882
Literary World, 13:259, 12 Aug 1882
In Cure of Her Soul
Critic, 49:287, Sep 1906
Dial, 41:37-8, 16 Jul 1906
Independent, 61:581, 6 Sep 1906
In the Three Zones
Dial, 14:218, 1 Apr 1893
Independent, 45:507, 13 Apr 1893
Literary World, 24:74, 11 Mar 1893
Jethro Bacon and the Weaker Sex
Critic, 43:92, Jul 1903
Independent, 55:157-8, 15 Jan 1903
King Noanett
Chautauquan, 24:384, Dec 1896
Critic, NS 26:314, 21 Nov 1896
Dial, 21:288, 16 Nov 1896
Harper's, 95:Literary Notes, 1-2, Jun 1897
Independent, 48:1174-5, 27 Aug 1896
Literary World, 27:259, 22 Aug 1896
Mrs. Knollys, and Other Stories
Chautauquan, 26:463, Jan 1898
Critic, NS 29:231, 2 Apr 1898
Independent, 50:123, 27 Jan 1898
Literary World, 29:3, 8 Jan 1898
Pirate Gold
Critic, NS 25:427, 13 Jun 1896
Dial, 20:335-6, 1 Jun 1896
Literary World, 27:172, 30 May 1896
The Residuary Legatee
Catholic World, 47:561-2, Jul 1888
Chautauquan, 9:63, Oct 1888
Critic, NS 10:17, 14 Jul 1888
Independent, 40:817, 28 Jun 1888
Literary World, 19:220, 7 Jul 1888
The Sentimental Calendar
By J. S. of Dale [pseud.].
Critic, NS 7:16, 8 Jan 1887
Literary World, 18:11, 8 Jan 1887
See also The King's Men.

[Stimtz, Stephen Conrad]
Mrs. Jim and Mrs. Jimmie
By Stephen Conrad [pseud.].
Independent, 59:986, 26 Oct 1905

Stirling, A. [pseud.]
See Kimball, Annie Lydia (McPhail).

Stockton, Frank Richard
The Adventures of Captain Horn
Catholic World, 61:700-1, Aug 1895

Critic, NS 23:432, 15 Jun 1895
Dial, 19:19, 1 Jul 1895
Independent, 47:1107, 15 Aug 1895; 47:1579, 21 Nov 1895
Literary World, 26:181, 15 Jun 1895
Westminster Review, 144:351, Sep 1895

Afield and Afloat
Critic, 37:468, Nov 1900
Independent, 52:2580-1, 25 Oct 1900
Literary World, 32:55, 1 Apr 1901

Amos Kilbright
Catholic World, 48:271-2, Nov 1888
Chautauquan, 9:434, Apr 1889
Critic, NS 11:29, 19 Jan 1889
Independent, 40:1685, 27 Dec 1888
Literary World, 19:365, 27 Oct 1888

Ardis Claverdon
Critic, NS 14:175, 11 Oct 1890
Dial, 11:240-1, Dec 1890
Independent, 42:1497, 23 Oct 1890
Literary World, 21:430, 22 Nov 1890

The Associate Hermits
Critic, NS 31:162, Feb 1899
Dial, 26:124, 16 Feb 1899
Harper's, 98:Literary Notes, 2, Mar 1899
Independent, 50:1869, 22 Dec 1898
Literary World, 30:6, 7 Jan 1899

The Bee-Man of Orn, and Other Fanciful Tales
Critic, NS 8:176, 8 Oct 1887
Literary World, 18:347-8, 15 Oct 1887

A Bicycle of Cathay
Critic, 38:86, Jan 1901
Literary World, 32:103, 1 Jul 1901

A Borrowed Month
Westminster Review, 128:784, Sep 1887

Buccaneers and Pirates of Our Coasts
Independent, 50:1345, 10 Nov 1898

Captain Chap
Chautauquan, 25:112, Apr 1897

The Captain's Toll-Gate
Critic, 43:189, Aug 1903
Dial, 35:158 [222], 1 Oct 1903
Independent, 55:2059, 27 Aug 1903
Literary World, 34:179, Jul 1903

The Casting Away of Mrs. Lecks and Mrs. Aleshine
Catholic World, 44:412, Dec 1886
Chautauquan, 7:191, Dec 1886
Critic, NS 7:27, 15 Jan 1887
Dial, 7:189, Dec 1886

The Christmas Wreck
Critic, NS 6:147, 25 Sep 1886

The Clocks of Rondaine
Independent, 44:1712, 1 Dec 1892

The Dusantes
Catholic World, 47:267, May 1888
Critic, NS 9:114, 10 Mar 1888
Dial, 9:67, Jul 1888
Literary World, 19:123, 14 Apr 1888

The Floating Prince
Critic, 1:337, 3 Dec 1881

The Girl at Cobhurst
Chautauquan, 27:428, Jul 1898
Critic, NS 29:343-4, 21 May 1898
Dial, 25:75, 1 Aug 1898
Harper's, 97:Literary

Stockton, Frank Richard (cont.)
Notes, 3, Jul 1898
Independent, 50:637, 1 Sep 1898
Literary World, 29:203, 25 Jun 1898
Literature, 3:160, 20 Aug 1898

The Great Stone of Sardis
Independent, 49:1662, 16 Dec 1897
Literary World, 29:10, 8 Jan 1898
Literature, 2:82-3, 22 Jan 1898

The Great War Syndicate
Critic, NS 11:167, 6 Apr 1889; NS 13:296, 14 Jun 1890
Dial, 11:13, May 1890
Independent, 42:629-30, 8 May 1890

The House of Martha
Dial, 12:278, Dec 1891

The Hundredth Man
Catholic World, 46:557, Jan 1888
Chautauquan, 8:198, Dec 1887
Critic, NS 8:229, 5 Nov 1887
Dial, 8:146, Nov 1887
Independent, 39:1425, 3 Nov 1887
Literary World, 18:382, 12 Nov 1887

John Gayther's Garden, and Other Stories
Critic, 42:564, Jan 1903
Independent, 55:44, 1 Jan 1903

Kate Bonnet
Critic, 41:90, Jul 1902
Independent, 54:1077, 1 May 1902
Literary World, 33:60, 1 Apr 1902

The Lady, or the Tiger? and Other Stories
Critic, NS 6:147, 25 Sep 1886
Dial, 5:67-8, Jul 1884
Westminster Review, 123 (NS 67):292-3, Jan 1885

The Late Mrs. Null
Catholic World, 43:272-4, May 1886
Chautauquan, 6:547, Jun 1886
Critic, NS 5:166, 3 Apr 1886
Dial, 7:15, May 1886
Independent, 38:527, 29 Apr 1886
Literary World, 17:182, 29 May 1886

The Merry Chanter
Critic, NS 14:57, 2 Aug 1890
Independent, 42:1133, 14 Aug 1890
Literary World, 21:254, 2 Aug 1890

Mrs. Cliff's Yacht
Chautauquan, 24:376, Dec 1896
Critic, NS 26:341, 28 Nov 1896
Dial, 21:288, 16 Nov 1896

Personally Conducted
Critic, NS 12:267, 30 Nov 1889
Independent, 41:1399, 24 Oct 1889

Pomona's Travels
Critic, NS 22:344, 24 Nov 1894
Literary World, 25:393, 17 Nov 1894

Rudder Grange
Chautauquan, 6:184, Dec 1885
Independent, 31:10, 29 May 1879; 37:1488, 19 Nov 1885
Westminster Review, 119:290, Apr 1883

The Rudder Grangers Abroad, and Other Stories
Catholic World, 53:606, Jul 1891
Critic, NS 16:17, 11 Jul 1891

Independent, 43:1219, 13 Aug 1891

The Squirrel Inn

Dial, 12:278, Dec 1891

Independent, 43:1844, 10 Dec 1891

The Stories of the Three Burglars

Independent, 42:630, 8 May 1890

Literary World, 21:238, 19 Jul 1890

The Story of Viteau

Chautauquan, 5:181, Dec 1884

Independent, 36:1356, 23 Oct 1884

A Story-Teller's Pack

Critic, NS 27:423, 19 Jun 1897

Dial, 23:93, 16 Aug 1897

Independent, 49:719, 3 Jun 1897; 49:851, 1 Jul 1897

Literary World, 28:260, 7 Aug 1897

The Vizier of the Two-Horned Alexander

Critic, 36:31-2, Jan 1900

Independent, 51:3171, 23 Nov 1899

Literary World, 30:377, 11 Nov 1899

The Watchmaker's Wife, and Other Stories

Dial, 16:147, 1 Mar 1894

Independent, 45:1653, 7 Dec 1893

What Might Have Been Expected

Critic, NS 13:15, 11 Jan 1890

Literary World, 21:41, 1 Feb 1890

The Young Master of Hyson Hall

Westminster Review, 153:113, Jan 1900

[Stockton, Louise]

Dorothea

Critic, 2:175, 1 Jul 1882

Dial, 3:13, May 1882

Literary World, 13:133, 22 Apr 1882

Stoddard, Charles Warren

For the Pleasure of His Company

Dial, 35:155 [219], 1 Oct 1903

Literary World, 34:180, Jul 1903

Stoddard, Elizabeth Drew (Barstow)

The Morgesons

Critic, NS 12:162, 5 Oct 1889

Independent, 41:1355, 17 Oct 1889

Literary World, 20:324, 28 Sep 1889

Two Men

Critic, NS 9:305, 23 Jun 1888

Independent, 40:1073, 23 Aug 1888

Literary World, 19:227, 21 Jul 1888

Stoddard, William Osborn

Chumley's Post

Literary World, 27:220, 11 Jul 1896

Esau Hardery

Literary World, 12:454, 3 Dec 1881

Little Smoke

Chautauquan, 14:510, Jan 1892

Montanye

Dial, 31:34, 1 Jul 1901

On the Old Frontier

Chautauquan, 19:247, May 1894

The Quartet

Critic, 1:276, 8 Oct 1881

Red Beauty

Critic, NS 6:249, 20 Nov 1886

The Red Mustang

Critic, NS 14:166, 4 Oct 1890

Harper's, 81:Literary Notes, 1, Jun 1890

Stoddard, William Osborn (cont.)
Independent, 42:788, 5 Jun 1890
The Red Patriot
Chautauquan, 26:461, Jan 1898
Success Against Odds
Chautauquan, 29:510, Aug 1899
The Swordmaker's Son
Chautauquan, 24:508, Jan 1897
Independent, 49:122, 28 Jan 1897
The Talking Leaves
Critic, 2:296, 4 Nov 1882
Harper's, 73:Literary Notes, 4, Aug 1886
Two Arrows
Harper's, 73:Literary Notes, 4, Aug 1886

Stokely, Edith (Keeley), and Marion Kent Hurd
Miss Billy
Catholic World, 83:122, Apr 1906

Stone, Mrs. C. H.
One of "Berrian's" Novels
Critic, NS 14:234, 8 Nov 1890

Stone, Mary E.
See Bassett, Mary E. Stone.

Stories by American Authors--I, II, and III
Literary World, 15:183, 31 May 1884

Stories by American Authors--IV
Independent, 36:1131, 4 Sep 1884

Stories by American Authors--V
Independent, 36:1324, 16 Oct 1884

Stories by American Authors--VI
Literary World, 15:328, 4 Oct 1884

Stories by American Authors--VII
Critic, NS 2:234-5, 15 Nov 1884

Stories by American Authors--VIII
Critic, NS 2:306, 27 Dec 1884

Stories of American Authors--VIII, IX, and X
Literary World, 16:202, 13 Jun 1885

Stories by American Authors--IX
Critic, NS 3:78, 14 Feb 1888

Stories of the South
Critic, NS 20:337, 25 Nov 1893

Storke, Francis Eugene
Mr. DeLacy's Double
Literary World, 30:54, 18 Feb 1899

Story, William Wetmore
Fiammetta
Catholic World, 43:132-3, Apr 1886
Critic, NS 5:43, 23 Jan 1886
Dial, 6:302, Mar 1886
Independent, 38:107, 28 Jan 1886
Literary World, 17:40-1, 6 Feb 1886

Stowe, Harriet Elizabeth (Beecher)
My Wife and I
Galaxy, 13:276-7, Feb 1872
Literary World, 2:97-8, 1 Dec 1871

Oldtown Fireside Stories
Literary World, 2:124, 1 Jan 1872
Pink and White Tyranny
Catholic World, 13:858-9, Sep 1871
Galaxy, 12:719-21, Nov 1871
Independent, 37:555, 30 Apr 1885
Literary World, 2:25-6, 1 Jul 1871
Poganuc People
Literary World, 9:13, 1 Jun 1879
Westminster Review, 110:273, Oct 1878
We and Our Neighbors
Independent, 27:10, 29 Apr 1875
Literary World, 6:7, 1 Jun 1875
See also Six of One, by Half a Dozen of the Other.

Streeter, John Williams
Doctor Tom
Critic, 46:190, Feb 1905

Strickland, Terésa Hammond
Under the Ban
Literary World, 29:188, 11 Jun 1898

Stringer, Arthur John Arbuthnot
The Silver Poppy
Dial, 35:156 [220], 1 Oct 1903
Literary World, 34:237, Sep 1903
The Under Groove
Independent, 65:268, 30 Jul 1908
The Wire Tappers
Critic, 49:288, Sep 1906
Dial, 41:38, 16 Jul 1906

Stuart, Eleanor [pseud.]
See Childs, Eleanor Stuart (Patterson).

Stuart, Henry Longan
Weeping Cross
Dial, 45:214-5, 1 Oct 1908
Independent, 65:550, 3 Sep 1908

Stuart, Ruth (McEnery)
Carlotta's Intended, and Other Tales
Critic, NS 22:186, 22 Sep 1894
Harper's, 89:Literary Notes, 1-2, Sep 1894
Literary World, 25:233-4, 28 Jul 1894
George Washington Jones
Critic, 44:94, Jan 1904
A Golden Wedding, and Other Tales
Critic, NS 19:377-8, 10 Jun 1893
Harper's, 86:Literary Notes, 3, Apr 1893
Independent, 45:507, 13 Apr 1893
Literary World, 24:89, 25 Mar 1893
Holly and Pizen, and Other Stories
Critic, 36:170, Feb 1900
Independent, 52:196, 18 Jan 1900
Literary World, 31:140, 1 Jul 1900
In Simpkinsville
Critic, NS 28:340, 4 Dec 1897
Harper's, 95:Literary Notes, 2, Sep 1897
Literary World, 28:298, 4 Sep 1897
Literature, 1:212, 4 Dec 1897
Moriah's Mourning, and Other Half-Hour Sketches
Critic, NS 30:395-6, Nov 1898
Independent, 50:264, 28 Jul 1898; 50:1424, 17 Nov 1898
Harper's, 97:Literary Notes, 2, Aug 1898

Stuart, Ruth (McEnery) (cont.)
Literary World, 29:269, 20 Aug 1898
Napoleon Jackson
Chautauquan, 36:336, Dec 1902
Critic, 41:584, Dec 1902
Dial, 33:332, 16 Nov 1902
The Rivers Children
Chautauquan, 40:592, Feb 1905
Critic, 46:190, Feb 1905
The Second Wooing of Salina Sue
Independent, 59:156, 20 Jul 1905
Solomon Crow's Christmas Pockets, and Other Tales
Critic, NS 27:251, 10 Apr 1897
Harper's, 94:Literary Notes, 4, Feb 1897
Independent, 49:250, 25 Feb 1897
Sonny
Chautauquan, 40:592, Feb 1905
Critic, NS 27:75, 30 Jan 1897; 46:285, Mar 1905
The Story of Babette
Critic, NS 23:141, 16 Feb 1895
Harper's, 90:Literary Notes, 2-3, Jan 1895
Independent, 47:737, 30 May 1895; 47:1579, 21 Nov 1895
Literary World, 26:42, 9 Feb 1895
The Woman's Exchange of Simpkinsville
Independent, 63:1473, 19 Dec 1907

Sullivan, Mrs. A. Shackelford
A Questionable Marriage
Dial, 22:312, 16 May 1897
Literary World, 28:355, 16 Oct 1897

Sullivan, James William
Tenement Tales of New York
Critic, NS 23:454, 22 Jun 1895
Literary World, 26:233, 27 Jul 1895

Sullivan, Thomas Russell
Ars et Vita, and Other Stories
Dial, 25:79, 1 Aug 1898
Independent, 50:797, 16 Jun 1898
Literary World, 29:205, 25 Jun 1898
The Courage of Conviction
Critic, 42:86, Jan 1903
Dial, 33:63, 1 Aug 1902
Literary World, 33:124, 1 Aug 1902
Day and Night Stories
Chautauquan, 11:649-50, Aug 1890
Critic, NS 14:16, 12 Jul 1890
Literary World, 21:201, 21 Jun 1890
Day and Night Stories/Second Series
Critic, NS 20:87, 5 Aug 1893
Dial, 15:94-5, 16 Aug 1893
Independent, 45:1282, 21 Sep 1893
Literary World, 24:210, 1 Jul 1893
Roses of Shadow
Literary World, 17:11, 9 Jan 1886
Tom Sylvester
Critic, NS 20:412, 23 Dec 1893
Dial, 16:20, 1 Jan 1894
Independent, 45:1654, 7 Dec 1893
Literary World, 24:452, 16 Dec 1893

Super, Mrs. Emma Lefferts
One Rich Man's Son

Chautauquan, 23:654, Aug 1896

Sutherland, Howard Vigne
The Legend of Love
Critic, NS 20:183, 16 Sep 1893

Sutphen, Van Tassel
See Sutphen, William Gilbert Van Tassel.

Sutphen, William Gilbert Van Tassel
The Cardinal's Rose
Literary World, 32:87, 1 Jun 1901; 32:103, 1 Jul 1901
The Gates of Chance
Dial, 36:371, 1 Jun 1904
Independent, 56:1336, 9 Jun 1904
Literary World, 35:229, Aug 1904
The Golficide, and Other Tales of the Fair Green
Harper's, 97:Literary Notes, 2, Jul 1898
Independent, 50:727, 2 Jun 1898
Literary World, 29:205, 25 Jun 1898
The Nineteenth Hole
Dial, 31:370, 16 Nov 1901
Independent, 53:2184, 12 Sep 1901
Literary World, 32:138, 1 Sep 1901

Swan, Annie S.
Fettered Yet Free
Independent, 47:1543, 14 Nov 1895
Twice Tried
Chautauquan, 18:255, Nov 1893

Swett, Sophie
See Swett, Sophia Miriam.

Swett, Sophia Miriam
Captain Polly
Harper's, 79:Literary Notes, 3-4, Sep 1889
Flying Hill Farm
Harper's, 85:Literary Notes, 3-4, Aug 1892
Pennyroyal and Mint
Critic, NS 27:255, 10 Apr 1897
Literary World, 28:57-8, 20 Feb 1897
Tom Pickering of 'Scutney
Chautauquan, 27:112, Apr 1898

Swett, Susan Hartley
Field Clover and Beach Grass
Critic, NS 27:255, 10 Apr 1897
Literary World, 28:58, 20 Feb 1897

Swift, Augustus M.
Cupid, M. D.
Critic, 2:309, 18 Nov 1882
Independent, 34:10-1, 16 Nov 1882

Taber, Harry Parson
See Wells, Carolyn, and Harry Parson Taber.

Taggart, Marion Ames
Aser, the Shepherd
Independent, 49:1661, 16 Dec 1897
Bezaleel
Independent, 49:1661, 16 Dec 1897
The Wyndham Girls
Catholic World, 76:550, Jan 1903

Talbot, Charles Remington
The Impostor
Chautauquan, 22:382, Dec 1895

Talbot, Ethelbert
My People of the Plains
Independent, 62:1036, 2 May 1907

Talcott, Hannah Elizabath (Bradbury) Goodwin
Dorothy Gray
Critic, NS 15:108-9, 28 Feb 1891
The Fortunes of Miss Follen
By Mrs. Goodwin-Talcott.
Galaxy, 22:429, Sep 1876
One Among Many
Literary World, 15:194, 14 Jun 1884
Our Party of Four
Critic, NS 9:67, 11 Feb 1888

Tales of Our Coast
By S. R. Crockett, Gilbert Parker, Harold Frederic, W. Clark Russell, and "Q".
Critic, NS 27:58, 23 Jan 1897
Independent, 48:1693, 10 Dec 1896
Literary World, 27:457, 12 Dec 1896

Tappan, Eva March
The Christ Story
Chautauquan, 38:414, Dec 1903

Tarkington, Booth
See Tarkington, Newton Booth.

Tarkington, Newton Booth
The Beautiful Lady
Critic, 47:286, Sep 1905
Independent, 59:580-1, 7 Sep 1905; 59:1153, 16 Nov 1905
Cherry
Chautauquan, 41:285, May 1905
Critic, 44:94, Jan 1904
Literary World, 35:50, Feb 1904
The Conquest of Canaan
Critic, 48:286-7, Mar 1906
Dial, 40:155, 1 Mar 1906
Independent, 59:1153, 16 Nov 1905
The Gentleman from Indiana
Critic, 36:91, Jan 1900
Independent, 52:67-8, 4 Jan 1900
Literary World, 30:455, 23 Dec 1899
The Guest of Quesnay
Independent, 65:1061, 5 Nov 1908: 65:1464, 17 Dec 1908
In the Arena
Critic, 46:479, May 1905
Monsieur Beaucaire
Critic, 37:552, Dec 1900
The Two Vanrevels
Critic, 41:584, Dec 1902
Dial, 33:327, 16 Nov 1902
Independent, 54:2771, 20 Nov 1902; 54:2838-9, 27 Nov 1902

Tascher, Julia M.
Arbutus and Dandelions
Independent, 35:11, 2 Aug 1883

Taylor, Bayard
Joseph and His Friend
Westminster Review, 95:275, Apr 1871

Taylor, Belle Gray
The Sardonyx Seal
Chautauquan, 13:552, Jul 1891
Critic, NS 15:237, 2 May 1891
Dial, 12:50, Jun 1891
Independent, 43:645, 30 Apr 1891; 45:1058, 3 Aug 1893

Taylor, Bert Leston
The Charlatans
Dial, 42:228, 1 Apr 1907
Independent, 62:562-3, 7 Mar 1907

________, and Alvin T. Thoits
Under Three Flags
Literary World, 28:43, 6 Feb 1897

Taylor, Emerson Gifford
A Daughter of Dale
Critic, 45:477, Nov 1904
Independent, 57:741-2, 29 Sep 1904
The Upper Hand
Dial, 43:63, 1 Aug 1907
Independent, 62:101, 10 Jan 1907

Taylor, Hobart Chatfield
See Chatfield-Taylor, Hobart Chatfield.

Taylor, Mary Imlay
Anne Scarlett
Independent, 54:167-8, 16 Jan 1902
Caleb Trench
Dial, 48:395, 1 Jun 1910
The Cardinal's Musketeer
Critic, 37:86, Jul 1900
Dial, 29:24, 1 Jul 1900
Independent, 52:953, 19 Apr 1900
The Cobbler of Nîmes
Dial, 29:498, 16 Dec 1900
Literary World, 32:38, 1 Mar 1901
The House of the Wizard
Dial, 29:24, 1 Jul 1900
Literary World, 30:456, 23 Dec 1899
An Imperial Lover
Dial, 24:81, 1 Feb 1898
Independent, 50:222, 17 Feb 1898
Literary World, 29:60, 19 Feb 1898
The Impersonator
Dial, 42:17, 1 Jan 1907
On the Red Staircase
Dial, 22:155, 1 Mar 1897
Literary World, 28:127, 17 Apr 1897
The Reaping
Catholic World, 87:407, Jun 1908
Dial, 44:246, 16 Apr 1908
A Yankee Volunteer
Independent, 51:426, 9 Feb 1899
Literary World, 30:38, 4 Feb 1899

Taylor, Winnie Louise
His Broken Sword
Critic, NS 10:17, 14 Jul 1888
Dial, 9:66-7, Jul 1888
Independent, 40:753, 14 Jun 1888
Literary World, 19:169-70, 26 May 1888

Teal, Angeline (Gruey)
John Thorn's Folks
Critic, NS 2:137, 20 Sep 1884
Muriel Howe
Independent, 42:1834, 22 Dec 1892
Literary World, 24:43, 11 Feb 1893
The Rose of Love
Independent, 45:1653, 7 Dec 1893
Literary World, 24:468, 30 Dec 1893

Teetzel, Mrs. Frances Grant
A Dynamite Cartridge
Critic, NS 12:186, 19 Oct 1889
Literary World, 16:209, 13 Jun 1885

Templeton, Faith [pseud.]
See Barber, Harriet Boomer.

Tenney, Edward Payson
Agamenticus
Independent, 30:12, 5 Sep 1878
Agatha and the Shadow
Critic, NS 7:101, 26 Feb 1887
Literary World, 18:58, 19 Feb 1887
Constance of Acadia
Independent, 38:1013, 12 Aug 1886
Literary World, 18:58,

Tenney, Edward Payson (cont.)
19 Feb 1887

Terhune, Albert Payson
Caleb Conover, Railroader
Independent, 62:1526-7, 27 Jun 1907
Columbia Stories
Literary World, 28:298, 4 Sep 1897
See also Terhune, Mary Virginia (Hawes), and Albert Payson Terhune.

Terhune, Mary Virginia (Hawes)
Eve's Daughters
Literary World, 16:290, 22 Aug 1885
A Gallant Fight
By Marion Harland [pseud.].
Catholic World, 48:549-50, Jan 1889
Independent, 41:402, 28 Mar 1889
Literary World, 20:59, 16 Feb 1889
Handicapped
By Marion Harland [pseud.].
Critic, 1:191, 16 Jul 1881
Dial, 2:88, Aug 1881
His Great Self
By Marion Harland [pseud.].
Critic, NS 17:276, 14 May 1892
Independent, 44:881, 23 Jun 1892
Literary World, 23:110, 26 Mar 1892
In Our Country
By Marion Harland [pseud.].
Critic, 40:281, Mar 1902
Literary World, 32:179, 1 Nov 1901
Jessamine
By Marion Harland [pseud.].
Galaxy, 17:425, Mar 1874
Literary World, 4:124, 1 Jan 1874
Judith
By Marion Harland [pseud.].
Independent, 36:748, 12 Jun 1884
Literary World, 15:5, 12 Jan 1884
Mr. Wayt's Wife's Sister
Catholic World, 59:135-6, Apr 1894
Critic, NS 22:38-9, 21 Jul 1894
Literary World, 25:58, 24 Feb 1894; 27:187, 13 Jun 1896
An Old-Field School-Girl
By Marion Harland [pseud.].
Chautauquan, 26:687, Mar 1898
Independent, 49:1695, 23 Dec 1897
Literary World, 28:399, 13 Nov 1897
The Royal Road
By Marion Harland [pseud.].
Chautauquan, 21:775, Sep 1895
Literary World, 26:11, 12 Jan 1895
True as Steel
By Marion Harland [pseud.].
Literary World, 2:181-2, 1 May 1872
When Grandmama Was New
By Marion Harland [pseud.].
Independent, 51:2570, 21 Sep 1899
With the Best Intentions
By Marion Harland [pseud.].
Catholic World, 51:833, Sep 1890
Chautauquan, 12:825-6, Mar 1891
Critic, NS 14:192, 18 Oct 1890
Independent, 42:1344, 25 Sep 1890
Literary World, 21:303, 13 Sep 1890

________, and Albert Payson Terhune
Dr. Dale
By Marion Harland [pseud.] and Albert Payson Terhune.
Catholic World, 72:408-9, Dec 1900

Critic, 38:85, Jan 1901

Teuffel, Blanche Willis (Howard) von
Aulnay Tower
Critic, NS 4:135, 19 Sep 1885
Dial, 6:179, Nov 1885
Literary World, 16:291, 22 Aug 1885
Aunt Serena
Dial, 2:150, Nov 1881
Literary World, 13:415, 19 Nov 1881
A Battle and a Boy
Chautauquan, 17:486, Jul 1893
Literary World, 24:26, 28 Jan 1893
Dionysius the Weaver's Heart's Dearest
Independent, 51:2964, 2 Nov 1899
The Garden of Eden
Critic, 37:278, Sep 1900
Literary World, 31:121, 1 Jun 1900
Guenn
Catholic World, 38:719-20, Feb 1884
Dial, 4:229, Jan 1884
Independent, 36:299, 6 Mar 1884
Literary World, 15:12, 12 Jan 1884
One Summer
Literary World, 6:18, 1 Jul 1875
Westminster Review, 120:279-80, Oct 1883
The Open Door
Chautauquan, 9:564, Jun 1889
Dial, 10:58, Jul 1889
Independent, 41:1217, 19 Sep 1889
Literary World, 20:156, 11 May 1889
Seven on the Highway
Literary World, 28:436, 27 Nov 1897
Tony, the Maid
Catholic World, 46:413-5, Dec 1887
Critic, NS 8:257, 19 Nov 1887
Dial, 8:268-9, Mar 1888
Harper's, 75:Literary Notes, 4, Nov 1887
Independent, 39:1587, 8 Dec 1887
Literary World, 18:461, 10 Dec 1887

_______, and William Sharp
A Fellowe and His Wife
Critic, NS 17:264, 7 May 1892
Literary World, 23:119, 9 Apr 1892
Westminster Review, 138:570-1, Nov 1892

Thanet, Octave [pseud.]
See French, Alice.

Thébaud, Augustus
Louisa Kirkbride
Catholic World, 29:719, Aug 1879

Theodora
Literary World, 11:264, 31 Jul 1880

Thickstun, Frederick [pseud.]
See Clark, Frederick Thickstun.

Thiusen, Ismar [pseud.]
See Macnie, John.

Thoits, Alvin T.
See Taylor, Bert Leston, and Alvin T. Thoits.

Thomas, Augustus
Arizona
Literary World, 30:376, 11 Nov 1899

Thomas, Chauncey
The Crystal Button
Catholic World, 52:934-6, Mar 1891
Critic, NS 15:168, 28

Thomas, Chauncey (cont.)
Mar 1891
Independent, 43:457, 26 Mar 1891

Thomas, Henry Wilton
The Sword of Wealth
Independent, 62:739, 28 Mar 1907

Thomas, Martha McCannon
Captain Phil
Critic, NS 2:148, 27 Sep 1884

Thomas, Reuen
Grafenburg People
Chautauquan, 7:254, Jan 1887
Independent, 38:1700, 30 Dec 1886

Thomas, Richard Henry
Penelve
Independent, 50:1344, 10 Nov 1898

Thompson, Adele Eugenia
Betty Seldon, Patriot
Chautauquan, 34:333, Dec 1901
Brave Heart Elizabeth
Chautauquan, 36:448, Jan 1903

Thompson, Mrs. Clara M.
Hawthorndean, or Philip Benton's Family
Literary World, 3:155, 1 Mar 1873

Thompson, Helen Stuart
Windy Creek
Critic, NS 32:845, Sep 1899
Independent, 51:2234, 17 Aug 1899

Thompson, James Maurice
Alice of Old Vincennes
Critic, 37:406, Nov 1900
Independent, 52:2804, 22 Nov 1900
At Love's Extremes
Catholic World, 53:440, Jun 1891
Critic, NS 4:17, 11 Jul 1885; NS 15:310, 13 Jun 1891
Dial, 6:123, Sep 1885
Literary World, 16:261, 25 Jul 1885
A Banker of Bankersville
Critic, NS 7:77, 12 Feb 1887
Literary World, 18:169, 28 May 1887
His Second Campaign
Independent, 35:12, 6 Sep 1883
Literary World, 14:228, 14 Jul 1883
Hoosier Mosaics
Literary World, 6:67, 1 Oct 1875
A King of Honey Island
Catholic World, 73:249-50, May 1901
Milly
Literary World, 32:59, 1 Apr 1901
The Ocala Boy
Chautauquan, 22:382, Dec 1895
Sweetheart Manette
Critic, 38:471, May 1901
Independent, 53:788, 4 Apr 1901
A Tallahassee Girl
Critic, 2:85, 25 Mar 1882
Dial, 2:293, Apr 1882
Independent, 34:12, 13 Apr 1882
Literary World, 13:98, 25 Mar 1882

Thompson, Maurice
See Thompson, James Maurice.

Thompson, Ray
A Respectable Family
Literary World, 11:112, 27 Mar 1880

Thompson, Vance
Spinners of Life
Critic, 42:564, Jun 1903
Dial, 35:157 [221], 1 Oct 1903

Thomson, Edward William
Old Man Savarin and Other Stories
Chautauquan, 21:775, Sep 1895

Thomson, Peter Gibson
Her Ladyship
Literary World, 11:112, 27 Mar 1880

Thornet, Teresa A. [pseud.]
See Holloway, Mrs. Anna.

Thorpe, Francis Newton
The Spoils of Empire
Dial, 34:376, 1 Jun 1903

Thorpe, Kamba [pseud.]
See Bellamy, Elizabeth Whitfield (Croom).

Thrum, Thomas George, comp.
Hawaiian Folk Tales
Independent, 62:1035, 2 May 1907

Thruston, Lucy Meacham (Kidd)
Called to the Field
Critic, 49:574, Jun 1906
Independent, 60:1219, 24 May 1906
A Girl of Virginia
Critic, 41:280, Sep 1902
Dial, 33:67, 1 Aug 1902
Literary World, 33:124, 1 Aug 1902
Jenifer
Independent, 63:635-6, 12 Sep 1907
Mistress Brent
Chautauquan, 34:324, Dec 1901
Where the Tide Comes In
Dial, 36:370, 1 Jun 1904
Independent, 57:512, 1 Sep 1904

Thurber, Alwyn M.
Quaint Crippen, Commercial Traveler
Independent, 48:1007, 23 Jul 1896
Literary World, 27:478, 26 Dec 1896

Thurston, Ida (Treadwell)
The Bishop's Shadow
Literary World, 30:347, 14 Oct 1899

Thwing, Eugene
The Man from Red Keg
Independent, 60:342, 8 Feb 1906
The Red-Keggers
Literary World, 34:262, Oct 1903

Tibbles, Thomas Henry
Hidden Power
Critic, 1:159, 18 Jun 1881

Ticknor, Caroline
A Hypocritical Romance, and Other Stories
Critic, NS 26:297, 14 Nov 1896

Tidball, Mary Langdon
Barbara's Vagaries
Harper's, 73:Literary Notes, 4, Jul 1886; 74:Literary Notes, 4, Jan 1887
Literary World, 17:367, 30 Oct 1886

[Tiernan, Frances Christine (Fisher)]
After Many Days
By Christian Reid [pseud.].
Literary World, 8:46, 1 Aug 1877
Armine
By Christian Reid [pseud.].

[Tiernan, Frances Christine (Fisher)] (cont.)
Catholic World, 39:570-1, Jul 1884

Carmela
By Christian Reid [pseud.].
Catholic World, 53:441, Jun 1891

Carmen's Inheritance
By Christian Reid [pseud.].
Independent, 25:1354, 30 Oct 1873

The Chase of an Heiress
By Christian Reid [pseud.].
Literary World, 29:339, 15 Oct 1898

A Child of Mary
By Christian Reid [pseud.].
Catholic World, 42:856-7, May 1886

A Comedy of Elopement
By Christian Reid [pseud.].
Critic, NS 19:215-6, 8 Apr 1893
Literary World, 24:74, 11 Mar 1893

A Daughter of the Sierra
By Christian Reid [pseud.].
Catholic World, 78:260-1, Nov 1903

Ebb-Tide, and Other Stories
By Christian Reid [pseud.].
Literary World, 3:76, 1 Oct 1872

A Gentle Belle
By Christian Reid [pseud.].
Literary World, 11:11, 3 Jan 1880

Heart of Steel
By Christian Reid [pseud.].
Critic, 3:93, 3 Mar 1883
Independent, 35:11, 17 May 1883
Literary World, 14:244, 28 Jul 1883

Hearts and Hands
By Christian Reid [pseud.].
Literary World, 5:157, 1 Mar 1875

"The Land of the Sky"
By Christian Reid [pseud.].
Critic, NS 23:461, 22 Jun 1895
Literary World, 7:24, 1 Jul 1876; 26:105, 6 Apr 1895

A Little Maid of Arcady
By Christian Reid [pseud.].
Catholic World, 57:435, Jun 1893

The Lost Lode
By Christian Reid [pseud.].
Catholic World, 56:725, Feb 1893

The Man of the Family
By Christian Reid [pseud.].
Independent, 49:1695, 23 Dec 1897
Literary World, 28:478, 25 Dec 1897

Miss Churchill
By Christian Reid [pseud.].
Critic, NS 7:241, 14 May 1887
Literary World, 18:102, 2 Apr 1887

Nina's Atonement, and Other Stories
By Christian Reid [pseud.].
Galaxy, 17:283-4, Feb 1874
Independent, 25:1256, 9 Oct 1873

The Picture of Las Cruces
By Christian Reid [pseud.].
Literary World, 27:330, 3 Oct 1896

Princess Nadine
By Christian Reid [pseud.].
Catholic World, 87:262-3, May 1908

A Question of Honor
By Christian Reid [pseud.].
Catholic World, 25:716-7, Aug 1877
Literary World, 6:50, 1 Sep 1875

Roslyn's Fortune
By Christian Reid [pseud.].
Critic, NS 3:137-8, 21 Mar 1885
Independent, 37:555, 30 Apr 1885
Literary World, 16:275, 8 Aug 1885

Valerie Aylmer
By Christian Reid [pseud.].

Literary World, 1:93, 1 Nov 1870
A Woman of Fortune
By Christian Reid [pseud.].
Independent, 49:57, 14 Jan 1897

Tiernan, Mary Spear (Nicholas)
Homoselle
Critic, 1:259, 24 Sep 1881
Dial, 2:101-2, Sep 1881
Literary World, 12:306, 10 Sep 1881
Jack Horner
Critic, NS 14:30, 19 Jul 1890
Dial, 11:13-4, May 1890
Literary World, 21:123, 12 Apr 1890
Suzette
Critic, NS 5:32, 16 Jan 1886
Literary World, 17:11, 9 Jan 1886

Tilton, Dwight [pseud. for George Tilton Richardson and Wilder Dwight Quint]
The Golden Greyhound
Independent, 61:213, 26 Jul 1906
Miss Petticoats
Dial, 32:392, 1 Jun 1902
On Satan's Mount
Chautauquan, 38:92-3, Sep 1903
Dial, 34:377, 1 Jun 1903
Independent, 55:1520, 25 Jun 1903
Literary World, 34:149-50, Jun 1903

Tilton, Theodore
Tempest-Tossed
Independent, 26:10, 4 Jun 1874; 35:12, 15 Mar 1883

Timsol, Robert [pseud.]
See Bird, Frederic Mayer.

Tincker, Mary Agnes
Aurora
Catholic World, 43:277, May 1886
Critic, NS 5:16, 9 Jan 1886; NS 16:128, 12 Sep 1891
Independent, 37:1565, 3 Dec 1885
Literary World, 16:465-6, 12 Dec 1885
Westminster Review, 125 (NS 69):597-8, Apr 1886
By the Tiber
Critic, 1:93, 9 Apr 1881
Dial, 2:18, May 1881
Literary World, 12:150, 23 Apr 1881
Westminster Review, 117:137, Jan 1882
The Jewel in the Lotos
Dial, 4:230, Jan 1884
Independent, 36:523, 24 Apr 1884; 42:1164, 21 Aug 1890
Literary World, 14:455, 15 Dec 1883
San Salvador
Catholic World, 55:286-9, May 1892
Chautauquan, 17:126, Apr 1893
Critic, NS 17:302, 28 May 1892
Independent, 44:664, 12 May 1892
Signor Monaldini's Niece
Independent, 31:12, 13 Mar 1879
Literary World, 10:53, 15 Feb 1879
Westminster Review, 114:278, Oct 1880
Two Coronets
Catholic World, 50:250-2, Nov 1889
Critic, NS 12:185, 19 Oct 1889
Dial, 10:216, Dec 1889
Independent, 41:1399, 24 Oct 1889
Literary World, 20:322, 28 Sep 1889

Todkill, Anas [pseud.]
See Cooke, John Esten.

Tomkins, Jane Harrison
Whose Fault?
By Jennie Harrison [pseud.].
Literary World, 21:289, 30 Aug 1890

Tomlinson, Everett Titsworth
The Boys with Old Hickory
Independent, 50:1059, 13 Oct 1898
Elder Boise
Independent, 53:2305, 26 Sep 1901
A Jersey Boy in the Revolution
Chautauquan, 30:321, Dec 1899
Old Fort Schuyler
Literary World, 32:107, 1 Jul 1901
Three Colonial Boys
Independent, 47:1405, 17 Oct 1895
Ward Hill, the Senior
Independent, 51:210, 19 Jan 1899

Tompkins, Elizabeth Knight
The Broken Ring
Critic, NS 28:34, 17 Jul 1897
Independent, 48:976, 16 Jul 1896
Her Majesty
Critic, NS 24:248, 19 Oct 1895
Literary World, 26:251, 10 Aug 1895; 26:389, 16 Nov 1895
Talks with Barbara
Critic, 37:550-1, Dec 1900
The Things That Count
Critic, 38:370-1, Apr 1901
Literary World, 31:172, 1 Sep 1900

Tourgee, Albion Winegar
Black Ice
Critic, NS 9:192, 21 Apr 1888
Independent, 40:753, 14 Jun 1888
Literary World, 19:106, 31 Mar 1888
Bricks Without Straw
Chautauquan, 1:285, Mar 1881
Dial, 1:110-2, Oct 1880
Independent, 32:11, 21 Oct 1880
Literary World, 11:374, 23 Oct 1880
Button's Inn
Critic, NS 8:164, 1 Oct 1887
Independent, 39:1424, 3 Nov 1887
Literary World, 18:291, 17 Sep 1887
'89
By Edgar Henry [pseud.].
Critic, NS 10:114, 8 Sep 1888
Figs and Thistles
Literary World, 11:11, 3 Jan 1880
A Fool's Errand
By One of the Fools.
Literary World, 10:375, 22 Nov 1879; 33:123, 1 Aug 1902
Hot Plowshares
Critic, 3:267, 9 Jun 1883
Dial, 4:66, Jul 1883
Independent, 35:11, 4 Oct 1883
Literary World, 14:349-50, 20 Oct 1883
John Eax, and Mamelon
Critic, 2:69, 11 Mar 1882
Dial, 2:264, Mar 1882
Independent, 34:11, 2 Mar 1882
Literary World, 13:81, 11 Mar 1882
The Man Who Outlived Himself
Chautauquan, 27:428, Jul 1898

Critic, NS 29:230, 2 Apr 1898
Independent, 50:693, 26 May 1898
Literary World, 29:155, 14 May 1898

The Mortgage on the Hip-Roof House
Chautauquan, 26:127, Oct 1897

Murvale Eastman, Christian Socialist
Chautauquan, 12:825, Mar 1891
Critic, NS 15:167, 28 Mar 1891
Independent, 43:273, 19 Feb 1891

Out of the Sunset Sea
Chautauquan, 18:638, Feb 1894
Critic, NS 21:237, 7 Apr 1894
Independent, 45:1653, 7 Dec 1893
Literary World, 24:367, 4 Nov 1893

Pactolus Prime
Catholic World, 55:606-7, Jul 1892
Critic, NS 13:259, 24 May 1890
Independent, 42:629, 8 May 1890
Literary World, 21:174, 24 May 1890

A Son of Old Harry
Literary World, 23:43, 30 Jan 1892; 24:59, 25 Feb 1893

Toinette
By Henry Churton [pseud.].
Galaxy, 18:855-6, Dec 1874
Literary World, 5:93, 1 Nov 1874

With Gauge & Swallow, Attorneys
Critic, NS 13:16, 11 Jan 1890
Independent, 41:1658, 12 Dec 1889
Literary World, 20:458, 7 Dec 1889

Townsend, Edward Waterman

Chimmie Fadden and Mr. Paul
Dial, 32:391, 1 Jun 1902
Literary World, 33:94, 1 Jun 1902

Chimmie Fadden Explains, Major Max Expounds
Critic, NS 23:459, 22 Jan 1895

"Chimmie Fadden," Major Max, and Other Stories
Critic, NS 23:218, 23 Mar 1895
Literary World, 26:75, 9 Mar 1895

A Daughter of the Tenements
Chautauquan, 22:510, Jan 1896
Critic, NS 24:301, 9 Nov 1895
Dial, 20:79-80, 1 Feb 1896
Independent, 47:1689, 12 Dec 1895
Literary World, 26:428, 30 Nov 1895

Days Like These
Critic, 39:183-4, Aug 1901
Dial, 31:27-8, 1 Jul 1901
Independent, 53:1620, 11 Jul 1901; 53:2778, 21 Nov 1901

Lees and Leaven
Independent, 55:741, 26 Mar 1903
Literary World, 34:142, Jun 1903

Near a Whole City Full
Critic, NS 29:413, 25 Jun 1898

A Summer in New York
Critic, 43:189, Aug 1903
Dial, 34:376, 1 Jun 1903
Independent, 55:741, 26 Mar 1903
Literary World, 34:138, Jun 1903

"Sure"
Critic, 44:563, Jun 1904

Townsend, George Alfred
The Entailed Hat
Critic, NS 1:231, 17 May 1884
Dial, 5:87-8, Aug 1884
Harper's, 81:Literary Notes, 3-4, Oct 1890
Independent, 36:747, 12 Jun 1884; 42:1641, 20 Nov 1890
Literary World, 15:159-60, 17 May 1884
Katy of Catoctin
Catholic World, 44:560-1, Jan 1887
Chautauquan, 7:506, May 1887
Critic, NS 7:52, 29 Jun 1887
Independent, 38:1700, 30 Dec 1886
Literary World, 18:19, 22 Jan 1887
Mrs. Reynolds and Hamilton
Independent, 42:1344, 25 Sep 1890

Townsend, Virginia Frances
A Boston Girl's Ambition
Critic, NS 7:191, 16 Apr 1887
Literary World, 17:392, 13 Nov 1886
Dorothy Draycott's To-morrows
Literary World, 28:479, 25 Dec 1897
The Hollands
Independent, 40:785, 21 Jun 1888
Mostly Marjorie Day
Critic, NS 16:347-8, 19 Dec 1891
Independent, 43:1762, 26 Nov 1891
One Woman's Two Lovers
Literary World, 5:124, 1 Jan 1875
A Woman's Word and How She Kept It
Literary World, 10:214, 5 Jul 1879

Townshend, Richard Baxter
Lone Pine
Literary World, 30:167, 27 May 1899; 32:11, 1 Jan 1901

Tracy, F. B.
See The Railroad.

Trafton, Adeline
See Knox, Adeline (Trafton).

Trail, Florence
Under the Second Renaissance
Critic, NS 23:203, 16 Mar 1895

Train, Arthur Cheney
The Butler's Story
Independent, 66:765, 8 Apr 1909
McAllister and His Double
Independent, 59:1232, 26 Nov 1905

Train, Elizabeth Phipps
Autobiography of a Professional Beauty
Independent, 48:770, 4 Jun 1896
Literary World, 27:154, 16 May 1896
Doctor Lamar
Chautauquan, 14:760-1, Mar 1892
Madam of the Ivies
Dial, 24:356, 1 Jun 1898
A Marital Liability
Independent, 49:948, 22 Jul 1897
Literary World, 28:279, 21 Aug 1897
Westminster Review, 152:355, Sep 1899
A Queen of Hearts
Dial, 24:356, 1 Jun 1898
A Social Highwayman
Literary World, 27:77, 7 Mar 1896

Trask, Kate (Nichols)
Free, Not Bound
Critic, 44:382, Apr 1904

Independent, 56:1450, 23 Jun 1904
John Leighton, Jr.
Critic, NS 28:278, 13 Nov 1897
Literary World, 28:464, 11 Dec 1897
Literature, 2:452, 16 Apr 1898
Lessons in Love
Critic, 38:183, Feb 1901
Independent, 53:332-3, 7 Feb 1901
White Satin and Homespun
Critic, NS 25:425, 13 Jun 1896
Independent, 48:976, 16 Jul 1896
Literary World, 28:145, 1 May 1897

Trask, Katrina
See Trask, Kate (Nichols).

Trebor [pseud.]
See Davis, Robert S.

Trimmer, Frederick Mortimer
The Golden Crocodile
Independent, 49:1695, 23 Dec 1897

Trotter, Ada M.
Bledisloe
Critic, NS 9:5, 7 Jan 1888
Literary World, 18:460, 10 Dec 1887

Troubetzkoy, Amélie (Rives) Chanler
According to St. John
Critic, NS 16:260, 14 Nov 1891
Athelwold
Harper's, 86:Literary Notes, 2, May 1893
Barbara Dering
Catholic World, 56:579-80, Jan 1893
Critic, NS 19:140, 11 Mar 1893
Literary World, 23:403, 19 Nov 1892
A Brother to Dragons, and Other Old-Time Tales
Catholic World, 47:694, Aug 1888
Critic, NS 9:228, 12 May 1888
Dial, 9:65-6, Jul 1888
Harper's, 76:Literary Notes, 1-2, Jan 1888
Literary World, 19:153, 12 May 1888
A Damsel Errant
Critic, NS 28:319, 27 Nov 1897
Independent, 49:1583, 2 Dec 1897
The Golden Rose
Independent, 65:153-4, 16 Jul 1908
Paris Mountain
Independent, 69:1092, 17 Nov 1910
Tanis, the Sang-Digger
Independent, 45:1653, 7 Dec 1893
Literary World, 24:351, 21 Oct 1893
Trix and Over-the-Moon
Independent, 68:318, 10 Feb 1910
Virginia of Virginia
Critic, NS 10:122-3, 15 Sep 1888
Independent, 40:1073, 23 Aug 1888
Literary World, 19:343, 13 Oct 1888

Trowbridge, John
The Great Match, and Other Matches
Literary World, 7:153-4, 1 Mar 1877
The Resolute Mr. Pansy
Chautauquan, 26:461, Jan 1898

Trowbridge, John Townsend
Coupon Bonds and Other Stories
Independent, 25:395, 27 Mar 1873

Trowbridge, John Townsend (cont.)
Literary World, 3:139, 1 Feb 1873
Cudjo's Cave
Critic, NS 15:27, 17 Jan 1891
Farnell's Folly
Independent, 37:75, 15 Jan 1885
Literary World, 16:31, 24 Jan 1885
Peter Budstone
Chautauquan, 8:198, Dec 1887
A Question of Damages
Literary World, 29:456, 24 Dec 1898
A Start in Life
Chautauquan, 9:189, Dec 1888
The Three Scouts
Critic, NS 15:180, 4 Apr 1891

True, John Preston
On Guard! Against Tory and Tarleton
Chautauquan, 38:520, Jan 1904
Scouting for Washington
Critic, 38:183, Feb 1901
Shoulder Arms
Chautauquan, 11:127, Apr 1890

Trumbull, Annie Eliot
A Cape Cod Week
Independent, 50:990, 6 Oct 1898
Literary World, 29:253, 6 Aug 1898
An Hour's Promise
Critic, 37:86, Jul 1900
Life's Common Way
Critic, 43:189, Aug 1903
Dial, 34:375, 1 Jun 1903
Literary World, 34:153, Jun 1903
Mistress Content Craddock
Critic, NS 32:748, Aug 1899
Independent, 51:2163, 10 Aug 1899
Literary World, 30:203, 24 Jun 1899
Rod's Salvation
Independent, 50:1060, 13 Oct 1898
Literary World, 29:269, 20 Aug 1898
White Birches
By Annie Eliot [pseud.].
Critic, NS 19:307, 13 May 1893
Harper's, 86:Literary Notes, 4, May 1893
Literary World, 24:148, 6 May 1893

Tucker, George Fox
Mildred Marville
Literary World, 30:92, 18 Mar 1899
A Quaker Home
Independent, 43:457, 26 Mar 1891

[Tunstall, Nannie Whitmell]
"No. 49"
Literary World, 15:217, 28 Jun 1884

Tupper, Frederic Allison
Moonshine
Critic, NS 2:306, 27 Dec 1884
Literary World, 16:63, 21 Feb 1885

Turnbull, Francese Hubbard (Litchfield)
The Catholic Man
Chautauquan, 12:285, Nov 1890
Independent, 42:493, 10 Apr 1890
The Golden Book of Venice
Dial, 29:498, 16 Dec 1900
Val-Maria
Critic, NS 20:100, 12 Aug 1893
Dial, 14:340, 1 Jun 1893
Independent, 45:1154, 24 Aug 1893

Literary World, 24:162, 20 May 1893

Turnbull, Mrs. Lawrence
See Turnbull, Francese Hubbard (Litchfield).

Turner, Alice
See Yardley, Alice Turner.

Twain, Mark [pseud.]
See Clemens, Samuel Langhorne.

Twells, Julia Helen (Watts)
By the Higher Law
Literary World, 33:73, 1 May 1902

Twombly, Alexander Stevenson
Kelea, the Surf-Rider
Critic, 38:183, Feb 1901

[Ulmann, Albert]
Chaperoned
Critic, NS 22:329, 17 Nov 1894

Underwood, Francis Henry
Doctor Gray's Quest
Dial, 19:94, 16 Aug 1895
Independent, 47:1170, 29 Aug 1895; 47:1579, 21 Nov 1895
Lord of Himself
Independent, 26:11, 2 Jul 1874
Literary World, 5:19, 1 Jul 1874
Man Proposes
Independent, 32:12, 26 Aug 1880
Literary World, 11:264, 31 Jul 1880
Quabbin
Chautauquan, 17:761, Sep 1893

Underwood, Mary Lanman
An American Mother, and Other Stories
Literary World, 29:141, 30 Apr 1898

An Unlaid Ghost
Catholic World, 47:122-5, Apr 1888
Critic, NS 9:115, 10 Mar 1888
Literary World, 19:91, 17 Mar 1888

Until Seventy Times Seven
Dial, 35:159 [223], 1 Oct 1903

Vachell, Horace Annesley
A Drama in Sunshine
Dial, 27:491-2, 16 Dec 1899
John Charity
Dial, 31:27, 1 Jul 1901
Judge Ketchum's Romance
Literary World, 26:122-3, 20 Apr 1895
The Procession of Life
Dial, 27:21, 1 Jul 1899
Literary World, 30:123, 15 Apr 1899
The Quicksands of Pactolus
Critic, NS 25:6-7, 4 Jul 1896
Dial, 21:20, 1 Jul 1896
Independent, 48:976, 16 Jul 1896
Literary World, 27:267, 22 Aug 1896

Vaile, Charlotte Marion (White)
The M. M. C.
Literary World, 30:92, 18 Mar 1899
The Truth About Santa Claus
Chautauquan, 38:412, Dec 1903

Valentine, Edward Abram Uffington
Hecla Sandwith
Critic, 46:479, May 1905
Independent, 58:1482, 29 Jun 1905

Valentine, Ferdinand Charles
Gotham and the Gothamites
Critic, NS 7:240, 14

Valentine, Ferdinand Charles (cont.)
May 1887

Valentine, Jane [pseud.]
See Meeker, Mrs. Nellie J.

Vanamee, Lida (Ostrom)
An Adirondack Idyl
Literary World, 24:386-7, 18 Nov 1893
Two Women
Chautauquan, 21:775, Sep 1895

Vance, Arthur Turner
The Real David Harum
Chautauquan, 32:334, Dec 1900

Vance, Louis Joseph
The Black Bag
Independent, 64:693, 26 Mar 1908
The Brass Bowl
Independent, 64:208, 23 Jan 1908
The Bronze Bell
Independent, 66:762-3, 8 Apr 1909
The Private War
Dial, 40:365, 1 Jun 1906
Terrence O'Rourke
Independent, 59:697, 21 Sep 1905

Vance, Susa S.
Katherine
Critic, NS 3:17, 10 Jan 1885
Literary World, 16:276, 8 Aug 1885

Vance, Wilson
Big John Baldwin
Dial, 47:387, 16 Nov 1909

Vandegrift, Margaret [pseud.]
See Janvier, Margaret Thomson.

[Van Deventer, Emma Murdoch]
Shadowed by Three
By Lawrence L. Lynch [pseud.].
Literary World, 11:111-2, 27 Mar 1880

Van Dyke, Henry
The First Christmas-Tree
Chautauquan, 26:463, Jan 1898
The Lost Word
Chautauquan, 28:421, Jan 1899
The Ruling Passion
Chautauquan, 34:318-9, Dec 1901
Critic, 40:180, Feb 1902
Dial, 32:89, 1 Feb 1902
The Story of the Other Wise Man
Harper's, 92:Literary Notes, 3, Dec 1895

Van Loon, Mrs. Elizabeth
The Mystery of Allanwood
Independent, 32:12, 23 Sep 1880
Literary World, 11:280, 14 Aug 1880

Van Rensselaer, Mariana (Griswold)
One Man Who Was Content
Critic, NS 27:351-2, 22 May 1897
Independent, 49:851, 1 Jul 1897

Van Rensselaer, Mrs. Schuyler
See Van Rensselaer, Mariana (Griswold).

Van Vorst, Bessie (McGinnis)
The Issues of Life
Critic, 44:472-3, May 1904
Independent, 56:1199, 26 May 1904
Literary World, 35:107, Apr 1904
Letters to Women in Love
Independent, 62:101, 10 Jan 1907

_______, and Marie Van Vorst
Bagsby's Daughter
Critic, 40:84, Jan 1902
Literary World, 33:28, 1 Feb 1902

Van Vorst, Frederick B.
Without a Compass
Literary World, 16:385, 31 Oct 1885

Van Vorst, Mrs. John
See Van Vorst, Bessie (McGinnis).

Van Vorst, Marie
First Love
Independent, 69:1090, 17 Nov 1910
The Girl from His Town
Independent, 69:362, 18 Aug 1910
Miss Desmond
Dial, 40:19, 1 Jan 1906
Phillip Longstreth
Critic, 41:375-6, Oct 1903
Dial, 33:64, 1 Aug 1902
Independent, 54:1668, 10 Jul 1902
Literary World, 33:76, 1 May 1902
The Sin of George Warrener
Critic, 49:288, Sep 1906
Dial, 41:114-5, 1 Sep 1906
Independent, 61:820-1, 4 Oct 1906
See also Van Vorst, Bessie (McGinnis), and Marie Van Vorst.

Van Zile, Edward Sims
Don Miguel, and Other Stories
Critic, NS 16:215, 10 Oct 1891
Independent, 43:1605, 29 Oct 1891
A Duke and His Double
Critic, 44:94, Jan 1904
The Last of the Van Slacks
Critic, NS 12:63, 10 Aug 1889
A Magnetic Man, and Other Stories
Critic, NS 16:77, 15 Aug 1891
The Manhattaners
Literary World, 27:220, 11 Jul 1896
Wanted--a Sensation
Critic, NS 6:99, 28 Aug 1886
With Sword and Crucifix
Independent, 53:333, 7 Feb 1901
Literary World, 31:140, 1 Jul 1900

Vaughan, Frank
Kate Weathers
Literary World, 9:47, 1 Aug 1878

Veeder, Emily Elizabeth (Ferris)
Her Brother Donnard
Critic, NS 15:208, 18 Apr 1891

Venable, William Henry
A Dream of Empire
Dial, 31:366, 16 Nov 1901
Independent, 53:1623, 11 Jul 1901
Tom Tad
Critic, 42:86, Jan 1903

Ventura, Luigi Donato
Peppino
Critic, NS 5:93, 20 Feb 1886

_______, and S. Shevitch
Misfits and Remnants
Literary World, 17:317, 18 Sep 1886

Verdendorp, Basil [pseud.]
The Verdendorps
Westminster Review, 115:157, Jan 1881

Victor, Metta Victoria (Fuller)
Passing the Portals
Independent, 28:9, 15 Jun 1876

Vielé, Herman Knickerbocker
Heartbreak Hill
Dial, 45:295, 1 Nov 1908
Independent, 66:375-7, 18 Feb 1909
The Last of the Knickerbockers
Critic, 40:151, Feb 1902
Dial, 31:370-1, 16 Nov 1901
Literary World, 33:60, 1 Apr 1902
Myra of the Pines
Critic, 41:280-1, Sep 1902
Independent, 54:1728, 17 Jul 1902

Vincent, Edgar LaVerne
Margaret Bowlby
Dial, 33:66, 1 Aug 1902

Vincent, Frank, and Albert Edmund Lancaster
The Lady of Cawnpore
Independent, 43:1844, 10 Dec 1891

Vinton, Arthur Dudley
Looking Further Backward
Critic, NS 14:218, 1 Nov 1890

Vynne, Harold Richard
Love Letters
Literary World, 30:268, 19 Aug 1899

Wagnalls, Mabel
Miserere
Chautauquan, 15:653, Aug 1892
Independent, 44:313, 3 Mar 1892

Wait, Frona [pseud.]
See Colburn, Frona Eunice Wait (Smith).

Waite, Carlton
A Silver Baron
Independent, 49:220, 18 Feb 1897

[Waite, Lucy]
Dr. Helen Rand
By Lois Wright [pseud.].
Critic, NS 16:261, 14 Nov 1891

Walcott, Earle Ashley
The Apple of Discord
Independent, 64:209, 23 Jan 1908
Blindfolded
Independent, 62:386, 14 Feb 1907

Wall, George A.
See Robinson, Edward A., and George A. Wall.

________, and George B. Heckel
Jacob Valmont, Manager
Catholic World, 50:258-9, Nov 1889

Wallace, Lewis
Ben-Hur
Catholic World, 38:572-4, Jan 1884
Harper's, 84:Literary Notes, 4, Dec 1891
Independent, 32:11, 30 Dec 1880
Literary World, 12:115, 26 Mar 1881
The Boyhood of Christ
Harper's, 78:Literary Notes, 4, Dec 1888
The Fair God
Chautauquan, 28:315-6, Dec 1898
Galaxy, 17:140, Jan 1874
Independent, 25:1256, 2 Oct 1873
Literary World, 4:51-3, 1 Sep 1873
The Prince of India
Catholic World, 58:133-6, Oct 1893

Chautauquan, 18:381, Dec 1893
Critic, NS 20:235-6, 14 Oct 1893
Dial, 15:226-7, 16 Oct 1893
Harper's, 87:Literary Notes, 1, Aug 1893
Literary World, 24:283-4, 9 Sep 1893

Waller, Mary Ella
Flamsted Quarries
Catholic World, 92:255-6, Nov 1910
Independent, 69:1219-20, 1 Dec 1910
Giotto's Sheep
Critic, NS 11:233, 11 May 1889
The Rose-Bush of Hildesheim
Critic, NS 11:233, 17 May 1889
Sanna
Independent, 59:209, 27 Jul 1905; 59:1154, 16 Nov 1905
The Wood-Carver of 'Lympus
Critic, 45:477, Nov 1904
Dial, 36:372-3, 1 Jun 1904
Independent, 56:1335, 9 Jun 1904
Literary World, 35:168, Jun 1904
A Year Out of Life
Independent, 66:1344, 17 Jun 1909

Wallis, John Calvin
A Prodigious Fool
Literary World, 12:200, 4 Jun 1881

Walsh, William Thomas
The Mirage of the Many
Catholic World, 92:104-5, Oct 1910

Walsingham, Charlotte
O'er Moor and Fen
Independent, 28:11, 6 Jan 1876
Literary World, 6:101, 1 Dec 1875

Walton, Eleanor Going
She Who Will Not When She May
Literary World, 29:322, 1 Oct 1898

Waltz, Elizabeth (Cherry)
The Ancient Landmark
Independent, 59:1229, 26 Nov 1905
Pa Gladden
Critic, 44:478, May 1904
Independent, 55:2875-6, 3 Dec 1903

Walworth, Jeannette Ritchie (Hadermann)
Against the World
Literary World, 3:163, 1 Apr 1873
The Bar-Sinister
Critic, NS 4:183-4, 17 Oct 1885
Independent, 37:1327, 15 Oct 1885
Literary World, 16:283-4, 22 Aug 1885
Dead Men's Shoes
Literary World, 2:162-3, 1 Apr 1872
Forgiven at Last
Literary World, 1:51-2, 1 Sep 1870
Fortune's Tangled Skein
Literary World, 30:91-2, 18 Mar 1899
Heavy Yokes
Independent, 28:12, 3 Aug 1876
The Little Radical
Independent, 42:788, 5 Jun 1890
The New Man at Rossmere
Catholic World, 54:143-4, Oct 1891
Critic, NS 6:136-7, 18 Sep 1886
Independent, 38:1520, 25 Nov 1886

Walworth, Jeannette Ritchie (Hadermann) (cont.)
Literary World, 17:315-6, 18 Sep 1886
An Old Fogy
Literary World, 27:75-6, 7 Mar 1896
On the Winning Side
Literary World, 29:124, 16 Apr 1898
The Silent Witness
Critic, NS 10:113-4, 8 Sep 1888
Independent, 40:1073, 23 Aug 1888
Southern Silhouettes
Chautauquan, 8:327, Feb 1888
Critic, NS 8:310, 17 Dec 1887
Dial, 8:154, Nov 1887
Independent, 39:1361, 20 Oct 1887
A Splendid Egotist
Critic, NS 11:307, 22 Jun 1889
That Girl from Texas
Critic, NS 11:29, 19 Jan 1889
Uncle Scipio
Literary World, 28:43-4, 6 Feb 1897
Without Blemish
Critic, NS 5:116, 6 Mar 1886
Independent, 38:366, 25 Mar 1886; 39:686, 2 Jun 1887
Literary World, 17:130, 17 Apr 1886

Ward, A. B. [pseud.]
See Bailey, Alice (Ward).

Ward, Elizabeth Stuart (Phelps)
Avery
Critic, 41:583, Dec 1902
Independent, 55:212-3, 22 Jan 1903
Literary World, 33:194, 1 Dec 1902
Beyond the Gates
Dial, 4:230, Jan 1884
Literary World, 14:361-2, 3 Nov 1883
Burglars in Paradise
Critic, NS 9:54, 4 Feb 1888
Doctor Zay
Critic, 2:325-6, 2 Dec 1882
Dial, 3:137, Nov 1882
Independent, 34:10, 16 Nov 1882
Literary World, 13:371, 4 Nov 1882
Donald Marcy
Critic, NS 20:182, 16 Sep 1893
Independent, 45:1018, 27 Jul 1893
Literary World, 24:163, 20 May 1893
The Empty House
Catholic World, 92:392-3, Dec 1910
Fourteen to One
Catholic World, 53:605-6, Jul 1891
Chautauquan, 13:552, Jul 1891
Critic, NS 16:64, 8 Aug 1891
Independent, 43:1283, 27 Aug 1891
Westminster Review, 136:697, Dec 1891
Friends: A Duet
Critic, 1:188, 16 Jul 1881
Dial, 2:66, Jul 1881
Literary World, 12:231, 2 Jul 1881
The Gates Between
Catholic World, 46:269-71, Nov 1887
Chautauquan, 8:125, Nov 1887
Critic, NS 8:244, 12 Nov 1887
Independent, 39:1622, 15 Dec 1887
Literary World, 18:343-4, 15 Oct 1887
Hedged In
Galaxy, 9:709-10, May

1870
Literary World, 1:7, 1 Jun 1870

Jack the Fisherman
Chautauquan, 8:125, Nov 1887
Critic, NS 8:244, 12 Nov 1887
Literary World, 18:369, 29 Oct 1887
Westminster Review, 128:1180-1, Dec 1887

Loveliness
Independent, 51:3300, 7 Dec 1899
Literary World, 30:377, 11 Nov 1899

The Madonna of the Tubs
Chautauquan, 7:253, Jan 1887
Critic, NS 7:27, 15 Jan 1887
Dial, 7:231, Jan 1887
Independent, 38:1556, 2 Dec 1886; 47:1728, 19 Dec 1895
Literary World, 17:438, 27 Nov 1886

The Man in the Case
Independent, 61:1116-7, 8 Nov 1906

An Old Maid's Paradise, and Burglars in Paradise
Chautauquan, 8:198, Dec 1887
Critic, NS 4:125, 12 Sep 1885; NS 6:102, 28 Aug 1886; NS 9:54, 4 Feb 1888
Independent, 39:1425, 3 Nov 1887
Literary World, 16:291, 22 Aug 1885

A Pair of Originals
Chautauquan, 14:761, Mar 1892

Sealed Orders
Independent, 31:10, 27 Nov 1879
Literary World, 10:341, 25 Oct 1879

The Silent Partner
Literary World, 1:165-7, 1 Apr 1871

A Singular Life
Chautauquan, 23:127, Apr 1896
Critic, NS 25:212, 28 Mar 1896
Dial, 20:80, 1 Feb 1896
Independent, 47:1690, 12 Dec 1895; 48:769, 4 Jun 1896
Literary World, 26:388, 16 Nov 1895

The Story of Avis
Galaxy, 24:855-7, Dec 1877
Literary World, 8:97-8, 1 Nov 1877

The Supply at St. Agatha's
Catholic World, 63:274-5, May 1896
Critic, NS 25:421, 13 Jul 1896
Independent, 48:628, 7 May 1896; 48:769, 4 Jun 1896
Literary World, 27:365, 31 Oct 1896

Trixy
Catholic World, 80:833, Mar 1905
Chautauquan, 42:577, Feb 1906
Independent, 58:99-100, 12 Jan 1905

Within the Gates
Catholic World, 75:262, May 1902
Chautauquan, 34:329, Dec 1901
Critic, 39:577-8, Dec 1901
Independent, 54:347, 6 Feb 1902
Literary World, 32:205, 1 Dec 1901

________, and Herbert D. Ward

Come Forth!
Catholic World, 52:448-50, Dec 1890
Chautauquan, 12:422, Dec 1890
Critic, NS 14:143, 20

Ward, Elizabeth Stuart (Phelps), and Herbert D. Ward (cont.)
Sep 1890; NS 15:54, 31 Jan 1891
Independent, 42:1497, 23 Oct 1890
Literary World, 21:355, 11 Oct 1890
Westminster Review, 134:692, Dec 1890
A Lost Hero
Chautauquan, 14:511, Jan 1892
Independent, 43:1762, 26 Nov 1891
The Master of the Magicians
Catholic World, 51:548-9, Jul 1890
Chautauquan, 11:649, Aug 1890
Critic, NS 14:2, 5 Jul 1890
Independent, 42:668, 15 May 1890
Literary World, 21:186, 7 Jun 1890

Ward, Herbert Dickinson
The Burglar Who Moved Paradise
Chautauquan, 26:239-40, Nov 1897
Independent, 49:719, 3 Jun 1897
Literary World, 28:227, 10 Jul 1897
The New Senior at Andover
Chautauquan, 12:826, Mar 1891
Critic, NS 15:193, 11 Apr 1891
Independent, 43:421, 19 Mar 1891
A Republic Without a President, and Other Stories
Literary World, 24:163, 20 May 1893
The White Crown, and Other Stories
Critic, NS 22:54, 28 Jul 1894
Dial, 16:368, 16 Jun 1894
Literary World, 25:167, 2 Jun 1894
See also Ward, Elizabeth Stuart (Phelps), and Herbert D. Ward.

Wardman, Ervin
The Princess Olga
Dial, 40:366, 1 Jun 1906
Independent, 61:579, 6 Sep 1906

Warfield, Catherine Ann (Ware)
Lady Ernestine
Independent, 28:8, 16 Nov 1876
Miriam Monfort
Literary World, 4:66, Oct 1873

Waring, George Edwin
Vix
Independent, 35:11, 13 Sep 1883

Warman, Cy
The Empress Messenger, and Other Tales of the Rail
Independent, 49:1695, 23 Dec 1897
Literary World, 28:359, 16 Oct 1897
Literature, 2:147, 5 Feb 1898
Frontier Stories
Literary World, 29:403, 26 Nov 1898
Short Rails
Critic, 38:183, Feb 1901
Independent, 52:2813, 22 Nov 1900
Literary World, 32:75, 1 May 1901
Snow on the Headlight
Critic, NS 32:1055-6, Nov 1899
Independent, 51:2230, 17 Aug 1899
Literary World, 30:267-8, 19 Aug 1899
The Story of the Railroad
Chautauquan, 28:316-7,

Dec 1898
Critic, NS 30:511-2, Dec 1898
Independent, 51:281, 26 Jan 1899
Tales of an Engineer
Independent, 47:1728, 19 Dec 1895
The White Mail
Independent, 51:2829-30, 19 Oct 1899; 51:3171, 23 Nov 1899

Warner, Anna Bartlett
Patience
Critic, NS 15:209, 18 Apr 1891
Independent, 43:456, 26 Mar 1891
West Point Colors
Critic, 44:189, Feb 1904
See also Warner, Susan Bogert, and Anna Warner.

Warner, Anne
See French, Anne (Warner).

Warner, Beverly Ellison
Troubled Waters
Chautauquan, 5:611, Jul 1885
Critic, NS 3:293, 20 Jun 1885
Independent, 37:1199, 17 Sep 1885
Literary World, 16:273-4, 8 Aug 1885

Warner, Charles Dudley
The Golden House
Critic, NS 23:236-7, 30 Mar 1895
Dial, 18:50-1, 16 Jan 1895
Harper's, 90:Literary Notes, 1, Jan 1895
Literary World, 25:464, 29 Dec 1894
A Little Journey in the World
Critic, NS 12:322, 28 Dec 1889
Harper's, 80:Literary Notes, 1-2, Jan 1890
Independent, 42:561-2, 24 Apr 1890
Literary World, 20:452-3, 7 Dec 1889
That Fortune
Dial, 27:75, 1 Aug 1899
Harper's, 99:Literary Notes, 1, Sep 1899
Independent, 51:1955, 20 Jul 1899; 51:3171, 23 Nov 1899
Literary World, 30:230-1, 22 Jul 1899
See also Clemens, Samuel Langhorne, and Charles Dudley Warner.

Warner, Ellen E. (Kenyon)
A Lucky Waif
Critic, NS 5:128, 13 Mar 1886
Literary World, 17:112, 3 Apr 1886

Warner, Susan Bogert
Diana
Literary World, 8:149, 1 Jan 1878
The End of a Coil
Independent, 32:11-2, 4 Nov 1880
A Red Wallflower
Independent, 37:1167, 10 Sep 1885
Stephen, M. D.
Independent, 36:171, 7 Feb 1884

________, and Anna Warner
The Gold of Chickaree
Independent, 28:8, 7 Dec 1876
Wych Hazel
Galaxy, 22:139, Jul 1876
Independent, 28:28-9, 11 May 1876

Warren, Charles
The Girl and the Governor
Critic, 37:569, Dec 1900
Literary World, 32:75,

Warren, Charles (cont.)
1 May 1901

Warren, Cornelia
Miss Wilton
Catholic World, 55:290-1, May 1892
Critic, NS 17:276, 14 May 1892
Independent, 44:881, 23 Jun 1892
Literary World, 23:87-8, 12 Mar 1892

Warren, Maude Lavinia (Radford)
Peter-Peter
Independent, 67:425, 19 Aug 1909

Warren, Thomas Robinson
Juliette Irving and the Jesuit
Catholic World, 61:564, Jul 1895

Warren, William Fairfield
The Story of Gottlieb
Chautauquan, 14:381, Dec 1891
Critic, NS 17:51, 23 Jan 1892

[Warriner, Edward Augustus]
Victor la Tourette
By a Broad Churchman.
Galaxy, 19:858-9, Jun 1875

Warth, Julian [pseud.]
See Parsons, Julia (Warth).

Wasson, George Savery
Cap'n Simeon's Store
Critic, 43:381, Oct 1903
Independent, 55:1349, 4 Jun 1903
Literary World, 34:178, Jul 1903
Home from Sea
Independent, 64:1351-2, 11 Jun 1908

Watanna, Onoto [pseud.]
See Badcock, Winnifred (Eaton).

Waterloo, Stanley
Armageddon
Independent, 51:209, 19 Jan 1899
The Launching of a Man
Dial, 27:174, 16 Sep 1899
Independent, 51:2162, 10 Aug 1899
An Odd Situation
Critic, NS 27:59, 23 Jan 1897
Dial, 14:217, 1 Apr 1893
The Seekers
Independent, 52:2460, 11 Oct 1900
The Story of Ab
Independent, 49:1544, 25 Nov 1897; 62:621, 14 Mar 1907
Literature, 2:388, 2 Apr 1898

Waters, Clara (Erskine) Clement
Eleanor Maitland
Critic, 2:113, 22 Apr 1882
Literary World, 13:415, 19 Nov 1881

[Watrous, Charles]
Told at Tuxedo
By A. M. Emory [pseud.].
Critic, NS 8:30, 16 Jul 1887

Watson, Augusta Campbell
Beyond the City Gates
Critic, NS 28:34, 17 Jul 1897
Dial, 23:285, 16 Nov 1897
Literary World, 28:203, 26 Jun 1897
Dorothy the Puritan
Critic, NS 20:298-9, 11 Nov 1893
Independent, 45:1453, 26

Oct 1893
Literary World, 24:226, 15 Jul 1893
Off Lynnport Light
Literary World, 26:253, 10 Aug 1895
The Old Harbor Town
Independent, 44:664, 12 May 1892
Literary World, 23:230, 2 Jul 1892

Watson, Lewis H.
Not to the Swift
Critic, NS 15:322, 20 Jun 1891

Watson, Thomas Edward
Bethany
Dial, 38:127-8, 16 Feb 1905
Independent, 58:209-10, 26 Jan 1905

Watts, William Courtney
Chronicles of a Kentucky Settlement
Independent, 49:719, 3 Jul 1897

Wayne, Charles Stokes
Mrs. Lord's Moonstone, and Other Stories
Literary World, 19:221, 7 Jul 1888
A Prince to Order
Independent, 59:576, 7 Sep 1905

Webster, Alice Jean Chandler
Jerry Junior
Independent, 63:163, 18 Jul 1907
Much Ado About Nothing
Independent, 67:199-200, 22 Jul 1909
The Wheat Princess
Critic, 49:94, Jul 1906
When Patty Went to College
Literary World, 34:123, May 1903

Webster, Henry Kitchell
The Banker and the Bear
Independent, 52:2582, 25 Oct 1900
The Duke of Cameron Avenue
Independent, 56:1448, 23 Jun 1904
A King in Khaki
Dial, 46:371, 1 Jun 1909
Roger Drake, Captain of Industry
Dial, 34:243, 1 Apr 1903
Literary World, 34:10, 1 Jan 1903
The Sky-Man
Dial, 48:398, 1 Jun 1910
Traitor or Loyalist
Dial, 38:15, 1 Jan 1905
The Whispering Man
Dial, 45:457-8, 16 Dec 1908
See also Merwin, Samuel, and Henry Kitchell Webster.

Webster, Jean
See Webster, Alice Jean Chandler.

A Week Away from Time
Ed. Mrs. James Lodge.
Critic, NS 7:319, 25 Jun 1887
Independent, 39:1231, 29 Sep 1887
Literary World, 18:182, 11 Jun 1887

Weeks, J. Hatton
The Tin Kitchen
Critic, NS 27:219, 27 Mar 1897
Literary World, 27:456, 12 Dec 1896

[Weitzel, Sophie (Winthrop)]
Counter-Currents
Literary World, 20:13, 5 Jan 1889
Justina
Critic, NS 6:172, 9 Oct 1886
Literary World, 17:211-2,

[Weitzel, Sophie (Winthrop)] (cont.)
26 Jun 1886

Wells, Carolyn
The Clue
Independent, 67:1507, 30 Dec 1909

_______, and Harry Parson Taber
The Matrimonial Bureau
Critic, 46:564, Jun 1905
The Gordon Elopement
Critic, 44:563, Jun 1904
Literary World, 35:111-2, Apr 1904

Wells, Catherine Boott (Gannett)
Miss Curtis
Critic, NS 8:336, 31 Dec 1887
Literary World, 19:25-6, 21 Jan 1888
Two Modern Women
Critic, NS 14:166, 4 Oct 1890
Independent, 42:1414, 9 Oct 1890

Wells, David Dwight
Her Ladyship's Elephant
Critic, NS 30:205, Sep 1898
Independent, 50:730, 2 Jun 1898
Literary World, 29:252-3, 6 Aug 1898
His Lordship's Leopard
Independent, 52:2521, 18 Oct 1900
Literary World, 31:157, 1 Aug 1900
Parlous Times
Dial, 31:33, 1 Jul 1901

[Wells, Eleanor P. Bell]
Madame Lucas
Critic, 2:22, 28 Jan 1882
Dial, 2:265, Mar 1882
Independent, 34:11, 2 Mar 1882
Literary World, 13:27, 28 Jan 1882

Wells, Kate Gannett
See Wells, Catherine Boott (Gannett).

Welsh, James
A White Baby
Critic, NS 24:407, 14 Dec 1895
Independent, 47:1690, 12 Dec 1895
Literary World, 27:203-4, 27 Jun 1896

Wendell, Barrett
The Duchess Emilia
Critic, NS 3:183-4, 18 Apr 1885
Literary World, 16:129, 18 Apr 1885
Rankell's Remains
Literary World, 17:453-4, 11 Dec 1886

Wendt, Frederick W.
Ocean Sketches
Independent, 49:650, 20 May 1897

Wentworth, Walter [pseud.]
See Gilman, Bradley.

West, Kenyon [pseud.]
See Howland, Frances Louise (Morse).

Westcott, Blanche
Jean
Independent, 31:12, 23 Jan 1879
Literary World, 10:119, 12 Apr 1879

Westcott, Edward Noyes
David Harum
Chautauquan, 29:206, May 1899
Critic, NS 30:303-4, Oct 1898; 38:87, Jan 1901
Independent, 50:1425, 17 Nov 1898; 51:1240, 4

May 1899; 51:1565, 8 Jun 1899
Literary World, 29:404, 26 Nov 1898
The Teller
Critic, 40:281, Mar 1902
Independent, 53:3091, 26 Dec 1901
Literary World, 32:177, 1 Nov 1901

Wetherill, Julie K.
See Baker, Julie Keim (Wetherill).

Wetmore, Elizabeth (Bisland)
A Candle of Understanding
Critic, 44:380, Apr 1904
Dial, 35:265, 16 Oct 1903

Wharton, Edith Newbold (Jones)
Crucial Instances
Independent, 53:1322-3, 6 Jun 1901; 53:2777, 21 Nov 1901
The Descent of Man, and Other Stories
Critic, 45:187, Aug 1904
Dial, 37:40-1, 16 Jul 1904
Independent, 56:1334-5, 9 Jun 1904
Literary World, 35:163, Jun 1904
The Fruit of the Tree
Dial, 43:317, 16 Nov 1907
Independent, 63:1226-8, 21 Nov 1907; 63:1436-7, 12 Dec 1907
The Greater Inclination
Critic, NS 32:747-8, Aug 1899; 37:173-6, Aug 1900
Dial, 27:76, 1 Aug 1899
Literary World, 30:220, 8 Jul 1899; 31:89, 1 Apr 1900
The Hermit and the Wild Woman
Independent, 66:265, 4 Feb 1909
The House of Mirth
Critic, 47:509-10, Dec 1905
Dial, 40:15-6, 1 Jan 1906
Independent, 59:150-1, 20 Jul 1905; 59:1151, 16 Nov 1905
Madame De Treymes
Independent, 62:1528, 27 Jun 1907; 63:1226-8, 21 Nov 1907
Sanctuary
Critic, 44:269-70, Mar 1904
Dial, 36:118-9, 16 Feb 1904
Independent, 55:2933-4, 10 Dec 1903; 57:1138, 17 Nov 1904
Literary World, 34:348-9, Dec 1903
Tales of Men and Ghosts
Independent, 69:1089, 17 Nov 1910
The Touchstone
Critic, 37:176, Aug 1900
Dial, 29:126, 1 Sep 1900
The Valley of Decision
Catholic World, 75:248-9, May 1902
Critic, 40:541-3, Jun 1902
Dial, 32:245-6, 1 Apr 1902
Independent, 54:639, 13 Mar 1902; 54:2770, 20 Nov 1902

[Wharton, Edward Clifton]
The War of the Bachelors
By Orleanian [pseud.].
Independent, 35:11, 17 May 1883
Literary World, 14:245, 28 Jul 1883

Wharton, Thomas Isaac
"Bobbo," and Other Fancies
Critic, NS 28:172, 25 Sep 1897
Harper's, 95:Literary

Wharton, Thomas Isaac (cont.)
Notes, 2-3, Aug 1897
Independent, 49:1149, 2 Sep 1897
Hannibal of New York
Catholic World, 44:412, Dec 1886
Critic, NS 6:147-8, 25 Sep 1886
Independent, 38:1412-3, 4 Nov 1886
Literary World, 17:315, 18 Sep 1886
A Latter Day Saint
Independent, 36:300, 6 Mar 1884
Literary World, 15:60, 23 Feb 1884

Wheatley, Louise Knight
Ashes of Roses
Critic, NS 20:298, 11 Nov 1893
Literary World, 24:369, 4 Nov 1893

Wheaton, Campbell [pseud.]
See Campbell, Helen (Stuart).

[Wheeler, Andrew Carpenter]
The Conquering of Kate
By J. P. Mowbray [pseud.].
Critic, 43:77, Jul 1903
Dial, 35:68, 1 Aug 1903
Literary World, 34:151, Jun 1903
The Primrose Path of Dalliance
By Nym Crinkle [pseud.].
Independent, 44:1130, 11 Aug 1892
Tangled Up in Beulah Land
By J. P. Mowbray [pseud.].
Critic, 41:583, Dec 1902
The Toltec Cup
By Nym Crinkle [pseud.].
Critic, NS 14:57, 2 Aug 1890
Independent, 42:1344, 25 Sep 1890
Literary World, 21:289, 30 Aug 1890

Wheeler, Esther Gracie (Lawrence)
Stray Leaves from Newport
Critic, NS 10:17, 14 Jul 1888
Independent, 40:817, 28 Jun 1888
Literary World, 19:188, 9 Jun 1888
A Washington Symphony
Critic, NS 20:87, 5 Aug 1893
Independent, 45:1018, 27 Jul 1893
Literary World, 24:179, 3 Jun 1893

Wheeler, Mrs. William Lamont
See Wheeler, Esther Gracie (Lawrence).

Wheelwright, John Tyler
A Bad Penny
Critic, NS 27:254, 10 Apr 1897
Literary World, 27:203, 27 Jun 1896
A Child of the Century
Critic, NS 7:192, 16 Apr 1887
Independent, 39:878, 14 Jul 1887
Literary World, 18:138-9, 30 Apr 1887
See also The King's Men.

Whitaker, Herman
The Planter
Dial, 47:48, 16 Jul 1909
The Settler
Dial, 44:45, 16 Jan 1908

White, Caroline (Earle)
Love in the Tropics
Critic, NS 13:269, 31 May 1890
Independent, 42:967, 10 Jul 1890
A Modern Agrippa [and others]

Literary World, 24:194, 17 Jun 1893

White, Eliza Orne

A Browning Courtship, and Other Stories
Dial, 24:81, 1 Feb 1898
Literary World, 29:28, 22 Jan 1898

The Coming of Theodora
Independent, 47:1543, 14 Nov 1895; 47:1579, 21 Nov 1895
Literary World, 27:87, 21 Mar 1896

Ednah and Her Brothers
Chautauquan, 33:544, Aug 1901

John Forsyth's Aunts
Critic, 40:376, Apr 1902
Independent, 54:816, 3 Apr 1902
Literary World, 33:27-8, 1 Feb 1902

Lesley Chilton
Critic, 44:94, Jan 1904
Dial, 35:264, 16 Oct 1903

A Lover of Truth
Independent, 50:1704, 8 Dec 1898
Literary World, 29:400-1, 26 Nov 1898
Literature, 3:524, 3 Dec 1898

Miss Brooks
Critic, NS 14:165-6, 4 Oct 1890
Independent, 42:1133, 14 Aug 1890
Literary World, 21:206, 21 Jun 1890

Winterborough
Catholic World, 56:430-1, Dec 1892
Critic, NS 19:96, 18 Feb 1893
Literary World, 23:470-1, 17 Dec 1892

White, Hervey

Differences
Independent, 52:2813, 22 Nov 1900
Literary World, 31:69, 3 Mar 1900

Quicksand
Catholic World, 74:107-8, Oct 1901
Literary World, 32:103, 1 Jul 1901

When Eve Was Not Created, and Other Stories
Independent, 53:1624, 11 Jul 1901

White, Richard Grant

The Fate of Mansfield Humphreys
Dial, 5:65, Jul 1884
Independent, 36:1131, 4 Sep 1884
Literary World, 15:224-5, 12 Jul 1884

White, Stewart Edward

Arizona Nights
Independent, 63:1473, 19 Dec 1907

The Blazed Trail
Critic, 41:281, Sep 1902; 46:190, Feb 1905
Dial, 32:387, 1 Jun 1902

Conjuror's House
Critic, 43:189, Aug 1903
Literary World, 34:121, May 1903

The Forest
Literary World, 34:349, Dec 1903

The Riverman
Independent, 65:1065-6, 5 Nov 1908

The Silent Places
Critic, 45:95, Jul 1904
Dial, 36:370, 1 Jun 1904

The Westerners
Critic, 40:180, Feb 1902
Independent, 53:3021-2, 19 Dec 1901
Literary World, 32:218, 1 Dec 1901

________, and Samuel Hopkins Adams

The Mystery

White, Stewart Edward, and Samuel Hopkins Adams (cont.)
 Independent, 62:970, 24 Apr 1907

White, William Allen
 A Certain Rich Man
  Catholic World, 90:249, Nov 1909
  Dial, 47:180, 16 Sep 1909
  Independent, 67:546-7, 2 Sep 1909
 In Our Town
  Independent, 62:1035, 2 May 1907
 The Real Issue, and Other Stories
  Critic, NS 27:269-70, 17 Apr 1897
  Dial, 22:24, 1 Jan 1897
  Independent, 49:57, 14 Jan 1897
  Literary World, 28:27, 23 Jan 1897
 Strategems and Spoils
  Critic, 40:471, May 1902
  Dial, 31:369, 16 Nov 1901
  Independent, 54:1192, 15 May 1902

Whitehouse, Florence Brooks
 The Effendi
  Dial, 37:212, 1 Oct 1903
 The God of Things
  Catholic World, 75:688-9, Aug 1902

Whiteley, Isabel (Nixon)
 The Falcon of Langéac
  Critic, NS 27:252, 10 Apr 1897
  Dial, 23:18, 1 Jul 1897
  Literary World, 28:193-4, 12 Jun 1897

Whitelock, Louise (Clarkson)
 How Hindsight Met Provincialatis
  Critic, NS 32:846-7, Sep 1899
  Literary World, 31:55, 17 Feb 1900
 A Mad Madonna, and Other Stories
  Critic, NS 25:291, 25 Apr 1896
  Dial, 20:174, 16 Mar 1896
 The Shadow of John Wallace
  Critic, NS 2:256, 29 Nov 1884
  Dial, 5:328-9, Apr 1885
  Independent, 36:1646, 25 Dec 1884
  Literary World, 15:385-6, 15 Nov 1884

Whitelock, William Wallace
 When Kings Go Forth to Battle
  Independent, 64:209, 23 Jan 1908

Whitlock, Brand
 The Happy Average
  Critic, 46:94, Jan 1905
 Her Infinite Variety
  Independent, 56:795, 7 Apr 1904
  Literary World, 35:107, Apr 1904
 The 13th District
  Dial, 32:389, 1 Jun 1902
  Independent, 54:1490, 19 Jun 1902
 The Turn of the Balance
  Dial, 42:314, 16 May 1907

Whitney, Adeline Dutton (Train)
 Ascutney Street
  Critic, NS 14:235, 8 Nov 1890
  Literary World, 21:398, 8 Nov 1890
 Biddy's Episodes
  Literary World, 35:379, Dec 1904
 Bonnyborough
  Catholic World, 44:413, Dec 1886
  Critic, NS 5:92, 20 Feb 1886
  Literary World, 17:24, 23 Jan 1886

A Golden Gossip
Chautauquan, 15:653, Aug 1892
Critic, NS 17:324, 11 Jun 1892
Independent, 44:881, 23 Jun 1892
Literary World, 23:127, 9 Apr 1892
Homespun Yarns
Critic, NS 7:124, 12 Mar 1887
Odd, or Even?
Catholic World, 31:720, Aug 1880
Dial, 1:14, May 1880
Literary World, 11:199, 5 Jun 1880
The Open Mystery
Independent, 49:1243, 23 Sep 1897
Real Folks
Literary World, 2:73-4, 1 Oct 1871
Sights and Insights
Literary World, 6:163, 1 Apr 1876
Westminster Review, 106:137, Jul 1876
Square Pegs
Independent, 51:2829, 19 Oct 1899
Literary World, 30:340, 14 Oct 1899
Zerub Throop
Literary World, 7:51, 1 Sep 1876.
See also Six of One, by Half a Dozen of the Other.

Whitson, John Harvey
Barbara, a Woman of the West
Dial, 34:374, 1 Jun 1903
Literary World, 34:123-4, May 1903
The Castle of Doubt
Dial, 42:379, 16 Jun 1907
Independent, 63:574, 5 Sep 1907
Justin Wingate, Ranchman
Dial, 38:392, 1 Jun 1905
The Rainbow Chasers
Critic, 45:477-8, Nov 1904
Dial, 36:370-1, 1 Jun 1904
Independent, 56:858-9, 14 Apr 1904
Literary World, 35:166, Jun 1904
Westminster Review, 164:234, Aug 1905

Whittaker, Frederick
The Cadet Button
Literary World, 8:217, 1 May 1878

Whittlesey, Elsie Leigh
The Hemlock Swamp and a Season at the White Sulphur Springs
Literary World, 3:166-7, 1 Apr 1873
Who Was She?
Literary World, 1:99-100, 1 Dec 1870

Wickersham, James Alexander
Enoch Willoughby
Chautauquan, 31:532, Aug 1900
Independent, 52:1019, 26 Apr 1900

Widdemer, Irene
Daisy Brentwell
Galaxy, 21:714, May 1876
Independent, 28:10, 23 Mar 1876

[Wiechmann, Ferdinand Gerhard]
Maid of Montauk
By Forest Monroe [pseud.].
Literary World, 33:94, 1 Jun 1902

Wiggin, Kate Douglas (Smith)
A Cathedral Courtship, and Penelope's English Experiences
Catholic World, 57:720, Aug 1893
Independent, 45:1282, 21

Wiggin, Kate Douglas (Smith) (cont.)
Sep 1893
Diary of a Goose Girl
Catholic World, 75:546, Jul 1902
Chautauquan, 35:622, Sep 1902
Dial, 32:392, 1 Jun 1902
Independent, 54:1726, 17 Jul 1902
Marm Lisa
Chautauquan, 26:240, Nov 1897
Critic, NS 26:360, 5 Dec 1896
Literary World, 27:478, 26 Dec 1896
New Chronicles of Rebecca
Catholic World, 85:693-4, Aug 1907
Independent, 63:574-5, 5 Sep 1907
The Old Peabody Pew
Independent, 63:1473, 19 Dec 1907
Penelope's English Experiences
Chautauquan, 32:454, Jan 1901
Penelope's Irish Experiences
Catholic World, 73:395-6, Jun 1901
Chautauquan, 34:344, Dec 1901
Critic, 39:78, Jul 1901; 42:285, Mar 1903
Independent, 53:1561, 4 Jul 1901
Literary World, 32:92, 1 Jun 1901
Penelope's Progress
Chautauquan, 28:216, Nov 1898
Critic, NS 30:101-2, Jul-Aug 1898
Harper's, 97:Literary Notes, 2-3, Oct 1898
Independent, 50:729, 2 Jun 1898
Literary World, 29:188, 11 Jun 1898
Literature, 3:113, 6 Aug 1898
Rebecca of Sunnybrook Farm
Dial, 35:264, 16 Oct 1903
Literary World, 34:306, Nov 1903
Rose o' the River
Catholic World, 82:266-7, Nov 1905
Chautauquan, 43:192, Apr 1906
Critic, 47:579, Dec 1905
Independent, 59:989-90, 26 Oct 1905
The Story of Patsy
Critic, NS 12:5, 6 Jul 1889
Independent, 41:834, 27 Jun 1889
A Summer in a Cañon
Critic, NS 13:28, 18 Jan 1890
Timothy's Quest
Critic, NS 15:28, 17 Jan 1891
The Village Watch-Tower
Literary World, 26:388, 16 Nov 1895
See also The Affair at the Inn.

Wilcox, Marrion
Real People
Independent, 38:1520, 25 Nov 1886
Señora Villena; and Gray
Critic, NS 8:245, 12 Nov 1887

Wildman, Rounseville
The Panglima Muda
Literary World, 26:105, 6 Apr 1895

Wildrick, Mrs. Marion White
A Zealot in Tulle
Catholic World, 45:132, Apr 1887
Critic, NS 7:282, 4 Jun 1887
Dial, 7:292, Apr 1887
Literary World, 18:140, 30 Aug 1887

Wilkes, Clement [pseud.]
See Goodwin, Henry Leavitt.

Wilkie, Franc Bangs
The Gambler
Literary World, 19:154, 12 May 1888
Pen and Powder
Critic, NS 11:5, 5 Jan 1889

Wilkins, Mary E.
See Freeman, Mary Eleanor (Wilkins).

Wilkins, William A.
The Cleverdale Mystery
Critic, 2:310, 18 Nov 1882
Dial, 3:140, Nov 1882
Independent, 34:13, 21 Dec 1882
Literary World, 13:401, 18 Nov 1882

Wilkinson, Florence
See Evans, Florence (Wilkinson).

Willard, Caroline McCoy (White)
Kin-da-shon's Wife
Chautauquan, 17:127, Apr 1893
Critic, NS 19:127, 4 Mar 1895
Independent, 45:53, 12 Jan 1893
A Son of Israel
By Rachel Penn [pseud.].
Independent, 50:222, 17 Feb 1898
Literary World, 29:75, 5 Mar 1898

Willard, Mrs. Eugene S.
See Willard, Caroline McCoy (White).

[Willard, Josiah Flynt]
The Little Brother
By Josiah Flynt [pseud.].
Chautauquan, 36:340, Dec 1902
Dial, 32:390, 1 Jun 1902
Independent, 54:1964, 14 Aug 1902
Literary World, 33:77, 1 May 1902
The Rise of Ruderick Clowd
By Josiah Flynt [pseud.].
Catholic World, 77:396-7, Jun 1903
Critic, 43:379, Oct 1903
Dial, 35:69-70, 1 Aug 1903
Literary World, 34:138, Jun 1903

Willetts, Sarah B.
Married Too Early
Literary World, 16:275, 8 Aug 1885

Williams, Egerton Ryerson
Ridolfo
Independent, 62:673, 21 Mar 1907

Williams, Francis Churchill
The Captain
Chautauquan, 37:110, Apr 1903
Dial, 34:376, 1 Jun 1903
Independent, 55:739-40, 26 Mar 1903
J. Devlin, Boss
Catholic World, 74:392, Dec 1901
Critic, 40:180-1, Feb 1902
Dial, 31:370, 16 Nov 1901
Independent, 53:2361-2, 3 Oct 1901
Literary World, 32:187, 1 Nov 1901

Williams, Francis Howard
Atman
Catholic World, 53:142-3, Apr 1891
Critic, NS 15:179, 4 Apr 1891

Williams, Frederick Benton [pseud.]
See Hamblen, Herbert Elliott.

Williams, George Forrester
Bullet and Shell
Chautauquan, 10:505, Jan 1890; 22:255, Nov 1895

[Williams, Harold]
Mr. and Mrs. Morton
Independent, 35:11, 7 Jun 1883
Silken Threads
By George Afterem [pseud.].
Critic, NS 4:137, 19 Sep 1885

Williams, Jesse Lynch
The Adventure of a Freshman
Independent, 51:3297, 7 Dec 1899
Princeton Stories
Critic, NS 23:439, 15 Jun 1895
Literary World, 26:218, 13 Jul 1895
The Stolen Story, and Other Newspaper Stories
Critic, NS 32:754, Aug 1899
Independent, 51:2569, 21 Sep 1899
Literary World, 30:140, 29 Apr 1899

Williams, Meade Creighton
Early Mackinac
Independent, 50:729, 2 Jun 1898

[Williams, Nathan Winslow]
A Master Hand
By Richard Dallas [pseud.].
Independent, 55:2354, 1 Oct 1903

Willson, Thomas Edgar
It Is the Law
Independent, 40:241, 23 Feb 1888

Wilson, Augusta Jane (Evans)
At the Mercy of Tiberius
Catholic World, 46:835-6, Mar 1888
Critic, NS 9:3-4, 7 Jan 1888
Infelice
Literary World, 6:118, 1 Jan 1876
A Speckled Bird
Critic, 41:479, Nov 1902
Dial, 33:333, 16 Nov 1902

Wilson, Elizabeth (Sargent), and J. L. Sargent
Sugar Pine Murmurings
Literary World, 30:279, 2 Sep 1899

Wilson, Harry Leon
The Boss of Little Arcady
Dial, 39:209, 1 Oct 1905
Independent, 59:579-60, 7 Sep 1905
The Lions of the Lord
Dial, 35:156 [220], 1 Oct 1903
Independent, 55:2118-9, 3 Sep 1903
Literary World, 34:167-8, Jul 1903
The Seeker
Critic, 46:190, Feb 1905
Dial, 37:211, 1 Oct 1904
Literary World, 35:282, Oct 1904
The Spenders
Catholic World, 75:835-6, Sep 1902
Critic, 41:281, Sep 1902
Dial, 33:65, 1 Aug 1902
Independent, 54:1609, 3 Jul 1902
Literary World, 33:124, 1 Aug 1902

Wilson, Henry R.
The Russian Refugee
Critic, NS 8:54, 30 Jul

1887
Literary World, 18:253, 6 Aug 1887

Wilson, Marian Calvert
Manuelita
Critic, NS 18:119, 3 Sep 1892

[Wilson, Richard Henry]
Mazel
By Richard Fisguill [pseud.].
Dial, 32:390, 1 Jun 1902
Literary World, 34:122, May 1903
The Venus of Cadiz
By Richard Fisguill [pseud.].
Dial, 39:115, 1 Sep 1905

Wilson, Robert Burns
Until the Day Break
Critic, 38:183, Feb 1901
Independent, 52:2452, 11 Oct 1900
Literary World, 32:103, 1 Jul 1901

Wilson, Sydney J.
Stanley Huntingdon
Literary World, 18:121, 16 Apr 1887

Wilson, Theodora B., and James Clarence Harvey
After Many Days
Critic, NS 21:166, 10 Mar 1894
Literary World, 24:257, 12 Aug 1893

Wilson, William Huntington
Rafnaland
Critic, 37:570, Dec 1900
Dial, 29:499, 16 Dec 1900
Literary World, 31:269, 1 Dec 1900

Wilson, William Robert Anthony
Good-for-Nothin'
Independent, 47:1690, 12 Dec 1895

Winchester, Carroll [pseud.]
See Curtis, Caroline Gardiner (Cary).

Winslow, Helen Maria
Salome Shepard, Reformer
Literary World, 24:193, 17 Jun 1893
Spinster Farm
Independent, 65:1247, 26 Nov 1908

Winslow, William Henry
The Sea Letter
Literary World, 33:61, 1 Apr 1902

Winston, Nannie B.
Waters That Pass Away
Critic, NS 32:758, Aug 1899

Winter, Alice (Ames)
The Prize to the Hardy
Critic, 46:381, Apr 1905

Wise, John Sergeant
The Lion's Skin
Dial, 39:42, 16 Jul 1905
Independent, 58:1132-3, 18 May 1905

Wister, Owen
The Dragon of Wantley
Independent, 47:1170, 29 Aug 1895
The Jimmyjohn Boss, and Other Stories
Literary World, 32:75, 1 May 1901
A Journey in Search of Christmas
Critic, 45:578, Dec 1904
Lady Baltimore
Dial, 40:365, 1 Jun 1906
Independent, 60:1159-60, 17 May 1906; 61:1158-60, 15 Nov 1906
Lin McLean

Wister, Owen (cont.)
Critic, NS 29:414, 25 Jun 1898
Dial, 24:81, 1 Feb 1898
Harper's, 96:Literary Notes, 3, Dec 1897
Independent, 50:629, 12 May 1898
Literary World, 29:155, 14 May 1898

Philosophy 4
Catholic World, 77:397, Jun 1903

Red Men and White
Critic, NS 24:428, 21 Dec 1895
Dial, 20:173, 16 Mar 1896
Harper's, 92:Literary Notes, 4, Dec 1895
Indianapolis, 47:1690, 12 Dec 1895
Literary World, 27:187, 13 Jun 1896

The Virginian
Critic, 41:358-9, Oct 1902
Dial, 32:392, 1 Jun 1902; 33:242, 16 Oct 1902
Independent, 54:1610, 3 Jul 1902; 54:2771, 20 Nov 1902
Literary World, 33:139, 1 Sep 1902

See also A Week Away from Time.

Witherspoon, Orlando
Doctor Ben
Catholic World, 48:553, Jan 1889
Critic, 2:269, 7 Oct 1882; NS 10:205, 27 Oct 1888
Dial, 3:116, Oct 1882
Literary World, 13:315, 23 Sep 1882

Wolf, Alice S.
A House of Cards
Independent, 48:629, 7 May 1896
Literary World, 27:250-1, 8 Aug 1896

A Wolf at the Door
Literary World, 8:164, 1 Feb 1878

Wolf, Emma
The Joy of Life
Critic, NS 26:361, 5 Dec 1896

Other Things Being Equal
Critic, NS 19:161-2, 18 Mar 1893
Literary World, 24:12, 14 Jan 1893

A Prodigal in Love
Critic, NS 22:136-7, 1 Sep 1894
Harper's, 89:Literary Notes, 3, Sep 1894
Literary World, 25:219, 14 Jul 1894

Wolfenstein, Martha
Idyls of the Gass
Chautauquan, 38:95, Sep 1903
Critic, 40:376, Apr 1902; 43:286, Sep 1903
Independent, 54:817, 3 Apr 1902
Literary World, 33:107, 1 Jul 1902

[Wood, Anna Cogswell]
Diana Fontaine
By Algernon Ridgeway [pseud.].
Critic, NS 16:63-4, 8 Aug 1891
Independent, 43:1142, 30 Jul 1891

[Wood, Charlotte Dunning]
A Step Aside
By Charlotte Dunning [pseud.].
Critic, NS 6:185, 16 Oct 1886
Independent, 38:1520, 25 Nov 1886
Literary World, 17:351, 16 Oct 1886

Upon a Cast
By Charlotte Dunning [pseud.].
Critic, NS 4:28, 18 Jul 1885
Harper's, 90:Literary Notes, 3, Feb 1895
Independent, 37:1230, 24 Sep 1885
Literary World, 16:269-70, 8 Aug 1885

Wood, Edith (Elmer)
Shoulder Straps and Sun Bonnets
Literary World, 33:61, 1 Apr 1902
The Spirit of the Service
Critic, 44:94, Jan 1904

Wood, Eugene
Folks Back Home
Independent, 64:1350, 11 Jun 1908

Wood, Frances Hartson, and Eva Paine Kitchel
Warp and Woof
Independent, 42:788, 5 Jun 1890

Wood, Henry
Edward Burton
Critic, NS 14:166, 4 Oct 1890
Independent, 42:965, 10 Jul 1890
Westminster Review, 134:219-20, Aug 1890
Victor Serenus
Independent, 50:729, 2 Jun 1898
Literary World, 29:204, 25 Jun 1898

Wood, John Seymour
A Coign of Vantage
Critic, NS 21:165, 10 Mar 1894
Dial, 16:20, 1 Jan 1894
College Days
Critic, NS 22:106, 18 Aug 1894
A Daughter of Venice
Critic, NS 19:364, 3 Jun 1893
Dial, 14:113-4, 16 Feb 1893
Literary World, 24:258, 12 Aug 1893
Gramercy Park
Critic, NS 18:177, 1 Oct 1892
Independent, 44:1229, 1 Sep 1892
Literary World, 23:310, 10 Sep 1892
An Old Beau, and Other Stories
Critic, NS 19:364, 3 Jun 1893
Literary World, 24:148, 6 May 1893
Yale Yarns
Critic, NS 24:179-80, 21 Sep 1895
Literary World, 26:218, 13 Jul 1895

[Wood, Julia Amanda (Sargent)]
The Brown House at Duffield
By Minnie Mary Lee [pseud.].
Catholic World, 24:860, Mar 1877
The Heart of Myrrha Lake
By Minnie Mary Lee [pseud.].
Independent, 25:843, 3 Jul 1873
Herbert's Wife
By Minnie Mary Lee [pseud.].
Catholic World, 21:719, Aug 1875

[Woodruff, Julia Louisa Matilda (Curtiss)]
Bellerue
By W. L. M. Jay [pseud.].
Critic, NS 15:322, 20 Jun 1891
Holden with the Cords
By W. L. M. Jay [pseud.].
Galaxy, 18:711-2, Nov 1874

[Woodruff, Julia Louisa Matilda (Curtiss)] (cont.)
Independent, 26:10, 8 Oct 1874
Literary World, 5:82, 1 Nov 1874

Woods, Kate (Tannatt)
A Fair Maid of Marblehead
Critic, NS 12:186, 19 Oct 1889
Literary World, 20:426, 23 Nov 1889
Mopsy, Her Tangles and Triumphs
Independent, 48:1494, 5 Nov 1896
That Dreadful Boy
Literary World, 17:219, 26 Jun 1886

Woods, Katharine Pearson
From Dusk to Dawn
Chautauquan, 17:125-6, Apr 1893
Critic, NS 19:216, 8 Apr 1893
Independent, 45:53, 12 Jan 1893
Literary World, 24:42, 11 Feb 1893
John, a Tale of King Messiah
Critic, NS 27:441, 26 Jun 1897
Independent, 49:57, 14 Jan 1897
Metzerott, Shoemaker
Chautauquan, 10:633, Feb 1890
Critic, NS 12:256, 23 Nov 1889
Dial, 10:215, Dec 1889
Literary World, 20:383-4, 9 Nov 1889
The Son of Ingar
Independent, 49:1662, 16 Dec 1897
Literary World, 29:188, 11 Jun 1898
A Web of Gold
Chautauquan, 12:825, Mar 1891
Critic, NS 17:209, 9 Apr 1892
Independent, 43:533, 9 Apr 1891

Woods, Virna
A Modern Magdalene
Literary World, 25:231, 28 Jul 1894

[Wood-Seys, Roland Alexander]
The Blacksmith of Voe
By Paul Cushing [pseud.].
Harper's, 85:Literary Notes, 3, Oct 1892
Cut with His Own Diamond
By Paul Cushing [pseud.].
Catholic World, 54:612-3, Jan 1892
Harper's, 84:Literary Notes, 3, Mar 1892
The Great Chin Episode
By Paul Cushing [pseud.].
Independent, 45:1018, 27 Jul 1893

Woolf, Philip
Who Is Guilty
Literary World, 17:252-3, 24 Jul 1886

Woolley, Celia Parker
A Girl Graduate
Chautauquan, 9:625, Jul 1889
Critic, NS 11:238, 11 May 1889; NS 12:17, 13 Jul 1889
Independent, 41:929, 18 Jul 1889
Literary World, 20:206-7, 22 Jun 1889
Love and Theology
Catholic World, 47:412-4, Jun 1888
Critic, NS 8:245, 12 Nov 1887
Literary World, 18:369, 29 Oct 1887
Roger Hunt
Catholic World, 55:131-2, Apr 1892
Chautauquan, 16:127,

Oct 1892
Critic, NS 17:252, 30 Apr 1892
Independent, 44:881, 23 Jun 1892
Literary World, 23:106-7, 26 Mar 1892

Woolley, Edward Mott
Roland of Altenburg
Dial, 37:312, 16 Nov 1904

[Woolsey, Sarah Chauncey]
Cross Patch
By Susan Coolidge [pseud.].
Critic, 1:337, 3 Dec 1881
For Summer Afternoons
By Susan Coolidge [pseud.].
Independent, 28:9, 15 Jun 1876
Just Sixteen
By Susan Coolidge [pseud.].
Chautauquan, 11:127, Apr 1890
A Little Country Girl
By Susan Coolidge [pseud.].
Chautauquan, 6:185, Dec 1885
Independent, 38:1237-8, 30 Sep 1886
What Katy Did
By Susan Coolidge [pseud.].
Literary World, 3:105-6, 1 Dec 1872

Woolson, Constance Fenimore
Anne
Critic, 2:187-8, 15 Jul 1882
Dial, 3:60, Jul 1882
Independent, 34:11, 7 Sep 1882
Literary World, 13:227, 17 Jun 1882
Castle Nowhere
Critic, NS 6:249, 20 Nov 1886
Harper's, 73:Literary Notes, 1-2, Sep 1886
Independent, 27:10, 29 Apr 1875; 38:1520, 25 Nov 1886
Literary World, 5:172, 1 Apr 1875; 17:466, 11 Dec 1886
Dorothy, and Other Italian Stories
Critic, NS 25:92, 8 Feb 1896
Dial, 19:385, 16 Dec 1895
Literary World, 27:188, 13 Jun 1896
East Angels
Catholic World, 43:561-4, Jul 1886
Critic, NS 6:111, 4 Sep 1886
Dial, 7:66-7, Jul 1886
Harper's, 73:Literary Notes, 1-2, Jun 1886; 74:Literary Notes, 3, Jan 1887
Independent, 38:1076, 26 Aug 1886
Literary World, 17:243, 24 Jul 1886
For the Major
Critic, 3:280, 16 Jun 1883
Independent, 35:11, 2 Aug 1883
Literary World, 14:260-1, 11 Aug 1883
The Front Yard, and Other Italian Stories
Dial, 19:385, 16 Dec 1895
Harper's, 91:Literary Notes, 4, Sep 1895
Independent, 47:1303, 26 Sep 1895
Literary World, 27:188, 13 Jun 1896
Horace Chase
Critic, NS 21:270, 21 Apr 1894
Dial, 16:366-7, 16 Jun 1894
Harper's, 88:Literary Notes, 1, Mar 1894
Literary World, 25:85, 24 Mar 1894
Jupiter Lights
Catholic World, 50:826-9,

Woolson, Constance Fenimore (cont.)
Mar 1890
Critic, NS 13:51, 1 Feb 1890
Harper's, 80:Literary Notes, 2-3, Jan 1890
Independent, 41:1576, 28 Nov 1889
Literary World, 21:41, 1 Feb 1890
The Old Stone House
By Anne March [pseud.].
Independent, 25:331, 13 Mar 1873
Rodman the Keeper
Catholic World, 44:708-9, Feb 1887
Critic, NS 7:17, 8 Jan 1887
Dial, 1:13-4, May 1880
Harper's, 74:Literary Notes, 4, Dec 1886
Independent, 38:1665, 23 Dec 1886
Literary World, 11:223, 3 Jul 1880
Two Women
Galaxy, 24:286, Aug 1877

Worth, Julian [pseud.]
See Parsons, Julia (Worth).

Wright, Harold Bell
That Printer of Udell's
Chautauquan, 38:520, Jan 1904
Critic, 43:286, Sep 1903
Literary World, 34:169, Jul 1903

Wright, Julia (McNair)
Cynthia's Sons
Independent, 48:1463, 29 Oct 1896
The Dragon and the Tea-Kettle
Critic, NS 3:257, 30 May 1885
The Pooles' Millions
Literary World, 28:12, 9 Jan 1897
Ragweed
Literary World, 26:90, 23 Mar 1895
A Wife Hard Won
Literary World, 15:130, 19 Apr 1884

Wright, Lois [pseud.]
See Waite, Lucy.

Wright, Mabel (Osgood)
At the Sign of the Fox
By Barbara [pseud.].
Critic, 47:381-2, Oct 1905
People of the Whirlpool
Independent, 55:1814-5, 30 Jul 1903
Poppea of the Post-Office
Dial, 47:183, 16 Sep 1909
Independent, 67:549, 2 Sep 1909
Tommy-Anne and the Three Hearts
Chautauquan, 24:375-6, Dec 1896
Literary World, 28:13, 9 Jan 1897
Wabeno, the Magician
Chautauquan, 30:331, Dec 1899

Wright, Mary (Tappan)
Aliens
Critic, 41:376, Oct 1903
Dial, 32:389-90, 1 Jun 1902
Independent, 54:1075, 1 May 1902
The Test
Critic, 45:279, Sep 1904
Dial, 36:370, 1 Jun 1904
The Tower
Independent, 60:1223, 24 May 1906
A Truce, and Other Stories
Critic, NS 25:442, 20 Jun 1896
Independent, 47:1170, 29 Aug 1895

Wyatt, Edith Franklin
Every One His Own Way

Critic, 39:375, Oct 1901; 39:578, Dec 1901
Dial, 31:32, 1 Jul 1901
Independent, 53:1747, 25 Jul 1901
True Love
Critic, 43:381, Oct 1903
Literary World, 34:74, Apr 1903

Wyman, Lillie Buffum (Chace)
Poverty Grass
Critic, NS 6:137, 18 Sep 1886
Independent, 38:1236, 30 Sep 1886

Wynne, Madeline (Yale)
The Little Room and Other Stories
Dial, 20:174, 16 Mar 1896

X., A. [pseud.]
See Mathews, Frances Aymar.

Yardley, Alice Turner
Yarns
Independent, 47:1728, 19 Dec 1895

[Yardley, Mrs. Jane Woolsey]
Little Sister
Critic, 2:339-40, 16 Dec 1882
Independent, 35:11, 1 Feb 1883
A Superior Woman
Critic, NS 3:293, 20 Jun 1885
Independent, 37:1103, 27 Aug 1885
Literary World, 16:209, 13 Jun 1885

Yechton, Barbara [pseud.]
See Krausé, Lyda Farrington.

Young, Julia Evelyn (Ditto)
Adrift
Chautauquan, 11:649, Aug 1890
Critic, NS 14:234, 8 Nov 1890
Literary World, 21:39, 1 Feb 1890

Young, Rose Emmet
Henderson
Independent, 56:795-6, 7 Apr 1904
Literary World, 35:73, Mar 1904

Z., Z. [pseud.]
See Doissy, Louise.

Zogbaum, Rufus Fairchild
Horse, Foot, and Dragoons
Harper's, 75:Literary Notes, 3, Nov 1887

INDEX OF TITLES